THOMAS G. BERGIN

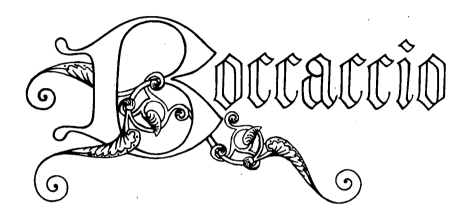

THE VIKING PRESS • NEW YORK

To Giuliano and Carla Vassalli

friends in war and peace

LIBRARY OF CONGRESS CATALOGING IN PUBLICATION DATA
Bergin, Thomas Goddard, 1904–
Boccaccio.
Bibliography: p.
Includes index.
1. Boccaccio, Giovanni, 1313–1375—Criticism and interpretation.
PQ4286.B4   858'.109   81-65281
ISBN 0-670-17735-0   AACR2

Printed in the United States of America
Set in Videocomp Bembo

Grateful acknowledgment is made to the following for permission to reprint copyrighted material:

AHM Publishing Corporation: One stanza of Petrarch's Rhymes 53, translated by Gilbert Cunningham, from *Petrarch: Selected Sonnets, Odes and Letters* (Crofts Classic Series), edited by Thomas G. Bergin (AHM Publishing Corporation, Arlington Heights, Ill., 1966).

Associated University Presses: Three stanzas from *Nymphs of Fiesole* by Giovanni Boccaccio, translated by Joseph Tusiani, Fairleigh Dickinson University Press, 1971.

Bobbs-Merrill Educational Publishing: A selection from *Boccaccio on Poetry*, translated by Charles G. Osgood, copyright 1930 by Princeton University Press, © 1956 by The Liberal Arts Press, Inc. Used by permission of The Liberal Arts Press Division of The Bobbs-Merrill Co., Inc.

Guido Guarino: Selections from *Concerning Famous Women* by Guido Guarino. Copyright © 1963 by Guido Guarino. Published by Rutgers University Press.

Indiana University Press: Selections from *Letters from Petrarch* by Morris Bishop, Indiana University Press, 1966.

Bernadette-Marie McCoy: Selections from *The Book of Theseus*, translated by Bernadette Marie McCoy, published by Medieval Text Association, 1974.

Yale University Press: Boccaccio's poem "To that fair kingdom," Sonnet 126, translated by Thomas G. Bergin, from *Lyric Poetry of the Italian Renaissance*, edited by L. R. Lind, Yale University Press, 1954.

CONTENTS

INTRODUCTION

or well over a century at least, in English-speaking countries, Boccaccio's name has been widely known, even though more often than not mentioned with a salacious snigger, for until our own emancipated times his *Decameron*, in general popular opinion, was simply "a dirty book" and its author a licentious, if admittedly entertaining, purveyor of bawdy anecdotes. Scholars, to be sure, had been cognizant of other aspects of his masterpiece, and many literary historians looking beyond the *Decameron* had learned to appreciate, particularly through his association with Chaucer, Boccaccio's significant contribution to the literature of the Western world. And in our own generation, with its renewed interest in the Middle Ages, the works of this gifted and versatile genius have been the object of scrupulous and perceptive attention.

Such studies have been, however, of a specialized nature; "boccaccisti" write for other "boccaccisti," assuming in their readers an easy familiarity with the canon of the master's works. Vittore Branca's excellent *Boccaccio: The Man and His Works* has recently become available, but its very virtues, abundance of detail, encyclopedic erudition, and analysis of literary-philosophical currents, make it a little forbidding for the kind of reader I have in mind. There is not currently available in English an introductory study of the great friend of Petrarch and admirer of Dante, in which the facts of his life and the nature of his poems, romances, and Latin works are systematically set forth. The monographs of Hutton, Chubb, and MacManus are out of print and outdated. It is the purpose of this book to fill that gap and to provide a general introduction to the man and his works.

To that end I have supplied two chapters of historical-biographical substance and then proceeded to an orderly presentation of all Boccaccio's works, including those written in Latin. In discussing the separate titles I have given brief summaries of their contents and added pertinent information on their sources and their genesis with some comment on their place in literary history, their influence on later writers, and the verdict of criticism on their merits—at least in broad outlines, for the history of Boccaccio criticism is a subject too vast for comprehensive coverage in a book of this nature. Where it seemed proper and not too hazardous I have ventured to express an opinion of my own. But I would stress that the raison d'être of my book is simply to present the author and survey his achievement and not to record the views of scholars over the centuries or to advance any original critical theories. In view of the public I have in mind, I have, as often as possible, called on English and American authorities for support or illumination. I hope that my book will be useful to the general reader who has heard something of Boccaccio and would like to know more; I dare, also, to hope that it may be of some use to scholars in the field as a kind of handbook.

A book of this nature is, of necessity, dependent on the labors of countless predecessors. My footnotes will indicate the scope of my debt. I should like to acknowledge my particular indebtedness to Vittore Branca. Not only have his authoritative studies, especially his *Profilo biografico*, been my principal source (so well has he absorbed and weighed the findings of early scholars that it is rarely necessary to look beyond his pages), but he has personally come to my aid in a number of emergencies, generously offering guidance or supplying information otherwise difficult for me to come by.

TGB
Madison, Ct. 1981

CHAPTER 1

BACKGROUND

occaccio's entire life span was cast in the fourteenth century. Since, like his contemporaries Dante and Petrarch, the author of the *Decameron* was not only a keen observer of events but an active participant in public matters, some acquaintance with the history of his times—political and cultural—is essential for a proper appreciation of his work.

Historians confront the fourteenth century with a certain uneasiness and, reluctant to pigeonhole it as either "medieval" or "Renaissance," commonly designate it as "a century of transition." Certainly the assurance, innocent or savage as it may seem to us, that characterized the High Middle Ages is gone. In the sphere of philosophy and faith the contrast between the thirteenth and fourteenth centuries may be illustrated by the works of the great doctors of the respective ages: the serenity—one might fairly say the optimism—of the great *Summa* of St. Thomas Aquinas was challenged by the scrutiny of Duns Scotus and William of Ockham, whose perceptions, however admirable in showing the way to a new world of intellectual emancipation, were *au fond* corrosive of traditional values.

In a humbler sector of human things too we may find not only the cause but also the justification for the troubled anxiety of fourteenth-century mankind. "Economic depression was to grip the age," a modern historian writes, "and the root of the difficulty lay in agriculture. Population had continued to rise since the eleventh century and by the end of the thirteenth it had clearly begun to exceed the available food supply . . . crop failures posed a constant threat and . . . from 1315 on bad harvests followed each other in rapid succession. Prices soared; disease reached epidemic proportions."[1] Nor was economic distress in any way alleviated by political guidance; the century was devastated by the Hundred Years' War, fought between two Christian nations, unchallenged and unrestrained by the once supreme and now enfeebled world authorities of Church and Empire. Needless to say, the costs of the war added soaring inflation to the tribulations of society.

Henri Pirenne, whose chapter on this period is entitled "The European Crisis," sketches its profile:

> Nothing more involved and bewildering and more full of contrasts can be imagined than the period extending from the beginning of the fourteenth to about the middle of the fifteenth century. The whole of European society, from the depth to the surface was as though in a state of fermentation. . . . A spirit of restlessness was abroad; it was a restlessness that almost amounted to mental confusion. The world was suffering and struggling, but it was hardly advancing. . . . Though they were badly shaken, the old ideals still survived; one finds them everywhere, modified, no doubt, or impaired, but still unchanged in any essential. . . . What is really new about this period, what strikes one immediately upon a general survey, is its revolutionary tendencies. They were nowhere triumphant, but they were felt in every department of life. No previous epoch had ever furnished so many names of tribunes, demagogues, agitators and reformers. . . . But there was no coherence in all this unrest, and no continuity.[2]

Petrarch, instinctively sensing the instability of his age—which matched and perhaps to some extent explained his own spiritual unease —did not hesitate to define it as the worst in all history, and if we recall that its chronicles are full of wars, endemic crime on a continental scale, to say nothing of recurrent famines and plagues, of which the Black Death is the most spectacular but not the only example, it is not hard to agree with him. Barbara Tuchman gives to her recent survey of the era the significant subtitle: "The Calamitous 14th Century."[3] There are, to be sure, colorful episodes that capture the imagination and still have about them an aura of glamor and romance: for those of the English-speaking family the battles of Crécy and Poitiers and the names of Edward and the Black Prince still glitter in memory, and the cometlike effulgence of Cola di Rienzi, "the last of the Tribunes," which fascinated Bulwer-Lytton and Wagner (whose *Rienzi* was Hitler's favorite opera) lingers on in Italy. Yet such shining names also aptly illustrate Pirenne's thesis. For in fact the Hundred Years' War had no victor; and Cola came to a sad end.

In terms of literary history, however, the contributions of the uneasy century are not to be scorned; out of its stress and turmoil emerged a number of writers without whom the realm of letters would be sadly impoverished: the great Italian trio, Dante (even though it may be argued that his formation must be credited to the thirteenth century), Petrarch, and Boccaccio; in England Chaucer and Langland; in Spain the ebullient Juan Ruiz and in Germany Meister Eckardt. For Italy especially the trecento holds an unrivaled preeminence. Not only did the *Divine Comedy*, the *Canzoniere*, and the *Decameron* bring the adolescent vernacular into assured maturity, but the perceptive industry of Petrarch and Boccaccio also brought about the reassessment of the Latin heritage and the appreciation of Greek literature, which are the components of humanism, a vital element in the Renaissance that lay ahead.

For Europe as a whole, politically and culturally, the century's instabilities derived in large part from the displacement of both of the main pillars of medieval life: the Empire and the Church. Dante, in the century's first decade, had placed all of his hopes for the renewed well-being of the Christian world on the success of the Emperor Henry VII. But Henry not only failed to bring imperial authority back to Italy, he died prematurely in 1313 (the year of Boccaccio's birth), and throughout the fourteenth century no emperor arose endowed with the personality and the competence to reassert his preeminence among the sovereigns of Europe. Ludwig of Bavaria, who dared to do battle with the Avignon papacy, was outmaneuvered, excommunicated, and eventually humiliated. When his successor Charles IV (who so graciously charmed Petrarch) went to Rome for his crowning in 1355 he took every care not to offend the pope. The old empire was dead.

The papacy to be sure lived on, but its universal pretensions were gravely flawed. It no longer spoke from Rome but from Avignon; to Italians in particular but in some degree to all good Christians, this dislocation seemed unnatural and made the authority of God's vicar suspect. The Babylonian Captivity lasted through most of the century (1309–1377); all of the popes during this period were French, the College of Cardinals (naturally enough, since its members were nominated by the pontiff) had a French majority; invariably the princes of the Church were sympathetic to the policies of the French monarchy.

It should be said, in all fairness, that the Avignon popes were not by any means the least able or the least worthy of the successors of St. Peter. Clement V (1305–1314) and John XXII (1314–1334; it was he who humbled Ludwig of Bavaria) were men of vision and political competence; Benedict XII (1334–1342) was a decent man of goodwill, famous for his charitable works and honestly eager to put an end to the Hundred Years' War; Clement VI (1342–1352) was an enlightened patron of the arts; Innocent VI (1352–1362) dealt boldly and efficiently with brigands—and his bishops; Urban V (1462–1470) was of such high character as to win subsequent beatification (he made an effort to bring the papacy back to Rome but, understandably, found the brawling anarchy of the Eternal City intolerable); Gregory XI (1370–1378), another well-intentioned pontiff, finally succeeded in bringing the Church back to its true home. (He did not long survive his translation, although only forty-five years old at the time of his death.)

But the damage had been done. No matter what might be the character of an individual pope, all of the Avignon succession was suspect; its claim to universality and impartiality was weakened. It must be said too that the court was consistently venal. The Avignon papacy scandalously commercialized religion by simony, the sale of indulgences, and similar practices. The source of the "Triple Schism" of the early fifteenth century was in the Babylonian Captivity—and the schism in its turn nurtured the seed of the Reformation. Indeed the Reformation had a kind of premature dawning in the emergence of such reformers as Wycliffe and Hus, and one aspect of Protestantism was clearly foreshadowed in the *De Monarchia* of Dante Alighieri, which would divest the pope of his temporal power, and the *Defensor pacis* of Marsilius of Padua, which would deny him his preeminence within the Church. And no follower of Luther or Calvin would ever write more scathingly on the subject of the venality and corruption of the Curia than Francis Petrarch; his sonnet (*Rhymes* 136), perhaps more forceful in the sixteenth-century English of an anonymous translator than in the original Italian, voices the scandalized indignation of honest Christians:

> Vengeaunce must fall on thee, thow filthy whore
> Of Babilon, thow breaker of Christ's fold,
> That from achorns, and from the water colde,
> Art riche become with making many poore
> Thou treason's neste that in thie harte dost holde
> Of cankard malice and of myschief more
> Than pen can wryte, or may with tongue be tolde,
> Slave to delights that chastitie hath solde;
> For wyne and ease which settith all thie store
> Upon whoredome and none other lore,
> In thye pallais of strompetts yonge and olde
> Theare walks Plentie, and Belzebub thye Lorde
> Guides thee and them, and doth thy raigne upholde;
> It is but late, as wryting will recorde,
> That poore thow weart withouten lande or goolde;
> Yet now hath golde and pryde, by one accorde,
> In wichednesse so spreadde thie lyf abrode
> That it doth stincke before the face of God.[4]

If the sonnet, as seems likely, may be dated as of about 1347 it was written only a year or less after Crécy, which brought to an end the first phase of the most memorable political phenomenon of the century, the Hundred Years' War. The struggle had begun in 1336 with Edward III's claim to the throne of France, motivated in part by characteristic medieval dynastic territorial greed and in part by the necessity to protect the English province of Aquitaine from being gradually absorbed by the dynamic French monarchy.

The great duel between the two best-armed and best-organized nations of the West fascinated and indirectly involved all of Europe.

It was not to end until nearly eighty years after Boccaccio's death; it raged, with intervals of uneasy peace while the combatants paused to draw breath, throughout his mature lifetime and its repercussions were felt in Italy as indeed throughout Christendom. We may here summarize the pattern of hostilities during the fourteenth century. Topography as well as his posture as claimant obliged Edward to take the offensive. He began with a campaign in the North, making allies of Ludwig of Bavaria and the Flemish clothworkers, who were willing to accept him as the lawful king of France. This phase (1339–1340) was inconclusive, although the English won a notable naval victory at Sluys (1340). For two years the scene of combat then shifted to Brittany where each monarch supported his own candidate for the dukedom; this episode too yielded no decisive result. In 1345 Edward turned his attention to the South where his generals were successful in recovering the English possession won by the French from his father; thus encouraged he turned his attention again to the northern flank and after a brilliant campaign in Normandy soundly defeated the forces of Philip at Crécy, famed in history for the triumph of the English longbow over the armor-plated chivalry of France. This phase of the war closed a year later with the capture of Calais by the British; the onslaught of the plague cooled the belligerent ardor of both parties. Philip died in 1350; the English had won most of the battles and were comfortably lodged on the Channel but the fate of Aquitaine was still uncertain.

Taking advantage of tensions between Philip's successor John II and his cousin the king of Navarre, Edward reopened hostilities a few years later. In 1355 the Black Prince raided Languedoc and the following year pressed up to the Loire in a campaign that culminated with the battle of Maupertuis (Poitiers), a repetition of Crécy, where again English tactical skill and the efficiency of the archers completely routed the French; this time the French king was taken prisoner, leaving his country to be ravaged at will by bands of English and their auxiliaries. The peasantry, maddened by their misery and disillusioned by the ineptness of their betters as displayed at Crécy and Poitiers, rose in revolt in the first great proletarian manifestation of the Middle Ages. The "Jacquerie"—as the exasperated peasantry was called—burned and pillaged their masters' castles; they evoked the sympathy of some burghers as well, including Étienne Marcel, spokesman for the third estate and in effect ruler of Paris, but the rising was abortive and after a few short months the nobility restored order—with a savagery no less barbarous than that of the rebellious peasants.

In 1359 Edward renewed the war; this time his opponent was the canny Du Guesclin who, like Fabius of Rome, refused pitched battle but bled the English by constant harassment; at the Peace of Brétigny (1360) Edward renounced his claim to the French throne, settling for the uncontested suzerainty of Aquitaine and a substantial ransom payment for the prisoner King John. It was after this truce that the "free companies" of mercenaries reached their pestilential apogee, devastating France south of the Seine, threatening the pope at Avignon, and passing on to spread their infection into Italy. The war meanwhile, under the new French king Charles V ("the Wise"), entered into a Spanish phase; the Black Prince was drawn into an alliance with the bastard brother of Peter the Cruel of Castile and although he won his usual victories, Du Guesclin, Peter's ally, eventually triumphed. In Aquitaine the nobles, unhappy with the taxes levied under English rule, revolted; in three years the province was recovered by the French crown and the Treaty of Bruges (1375) preserved for the English only Calais and a small coastal strip of Gascony. The death of Edward two years later closed a long chapter in the interminable struggle; ahead lay many more years of strife including the epic of Agincourt and the romance of Jeanne d'Arc. But such matters take us beyond the span of Boccaccio's lifetime.

Unless he was born in Paris (which, as we shall see, seems unlikely to scholars today) Boccaccio never set foot in France and never had a chance (as Petrarch did) to observe the traces of the ravages of war. But the great duel had deep and significant repercussions in Italy. First, as we have noted, the "free companies," essentially armed and disciplined gangsters, spawned by the struggle and otherwise unemployed during its recurrent truces, crossed into Italy and, as the century wore on, became an endemic political pestilence south of the Alps, sometimes taking service under various princes, sometimes acting independently, sometimes blackmailing cities; it was not long before the natives followed the alien example; the "free companies" are in fact the forerunners of the *condottieri* who were to plague the peninsula until the early years of the sixteenth century.

Another effect of the Hundred Years' War was of a different nature but felt very keenly by Boccaccio and the Italians of his class of society. War is an expensive business, and to finance their efforts the kings of both France and England turned to Italian—usually Florentine—bankers. The interest demanded was ruinous and for some hard-pressed monarchs repudiation was inevitable. The most spectacular case was that of Edward III; after his first campaign in Flanders (where he had needed large sums to buy the assistance of his allies) Edward was obliged to renege on his debt to the Peruzzi (1339); this marked the beginning of the collapse of the Florentine banking houses; by the mid-forties they were all in trouble, with effects on the commune that we shall remark below.

Italy, politically speaking, was still what it had been since the fall of Rome and would remain until the time of Garibaldi, a geographical expression, divided into a number of separate states struggling for supremacy or in some cases for survival. The dream of a "garden of the empire" in peaceful union with the rest of Christendom under a benevolent monarch, which Dante hoped to see realized, had vanished with the death of Henry of Luxembourg following his unsuccessful siege of Florence in 1313. Yet in spite of the instability of its institutions and recurrent conflicts of its rival states, the presence of Italy loomed larger in the Europe of the fourteenth century than it does in our time. Since America was yet to be discovered and the window on the Atlantic was as yet, as it were, unopened, Italy occupied a central position on the continent. In population too it ranked much higher than it does today. Census figures for the Middle Ages are difficult to establish with precision but it has been said that in 1300 of the five cities in Europe with a population of 100,000 or more four were Italian: Milan, Florence, Genoa, and Venice.[5] Their only rivals were Constantinople and Paris; such modern centers as Madrid and Berlin were mere villages or small towns.

The combined wealth of the peninsula's cities surpassed that of all Europe; the chivalry of the West had for some time looked to Italy

for the financing of its enterprises (we have but to recall the role of
Venice in the Fourth Crusade a century before Boccaccio's day) and,
as the techniques of banking developed, Italians and particularly Florentines had a hand in all the major political events of Europe. The
significance of their contribution was symbolized by the alliances
between the wealthy families of the communes and the most ancient
aristocratic houses of the continent. We do not have to wait until the
Renaissance exports its Medici heiresses to France; in Boccaccio's time
(1360) Galeazzo Visconti "bought" a princess of France as a bride for
his son Gian Galeazzo by the payment of the ransom demanded by the
English for the return of John II. (Gian Galeazzo's daughter, later in
the century, marrying the duke of Orleans, would be the mother of
the graceful poet Charles d'Orléans, as much Visconti as Valois). The
cultural preeminence of Italy was reinforced by the tradition of Rome,
seat of Europe's only faith and rich also in its monuments and its
classical memories. The splendor of the Renaissance was yet to come
but the works of Giotto and Arnolfo di Cambio were its harbingers.
Italian traders and merchants traveled to all corners of the world
(Marco Polo even to far Cathay) and a countercurrent of pilgrims
from every country in Europe flowed incessantly to the Holy City.
Italy had been the mother of the oldest universities in Europe and
although by the fourteenth century Paris and Oxford afforded healthy
competition, Bologna, Pisa, and Padua still maintained their prestige,
and Italian scholars—as well as churchmen—held prominent positions
abroad.

Yet if the word "Italy" in the Middle Ages carried a connotation
far richer than the purely topographical, it must be admitted that
politically it was meaningless. "France" or "England" could convoke
assemblies, make laws, or embark on wars but "Italy" could not speak
with one voice. Since the defeat of the Lombards by Charlemagne
there had been no power on the peninsula sufficiently dominant to
serve as a nucleus for nationhood. The land had become the battle-
ground for the claims of two worldwide authorities, the pope, defended by his ultimately victorious Guelphs, and the emperor, backed
by his tenacious Ghibellines. Both were well entrenched and neither
was able to unite the faction-ridden land under his own exclusive

control—indeed for neither was the unity of Italy a primary objective. The result of the rivalry had been to exacerbate regional tensions and thwart every possibility of union. The South to be sure had been unified under the aggressive Normans who created the Kingdom of Naples and Sicily; coming into the hands of the Hohenstaufens under the able leadership of Frederick II it might have served as the Prussia or Piedmont of its time, but papal opposition frustrated Frederick's design and his successors were either ineffectual or, absorbed in problems of their own domains, not very much interested in the "garden" of their empire. Throughout Boccaccio's lifetime neither pope nor emperor was resident in Italy but the fragmented political condition of the land was a lasting legacy of the centuries of strife between the two institutions they represented.

An outline of political developments in fourteenth-century Italy must in the nature of the case require a survey of the fortunes of the more important independent states that had burgeoned, as it were, in the interstices of the papal-imperial pretensions. Although these states were all small when compared to such kingdoms as France and England, they were nevertheless centers of power and prestige, viable political units and significant in the councils of Europe. In Boccaccio's time the most powerful of these were the despotism of Milan, the republics of Venice and Florence, and the ancient feudal Kingdom of Naples (officially known as the Kingdom of Sicily). Of these the Milanese state was the richest and most aggressive.

In the early Middle Ages the Commune of Milan had earned fame and respect for its stalwart resistance to the German emperors; it had been the moving spirit of the Lombard League and had defeated the great Barbarossa at Legnano (1176). In the course of the thirteenth century, in keeping with the pattern of all Italian communes, Milan had ceased to be a democracy and had become a signoria, under the lordship of the Della Torre family. But in the last years of the century the vigorous Archbishop Otto Visconti had displaced the older family and established a dynasty that was to dominate the city and its far-reaching domain for well over a hundred years. In 1294 the archbishop's nephew Azzo succeeded him; his loyal services to the Ghibelline cause were rewarded by Henry VII who, on coming to Italy in

1310, made him imperial vicar of Lombardy. Azzo's prowess on the field of battle was matched by his diplomatic skill; under his rule Piacenza, Pavia, Bergamo, and Cremona—among other lesser communities—were annexed by the Milanese state. Azzo was excommunicated by John XXII and abdicated in favor of his son Galeazzo I, famous for his defeat of the papal forces at the battle of Vaprio (1324).

A misunderstanding with the Emperor Ludwig of Bavaria led to Galeazzo's incarceration a few years later; he was, however, soon released and on his death his son Azzo II again secured the title of imperial vicar from the emperor. The seven-years' rule of the second Azzo was distinguished by yet further extension of the power of Milan through Lombardy and (perhaps more usefully for the security of the line) by Azzo's murder of his uncle (who had conquered Pisa and Lucca) and defeat of his cousin, thus doing away with any possibility of dynastic feuds. On Azzo's death he was succeeded by his two uncles, in turn, Lucchino and Giovanni. The former thrust the hand of the Visconti yet deeper into Italy; first making his peace with the Church he proceeded to purchase Parma from the house of Este and solidified the grasp already established on Pisa, to the disquiet of the Florentines. He died, poisoned by his wife, in 1349; his brother Giovanni, already archbishop of Milan, succeeded him.

Petrarch, who accepted the hospitality of the archbishop, professed great admiration for his host and the verdict of historians is no less favorable. Though Giovanni ruled for only five years (1349–1354), his prudent administration and considerable enlargement of his inheritance are credited with making the Milanese state a respected and enduring power in Northern Italy. Genoa was taken under his wing, Bologna was occupied, and at the time of his death most Northern Italian lands, with the exception of the smaller states of Mantua, Verona, and Ferrara, had come under the sway of the Visconti. So large had its domain become, in fact, that on the archbishop's death it was partitioned among the three sons of his brother Stefano. Such fractionalizing might have been fatal, but happily for Milan—if not her neighbors—it was not destined to be permanent. Matteo, something of a monster, was assassinated within a year by agents of his brothers, Galeazzo II and Bernabò.

Galeazzo II, who held court at Pavia, was already the typical Renaissance prince; he too extended his patronage to Petrarch, founded the University of Pavia, and was renowned for his charm and diplomatic skill. We have noted how he arranged the marriage of his son with a daughter of the House of France; later (1368) he gave his daughter's hand (with a dowry of 200,000 florins) to Lionel, duke of Clarence, the son of Edward III. The ceremony was marked by regal splendor. "Such was the profusion of the banquet," writes the chronicler Giovio, "that the remnants taken from the table were enough and to spare for 10,000 men."[6]

Meanwhile, for his brother, who had inherited Milan itself, things did not run so smoothly. Constant wars with both the Church and the emperor led to oppressive taxation of the citizens; nor did Bernabò have either the graces or the statesmanlike skills of his brother. He survived Galeazzo by seven years and plotted to make himself sole master of the state; but he was outmaneuvered by Galeazzo's son, the wily and somewhat enigmatic Gian Galeazzo, who had his uncle executed in 1385, thus bringing the archbishop's inheritance once more under single administration.

Gian Galeazzo was to be one of the ablest and most distinguished personages of his time; his death in 1402 was perhaps a misfortune for Italy—although a great relief to Venetians and Florentines; it is probable that he might have established a united kingdom of Northern Italy, anticipating the laborious and half-fortuitous achievement of the House of Savoy four and a half centuries later. Boccaccio did not live to see the high tide of the Visconti fortunes; it was, however, evident to him as to others that during his whole lifetime the state of Milan was on the march. It is significant that the chronicles of Milan during this period contain no such allusions to class warfare and economic contention as we find in Florence. Save for oppressive taxation and occasional wanton acts of tyranny the burghers and folk of Milan seem to have been content with their state.

West of Lombardy, already dominated by the Visconti, lay Piedmont, in the fourteenth century still feudal but well integrated and ably ruled by the House of Savoy. Destined five centuries later to play a leading role in the creation of the Italian nation, Piedmont, during the years of which we write here, could hardly be counted an Italian state; the contribution of the region to the cultural development of the Renaissance was minimal and its political intervention in peninsular matters relatively negligible. Looking eastward from the city of St. Ambrose, however, the inquisitive eyes of the aggressive Milanese could envisage potential fields for further conquests and, past the waterline, look upon the face of a rival, with whom in the quattrocento the rulers of the city would be locked in a grueling struggle. For close to the Adriatic shore lay the *Serenissima* Republic of Venice, rich, resourceful, and well disciplined.

The Republic of St. Mark, as it had come to take form in the Middle Ages, was politically and socially sui generis; indeed something of a paradox. It was a republic, yet ruled by an oligarchy; the people, regulated and regimented, had little to say about their destiny. It could be called a tyranny—but without a tyrant. Situated on a complex of tiny islands, Venice had had a unique history that set it apart from other Italian states. It had never been a monarchy, nor in fact, ever been a part of the medieval feudal order. It was thus spared the civil strife that sprang up—in the states of Romagna and Tuscany for example— between the old aristocracy and the new bourgeoisie. Venice had escaped too the contagion of the Guelph-Ghibelline rivalry and had shrewdly worked out a constitutional pattern that prevented prominent families from challenging the state. It never followed the sequence of feudal dependence to commune to signoria that characterized almost every other Northern Italian state. Almost from the beginning the affairs of the republic had been administered by an oligarchy of the wealthy trading families; the doge to be sure was the supreme magistrate but he was responsible to the grand council and his office was not hereditary. (In 1335 Marin Faliero, suspected of trying to make it such, was convicted and executed.) In effect Venice was a totalitarian state in which even the members of the patrician families were subject to the discipline they had imposed upon their fellow citizens. An island people, the Venetians were fiercely nationalistic; even the clergy of the city was required to be of Venetian blood. It would not be incorrect to call the state in some sense "communist," for the chief means of production, the great trading galleys, were state property and could be leased but not owned by the merchants who sailed them. Finally, it should be noted the Venetians were rich. From the time of the city's founding in the fifth century it had cultivated commercial relationships with the East, gradually coming to own "concessions" as we would call them in all the principal cities of the Levant; it had also profited enormously from the lucrative business of ferrying crusaders to the Holy Land.

In 1310, three years before Boccaccio's birth, two decisive events took place in the City of the Lagoons. The pages of the *Libro d'Oro* had been closed; that is to say, the number of the families eligible for membership in the grand council was fixed forever, and, as a result of a conspiracy against the state, the Council of Ten was instituted. This council, working in secret, was given absolute power in matters of state policy; originally it was set up on an ad hoc basis, but it soon became permanent. Drawn from the membership of the council and working in cooperation with the doge who was himself a member, this small and therefore effective group was to guide the republic through its triumphs in the embattled centuries that lay ahead. If it inspired terror, it also commanded respect. It need hardly be added that membership on the council was not for life nor was it hereditary. And if the decisions of the council were secret and its actions final and without appeal, it must be said that over the years its patriotism, its judgment, and its impartiality were above suspicion. "Against the decrees of the Council," J. A. Symonds writes,

> "arbitrary though they might be, no one sought to rebel. The Venetian bowed in silence and obeyed, knowing that all his actions were watched, that his government had long arms in foreign lands, and that to arouse revolt in a body of burghers so thoroughly controlled by common interests, would be impossible. Further security the Venetians gained by their mild and beneficent administration of subject cities and by the prosperity in which their population flourished. . . . At home, the inhabitants of the island city, who had never seen a hostile army at their gates, and whose taxes were light in comparison with those of the rest of Italy, regarded the nobles as the authors of their unexampled happiness. Meanwhile these nobles were merchants. Idleness was unknown in Venice. Instead of excogitating new constitutions or planned

vengeance against hereditary foes the Venetian attended to his commerce on the sea, swayed distant provinces, watched the interests of the state in foreign cities, and fought the naval battles of the republic."[7]

Thus the political history of the *Serenissima* during the fourteenth century hinges on foreign policy. The overriding objective of the Venetians during the life span of Boccaccio was the attainment of supremacy in the Mediterranean; this meant, in effect, the destruction of the sea power of Genoa, its only rival. The long struggle ended, after many vicissitudes, with the Peace of Turin some years after Boccaccio's death; the war had bled both republics dry, but while Venice soon recovered Genoa never did. A portent of the final decision could be seen in the Venetian naval victory of Alghero (1352); it was their defeat on this occasion that threw the Genoese into the arms of the Visconti; although they survived to carry on the war, their vulnerability was apparent and the Visconti had only to bide their time.

A corollary of the century-long duel was a major change in Venetian policy. Until the fourteenth century the sons of St. Mark had, generally speaking, turned their backs on mainland Italy and sought their conquests in the East. The specter of a siege by the Genoese (which in fact the *Serenissima* underwent toward the end of the struggle in the War of Chioggia) compelled them to seek some convenient granary on the mainland; the island state could not grow its own food supply. Taking advantage of its role as a partner in an alliance against the tyrant Mastino della Scala of Verona in 1339, the republic occupied Treviso. It was the first step in a *Drang nach Westen* that would, in the succeeding century, see the banner of the lion floating triumphantly over Padua and Verona. These two states, independent *signorie* under the lordship respectively of the Scaligeri and the Carrara, led an uneasy existence during the fourteenth century; on the death of Mastino the Signoria of Verona disintegrated and was promptly annexed by the Visconti and a similar fate overtook Padua which, in effect, lost its independence at the time of Mastino's defeat in 1339. These once powerful centers did not have the wealth or the manpower to survive, placed as they were between the two great powers of the North. Both were annexed by the *Serenissima* in the early quattrocento (1404–1405) and remained a part of the Venetian Republic until its extinction in 1797.

As the Milanese thrust to the East moved the Visconti nearer to confrontation with the *Serenissima*, so their expansion southward seemed, during the years of the fourteenth century, to endanger the liberty of yet another vigorous Italian state, the Commune of Florence. The history of the Tuscan capital during the lifetime of Boccaccio reflects, in fact, both the struggle within the walls among the various social classes for political power and a share in the new wealth growing out of the wool trade and the successful banking and commercial enterprises and, concurrently, the efforts of all classes to maintain their independence against the pressures of foreign neighbors in a permanently unstable political situation. The story of Florence, chronicled by writers of rare talent from Dante to Guicciardini, is of particular interest because of the city's unique contributions to arts and letters; considering its bountiful gifts to mankind, as well as the contentious vivacity of its citizens, Florence may fairly be compared to classical Athens.

During the period we are here surveying Florentine foreign policy (with its inevitable repercussions on events within the walls) was in the main defensive and to a great degree shaped by an underlying legal disability. In the feudal chain of command during the Middle Ages Florence had been simply a part of the patrimony of the rulers of Tuscany, in theory dependent on the emperor but, by a legacy of Matilda of Tuscany (the humbler of Henry IV at Canossa), it had been put under the protection of the pope. Hence, recurrently, the city was obliged to appeal to one "protector" or another within the traditional feudal framework. It became the charge of magistrates as the years passed and Guelph and Ghibelline battled for supremacy, to preserve the city's independence against those who sought to destroy it and simultaneously to keep a wary eye on those who, under the guise of protecting its integrity, would hope to dominate it.

In 1313, the year of Boccaccio's birth, the Black Guelphs, who for a decade had been supreme in the city, had special cause to rejoice. Henry VII, beloved of Dante, died of a fever at Buonconvento, having failed in his effort to restore imperial power on the peninsula and, incidentally, to displace the Guelphs and put his own Ghibellines (and schismatic White Guelphs of which Dante was one) back into power. In their time of danger (1310) when Henry came to Lombardy, the rulers of Florence had invited Robert of Anjou, king of the Two Sicilies (i.e., Naples) and champion of the papal cause, to be their defender for a five-year period. After the death of Henry, the aggressive campaign of Uguccione della Faggiuola, another Ghibelline leader, posed yet another threat. Following Uguccione's capture at Lucca the Florentines urged Robert to send his brother, Piero, to lead their armies; he was, however, defeated and slain at the Val di Nivole. His successor, Count Novello d'Adria, was extremely unpopular and the anti-Neapolitan faction (even in crisis the Florentines were rarely at one in their sympathies) displaced him and put in his stead Lando d'Agobbio, who immediately abused the power vested in him and made himself a tyrant; he maintained himself until 1321 when a Neapolitan intervention in its turn overthrew him. It should be stressed that the parade of dictators within the city was occasioned by the constant menace from without, first from Uguccione, later from the even more aggressive Castruccio Castracani, self-made despot of Lucca (1281–1328), who at his death held Pistoia and Pisa, too close to Florence for comfort.

It was immediately after the downfall of Lando d'Agobbio that Castruccio made his thrust toward the city, putting nearby Prato under siege. The Florentines, now free from Neapolitan "protection," had reorganized their government and were striving to unite the factions, even promising to invite the exiles to return. A large army was sent to the relief of Prato; Castruccio withdrew and the victors fell to quarreling over the advisability of pursuing him. According to Machiavelli the people favored pursuit but the "signori" wished to retire to Florence. So not only did Castruccio escape, but he left in his train a rancorous division between the people and the magnates of Florence. The promise of reinstatement of the exiles was withdrawn and a new charter of the city was drawn up providing for a somewhat broader base of representation and longer terms in office.

The familiar pattern was repeated a few years later when Castruccio seized Pistoia and once more alarmed the Florentines. Their defeat at

Altopascio obliged them once more to turn to the House of Naples
for a protector; this time it was the young prince, Charles of Calabria.
Happily for the freedom of the city, in 1328 both Castruccio and
Charles died; so for a dozen years the commune was spared the dangers
of invasion and benevolent intervention and was relatively free of
factionalism as well. (These were, roughly speaking, the years of
Boccaccio's residence in Naples; Machiavelli notes that during these
years too Giotto's campanile was finished and the Arno overflowed its
banks in a vast inundation [1333]).

Dissension between the classes arose again in 1341 when the people,
enraged at the ineptitude of the administration, which had let slip a
golden opportunity to occupy Lucca, called for the overthrow of the
government. Manipulated by the nobles and a few of the powerful
merchants, the mob proclaimed Walter of Brienne, so-called duke of
Athens, in the service of Naples, ruler for life. Within a year however
Walter had managed to antagonize all classes and was compelled to
flee the city. Again the commune was reinstated with a new charter,
this time to the advantage of the merchant class over the nobles. The
latter took to arms in protest and were so completely defeated that,
says Machiavelli, "never afterward did they dare to take up arms
against the people."[8] A decade of tranquility ensued, marred by the
great famine of 1343 and the Black Death, which came to the city in
the spring of 1348 and carried off, according to Machiavelli, some
96,000 souls[9]—probably an exaggerated figure but indicative of its
impact.

It must be remembered as we follow the affairs of the city through
these years that behind the official framework of government, the
council, the priors, and the various elected officers (frequently reorganized and reshuffled as the humbler elements of the citizenry, the lesser
guilds, and the *popolo minuto* pressed their claims for representation)
there was another body, extralegal but often the true arbiter of the
commune's destinies from the time of Dante: the *Parte Guelfa*. The
function of the party, something like that of the Communist party in
Russia or the Fascist party under Mussolini's regime, was, in effect, to
see that the commune remained loyal to its traditions; in this case
opposition to the emperor and close association with the pope. To be

sure, in moments of emergency political expediency might be allowed to prevail over pious devotion to principle, but the *Parte Guelfa,* whose core was the wealthy merchant class, remained inviolate. In the years following the plague—marked by an uprising of the lower classes who had suffered greatly from the hardships attendant on the calamity— the party prevailed upon the commune to institute a policy of issuing "warnings" to citizens suspected of subversive plotting with Ghibel- lines. These "warnings" were in effect proscriptions and a "warned" citizen was usually fined or banished, with confiscation of his property by the state. According to Machiavelli the device was invented by a few powerful families as a useful method of ruining their potential rivals, but of course the security of the state was regularly invoked. The more liberal members of the merchant class who were not in sympathy with the policy of "warnings" were of course suspect and liable to be "warned" themselves. The issuance of "warnings" was first sanctioned by the magistrates in 1357; by 1366 the system had become generally unpalatable but in the intervening years "warnings" were recurrently given out, notably in 1359–1360, when some of Boccaccio's friends, conspiring to attack the ruling faction, were banished.

To follow the events that fill the chronicles of the "great town by the Arno" year by year during Boccaccio's lifetime would be to survey what seems to be an endless succession of factional quarrels within the walls and petty wars abroad. Yet through it all the commune flour- ished. It recovered not only from the devastation of the plague but, perhaps more surprisingly, also from the economic disaster caused by the collapse of the great banking houses in the forties. It was diplomati- cally and militarily strong enough to hold off the Visconti when they occupied Bologna fifty miles north in 1350. By the sixties the tenor of life had improved and the commune had prepared its defenses by annexation or dominance over the neighboring Tuscan towns, such as Pistoia, Prato, and San Gimignano. It withstood successfully the incur- sion of the Great Company in 1358–1359 and the even more alarming forays of the *condottiere* Hawkwood in alliance with the Pisans (1362– 1364). (In 1379, four years after Boccaccio's death, "Giovanni Acuto" would bring his White Company into the service of the Florentines; his portrait, by Paolo Uccello, adorns the inner facade of the Duomo.)

One rather surprising political shift may be noted. In 1375 the pope's legate in Romagna held up the city's grain supply and encouraged further ravages on the part of the doughty Hawkwood; there is reason to believe that the legate, if not his master, was thinking of adding Florence to the patrimony of Peter. Incensed by such behavior, the commune, hitherto proud of its fidelity to the pope, turned about and declared war on the papacy. The war, administered by a special council known as "the Eight Saints," was a popular one and was vigorously waged. It ended, however, in a stalemate, with the commune paying a fine for its contumacious action.

Beyond, as the century waned, lay the proletarian rising of the Ciompi, the conservative reaction, and the political climate that would prepare the way for the Medici. But all of this was after Boccaccio's time. So too were the great artistic and cultural triumphs of the Renaissance, but for all that the cultural life of fourteenth-century Florence, still free and undisciplined, is not to be despised. Giotto's tower was finished, the first doors were put on the Baptistery, the university was founded. And if Dante died in exile and Petrarch avoided the town of his ancestors, yet the roll call of Florentine men of letters is impressive: Pucci, Sacchetti, the succession of the chroniclers Villani, and more. And Giovanni Boccaccio.

A twentieth-century political scientist, reading the story of Florence in the years of which we are writing, would find the pattern of events easy to understand and in many ways surprisingly "modern." The struggle for power—and the economic opportunity that accompanies it—is a phenomenon familiar to all of us; it continues today. We can understand the aspirations of the Florentine *popolo minuto* and the uneasiness of the magnates in the face of their demands. We can sympathize with the ideal of liberty to which all Florentines (and the majority probably quite sincerely) professed devotion. In spite of the measures sometimes employed to suppress dissidents (and it is fair to remember that out of necessity the commune was a kind of garrison state during most of the turbulent century) it is undeniable that the burghers of the City of the Lily enjoyed a greater liberty of thought, of speech, and even of action, than prevailed in any other Italian state —greater by far than anything that the Visconti would tolerate or that could hope to flourish under the watchful eye of the Venetian Council of Ten.

To move from Florence to the Kingdom of the Two Sicilies (for so it was styled, though somewhat inaccurately since Sicily had broken away from the Angevin state in 1282; the twain would not be joined again until the eighteenth century) is to move into a completely different social order. The kingdom was the largest political unit on the peninsula and Naples, its capital, was a large and busy city. But the social structure of the realm was still feudal—indeed perhaps more so than a century earlier, for Charles of Anjou, who had displaced the Swabian line, had by his legislative measures augmented the privileges already enjoyed by the nobility and the clergy.

The economy was primarily agricultural; the kingdom possessed, as it does today, few exploitable natural resources. Trade was largely in the hands of foreigners among whom Florentines were prominent; Catalans, Genoese, Venetians, and Marseillais also plied their trades of banking and merchandising. The middle class, in Florence the seedbed of social progress and the cult of liberty, was in the kingdom relatively small and impotent. Underneath it the great mass of the peasantry lived in abject misery, relieved sporadically by savage uprisings, savagely repressed. In the kingdom too as in the North the mercenary "companies" were a scourge; veterans of the recurrent wars in Sicily as well as adventurers from the North ravaged the countryside, which indeed did not lack brigands of its own spawning; brigandage in fact became a tradition of the kingdom; in such regions as Lucania and Calabria specimens are still to be found. At the top of the ladder was the nobility, a large and parasitic element, arrogant, punctilious, and inept. During the reigns of Robert and Joan, foreigners, who as noted dominated the world of commerce, also rose high in the councils of the state; the native ruling class had as little talent for politics as for finance. The most able statesman in the service of the Angevin rulers during Boccaccio's lifetime was his fellow Florentine, Niccolò Acciaiuoli. Neapolitan history therefore is not the story of class rivalry or of a striving for social progress or liberty; it is hardly the history of a community at all; it is a dynastic chronicle. The story of the monarchy is the story of the monarch.

In Boccaccio's years there were but two rulers of the kingdom: Robert, surnamed the Wise, who reigned from 1309 to 1343, and his granddaughter Joan, who succeeded him and came to a wretched end, murdered by order of her cousin and successor six years after Boccaccio's death. Under both sovereigns the principal objective of foreign policy was to recover Sicily from the Aragonese who had been firmly entrenched on the island since the "Sicilian vespers" of 1282 had driven out the Angevins. As to internal policy, there was none to speak of save, perhaps, for Joan, survival on the throne.

In the early years of his reign Robert was an important figure in the affairs of the peninsula. On the occasion of Henry VII's invasion of Italy the pope had made Robert his vicar, Florence had put herself under his protection, and he became, in effect, the leader of all Italian Guelphs. The death of Henry spared Robert a confrontation with the imperial invaders, which may have been fortunate for him; two years later, in alliance with the Florentines at Montecatini he was badly beaten by the Ghibelline chieftain Uguccione della Faggiuola. Serving also as the pope's vicar against the aggressive Visconti, for a time he had some success promoting and controlling a Guelph rising in Genoa (1318), but in the end the Visconti came out on top. Since Robert was not only king of Naples but also count of Provence (a part of the Angevin patrimony) he had a legitimate interest in the affairs of Northern Italy. But his abiding concern was the reconquest of Sicily; perhaps his seven humiliating years as hostage in the Aragonese court during his adolescence added a personal incentive to his dynastic purpose. In any case between 1314 and 1342 he made no fewer than five attempts to recover the island; all were failures and all signified the even greater impoverishment of the kingdom and resulted in even more crushing taxes for its people.

History's verdict on Robert is somewhat ambivalent. In his own day, if Dante did not think much of him, Petrarch admired him greatly, seeing in him not only the perfect ruler but also the illuminated patron of arts and letters. Robert gave cordial welcome to Laura's liege man and was instrumental in his coronation as poet laureate. The king also embellished his capital, inviting Giotto to work in the city; the Royal Library flourished under his aegis if not direction; he even wrote a book (of devotional nature) himself. His court was notable for its splendor, and the city—at least the upper classes—prospered under him. Boccaccio, who knew Naples in the last decade of Robert's reign, compares the order and elegance of urban life in the Angevin capital very favorably with the incessant restlessness and relative bourgeois shabbiness of Florence.

And in fact Boccaccio's sojourn coincided with a prosperous period in the life of the capital; Fausto Nicolini estimates that the population grew from 40,000 to 60,000 between 1280 and 1340,[10] and though wars were waged abroad the city thrived untroubled by the factional disputes that seemed endemic in Boccaccio's Florence. But with the death of Robert in 1343 the years of tranquillity in glamorous Naples came to an end.

Both of Robert's sons predeceased him. In order, so he thought, to avoid dynastic rivalries (he was himself a descendant of a cadet branch and his kinsman, the king of Hungary, might have pressed a claim to the throne, he had his granddaughter Joan betrothed to his elder brother, Charles Martel's grandson Andrew of Hungary; both children were seven years old when the engagement took place (1333). The marriage was solemnized in 1342; it was a brief and unhappy alliance. In 1345, in circumstances that still remain mysterious after six centuries, the young prince was murdered; many suspected that the queen, said to be in love with her cousin Louis of Taranto, had a hand in the affair. It was the end of peace in Naples. The prince's brother, Louis, king of Hungary, twice invaded the kingdom (1348 and 1350–1352); on the second occasion his armies occupied the capital but in the face of general hostility could not hold it. Meanwhile Joan had been obliged to flee to her county of Provence; there, ably guided by Acciaiuoli, she managed to get the pope's absolution and also his blessing on her marriage to Louis of Taranto (although she had to cede Provence to the papacy as a part of the bargain). The royal pair returned in triumph and were crowned in the capital in 1352. A decade of relative serenity ensued, although the king and queen were each jealous of the other's prerogative. Inevitably the reconquest of Sicily was essayed; under

Acciaiouli's leadership it promised to be successful; a six-year campaign of attrition and negotiation with the slippery baronage of Sicily ended in failure however when Louis died (1362), leaving the kingdom once more unstable. Joan's third husband, James III of Mallorca, had little interest in the affairs of the kingdom, or, for that matter, in the queen. Acciaiuoli died three years later and the last years of Joan's unhappy reign were dedicated to keeping her throne secure against the intrigues of the rival branch of the family, the clan of Durazzo, destined to succeed her in the end. At long last a treaty in 1372 put an end to the ninety-year-old effort to recapture Sicily.

The foregoing survey may suffice to indicate the principal developments in the most prosperous and politically significant states of Italy; many of these events were witnessed at first hand by the author of the *Decameron.* Another large area of the peninsula with which he had frequent contact was the patrimony of Peter: the lands of Emilia, Romagna, and the Marches, over which the Holy Father was temporal lord. In these provinces, although there was plenty of activity, much of it violent, one cannot detect any special direction, nor do the congeries of petty signorie have any collective goal. The pope was, in the fourteenth century, an absentee landlord and in his absence disorder reigned. "Tyrants like the Malatesta of Rimini, the Ordelaffi of Forlì ... and the Manfredi of Faenza pursued their schemes in defiance of the Papacy"[11] and Bologna, as we have noted, fell for a while into the hands of the Visconti. Finally, in 1353, Innocent VI sent the Spanish Cardinal Albornoz to Rome and Romagna; Albornoz was both soldier and statesman and he soon brought the contentious despots to heel; he was obliged to make a second incursion (1358–1363), however, before his master's authority was firmly reestablished.

The Eternal City itself, during the Babylonian Captivity, had fallen to low estate. Its population shrank drastically—some historians say to a mere 20,000—and it was ineffectually administered by a papal vicar and a quarrelsome senate, composed of representatives of the Roman nobility who made the city and the surrounding countryside the scene of incessant feuding and brigandage. The monuments of antiquity— the Colosseum, the Theater of Marcellus, and the like—served as fortresses for the embattled clans.

Vulture and serpent, lion, wolf and bear,
on a high marble column work their will,
Yet, gnawing it, likewise themselves devour,

as Petrarch poetically puts it.[12] This dismal chaos provided the background and the motivation for one of the most spectacular events of the century, the seizure of power by Cola di Rienzi who, though of lowly origin, managed by a coup to dislodge the nobles and make himself master of Rome, assuming the ancient title of Tribune. For a few brief months in 1347 Cola ruled the city, applauded by Petrarch and doubtless by many other men of goodwill. His own vanity and the machinations of the great families brought him down; he returned briefly with Albornoz in 1354 but once more became too arrogant for the tolerance of the people on whom he depended, and was murdered by the mob at the foot of the Capitol. But his dream of restoring the glory and dominion of Rome and its people left its mark on men's memories; like Hus and the Jacquerie he seems— looking back—a portent of things to come. As far as pacifying the city was concerned, however, Cola's labors were fruitless; when Urban V returned he found the anarchy and violence as intolerable as ever.

As in political and social matters the fourteenth century was a time of agitated stagnation wherein it is difficult for the historian to trace any clear lines of development, much less "progress," so too in matters of technology it is a relatively barren age. Pirenne, granting that during the century "bigger ships were built and they made longer voyages," yet comments wryly that the chief technological advance was the discovery of a method for salting herring.[13] Perhaps this is a little harsh; there were improvements in papermaking and in bookkeeping; spectacles (though an invention of the thirteenth century) came into wider use and must have considerably enlarged the reading public. Arabic numerals replaced the clumsier Roman symbols. And it was "towards the beginning of the fourteenth century," Marc Bloch reminds us, that "counterpoise clocks brought with them at last, not only the mechanization of the instrument, but, so to speak, time itself."[14] Gunpowder came to Europe in Boccaccio's day, too, portending the doom both of the French knight and the sturdy English bowman—but its triumph was some time in the future.

Boccaccio's imagination was stirred by reports of the rediscovery (in 1342) of the "Fortunate Isles" (the Canaries), but the age of the great explorers was still to come, even as the splendors of the Renaissance. Yet the contributions of the fourteenth century are not contemptible. Aside from the great creative writers in the various vernaculars that we have mentioned, the century also produced in music the great champions of the *ars nova:* Philippe de Vitry and Guillaume Machaud in France and Francesco Landini in Italy. And it is the century too of Giotto, Andrea Pisano, Duccio, and Simone Martini.

A survey, even capsular, of the technology of the fourteenth century may serve to remind a twentieth-century reader of what is so often forgotten or discounted as he follows a political or aesthetic thread through the tangled skein of the past: the day-to-day texture of medieval life. Yet, as we make our way through the *Decameron* or savor the tales of Chaucer's blithe companions, it may add a dimension to our appreciation if we call to mind what kind of world it was in which their great creators lived and wrote. If we can, that is—for in fact the conditions of life in the Middle Ages were certainly much closer in existential respects to those of the Homeric or even the biblical age than to anything we have known since the industrial revolution.

The gulf between our way of life and that of medieval men is so great as to call for some imagination to bridge it. It is not merely a matter of such recent amenities as airplanes, radio, or television. Boccaccio's time not only knew nothing of trains; it was likewise ignorant even of stagecoaches. There was in fact no public transportation. A journey was an exercise in private enterprise, calling for one's own horse or mule; impedimenta were carried on the back of sumpter animals, rarely and exceptionally on wagons. The traveler was not sheltered from the elements; he was furthermore exposed to the endemic brigandage of the times and, in Italy at least, also liable to run afoul of the soldiery of the warring communes. Travel by sea was perhaps more hazardous—Petrarch, after one narrow escape, permanently foreswore ships. The sailing craft of his day were powerless against head winds, vulnerable to storms—and, like brigandage ashore, piracy at sea was a recognized, quasi-respectable career, as several tales of the *Decameron* make evident. To take an example from another field: it was not simply that the Middle Ages had no telephones or telegraph; there was not even a postal service. Letters were carried by friends—and subject to all the risks of travel mentioned above. Or, to glance at another sector, it was not simply a matter of lack of central heating; for many a well-to-do household there was only a rudimentary kind of fireplace, imperfect in draft; even the halls of the great castles smoked and were warm only in the proximity of the fire itself. The man of the Middle Ages, even of the upper classes, shivered in winter even as he sweated in an insect-infested summer.

With regard to food, although we have many records of sumptuous banquets, often with entrées of game that has become scarce or unavailable nowadays, the day-by-day fare of the overwhelming majority was limited in range. Bread was the staple for the masses; not the white bread we know but dark and coarse, made more often of rye, barley, or maslin (a mixture of rye and wheat) than of wheat. Lack of refrigeration made meat in some months unavailable, at all times potentially hazardous. Not only were such alleviating beverages as coffee, tea, and chocolate still unknown; medieval Europe had yet to know the sustaining and, as it now seems, basic bounties of the New World: tomatoes, potatoes, corn. (It is strange to think that Boccaccio never sat down to a plate of *polenta,* the daily fare of wide regions of Italy nowadays.)

Men had not yet learned how to control—or cooperate with—the forces of nature; famines, floods, and plagues are recorded with inexorable recurrence in the chronicles of all nations and communities. Matters of medicine and sanitation scarcely bear thinking about; it is doubtful that the average man of the twentieth century could survive a week of life in a medieval town. Save for the torches of festive occasions cities were dark at night; the streets were narrow, noisy, and carpeted with dung. Florence, to be sure, had more amenities than the average town of the times; it could offer paved streets, hospitals, and schools. Indeed Villani gives an impressive account of the educational facilities available—to the better classes. Even so the vast majority of Europeans could neither read nor write. Writing was indeed a special-

CHAPTER 2

LIFE

ny "Life" of Boccaccio is bound to be, for the most part, a tissue of conjectures. Although the poet spoke often of himself his testimony is suspect and objective documentation is scanty.[1] To begin with, we cannot be absolutely certain about either the time or place of his birth. The nearest thing we have to a birth certificate is Petrarch's statement (in *Seniles* [hereafter *Sen.*] 8.1) that he (Petrarch) anticipated by nine years his disciple's arrival in this world. This would mean that Boccaccio was born in 1313 and presumably—if nine years is an accurate measure—some time in early summer of that year, for Petrarch was born on July 20.[2] In the *Amorous Vision* (14, 42–46) Boccaccio refers to his legitimization by his father —probably in 1319 or 1320. Thus we may be sure of his paternity.

The roots of Boccaccio's line were in Certaldo, a small town twenty-three miles southwest of Florence; his grandfather Chelo was a prosperous member of the merchant-banking middle class who, as his business prospered and his horizon widened, set up residence in Florence.[3] His son, Boccaccino, carrying on the family business, made a number of trips to Paris, and for many years it was believed that our Giovanni was born of a liaison between Boccaccino and a Frenchwoman. In his romance, *Filocolo*,[4] Boccaccio, though in veiled terms and using fictitious names, gives a circumstantial account of the seduction of his mother by a Tuscan and of his own birth as a result of that union. He tells much the same story in the *Comedy of the Florentine*

Nymphs. [5] And in the Italian version of the first biography of our poet written by Filippo Villani, a contemporary, it is also affirmed that his mother was a "giovinetta parigina," of good social standing and furthermore, "as readers of Giovanni's works would have it," that Boccaccino had actually married her.[6]

Scholars today see the French mother as pure fiction. She is, they assert, the poet's own poetic creation, and as for Villani's testimony it is noteworthy that no French mother appears in the first version of his sketch; her intrusion into the vernacular version is evidence simply that the biographer was drawing on those same dubious romances for his information. Branca speaks for the overwhelming majority of critics nowadays when he affirms that Boccaccio was born "of an illegitimate relationship" not in Paris but in either Certaldo or Florence—probably the latter.[7] Yet some uncertainty must persist. Granting that modern scholarship has demolished the claims of Boccaccio's own fancy in the matter, it has been unable to produce any positive proof of its own. If one could date precisely the visits of Boccaccino to Florence one might, accepting Petrarch's rather loose chronological allusion, make a reasonably firm hypothesis with regard to the "parigina." But until further evidence is available we must say with Sapegno that Boccaccio's mother was a woman "of whom we know nothing."[8]

In any event whether his father took him from Paris home to Italy or simply brought him into the house from some nearer birthplace, young Giovanni grew up as one of the family. He soon had a stepmother (his father married in 1320) and, what was no doubt worse, a stepbrother; in the same passage already referred to in the *Filocolo* he speaks of "two ferocious bears" that barred his entrance into his father's house and obliged him to turn away and seek his fortune elsewhere. But this seems a little unlikely. His father, in truth, seems to have done very well by him, not only legitimizing him but giving him a sound education. Boccaccio's childhood years (which he recalls nostalgically in the less fanciful pages of the *Genealogie deorum gentilium*) were neither shameful nor poverty-stricken. Indeed the ursine stepmother may have had her uses. She was one Margherita dei Mardoli, daughter of Lippa de' Mardoli who was a close kin to Dante's

Beatrice and may have been the "reliable source" who later provided him with much information on the youth of Dante.

As to schooling Boccaccio himself tells us that before he was seven he had learned the first elements of letters.[9] Villani adds that the lad went to school under the mastership of Mazzuoli da Strada, father of Zanobi da Strada, destined for a distinguished career.[10] He and Boccaccio were contemporaries and classmates. Under the guidance of the elder da Strada young Giovanni not only learned Latin grammar and read Ovid but concurrently, at his father's bidding, learned "arismetica" or, as we should say, accounting. Clearly Boccaccino had plans for his love child.

As trade and commerce flourished the bankers of Florence and their merchant associates prospered. The link between Florence and the royal House of Naples was particularly strong for, as we have seen, the king of Sicily was the Guelph champion and defender of the commune against imperial aggression; on his part the protector of the city's liberties had frequent need of financial support. Hence the bankers of Florence were sure of welcome in Naples. In 1327 Boccaccino made his way to the Angevin capital, taking young Giovanni with him.[11] Boccaccino had become known to Charles of Calabria the previous year when the prince had been called in as protector and lord of Florence. Branca suggests that Barbato da Sulmona and Giovanni Barili, two gentlemen of prominence, destined to become known both for their offices and for their friendship with Petrarch, attested in his correspondence, may have been charmed by the precocious and doubtless attractive son of Boccaccino. Boccaccino seems to have been the representative of or at least associated with the banking house of the Bardi; the king was pleased with his services and bestowed upon him the titles of counselor and chamberlain, indications of esteem if not in themselves particularly significant or lucrative appointments. Young Giovanni was put to work at once; he received clients, dealt with letters of credit and similar transactions, and had frequent occasions to visit the busy port, a meeting place of all classes and nationalities. The scene of his employment was the region of Portanuova, near the Castelnuovo.[12]

He found the life of the city much to his taste. In the fifth book of his *Fiammetta*, speaking through the persona of that love-stricken lady, he describes Naples as abounding above all other Italian cities in joyous feasts, offering in addition to the delights of sea bathing many pastimes and spectacles, going on to chronicle rapturously the carefree celebrations of springtime, with the assembly of "lusty young lords and cavaliers" in the "greatest and most stately houses of noblemen" where they pay court to "the bravest and most honorable ladies, shining in glittering gold and adorned with their precious and most rare jewels." It seems likely that of such captivating scenes young Giovanni was no mere spectator. Years later he recalled with complacency that he associated with the young nobles of his age, who he recalls were not ashamed to come to his house which was, along with its furnishing, and in accordance with his means, "quite splendid."[13] His standing was something higher than what one would associate with his occupation; not so much that of a clerk or accountant but rather that of a member of a prominent and wealthy banking clan, enjoying the favor of the king. He speaks of seeing the monarch himself "on his throne"[14] and he probably had the entrée not only to the court but also to the homes of the royal kinsmen of the competing houses of Taranto and Durazzo.

A companion and to some degree a mentor of the youthful Boc-caccio in these happy days of young manhood was his compatriot Niccolò Acciaiuoli, destined to play a prominent role in the history of Naples and, for that matter, in the life of our subject. Like the Bardi and the Peruzzi the Acciaiuoli were bankers of some importance; the family, originally from Northern Italy, had been for some time resi-dent in Florence: the Acciaiuoli were thought of as Florentines. And also, even as the Bardi and the Peruzzi, they enjoyed close relations with the royal House of Naples and maintained their own banking house in the capital of the realm. Some scholars have suggested that Boccaccio may have been employed in their countinghouse rather than in that of the Bardi. Young Niccolò, who came to Naples about 1330, was already well known to Boccaccio. He was three years older than our subject but had been his schoolmate under the mastership of Mazzuoli da Strada. Acciaiuoli's father too had won the favor of King Robert and enjoyed the titles of counselor and chamberlain even before they had been conferred on Boccaccino.

Young Niccolò was shrewd, able, and ambitious and, in spite of his small stature, of attractive and even imposing social presence. In 1334 his services were called upon in a matter of some importance. Robert's sister-in-law, Catherine de Courtenay, exchanged her duchy of Durazzo for the Kingdom of Achaia (the Peloponnesus); the additional payment demanded of her was negotiated through the house of Acciaiuoli. The conduct of these negotiations was entrusted to young Niccolò; the affair afforded him the foothold he had long been seeking. To quote Villani: "He began to frequent the court of the Empress of Constantinople [Catherine de Courtenay]. And since his affable wisdom greatly pleased that most prudent lady, he came to enjoy such high and honorable favor with her that she entrusted to him her entire family and freely committed to him the charge of her household. On his part, recognizing the importance of the duties imposed upon him he took it upon himself to instruct the children, previously neglected, as is the custom in Naples, with regard to the manners, habits and discretion suitable to their royal station."[15] Villani dismisses the tale of illicit relations between the empress and her young steward as the mere envious gossip of jealous courtiers; more recent historians have permitted themselves some doubts.[16] In any case, shortly after his arrival in Naples, Acciaiuoli had laid the foundations for a distinguished career. His sponsorship may have opened for his young compatriot the doors of many of the noble families in the entourage of the great lady. Henri Hauvette[17] speculates that Acciaiuoli must have been for young Giovanni what Pandarus was for the tender Troilus of the *Filostrato*—a slightly older and trusted companion to whom the younger man could turn for guidance.

Acciaiuoli was not, to be sure, Boccaccio's only companion in these golden days. Branca plausibly postulates: "In this merry and refined society Boccaccio, always thirsting for affection, must have formed friendships destined to endure through his lifetime: with such young men as the carefree Niccolò da Montefalcone, later a Carthusian, Pietro Canigiani, agent of the princes of Taranto, Niccolò da Cigano, agent of the Frescobaldi, Americo Cavalcanti, already in 1334 chamberlain of King Robert, or more mature men such as Marino Bulgaro, an old Ischian sea-wolf, or Costantino della Rocca, treasurer and negotiator of military loans";[18] all names that appear in sundry works of our subject, including the *Decameron*.

We may imagine that not all of the companions of the warm-hearted young poet were male. In the *Caccia di Diana* we shall find a long list of Neapolitan ladies, a roll call of lovelies without rival in the literature of the times. This too is the time of the appearance of the irresistible if enigmatic Fiammetta, inspiration of the youthful works, *croce e delizia* of the poet's young manhood. So appealing, not to say convincing, is our hero's account of his meeting with this devastating charmer that it would be a pity not to record it here. The details of that unforgettable encounter are set forth in the *Filocolo,* wherein, after a lengthy introduction describing the fortunes of the House of Naples and concluding with the story of the birth of Fiammetta, illegitimate daughter of Robert of Naples and a noblewoman, the author goes on to say:

It befell that one day, the first hour of which had been dominated by Saturn, at a season when Phoebus with his horses had reached the 16th degree of the Celestial Ram, and on which the glorious departure of the Son of Jove from the despoiled Realm of Pluto was being celebrated, I, the composer of the present work, found myself in a gracious and fair temple in Parthenope, named after him who to be deified had permitted himself to be sacrificed upon the griddle [St. Lawrence]. There I was listening to the office, accompanied by a song of sweet melody, which is sung on that day, celebrated by the priestly successors of him who first girt himself with the cords, exalting and following the rules of poverty [the Franciscans]. And as I stood there, at a time, as I reckoned, when the fourth hour of the day had already risen over the eastern horizon, the marvelous beauty of the aforementioned young woman appeared before my eyes, for she had come to that place to hear what I was attentively hearing. And no sooner did I see her than forthwith my heart began to beat so strongly that every smallest pulse of my body responded with immoderate force. And not yet knowing the reason, nor feeling yet what my heart was already imagining would befall it as a result of that vision, I began to ask myself: "Ah me, what can this be?"—and I greatly feared lest it be some other kind of harmful mischance. But after an interval being reassured,

I plucked up a little courage and began to look attentively into the eyes of the winsome lady. And gazing therein steadily I beheld Love and in such a tender attitude as to cause me—whom he had long spared to endure in my tranquil state—to desire once more to become his subject for the sake of that beautiful lady. And being unable to satiate myself with the sight of her I fell to addressing him, saying: "Valorous Lord, whose strength the gods could not resist, I thank you, for you have placed my beatitude before my eyes, and now, feeling the sweetness of your rays, my cold heart is already becoming warm. Wherefore I, who have long in fear evaded your Lordship, now pray you, through the virtue of the beautiful eyes wherein you dwell so tenderly, to enter me with your godhead. I can no longer escape you and no longer do I wish to, but rather devoutly and humbly I submit to your pleasures." No sooner had I uttered these words than the shining eyes of the fair lady, all sparkling, looked into my own eyes with a piercing light. Through that light I could see come forth a fiery arrow, golden, it seemed to me, which, passing through my eyes, struck my heart so deeply with the beauty of that fair lady, that it resumed its earlier trembling which still endures. Within my heart that arrow lighted a flame, unquenchable I believe, and of such potency that it has turned the faculties of my soul to dwelling on the marvelous beauties of that winsome lady.[19]

All of which is to say, translating the syncretistic mythology and the stylized allegory that betrays a familiarity with the *Vita nuova* of Dante, that on Easter Saturday, in the Franciscan Church of San Lorenzo in Naples, Boccaccio first beheld the lady of his heart, Maria d'Aquino, love child of the king of Naples. Unlike Petrarch, who documents a *coup de foudre* suffered under circumstances of remarkable similarity, Boccaccio does not disclose the year. The exact date is also a matter of dispute; it hinges on what day the sun entered the sign of the Ram—or more properly on what date Boccaccio thought it did. March 14 and April 3 have been suggested; it is enough to know it was spring and so in full consistency with medieval propriety in these matters—and not only medieval, as Tennyson reminds us. We may note here that the occasion of the enamorment is also the subject of allusions in other works of our poet, notably the *Ameto* and the

Amorosa visione and for what it is worth we may remark that the references are consistent with what is said here. "An entirely mannered and traditional description,"[20] Quaglio observes, citing the literary examples of Andreas Capellanus and Dante. He might have cited too, as we have noted, the case of Petrarch, also overwhelmed by passion on a day of solemnity, an even less appropriate one than the day chosen by Boccaccio's assailant. (Curiously enough, in both cases there is some ambiguity with regard to the actual date.)

Granting the recognizable and traditional pattern of the encounter, questions still remain to tease the critic. Conventional and stylized though the circumstances may be, the event need not necessarily be fictitious. Lovers, especially in Latin countries, have met in churches before and since. Was there then truly a specific lady whose charm vanquished the poet (perhaps sometime between 1331 and 1333 and perhaps in the Church of San Lorenzo)? Was her name Maria? And was she an illegitimate daughter of Robert of Naples? In recent years Vittore Branca—to take the last question first—has established to his own satisfaction and that of most critics of our time that there never existed such a winsome by-blow of the wise king; there is, to be sure, no documentation certifying to her existence. (Which does not exclude the possibility that there may have been in the society of the court a young woman who believed herself to be such or was commonly rumored to be such or whom Boccaccio truly believed to be such.)

The erudition applied to the solution of this tender problem is impressive and shrewd but in the last analysis it is impossible to prove the negative case. Even as historians, dubious about the origin and social condition of Boccaccio's mother, must stop short of affirming he had no mother at all, so it would seem that skeptics must refrain from denying to the passionate Giovanni the flesh and blood inspiration of his young manhood, almost as dependable a postulate as motherhood in the mores of the day and in the pattern of the lives of ardent young poets through the centuries. Somewhat ironically the identification of Dante's Beatrice as the daughter of Folco Portinari is commonly if not universally accepted nowadays and that identification depends on Boccaccio's account. Perhaps, all things considered, one may be permitted to believe that Fiammetta really existed and that she was a lady of good social status even though probably not Robert's daughter. Branca himself concedes that sweeping skepticism may be no less misleading than blind credulity in these delicate matters.[21] As to the specific details of what went on in San Lorenzo that Holy Saturday over six hundred years ago, let us call it poetic truth, as valid as the encounter of the nine-year-old Dante with his *beatitudine* or the shameless trick that love played on the unsuspecting Francis in Avignon on Good Friday of 1327.

Sometime before the inspirational intervention of Fiammetta (be she flesh or fancy) the young Boccaccio had abandoned his business career and turned to the study of canon law. He confesses that he had not been happy in the bank—he felt himself born for poetry and poetry alone—perhaps we may suspect that his enrollment at the University of Naples represented the elder Boccaccio's desire to meet the ambitions of his son at least halfway. Law to be sure was hardly poetry but it was somewhat closer to the Muses than money changing. And in fact the study of law, pursued it would seem without any great enthusiasm by the young Giovanni, served to bring him into contact with men of distinction in the world of letters.

Preeminent among them was Cino da Pistoia, a lawyer of great prestige but better known to posterity and no doubt more significant to Boccaccio as a friend of Dante, a poet himself, a legitimate disciple of the *dolce stil nuovo* (the "sweet new style"), a living link between the great Alighieri and his already devoted admirer. One may suspect that from him, surely by example and possibly from precept, the novitiate law student learned more of poetry than of law. Years afterward in his sonnet on the death of Petrarch he memorializes his old master, placing him in the company of Dante, Petrarch—and incidentally his own Fiammetta—in the happy eternity of lovers.

It was perhaps during his university years—although other contacts may have earlier opened its doors to him—that the young scholar-poet began to frequent the Royal Library, a treasure house of learning and letters, containing not only works of science and theology but also manuscripts of romances in such vernaculars as Old French and Provençal. The royal house was of French origin and at the time of Boccaccio's sojourn in the capital Provence, as we have noted, was a

part of the domain of the king. And in the circle of scholars connected
with the library Boccaccio found many masters whom in his later years
—specifically in the last, autobiographical, chapters of the *Genealogies
of the Pagan Gods*—he will remember with gratitude. Among them we
may cite Paolo da Perugia, the royal librarian, an encyclopedist and
compiler (as Boccaccio himself was destined to be); the astrologists
Paolo dell'Abaco and Andolò del Negro; and Paolino Minorita, bishop
of Pozzuoli and prolix commentator on matters of history. Of special
importance in the formation of the young scholar's interests was the
Augustinian, Dionigi di Borgo San Sepolcro, a master of rhetoric and
poetics, whose own special niche in literary history stems from his gift
to Petrarch of the *Confessions* of Augustine, the very volume that the
singer of Vaucluse carried with him on his ascent of Mt. Ventoux.
Unquestionably the acquaintance with Dionigi, which verged on intimacy, intensified if it did not originally inspire, the devotion of
Boccaccio to his slightly older contemporary, Petrarch.

A link with Dante was forged too by the contact with Graziolo dei
Bambaglioli, who had already written a commentary on the *Divine
Comedy*. In this circle Boccaccio also met the Calabrian monk Barlaam,
"learned in Greek letters"; from this meeting sprang Boccaccio's fasci-
nation with Greek, his resolve to learn the language, and very likely
the Hellenized titles of his early works—including the *Decameron*.
Since the author tells us that he began his somewhat lengthy *Filocolo*
while still enrolled at the university we may well imagine that most
of his time was dedicated to extracurricular reading rather than the
perusal of legal tomes. Such deviation, Branca speculates, may have
been facilitated by the absence of the elder Boccaccio, whose business
affairs called him to Paris in 1332 for a lengthy stay. For the record
we may note here that the years of legal study are the years of the early
literary productions of the young student: the *Filocolo*, the *Caccia di
Diana*, the *Filostrato* may all be dated between 1333 and 1339 and it
may be that the *Teseida* was begun before Boccaccio left Naples.

The departure from Naples was a matter not of choice but necessity.
It is clear that Boccaccio left the city of Fiammetta with its sparkling
bays, its enchanting ladies, and its ever-widening cultural horizons
with regret. But, either in late 1340 or early 1341, he was obliged to

leave it all behind him. He had no independent means of support; his fortunes were still dependent on his father's career and it is evident—although the reasons are not entirely clear—that for Boccaccio *père* life in the Angevin capital had become difficult. In 1338 his association with the company of the Bardi had terminated and there is a record of the sale of a house the following year; this may be taken as evidence of financial stringency. Life was, in fact, becoming less pleasant for all the Tuscan banking companies in Naples; King Robert, at least temporarily on a sound financial basis, had less need of their services and political developments were beginning to strain the Angevin-Florentine bond. To the elder Boccaccio it was clear that the time had come to return to Tuscany and the son, however reluctant, was obliged to follow. It would be pleasant to think that the embryonic poet was able to remain in the city long enough to hear his revered Petrarch undergo his public examination for the laurel crown (which took place in Naples in December of 1341) but this seems unlikely; by the end of 1341 Boccaccio was almost certainly back in Tuscany.

If taking leave of a city that had nourished his formative years and opened to him its resources, social, cultural, and no doubt erotic, was painful, his distress must have been compounded by the circumstances attendant on his return. For about this time his father married again and the young man was given a new stepmother, apparently no more appealing to him than her predecessor. Some unflattering lines characterizing his father in the *Comedy of the Florentine Nymphs* written at about this time—"a cold-hearted, coarse and stingy old man" is the phrase applied to Boccaccino[22]—seem to indicate a certain tension in the family. There was also, of course, the problem of securing honorable and gainful employment. The early forties brought a time of uneasiness for bankers—the great crash of the Bardi and the Peruzzi was to take place a few years later; the political climate in Florence was fluid and potentially explosive; the city too was still recovering from the plague of 1340, which had taken off about one-sixth of the population. In such gloomy circumstances a refugee from Naples might well wonder where to look for preferment; such hopes as the young poet had were probably for a return to the kingdom, the sooner the better.

His letter to his friend Acciaiuoli, who had distinguished himself on a political-military mission to Greece on behalf of his patroness, indicates clearly the state of mind of the young exile—for such he thought himself to be. On the twenty-eighth of August 1341[23] he writes to his old friend and putative patron a letter that reads, in part, as follows:

> Niccolò, if one may put trust in the words of wretches, I swear to you by my sorrowful soul, that the departure of Trojan Aeneas was no more painful to Carthaginian Dido than yours was to me, although you may have been unaware of it. Nor was the return of Ulysses awaited with more eagerness by Penelope than I awaited yours. Now that I learn that it has recently taken place I have rejoiced though deep in the gloom of my cares as greatly as did the Patriarchs in Limbo, when from the lips of St. John they learned of the coming of Christ through which they were looking forward confidently to be soon granted their long-expected deliverance. Wherefore as soon as I see you—if I am to live long enough to see you—I can address to myself the words of Isaiah when he said: "Lo, light has been borne unto the people who were straying in darkness." Of my being in Florence against my will I shall tell you nothing for it would have to be set forth not in ink but in tears. This much only I shall tell you: that even as Alexander changed the fortunes of the pirate Antigonos from bad to good, so I hope you too will change mine. This is not a new hope but rather an old one, since my reverend father and master Dionysius—perhaps for the best—was taken from me by God.

The letter is signed "your Giovanni Boccaccio of Certaldo—and Fortune's enemy."

If they were times of financial—and perhaps social—unease yet the years of the early forties were rich in literary production. Boccaccio, with his gifts for adaptability and assimilation, soon made himself at home among the social and intellectual groups of Florence, the latter probably included more and subtler minds than had graced the court circles of Naples. Although the dating of all of Boccaccio's works is tentative it seems likely that the *Ameto* was composed in 1341–1342, followed shortly (later in 1342) by the *Amorosa visione*. The *Elegy of Madonna Fiammetta* is of 1343–1344; the *Nymph Song of Fiesole* probably of 1344–1346.[24] These are all substantial—if not in fact in some

cases downright prolix—works, the composition of which would seem
to indicate that this time of adjustment provided the young fortune
seeker ample leisure without sapping his creative vigor. If he was still
associated with his father in business enterprises, as seems likely, his
labors cannot have been too onerous.

Unemployment afforded time for reading as well as writing; the
works of the period indicate new sources, not all among the classics.
Branca opines[25] that in the businessman's milieu of the Tuscan capital
Boccaccio must have read many journals and reports of commercial
travelers, accounts of company operations and missions; on such reading—and possibly abetted by the example of Livy, some of whose
passages he translated at about this time—he may in some degree have
honed the crisp prose that would characterize some of the narration
in the *Decameron*, even as other sections of that multicolored tapestry
betray acquaintance with the subtler rhetoric of medieval tradition.

With no immediate prospect of a return to Naples and as yet unable
to establish himself in Florence, Boccaccio, late in 1345, made his way
to Romagna, either by invitation or otherwise. He stayed first in
Ravenna, a city still full of memories of Dante, still under the lordship
of the House of Polenta. Here, whatever his employment may have
been, he enlarged his acquaintance among men of letters; particularly
noteworthy among them was Donato degli Albanzani, a scholar and
classicist to whom Petrarch would later dedicate the polemical essay
On His Own Ignorance and That of Others. Although there is reason to
believe—on the basis of a letter of dedication preceding the aforementioned translation of Livy attributed to Boccaccio—that the young
poet found service in the court of the Polenta, it can hardly have been
a satisfactory appointment for two years later (perhaps toward the end
of 1347) he moved on to Forlì. There he seemed for a brief time, under
the aegis of Francesco Ordelaffi, lord of the town, to have found the
position of prestige and security that he had been seeking. Evidence
of his high station—or possibly great expectations—is found in a letter
written at that time to his old school friend Zanobi da Strada.[26]

The letter is indicative too of a rather remarkable change in Boccaccio's attitude toward Acciaiuoli, to whom he had written so affectionately a few years earlier. In the interval political events had interv-

ened to alter the relationship between the two happy companions of Neapolitan times. King Robert had died in January of 1343; the realm passed to his granddaughter, the young Joan. The murder of her husband, the youthful Andrew of Hungary, which took place in 1345, under circumstances still obscure, had thrown the kingdom into confusion. Acciaiuoli came to the fore as a partisan and adviser of the queen's cousin, Louis of Taranto; it was he who encouraged and probably actually arranged their marriage (1347). Meanwhile the brother of the unfortunate Andrew, having his own claim to the throne and well aware of the fierce factionalism in the court, moved to invade the kingdom. Joan was obliged to flee the capital and take refuge in Provence (also a part of her kingdom, which she was however compelled to cede to the pope in recognition of his exoneration for her supposed guilt in the slaying of her husband). So it was that in 1347 Louis of Hungary on his march to Naples passed through Romagna, where he was cordially received by the lords of that turbulent region. No doubt they saw in his coming an opportunity to win greater independence from the papacy, to which they were all in theory subject. Ordelaffi, Boccaccio's new patron, joined the Hungarian army and in the letter we have mentioned Boccaccio proudly informs Zanobi that he is to accompany his master not as a simple soldier but rather in the role of "arbiter rerum"—a designation as ambiguous as it is pompous and probably meant to signify something like "counselor" or "political adviser," as we should say nowadays. There is surely a suggestion that Boccaccio would hold in the entourage of the Ordelaffi a position similar to that of Acciaiuoli in the Angevin court. In the same period in which the letter was written the Third Eclogue, "Faunus," was composed; in its verses, under the customary allegorical veil, Louis of Hungary is represented as the righteous avenger of his slain brother; and among those who are seen as accomplices in the murder of Joan's spouse there is adumbrated the figure of Acciaiuoli himself.

Boccaccio did not, however, maintain his pro-Hungarian posture for long. Like his master he was disillusioned by the failure of the invader to establish himself firmly in the capital (Louis in fact withdrew after a few months of uneasy occupation) and perhaps a little disgusted by the rapacious savagery of the Hungarian army. Acciaiuoli meanwhile had been successful in reconciling Clement VI with the errant Joan; her marriage to Louis of Taranto received official blessing and the realm was once more restored to the good graces of the papacy. Acciaiuoli returned to Naples in glittering triumph as count of Terlizzi and Grand Seneschal of the Realm. Boccaccio's Fourth Eclogue reflects —a little regrettably for the good name of the author—the new state of affairs. In this composition the killing of the young prince is seen as deplorable to be sure but a logical consequence of his tyrannical conduct; the king of Hungary is given the name "Polyphemus" and represented as a violent savage. The character who comes out best is "Pythias"—Acciaiuoli—whose fidelity to his sovereign is extravagantly lauded. Indeed those who sided with Polyphemus are now severely criticized for their error. "Il serait difficile de pousser plus loin l'impudeur ou l'oubli," as E. G. Léonard justly observes.[27] The two successive eclogues, dedicated respectively to sharp criticism of Polyphemus and fulsome praise of "Alcestis" (Louis of Taranto, Joan's new husband), with a delicate suggestion that the poet, whose attitude in eclogue 3 is explained by his fear of the barbarous Polyphemus, might fairly expect some reward for his verses.

While it can hardly be said that such tergiversations do the poet much honor, they provide unmistakable evidence of his anxious uncertainties in these times of crisis and of his desire, natural enough under the circumstances, to find employment worthy of his gifts. Clearly the later eclogues we have cited indicate too that their author no longer had high expectations of advancement in Romagna nor perhaps even any desire for it since Naples seemed to be beckoning again. In any event Boccaccio left Romagna in time to be back in Florence at the high tide of the Black Death (March and April of 1348).[28] Among the victims of the scourge was his recently acquired stepmother; his father seems to have succumbed not very long afterward, for in 1350 Boccaccio was named his father's principal legatee and guardian of his half brother Jacopo (a responsibility he conscientiously and at times painfully discharged for the rest of his life). And during the years between 1348 and 1352, in the general opinion of critics, he composed his great masterpiece, the Decameron.

• • •

THE early fifties were a time of notable political and social involvement for Boccaccio. His various appointments added to his prestige,
undoubtedly improved his financial situation, and brought him personal contacts of a rewarding and enduring nature. In 1350 he returned
to Romagna but this time as an ambassador of the Commune of
Florence. The precise purpose of his political mission is not known;
it is recorded however that on this occasion he visited Ravenna,
carrying on behalf of the Company of Or San Michele of Florence
a gift of ten gold florins to Dante's daughter, Suora Beatrice, a nun
in the convent of Santo Stefano dell'Uliva. It was probably during this
visit too that an old Neapolitan friend, Bechino Bellincioni, a courtier
of King Hugo of Cyprus, reminded the poet that he had promised to
dedicate to his sovereign a study of the pagan divinities (later to take
form as the *Genealogie deorum gentilium* (the *Genealogies of the Pagan
Gods*).

Returning to Florence in September, Boccaccio learned that his
revered Petrarch was expected to pass through the city en route to
Rome. (It was a jubilee year and Petrarch was making his pious
Christian pilgrimage, for which special indulgences were given. It
would also mark his first sojourn in the city of his fathers.) Perhaps
1350 should also be remembered as a jubilee year in the history of
letters; within a few short months the author of the *Decameron* encountered the daughter of the writer of the *Divine Comedy* and the poet
of the immortal *Canzoniere*— thus bringing the great triumvirate into
a kind of existential synchronism. We may imagine with what ecstatic
joy the younger man went forth to meet the master whom he had
admired for years. Petrarch has left us a grateful and affectionate record
of that historic encounter between the "dioscuri" of European letters,
as Branca aptly calls them. Writing some nine years later the laureate
reminds his disciple:

> I cannot forget the occasion when I was hurrying across Italy and
> you not merely sent me affectionate greetings, which are like the
> footsteps of the soul, but you came in person with all haste, on the heels

of your admirable poem, moved by a laudable desire to meet a perfect stranger. Thus you showed first the face of your character, then that of your physical person, to one whom you had made up your mind to love. It was late in the day and already half dark when, after long exile, I was at last received within the walls of my homeland. You welcomed me with respect and reverence far beyond my deserts; you renewed for me the poetical encounter of Anchises and the King of Arcadia, who "in the first flush of youth longed to greet the hero and clasp him by the hand." Although I did not, like him, outtop all others, but rather stood below them, your spirit was none the less enthusiastic for that. You brought me, not "within the walls of Pheneus," but rather within the secret shrine of your friendship. Nor did I give you "a splendid quiver with Lycian arrows" but my constant and sincere affection.[29]

And in fact Boccaccio not only brought his "elder brother" into his own home but introduced him to a circle of admirers, including Zanobi da Strada and Francesco Nelli, thus initiating one might say the Florentine "cell" of Petrarch admirers.

Petrarch had been on his way to Rome when the first meeting between the two poets took place; he made another brief visit on his way back from the Eternal City two months later (in December of 1350). The following spring it was Boccaccio's privilege to bear to his "preceptor," at the time living in Padua, the formal document issued by the Commune of Florence (and probably drawn up by Boccaccio himself) revoking the action taken against Petrarch's father and restoring him to citizenship. Nor did the commune's indulgence stop at mere reinstatement; Boccaccio was empowered also to invite his illustrious colleague to accept a professorship in the recently founded (1349) University of Florence—an invitation courteously and perhaps wisely refused by Petrarch.

In spite of his refusal the visit was a happy one, giving both scholar-poets a chance to learn to know each other better and to exchange opinions on a variety of literary and poetic topics. Boccaccio made copies of his master's works, spoke of his own projects, and, as he records in his Ninth Letter, had a political discussion with Petrarch on the state of Italy and the delicate position of their native Florence before the ever-encroaching Visconti (who in that year occupied Bologna).

Between the second and third meetings with his master Boccaccio carried out another charge laid on him by the commune, which may have afforded him as much pleasure—although of a different nature. His star was on the rise now; in January of 1351 he was given the title of *camerlengo della camera* of the commune; his duties included overseeing certain municipal expenses and in virtue of that function he served on a committee negotiating the acquisition of the town of Prato, hitherto held by Naples; the seller was none other than Acciaiuoli, reluctantly obliged to cede the town by the pressing needs of the recently and precariously enthroned royal pair, Louis of Taranto and Queen Joan. (For the Florentines the redemption of Prato was no less urgent; under the shadow of the Visconti they could no longer permit a stronghold so close to their walls to remain in alien, even if traditionally friendly, hands.) Since only a few months earlier Acciaiuoli had called Zanobi da Strada to his service to occupy the prestigious and lucrative post of secretary instead of Boccaccio, who might reasonably have expected the appointment, the transaction must have afforded the scorned competitor a good deal of satisfaction; it no doubt seemed to him a way of "getting even."

Boccaccio's persistent—or recurrent—sense of injury—if we may here briefly anticipate chronology—vis à vis his Neapolitan friends comes out clearly in a letter written two years later to Zanobi. The occasion of the epistle was the death or, more accurately, the funeral of Acciaiuoli's son Lorenzo, who was buried amid great pomp in Florence on April 7, 1353. Returning from the ceremony "plunged in old memories and also in the warm complacency of his own emotions" (as Acciaiuoli's biographer puts it) Boccaccio learned that the father, on hearing of his son's death, had affected the serene detachment of a philosopher. This bit of news spurred him to write a scathing letter; he accuses Zanobi of neglecting him and forgetting their old friendship and he reproaches Acciaiuoli—"your Great Man" he calls him—for his inhuman coldness. But the letter also provides the writer with the occasion to refute the charge against him implied in Acciaiuoli's definition of him as "Iohannes tranquilitatum"—"John of the quiet times," in which Boccaccio, probably correctly, divines the accusation "fair weather friend." This charge the wounded poet indignantly denies, conveniently forgetting the evidence provided by the eclogues written a few years earlier. The letter also dwells at some length on the contrast between the rich and powerful status of Acciaiuoli and the humble but honest poverty of the writer.[30]

There were other missions and offices in these busy years. Toward the end of 1351 Boccaccio went to the Trentino and perhaps Friuli as the commune's envoy to Ludwig of Bavaria, with the intention of arresting the progress of the Visconti; in 1353 with the same end in view he was sent to Forlì and Ravenna. It was in the latter city that Boccaccio heard the shocking news of Petrarch's move to Milan (that same May) where the great laureate was basking comfortably under the protection of the same Visconti whose tyrannical style and predatory greed he had condemned during those twilight talks in Padua scarcely two years before. In the second part of the letter (from which we have quoted above), recalling those happy hours Boccaccio sadly but unsparingly accuses his friend of betraying his principles and suggests that he may have lost his sanity as well as his dignity.[31] Petrarch—perhaps because of a guilty conscience, perhaps because he had received similar letters from others of his circle—did not take offense and eventually Boccaccio became reconciled to his friend's unbecoming choice of patron. Returning to Florence in October of 1353 Boccaccio seems to have been for some months without employment; in a letter of that time he speaks of his difficult financial straits. But he may have made good use of the unemployed months to work on his Genealogies—or to woo the merry widow of the Corbaccio.

The respite, however, was short. In April of 1354 he was chosen once more to serve as the commune's ambassador; this time the mission was delicate and of the highest importance. It was known that the Emperor Charles IV was planning a visit to (or was it an invasion of?) Italy. The Florentines had at first looked forward with pleasure to the emperor's coming, hoping that it might prove troublesome to the Visconti. However, they had recently concluded a treaty with the Milanese and now shared the general and chronic uneasiness of Italian states at the prospect of imperial intervention. The pope's attitude was

enigmatic. It would be Boccaccio's task in Avignon to express the
Florentine concern, to ascertain the pope's views and intentions (if any)
with regard to the impending visit, and to make sure, if possible, that,
as in the past, the faithful commune could count on the Holy Father's
protection. Forty-five days were allowed to the mission; it actually
occupied sixty, and its dignity was indicated by the terms of the
ambassador's appointment: Boccaccio was accompanied by an assistant,
he was given four florins and three soldi per diem, and assigned three
horses. How successful Boccaccio was in this rather shadowy mission
is hard to assay; at least his report must have reassured the Florentines
that no serious dangers loomed.

But from a purely personal point of view the visit to Avignon must
have been a happy one for the ambassador himself. It was his first view
of the city so closely associated with the life of his revered master; it
seems fair to assume (although no letters between the two of that
period survive) that he was well received by Petrarch's Avignonese
circle, Guido Sette, Ludwig van Kempen, Lello Tosetti, and others.
Branca speculates that he may even have made a pilgrimage of piety
to Vaucluse[32] (the Sorga will receive affectionate annotation in the
De montibus of later years). And whatever the result of the mission
Boccaccio made a good impression on the pope, who speaks of him
six years later as a "dilectus filius."

Scarcely had he returned from Provence when he was sent forth on
another errand for the commune; this time to his home town of
Certaldo, menaced by the condottiere "Fra Moriale" who was terroriz-
ing the countryside. Boccaccio, either by bribery or threat of military
action on the part of the commune, was to get rid of this wellborn
brigand. He was successful in his efforts, pursued, it would seem, by
appeal to the purse rather than the sword; Fra Moriale withdrew his
forces and went elsewhere—not long afterward he was beheaded by
Cola di Rienzi. These appointments and others in the service of the
commune if they did not make the poet rich at least considerably
improved his financial condition; he was able to buy and send to
Petrarch at this time a precious manuscript of St. Augustine's commentary on the Psalms.

In this same busy year circumstances revived the dormant hope still lingering in the breast of Fiammetta's old worshiper of a return to Naples—and in becoming dignity. In May and June of 1355 Boccaccio was serving on a committee of the commune charged with payment of the militia, a post that, incidentally, gave him the opportunity to meet the emperor as the latter was returning from Rome; Boccaccio's silence on the encounter seems to indicate that he was much less impressed by the imperial presence than Petrarch who, meeting the sovereign earlier in the year, had rapturously recorded the details of their colloquy, and found Caesar all but incredibly "cordial" and "human."[33] But of much greater significance, we may be sure, was the encounter with his old friend Acciaiuoli, who came to Florence in late May to seek the aid of the commune in his dynastic battles. Although Boccaccio made no attempt to disguise his displeasure at the coronation of Zanobi da Strada as poet laureate—the candidacy had been instigated by Acciaiuoli and the emperor himself had placed the crown on Zanobi's brow in Pisa only a month earlier (April 15), thus affronting all friends of Petrarch, the true laureate—their contact seems to have been friendly, cordial enough at least to give Boccaccio reason to believe that he might be called to take Zanobi's recently vacated post of secretary to the seneschal. (Having served his master well in a position of great difficulty and constant tension, the modest Zanobi had gladly moved to the less demanding office of assistant to the bishop of Montecassino, Acciaiuoli's brother.)

In any event, in September of 1355, when his appointment on the military committee ran out and after a serious bout of illness in the summer, Boccaccio set out for Naples, as he indicates in his Eighth Eclogue. Something went wrong; it may well be that there was no firm commitment; what is clear is that Boccaccio was not received by Acciaiuoli and may indeed not even have reached Naples. Thanks to Zanobi, however, a forgiving friend and a faithful one in spite of Boccaccio's occasional invectives, the frustrated pilgrim did get to Montecassino where he had an opportunity to examine the treasures of the library. It was, says Branca,[34] a memorable visit, decisive for Boccaccio's classical interests; he was able to look upon ancient texts of vital importance to humanism and also to copy a number of items that he duly sent to Petrarch, along with a letter complaining of the treatment accorded him by Acciaiuoli; we have Petrarch's words of consolation in reply.[35] It is possible that out of this frustrating experience came also the embittered Eighth Eclogue, in which Acciaiuoli is accused of all sorts of misbehavior, including sodomy and complicity in the murder of Andrew of Hungary, although some of the details in the poem may have been added after the even more catastrophic sally to Naples seven years later.

Somewhere in this period Boccaccio had cause to mourn the death of his daughter Violante, touchingly evoked in the Eleventh Eclogue, "Olympia." In this poem we learn the fact, not stressed by most biographers of our subject and ignored by some, that he fathered five children. The avowal is intriguing. In fact it seems a little paradoxical that we know so little of the amatory activities of a man who, in his masterpiece, cheerfully and polemically professes his devotion to the ladies. One may be permitted to wonder why he never married; given his class and circumstances marriage might have seemed more predictable than bachelorhood; it might indeed even have provided him with some financial security. And it is strange too, that, save for the mysterious and to some degree at least fictitious Fiammetta, we do not know the names of any of his mistresses, not even that of the heartless widow who inspired the *Corbaccio*—and most probably the unforgettable tale of the scholar's revenge (*Decameron,* day 8, story 7). Some biographers suggest that some of the otherwise unexplained sorties to Romagna may have had amorous motivation but the lady—or ladies—concerned have eluded identification.[36] Indeed of the five children mentioned in the eclogue we cannot say whether they were born of one mother or not. Of Violante her father speaks with deep affection, not only in the eclogue but also in the moving and intimate letter wherein he tells Petrarch of his feelings on meeting the latter's granddaughter, little Eletta. A few lines bear quotation. Recalling his visit to the house of Petrarch's daughter in Venice in 1366, Boccaccio writes:

> Your Eletta, my delight, greeted me with a smile although she did not know who I was. I was not only overcome with joy; I took her into my arms, eagerly imagining that I was holding my own little girl. What can I say—? If you think I exaggerate, ask William of Ravenna

or our Donato [degli Albanzani], for they both knew her. Your child
has the identical aspect of the child who was my Eletta, the same
expression, the same light and laughter in her eyes, the same gestures
and walk, the same fashion of carrying her little self, save that my Eletta
was somewhat taller for her age at five and a half, when I saw her for
the last time. She has the same way of talking, the same vocabulary.
She has the same simple manner. In truth there is no difference between
them except that your little one has golden hair while mine had locks
of chestnut. Ah, how often, holding your child in my arms and listening to her prattle, the memory of my own lost little girl has brought
to my eyes tears that I conceal from all.[37]

The warmth of Boccaccio's words here calls to mind Petrarch's
lament for his dead grandson, "the solace of our lives, our hope, the
joy of our house."[38] Affectionate and even doting fathers (or grandfather, in the case of Petrarch) as both poets were (although to be sure
Petrarch had his troubles with his firstborn), it is the more strange—
at least to us today—that neither one seems to have the slightest
concern for, or even memory of, the mothers of their children. Boccaccio was not destined ever to know the placid delights of grandfa-
therhood; the eclogue makes it clear that none of his children survived
to full maturity.

The later years of the fifties were less demanding than the earlier
part of the decade; most of the time of the now well-established and
respected man of letters was spent at home, either in Florence or
Certaldo, fully occupied with literary pursuits. To be sure, the first
draft of the *Life of Dante* dates back to 1351; a new version, however,
was composed in 1360. A revised draft of the *Amorosa visione* was
prepared at some time between 1355 and 1361; there is also reason to
believe that, no doubt following the scholarly example of his master,
Boccaccio was hard at work on his learned Latin compilations, notably
the *Genealogies of the Pagan Gods*. In which connection it is possible
to speculate, a little heretically, on the effect of the intimacy with
Petrarch on the direction of the disciple's literary development.

It is undeniable that the association with Petrarch sharpened Boccaccio's scholarly and critical perceptions and enlarged his understand-

ing and appreciation of philosophy and literary theory. It also improved his Latin style and, as he tells us, provided him with spiritual
guidance, at once consoling and refining; in the Fifteenth Eclogue
Petrarch is given the name "Phylostropos"—"loving converter" in
Boccaccio's Greek—and plays the role of savior. On the other hand
one may suspect that something may have been lost in the conversion.
Up to the time of the great encounter in 1350 Boccaccio had written
works, either in prose or verse, that were essentially creative. From the
Filocolo to the *Decameron* he was the liege man of fancy. After the
friendship with Petrarch was born the record shows no production of
like nature, save for the sour and misogynistic *Corbaccio* (in spirit a
repudiation of the *Decameron*). One may clearly remark a turning
away from the creative and toward the scholarly or critical. Concurrently and inevitably, given the nature of the works, Latin displaces
the vernacular. Up to the time of the meeting with Petrarch the canon
shows no Latin works—save for an occasional *epistola* and some of the
earlier eclogues; all the major productions are written in Italian. But
after that crucial moment Latin predominates. Only the cult of Dante
and the admiration for his *Comedy* led Boccaccio in his last years to
return to the Tuscan that had so well served him in his young manhood.

   To what degree this change of direction—good or bad—was Petrarch's doing is hard to say; for some time after the years of the
composition of the *Decameron* there is evidence of a kind of "conversion" in our subject. A certain melancholy *timor mortis* is recurrently
detectable and a growing spiritual uneasiness, causing the poet to
contemplate at times with dismay the productions of his youthful
Muse. Somewhere during the late fifties—probably in 1357—Boccaccio took orders, though of precisely what nature is not certain.
Whatever kind of clerical office he held, however, it is clear that he
was enjoying it by 1360, when the pope, entrusting him with the care
of souls, addresses him as already a "clericus."[39] Perhaps the appointment was of the purely formal sort, intended to make Boccaccio
eligible for some kind of benefice or privilege, but whatever the nature
of the designation, in his midforties the eloquent and mordant critic

of friars—as he shows himself in the *Decameron*—took service in the robed army of the Church.

In the spring of 1359 he was off to visit Petrarch again, overcoming his distaste for the city of the tyrannical Visconti under whose protection his master was living in snug content. The occasion was recorded by the host, who noted in a tone of festive joyousness the presence of his friend at the planting of an olive tree in his garden.[40] The visit lasted for some weeks, giving the poets ample opportunity for exchange of ideas and discussion of their various literary projects. Boccaccio, as was his custom on such occasions, copied a number of his master's works, including the *Bucolicum carmen,* and again urged on his friend the reading of Dante. On his return to Florence in early April Boccaccio, no doubt inspired by the transcription of his mentor's verses, took up once more his own *Carmen;* the fifteenth of his eclogues was written at this time. In June of that same year he was again designated by the commune as ambassador to the Visconti; whatever duties may have been involved in such an appointment must have been discharged in Florence, for there is no record of another journey to Milan.

Among the topics of conversation during the visit with Petrarch, Greek matters had loomed large. Petrarch proudly showed his guest some manuscripts of Homer and Plato that had come into his possession, and both men of letters deplored their ignorance of Greek. Petrarch mentioned a meeting in Padua with one Leontius Pilatus whom he had requested to translate sections from Homer. Boccaccio, with characteristic zeal, seized on the occasion and in 1360 not only invited Pilatus to come to Florence but lodged him in his own house and managed to have him appointed professor of Greek in the University of Florence, the first such appointment in Western Europe. It was in Boccaccio's house that this strange, unkempt, untidy, and irascible Calabrian "wild man" began the translation of Homer. The Florentines were persuaded to grant him his professorship because they hoped to have instruction in "practical" Greek, useful for their commercial enterprises. When it turned out that such was not the notion—or perhaps the competence—of their professor they lost interest and at the end of two years the appointment lapsed.[41] His tenure, however, marks a significant moment in the cultural history of the West. Boccaccio's *Genealogies of the Pagan Gods* owes a good deal of its substance to the lore of Leontius, who is frequently quoted in its pages. And the *Genealogies*—to anticipate our further comment on the work—was destined to serve European scholars and poets for some two centuries and more. One may be permitted to see a happy allegory in the planting of that olive tree in Petrarch's garden.

In December of 1360 an unsuccessful conspiracy against the intransigent and reactionary Guelph faction that governed the city of Florence resulted in the downfall and exile of some of Boccaccio's most powerful friends and put an end, temporarily, to his public career. He retired to Certaldo, apparently well content with the tranquil delights provided by nature and the leisure afforded him for the cultivation of his own interests. He writes to his friend Pino de' Rossi, who suffered exile and sequestration of his considerable property as a result of his participation in the conspiracy, a letter of consolation in which he avers:

> Returning to Certaldo I have begun with much less difficulty than I had expected to find solace in life. I am beginning to enjoy rough country clothes and peasant fare. Being out of sight of all the ambitious, distasteful and vexing activities of our fellow citizens is such a comfort to my spirit that if only I could manage not to hear about them I am sure my tranquility would be even greater. In place of the interminable and pressing projects and schemes of city-dwellers I look upon fields, hills, trees clothed with green leaves and flowers of various hues: things that nature brings forth with simplicity, whereas the deeds of town folk are all artificial. I hear the song of nightingales and other birds . . . and when I feel like it I can hold discourse with my little books freely and without hindrance.[42]

Yet a year later the lover of rustic solitude was on the road again. In the winter of 1361–1362 we find him in Ravenna; it was to be his last visit to the town associated with Dante and perhaps more intimate memories of our subject. At the request of Petrarch he sought out, found, and transcribed a life of St. Peter Damian that his master had need of (the latter had gone back to work on his *De vita solitaria*), but the main purpose of this unofficial visit to what Boccaccio now styles "the Cisalpine sewer" is obscure. He speaks of being there under unfortunate circumstances but the nature of the circumstances is not further defined. He may be referring to the recent political events in Florence, so painful to his friends. Some have suspected a covert allusion to a purely personal tribulation, perhaps affecting the mother of his illegitimate children, who may have been a woman of Ravenna. Perhaps the relationship was terminated, possibly even by the death of his mistress. It is a tempting hypothesis, for the depression created by some such sad occurrence would surely linger and so to some extent explain the agitated reaction to an episode that occurred not very long after his return from Ravenna and that has its own significant place in literary history.

Petrarch is our authority for the story. In the spring of 1362 a holy man called upon Boccaccio, purporting to be an emissary of the sainted Peter of Siena, known as the Blessed Petroni and enjoying a wide popular cult in Tuscany. According to his self-styled agent, the venerable Peter had been vouchsafed on his deathbed a prophetic vision, which among other matters carried a dire warning for Petrarch and Boccaccio; Jesus himself had told the dying saint that such poets should know that death would soon overtake them and they would do well to give up the cult of poetry and turn their minds to divine things. Petrarch's letter (*Sen.* 1.5), written in answer to his terrified friend, is dated May 28, 1362. We do not have Boccaccio's letter; we may deduce that he had affirmed that he was preparing to abandon all literary activity and that he proposed to send his library to Petrarch.

The older scholar's reply is wise, patient, and affectionate—and is in its way a proclamation of cultural emancipation from clerical bondage. Petrarch begins in a rather matter-of-fact tone by conceding that the vision vouchsafed to the dying Peter "is a very great thing—if it is true. But it is an ancient abuse, that an air of divinity should draw a veil of religion over lies and falsities. . . . But I shan't make any statement about this until the deputy of the dead saint comes to see me. . . . When he gives me my share of the revelation I shall decide how much faith to put in him." As for the prediction that Boccaccio's life was nearing its end, his counselor goes on to say, that is hardly a matter for surprise or consternation; death is the common lot and no cause for dread. With regard to the monk's caution against the study of poetry he charges his shaken friend: "Be reasonable. I know of many who have attained the highest saintliness without literary culture; I don't know of any who were excluded from sanctity by culture. . . . All good men have the same goal, but there are numberless ways thither, and much variety for the pilgrim. . . . Every such journey is a blessed one, but the way of knowledge is certainly more glorious, illumined and lofty. Hence there is no comparison between the simple piety of a rustic and the intellectual faith of a scholar. Give me an example of a saint who arose from the mass of the unlettered, and I will match him with a greater saint of the other sort."

We may remark in this passage the unspoken equation of "poetry" and "culture." For both Petrarch and Boccaccio the cult of poetry signified devotion to learning, and, one may add, learning not limited to the sector of Christian theology. And Petrarch's affirmation here is, for a man of the Middle Ages and of staunch orthodox faith, a courageous one. For a true Christian the focus of interest should be on things divine and not on the glittering deviations offered by "poetry," implying as often as not a study of pagan mythology and history. Medieval poets were always painfully aware of this dilemma. Even Petrarch himself, for all his brave words here, asks God's forgiveness, in the final sonnet of his *Rhymes*, for his error in not using his talents for a higher purpose than the exaltation of Laura, which is to say "poetry."

As for the books, the laureate goes on to say, he is grateful for Boccaccio's offer of his library; if indeed Boccaccio is eager to get rid of it then he will consider purchasing it, for he would not like to see his friend's collection scattered. He asks for an itemized list to set a fair price. And, he adds, "if ever you should decide to spend with me our few remaining days, as I have always hoped and as indeed you once promised, you will find these books assembled, together with my own, which are yours as well."[43]

Such reassurances must have restored Boccaccio's peace of mind and, more important for the world of letters, have encouraged him to go on with such works of "poetry" as he was engaged in. Yet even so fortified and solaced, as he affirms himself to be, by the pastoral charms of Certaldo, the restless scholar could not bring himself to refuse another offer to return to Naples. This time the prospects seemed promising. Francesco Nelli, a friend of both Boccaccio and Petrarch, had replaced Zanobi da Strada in the service of the great Acciaiuoli, who was at this time riding on the high tide of his fortunes after military and diplomatic victories that had definitively secured the tottering throne of Queen Joan, now widowed of Louis of Taranto. More than ever did the grand seneschal feel the need of a court *literatus;* Petrarch was invited—not for the first time—to grace the Angevin capital with his presence. On his refusal Nelli suggested the name of Boccaccio and presently both from him and his master cordial and flattering invitations reached Certaldo.

In spite of his disillusioning experience a few years earlier Boccaccio accepted, and in October of 1362 once more made his way south, sufficiently sure of his welcome and expectant of a long sojourn to take with him his half brother and his library. This time, he felt certain, he would be given a position of prominence and dignity, prestigious, and no doubt lucrative as well. He probably envisaged some such role as that of Dante at the court of Can Grande or the Polenta or the status of Petrarch under the protection of the Visconti. He was prepared to reciprocate as a *literatus* should; his baggage contained two recently completed works, the *De mulieribus claris*, dedicated to Acciaiuoli's sister, and the *De casibus virorum illustrium*, originally dedicated to Louis of Taranto; it is reasonable to surmise that it was now meant for the grand seneschal himself. But this was not to be; the visit was destined to follow the pattern of the abortive excursion of 1355—but this time with even more painful humiliation.

The details of the shabby treatment accorded the distinguished and sanguine guest are set forth in his letter to Nelli,[44] written soon after the end of the unhappy chapter. Arriving at Nocera, where Acciaiuoli was holding court, Boccaccio and his brother were obliged to share one room—and a room of such a sort as to cause the writer to speak of it as a "sewer." And not only was the room to be shared with Jacopo but the bed as well—with bedding previously used by a muleteer. The furniture of the cobweb-infested cubicle consisted of a ramshackle table and a three-legged chair; the description suggests indeed that the room was a kind of scullery, a passageway for servants and "household rats." Happily, Mainardo Cavalcanti, brother of a deceased friend of the desolate pilgrim, and himself a high-ranking servant of the kingdom, was moved to compassion; he took Boccaccio out of his filthy lodgings and made him a guest in his own home. But worse was to come. Acciaiuoli suddenly moved from Nocera to a small villa near Baia and Boccaccio, along with the rest of the great man's entourage, was obliged to follow him. Here once more shabby and sordid lodging was offered him (again a friend came to his aid but this time only to supplement the furnishing of the squalid abode) and again, brusquely, Acciaiuoli took off—leaving the much-abused poet in solitude with no facilities even for moving his library and his few belongings. It is no wonder that, invited back to the same kind of quarters that he had been given at Nocera, Boccaccio refused and left the court and the kingdom, making his way back through Aversa and Sulmona—possibly with a pause at Montecassino—to seek consolation from Petrarch in Venice, arriving shortly after the middle of March (1363).

Petrarch welcomed his friend warmly, approved of his departure from the Angevin court, and no doubt would have effectively soothed his injured feelings. But a few weeks later there came a letter from Nelli, reproaching the wandering scholar for his precipitate flight from Naples and calling him "a man of glass," unstable and overly sensitive. It was Nelli's letter in fact that called forth from Boccaccio the indignant epistle from which we have quoted. This lengthy and vitriolic communication contains not only the details of the unseemly reception given the guest of Acciaiuoli but, in its second part, treats amply of the limitations, pretensions, and general grossness of the grand seneschal. Boccaccio reveals that he had apparently been expected to write a panegyric of the great man, probably a kind of laudatory biography, but such a task was impossible when there was, on the record, no evidence of distinction in either military or civil life but on the other hand all too patent proof of empty vanity, arrogance, and sundry other weaknesses.

Passion gives to this colorful epistle the status of literature, and the story it tells looms large in the chronicles of our subject. Certainly, considering the high hopes of glory and the confident expectation of substantial reward with which the *literatus* set forth, the episode must have been bitterly disappointing. Six centuries afterward biographers of Boccaccio still find the incident puzzling. Was Acciaiuoli simply too busy with affairs of state to take proper care of an invited and honorable guest? Was it a calculated revenge?—for the seneschal cannot have been unaware of the scathing criticisms made of him in the past by his old schoolmate. Acciaiuoli has not lacked for his defenders and the fact that Nelli, a man of goodwill and patient understanding, thought it fitting to reproach Boccaccio for his impatience suggests that the account the latter gives us may not tell us everything about the affair. One may hazard the guess that, as Boccaccio himself reveals, it was part of his assignment to prepare a flattering biography of his protector, that when it came to the point he found he couldn't, and that Acciaiuoli, understandably if callously, simply lost interest in him. Nelli, as far as is known, made no answer to Boccaccio's diatribe; it is quite possible that Petrarch persuaded his bitterly offended and all too eloquent disciple not to send it.

For the rest the sojourn on the Riva degli Schiavoni where the sage of Vaucluse had established his residence (he had parted, on good terms, with the Visconti in 1361), was consoling and restorative. Petrarch was, at the time, engaged in putting his *Rhymes* in order; we may imagine that Boccaccio advised, aided, and transcribed. There were gondola rides through the canals and the renewal of old friendships, especially with Donato degli Albanzani, now established in Venice and a frequenter of Petrarch's house. And once more Petrarch invited his most famous disciple to share his home for the few years remaining to them. And once more—out of delicacy? out of an instinctive feeling that too close an intimacy might mar the friendship?—Boccaccio refused. It is noteworthy that although he visited his master as often as he found it possible Boccaccio's stays were always relatively brief; on this occasion, as Petrarch notes, it was three months—longer than any other.

In mid-July the wanderer was once more installed in his rustic retreat in Certaldo; he had been absent for some ten months. The tenor of life among the charms of nature did not on this occasion call forth the expressions of serene content that had warmed the pages of his letter to Pino de' Rossi a few years earlier. Jacopo, the dependent half brother, had married for the second time (proving himself "twice stupid" as the author of the *Corbaccio* puts it)[45] and had brought his new wife to share the rather restricted quarters of the ancestral home. In spite of this inconvenience and even while complaining of failing energy Boccaccio threw himself once more into intense literary activity. He composed a third and definitive draft of the *Life of Dante* and gave final form to the *Corbaccio*. He also wrote the last two books of the *Genealogies*, the most significant and human part of the compilation, containing what may be called his "defense of poetry" and much incidental autobiographical material. Gradually his manner of life grew more monkish, if not monastic, with regular readings of the Breviary and a pious cult of the Virgin (the latter indicated in some of the poems of this period; the former activity revealed by a passage in the *Corbaccio*). He was busy too with the transcription of such elevating works as those of the "moral Seneca" and the patient and taxing editing of the translations from the Greek that Pilatus had left with him.

Meanwhile the volatile politics of Florence had taken yet another turn. The successful conclusion of the war with Pisa, a wave of prosperity, and the manifest goodwill of the new Pope Urban V (elected September 1362) had mellowed the intransigence of the ruling faction; the ordinances against sedition, real or imagined, were relaxed, and the exiles of 1360 were invited to return. For Boccaccio this signified that his friends once more were in positions of influence and consequently his own services were again sought by the commune. In the first part of 1365 he was again appointed to the *condotta,* the committee charged with military expenses, and in August of that year another embassy of importance was entrusted to him. He was sent once more to Avignon where, as all Italians rejoiced to learn, Urban was preparing to bring the papal court back to its true home in the Eternal City. Boccaccio was to assure the pontiff of the enduring devotion of his faithful Florentines and to suggest delicately that the intervention of the emperor would not be necessary to insure him safe passage to Rome. Although he was now beginning to feel the weight of his years (and of his flesh, too, for he grew extravagantly corpulent with age) and was not in the best of health, Boccaccio willingly accepted the assignment. It is significant that before his departure he made his will. The mission was accomplished apparently to the satisfaction of all parties—including Petrarch who wrote a commendatory letter.[46] The visit to the papal court provided an opportunity for renewing contacts with such old friends of the Petrarchan circle—which was now his disciple's circle as well—as Francesco Bruni, now papal secretary and enjoying high prestige, and Philippe de Cabassoles, still wistfully eager to see the *De vita solitaria*, which Petrarch had dedicated to him twenty years earlier and which still awaited completion.

On the conclusion of his embassy the commune's emissary returned to Certaldo—it was now November—following "the paths beset by dangers" through rough and brigand-ridden Liguria; Petrarch, so he writes a month after his friend's return home, could find peace neither night nor day out of concern for his safety. Later too from the same source came the joyous letter celebrating the arrival of the Latin version of Homer that Boccaccio had sent a year earlier—and passing on the news that Leontius Pilatus, "the animal man," had been cut down by a lightning bolt.[47] In the same year news came to Certaldo of the death of Niccolò Acciaiuoli.

In the spring of 1366 the aging but still restless poet took to the road again. He made his way to Venice where he expected to find his master; Petrarch, as it happened, was not in residence. Boccaccio, meeting by chance the laureate's son-in-law, Francescuolo da Brossano, was invited to visit Petrarch's daughter, Francesca, who was occupying her father's house on the Grand Canal. (It was here that the meeting with the child Eletta, bringing back memories of the lost Violante, took place.) Though delicacy prevented him from accepting the hospitality offered by Francesca—she was living alone in the house—Boccaccio spent a happy month in the City of the Lagoons, enjoying the companionship of Petrarch's kinsmen and his old friends; no doubt he took full advantage of the resources of Petrarch's impressive library.

The wanderer came home again in June but in December of the same year set forth once more, this time on a diplomatic mission to Rome where Urban had—alas, only temporarily, as it turned out—taken up residence. Since Boccaccio was again appointed to the *condotta* in the fall of 1367 he found himself obliged to live for a while in Florence, returning to rustic Certaldo in March of the following year. That fall he paid another visit to Petrarch; this time he found his master installed in a new home in Padua; as in the past he copied some of Petrarch's works and probably discussed with him once more the arrangement of the poems in the *Canzoniere*, an editorial task of which Laura's liege man never wearied.[48] In October Boccaccio pressed on to Venice to pay a visit of condolence to Donato degli Albanzani, recently bereaved of a son;[49] at the end of the month he made his way back to Tuscany.

Some time in the autumn of 1370 the aging poet made his last pilgrimage to Naples; this time, apparently, with no specific intention of seeking preferment although he may have been hoping for suitable shelter. The hospitality he had expected failed to materialize, for his putative host, Niccolò da Montefalcone—in accordance with the pattern of the sorties to Naples—inexplicably failed to appear. Yet the visitor seems to have been well taken care of; he remained until the following spring, surrounded, and one might say even courted, by a circle of his admirers to whom he read—under seal of secrecy, promptly broken—his *Genealogie deorum*. Ironically, on this occasion he was given by Mainardo Cavalcanti and by Queen Joan herself a pressing invitation to remain in the kingdom as a guest of the court. The invitation came too late; he replied that since he had declined Petrarch's offer of hospitality it would not be seemly to accept it from any other source; furthermore, "old and unwell" (as he puts it in *Ep.* 17), he was anxious to return to his house and his books (which, this time, it would seem he did not take with him).

Once back in his own little nest he carried on a brisk correspondence with his Neapolitan admirers and of course with Petrarch. He also found time to recopy, with stylistic revisions, his *Decameron*. Apparently the passage of the years had reconciled him with his youthful and irreverent masterpiece and the palinodic revulsion occasioned by the Blessed Peter's dour emissary had passed. It is true that (in 1372) he wrote Mainardo Cavalcanti, suggesting that the carefree pages be kept from the women of his friend's household, lest they deem the writer "a dirty man and a foul-mouth narrator of others' crimes," but the tone of the letter is lighthearted and the writer concludes that after all the book was written in youth and "under the compulsion of a greater man" (of which duress nothing is said in the work itself).

Perhaps he sent the new version of the work to Petrarch (or perhaps Petrarch had only recently found time to look at an earlier copy) for in 1373 his master wrote him[50] that he had derived much pleasure from "a hasty perusal" of the work. He does not claim to have read all of it, for it is "a very big volume, written in prose and intended for the masses." The tone of the work, "at some times too free," may be excused, he writes, "in consideration of your age at the time and in view of the public to whom the book is addressed." The indulgent critic is happy to add that "among much that was amusing he found "some serious and edifying matter as well"; he admires the description of plague-stricken Florence and he avows that he was so deeply fascinated by the story of Griselda that he felt moved to translate it into Latin. (It was Petrarch's version that came to the attention of Geoffrey Chaucer and thus gave yet wider resonance to the name and the virtue of the exemplary female.)

In the summer of 1372 Boccaccio suffered a severe illness—or more properly, as the half ironic, half petulant description of his symptoms suggests, a combination of illnesses, and was for a while close to death. It may have been that his major affliction was dropsy; as we have noted he had become grossly overweight. In spite of ill health he finished (in 1373) the writing of his *De casibus virorum illustrium*—Petrarchan in inspiration and in its way a companion piece to the *De mulieribus claris*—and dedicated it to Mainardo Cavalcanti, who had befriended him in the dark days in Naples a decade earlier.[51] In the autumn of the same year, at the invitation of the Commune of Florence, he began his public exposition and explication of the *Divine Comedy*. It was a task undertaken with love and devotion and his "commentary," so far as it goes, is invaluable, if also rambling and capricious. But the charge was full of tensions and even dangerous. Some Florentines had good reason to wish the pages of the *Comedy*, with their biting invective and their unsparing naming of names, to remain forever unglossed—if not forgotten. At the other extreme there were already abroad cultists of Dante who felt that the great poem was of such an exalted nature as to be approached only by an intellectual elite and therefore that public lectures on its substance and significance somehow vulgarized the work and demeaned its author. Boccaccio himself was eventually persuaded to adopt this precious attitude, as he indicates in his *Rhymes* (122, 123). And on this account and perhaps also because his health was rapidly failing, he gave up his course of lectures in the spring of 1374, retiring once more—and for the last time—to the simple rhythm of life in Certaldo.

The sale of a farm, recorded in January of 1374, would seem to suggest that the old scholar's financial state was no less precarious than his physical condition. He was deeply shaken by the news of the death of Petrarch, which occurred in July of that year.[52] Shortly after the sad tidings reached him he once more made his will, a document that, it may be said, reveals the characteristic thoughtfulness of this kind and unpretentious man, for he did not forget his faithful maidservant who had cared for him through the years.[53] His last year was spent, according to the testimony of a visitor, "in the company of the Lofty Muses and Divine Philosophy"—saddened, it may have been, if not embittered, by the alliance of the Commune of Florence with the Visconti and against Pope Gregory XI, a pact against all the traditions—and the best interests—of the Guelph city. But actual details of the poet's last year are scanty. We do know that he died on December 21, 1375, leaving orders that over his tomb (in the Church of Sts. Michael and James) the following verses should be inscribed:

> Under this stone lie the bones and ashes of John; his spirit
> stands in the presence of God, adorned with the merits his mortal
> labors on earth have earned him. Boccaccio sired him; his native
> Fatherland was Certaldo; he cherished the nourishing Muses.

To this brief epitaph Coluccio Salutati added an appendix, scrupulously listing the works destined to assure the poet's immortality. (No vernacular work is mentioned.) It runs as follows:

> Why, O illustrious poet, do you speak of yourself so humbly?
> You with your limpid notes have exalted pastoral verses;
> You with your arduous labors have numbered the hills and the mountains;

You have described the forests and springs and the swamps and marshes;
Aye, you have counted the names of the seas and the lakes and the rivers.
You bring before us great princes, relating their trials and downfalls,
From our first father Adam down to the magnates of our times.
You, in most lofty measures, celebrate notable matrons;
You have traced all the immortals to their dark and unknown beginnings,
Filling fifteen golden volumes, second to none of the ancients.
Labors past counting have made you famous among all the people
Nor will an age ever come that will pass over you in silence.[54]

Centuries later a strange and distressing event would bring yet
another tribute from the pen of a great writer to the memory of
Certaldo's gifted son. In 1783 the tomb was opened and found to
contain only a skull and a metal tube enclosing thirteen illegible pages
of parchment. Neither item was preserved.[55] Byron, some years later,
deploring the absence of a cenotaph in Santa Croce (the Westminster
Abbey of Florence) castigated the ungrateful Florentines in a noteworthy passage of *Childe Harold's Pilgrimage* (canto 4, stanza 58):

Boccaccio to his parent earth bequeath'd
His dust,—and lies it not her great among,
With many a sweet and solemn requiem breathed
O'er him who formed the Tuscan's siren tongue?
That music in itself, whose sounds are sung,
The poetry of speech? No;—even his tomb
Uptorn, must bear the hyaena bigot's wrong,
No more amidst the meaner dead find room,
Nor claim a passing sigh, because it told for whom![56]

There is no contemporary portrait of Boccaccio. However Filippo
Villani, describing the poet's physical appearance (presumably in his
prime), tells us that he was tall and somewhat corpulent, having a
round face, full but handsome lips, and a nose a little "depressed" above
the nostrils. He adds that Boccaccio had a dimpled chin, pleasant to
see when he laughed, and that his aspect was always merry and cheerful. The poet, we learn, was "fond of conversation and eager to make
friends, of whom he had many."[57] It is not hard to believe.

CHAPTER 3

DIANA'S HUNT

t is impossible to assign specific and authenticated dates to Boccaccio's early works. Thus we cannot say with certainty which of the artifacts of his youthful apprenticeship is truly the "first" product of his pen. Two Latin exercises, copied in the *Zibaldone laurenziano*—the *Elegy of Costanza*, a paraphrase of a Latin epitaph, and the so-called *Mythological Allegory*, an Ovidian catalog overlaid with moralizing interpretations—are, it would seem, items of very early composition.[1] Of slight intrinsic merit and never circulated, they are chiefly interesting as revealing the attraction that Latin letters and the study of mythology had for the young man who was later to undertake the massive *Genealogies* and to celebrate, in the classical tongue, the deeds of famous women and the trials of illustrious men. We may be tolerably sure too that at least some of the lyric poems that have come down to us predate the first narrative efforts of the aspiring author. We shall leave the consideration of such verses to our discussion of the collective *Rhymes* (see chapter 12).

With due respect for such obscure beginnings, we may legitimately begin our survey with what is assuredly the first narrative work of Boccaccio: *Diana's Hunt*, written, it would seem, shortly after the author had abandoned his business career to enter the university. Branca would date its composition to a time "before 1334,"[2] probably 1333; the latest possible date, on the basis of internal evidence, would be 1339.[3] It is noteworthy—and suggestive of early composition—that the work is not dedicated to Fiammetta, who is in fact not even mentioned in the poem. (There is, to be sure, an allusion to a pair of ladies so dazzlingly beautiful as to seem "due fiammette"[4] but the term is one of purely conventional courtly idiom and the charmers so described have no special prominence in the narrative.)

Formally the *Hunt* is composed of eighteen cantos of terza rima, all but one of fifty-eight lines; thus the standard canto contains nineteen terzine with a line added to rhyme with the second line of the last terzina. The poem tells, with directness and economy, a story simple in pattern, realistic in detail, and allegorical in purpose. Speaking in his own persona, the poet tells us that "in the sweet season when the tender grass clothes every meadow," while he stood pondering on his love sufferings, he seemed to hear a voice from above inviting certain fair ladies to the high court of Diana. The voice in fact summons thirty-three Neapolitan gentlewomen of the nobility or wealthy bourgeoisie; thirty-two are mentioned by name; the last of the roll call, "she whom love honors above all others," is not named. Diana welcomes the ladies and then divides them into four hunting parties (one of which is captained by the Unnamed Beauty) and dispatches them to hunt in the valleys and hills and streams. These preliminaries occupy the first two cantos. The following thirteen are devoted to a description of the hunt, including a catalog of the kinds of animals, birds, and fish slain by the intrepid and winsome huntresses. Their prey is varied; it includes not only hares and rabbits and mountain goats but also such exotic game as an elephant and a unicorn. The account of the hunt, "exploiting the bestiaries" as Muscetta remarks,[5] abounds in naturalistic detail, with ample description of the weapons used, the manner of the slayings, and the lively reactions of the noble participants. During the course of the chase twenty-six more of Diana's followers are identified; a late arrival brings the grand total to sixty.

Finally, as noon comes on, the goddess gives the order to abandon the chase and the ladies return, each bringing her catch to the meadow where Diana holds court. The huntress goddess bids them to sacrifice their prey to Jove, in her honor. But at this point the Unnamed Beauty arises and, speaking for all the band, refuses to perform the rite. For, she proclaims, all the ladies of the hunt have now been converted from

Diana's service by "another life"—clearly that of Venus. This some-what unexpected turn of events takes place in canto 16, at the end of which Diana takes her leave, understandably "perturbed." The Un-named Beauty then takes charge of the proceedings; she suggests that the slain animals be made burnt offerings to Venus. The others en-thusiastically consent; the animals are placed on the fire and the anony-mous leader offers a prayer to the Love Goddess, asking her to purify their spirits, open their hearts, and grant them happiness in love. Venus appears and assures her new devotees that their prayers will be granted; turning then to the fire, she changes the animals offered for sacrifice into handsome young gallants who forthwith run from the flames, immerse themselves in the waters of a nearby stream, and emerge again, each clad in a vermilion mantle. Venus then charges them to be loyal lovers of their ladies, after which she departs. In the last canto the narrator, who has witnessed these metamorphoses, suddenly finds that he too is wearing a red mantle and has apparently come forth from the flames like the rest, changed from a deer to a young man and "offered" to the mysterious unnamed lady. He expresses his delight at having this opportunity to serve such a noble and vírtuous mistress, whose effect on him has been to change him from beast to man. He asks all lovers to pray for his happy enjoyment of her love and, promising to say more of her in a more appropriate place, he ends his narrative.

The *Hunt* is hardly an important work. It is in some sense an "occasional" verse; it is not unreasonable to see it as a kind of lyric documentation of the delight of a young poet at finding himself a part of a glamorous and patrician society—for the register of names would seem to indicate familiarity if not intimacy with the leading families of the Angevin court. In its design the work seems to follow that of a late medieval genre (of which the *carros* of the troubadour Raimbaut de Vaqueiras is the best-known example), wherein a catalog of high-born ladies is enumerated, half playfully, half admiringly, costumed, as it were, as warriors or jousters. It seems probable that the famous lost *sirventes* of Dante, celebrating the sixty fairest ladies of Florence, was of that stamp and may have inspired Boccaccio. Branca sees too, in the pattern of the *Hunt*, the legacy of another popular form of verse, called precisely a *caccia*, which describes the various aspects of a realistic hunting expedition with erotic or social commentary; he does not, however, cite any particular model for Boccaccio's poem.[6] In the contest between Diana and Venus, which has Alexandrine and even classical precedents, one may also hear an echo of the medieval rhymed debate between such antagonists as Virtue and Lust, Sacred and Profane Love, and the like. But such a legacy is merely adumbrated in Boccaccio's verses, wherein there is in fact no confrontation between the two goddesses. Indeed the arguments of the Unnamed Fair suggest not so much opposition as transition; in effect she tells Diana: heretofore we have been your votaries but now we feel a more compelling loyalty. Nor does Diana stay for debate.

The use of hendecasyllabic terza rima, taken together with the division into cantos and a number of verbal echoes of the *Comedy*, provides clear evidence of Dantean influence. Perhaps the example of the master is also responsible for the discipline in the treatment of the theme; as we have seen, all the cantos, save one, have a like number of lines, nor is the reader disturbed by the digressive tendency or the disproportionate inflation of descriptive elements that characterize some of the more pretentious works of the "Neapolitan" Boccaccio. And if it be not too ponderous to remark of what is *au fond* a lighthearted courtly exercise one may say too that the mixture of realism and allegory is essentially Dantean; we find in this little work, as we find in the *Comedy*, a privileged vision, a parade of characters taken from life, and the climactic resolution of a fictitious narrative into an allegory with a moral—in this case, anticipating similar lessons to be offered in the *Amorous Vision* and the tale of Cymon in the *Decameron* (day 5, story 1), the civilizing influence of sexual love.[7]

The quest for sources and influences, however legitimate, should not lead us to overlook the existential genesis of Boccaccio's first fruit, clearly meant to celebrate the gallant society of the court and his own youthful participation in its fashionable pastimes. The names in the text, most of them readily identifiable, are recorded, one may believe, with the confidence that his tribute will be welcomed. No doubt the register of gracious ladies gave the work wide circulation when it was written; today the enumeration of so many long-forgotten names, all calling for footnotes, cannot be expected to afford the same pleasure. Even so, the *Caccia* is not without appeal. The narrative moves along at a good pace, the events of the hunt are varied and colorful, and the climax has a pleasing element of surprise.

The Unnamed Fair, the object of the author's special devotion, has not been identified. Branca affirms that she cannot be Fiammetta since the *senhal* (i.e., allusive pseudonym) is missing—indeed the absence of any reference to Fiammetta is one of the reasons for arguing that the *Caccia* is a very early work. One could reply that the lack of the *senhal* would not of itself exclude Fiammetta's candidacy for the special role, for the pet name may have come at a later point in their relationship. There are, however, other evidences of a predecessor of Fiammetta on our poet's altar (possibly one Giovanna, the "fair Lombard" of the *Amorosa visione*, 11.64); it may well be she who is Diana's aide and subsequently renegade and who transmutes her lover from beast to man or from bank clerk to poet. For Branca, she is more probably a "literary silhouette."[8]

For many years scholars were reluctant to attribute the *Hunt* to Boccaccio; their skepticism was based primarily on the absence of any allusion to the poem during the poet's lifetime or for many years after his death; it was in fact first mentioned only in 1521. Since Branca's study of the work in 1938, however, Boccaccio's paternity has been generally acknowledged.[9] The nature of the theme, the manner of treatment, and the abiding presence of Dante surely suggest kinship with other works of the author. In fact, specifically, such ingredients as nympholepsy, erotic allegory, and the parade of contemporary ladies of high degree will serve our poet well in the preparation of more pretentious and substantial confections.

Finally, although the little work bears no dedication, we may reasonably assume that a book about ladies is meant to be read by ladies. This would certainly be in accord with the author's subsequent practice; practically all his creative works—very explicitly the *Decameron*—are written ostensibly for the perusal of the fair sex. On this point Giorgio Padoan observes: "The continual appeal to women and the placing of the feminine element as an animating center, direct or indirect, seem to indicate, in all likelihood, the persistence in the author of a cultural attitude acquired in the Neapolitan rather than the Florentine ambiance. The same may be said, at least initially, for the design, so dear to Boccaccio, of a band of male and female story tellers."[10]

CHAPTER 4

THE FILOCOLO

he *Filocolo*, Boccaccio's first venture into the field of prose narrative, was written, so he tells us, at the suggestion of Maria d'Aquino, his Fiammetta, and it is certainly, whatever be its true genesis, the product of his Neapolitan sojourn both with regard to its conception and probably the actual writing of most of the lengthy and prolix tale. Antonio Enzo Quaglio, the book's most recent editor, does not hesitate to call the novel Boccaccio's "opera prima" and affirms that it was written "around 1336–1338."[1] Branca concurs;[2] Muscetta[3] believes that the author worked on his book "between 1336 until at least 1339." Some older authorities, taking into consideration Boccaccio's statement that he had labored over the task for many years, theorized that the work was not finished until after the author's return to Tuscany.[4] Such a theory is not implausible; indeed, if impressionistic criticism were permissible one might see a certain affinity in the epic coloring of the last part of the *Filocolo* and that of the *Teseida*. The dates of most of Boccaccio's works are all to some degree conjectural; perhaps we may be safe in saying that the *Filocolo* was of Neapolitan inspiration and probably was at least begun and quite possibly finished before the *Filostrato*.

For scholars of literary history as well as "boccaccisti" the work has special interest; the average reader of our century and perhaps of the author's own time might well contemplate the tale with mixed feelings. Yet, though its flaws are many and obvious, the *Filocolo* is not a work that can be ignored. Thomas C. Chubb a generation ago called it "perhaps the first novel of modern Europe"[5] and the scholarly Branca has recently expressed the same opinion in almost identical words.[6]

Boccaccio introduces his story with a survey of the historical events that culminated in the installation of Charles of Anjou as ruler of the Kingdom of Naples. This summary is couched in rather turgid and sometimes surprising allegorical terms; with a syncretism as bold as Dante's, Boccaccio makes the pagan goddess Juno stand for the Christian Church; she descends from Heaven (as she had in the *Aeneid* to incite Aeolus against Aeneas) to stir the pope to action against the wicked Manfred. The purpose of this cumbersome machinery is to bring on stage Maria d'Aquino, the illegitimate daughter of Robert of Naples, of whom the young author became enamored under the circumstances we have described in chapter 2. After this first meeting, Boccaccio tells us, a second encounter with the lady took place in a convent where she was dwelling. And it was on this occasion that she expressed her interest in the old story of Florio and Biancifiore and requested of her admirer that he should make a little book in the vernacular of the birth, vicissitudes, and end of the celebrated pair. Boccaccio set to work eagerly and assiduously; the resultant product was a good deal more generous in scope than the "picciol libro" Fiammetta asked for.

The long story is divided into five books, in turn subdivided into 459 chapters. Its central theme is the romantic adventures of the star-crossed lovers who had aroused Fiammetta's interest and who had been the subject of Byzantine romances that had come into Europe to be subsequently recast in Old French versions and in a ballad of popular tone, all familiar to Boccaccio.[7] But the main plot is in fact only the framework for a narrative of baroque luxuriance, drawing on many other sources for its numerous digressive subplots. The story of the faithful lovers' adventures does not begin until the second book and effectively concludes with the end of the fourth; the three central books themselves are full of motifs and episodes of varied provenance. In Quaglio's words: "Fused in the crucible of the author's enthusiasm we find Ovid and Valerius Maximus, Lucan and Dante, Statius and Virgil,

The Wonders of Rome and *The Golden Legend*, classical and medieval sources ambiguous and fantastic,"[8] and seasoned, we may add, with slices of fictionalized autobiography.

As Boccaccio tells the tale, it runs as follows: A Roman patrician, Quinto Lelio Africano, a descendant of Scipio and a Christian, has taken to wife Julia Topazia, a descendant of Julius Caesar. This noble and mutually devoted pair have, as the action begins, lived for five years in conjugal bliss marred only by their inability to have children. Lelio calls on St. James to help him in his need, promising to make a pilgrimage to the saint's shrine in Compostela if his wish for progeny is granted. And shortly afterward his wife informs him that she is at last pregnant. Learning of her husband's vow, she insists on undertaking the pilgrimage with him, and with appropriate retinue, they set off (1–8). Satan, jealous of the devotion accorded a Christian saint, intervenes. After calling a council of his henchmen, he takes the form of the governor of Marmorina (Verona),[9] a fief of Felice, the pagan king of Spain, and appears before the monarch, reporting that the troops of Rome have pillaged and burned the city.

Felice, losing no time in setting forth to revenge this outrage, meets the innocent Lelio on the road and kills him and all of his party, save for Julia and a few female attendants (9–27). After the slaughter, Felice learns that the devil has deceived him and, properly repentant, brings Julia back to his court in Seville, where in due course she is delivered of a beautiful daughter. Coincidentally, on the same day, the queen of Spain, Felice's wife, gives birth to a boy. Julia does not long survive the birth of her daughter, who is immediately adopted by the queen, and the two children are brought up together in the royal court (28–42). Felice, in fact, gives the children their names, Florio and Biancifiore, and after Julia has been given honorable burial, summons two learned members of his household, charging them with the education of the two children. "Let them be to you as your children. No custom or practice pertaining to gentlemen and ladies shall you overlook in your instruction; all my hope is fixed on them and they are the final end of all my desires." Their teachers obey the king's commands, and the children are given an education befitting their station. Before long they are reading "the psaltery and Ovid," of which the latter proves the more influential in their subsequent development (43–45, end of book 1).

As if the reading of Ovid were not enough, Venus, observing the young pair so clearly destined for her service, dispatches Cupid to earth. He takes the form of Felice, and fondling both of the children in turn, infects them with reciprocal love so that from that day forth they never wish to be parted. Their innocent kisses and caresses are witnessed by their tutor who reports to the king and queen. At this point the sovereigns, previously so well disposed to Biancifiore, turn against her. Apparently forgetting her distinguished ancestry, they think of her as simply the daughter of a captive foreign woman, therefore unworthy to become the bride of their son and heir. Their solution is to send Florio away to a town called Montoro,[10] under the pretext of completing his education. Both the young people are in tears and protest vigorously not to say copiously, but finally Florio consents and, accompanied by his mentor, Ascalion, he takes his leave (1–22). Since even distance does not avail to weaken his son's affections, the king feels obliged to plot the death of Biancifiore. In collusion with his steward, he makes it appear that Biancifiore has tried to poison him, and she is doomed to die at the stake (23–39). Alerted by Venus and aided by Mars, Florio (though in disguise and not revealing his identity) appears in the nick of time, defeats the wicked steward who, dying, confesses that Biancifiore was innocent; he makes no mention of the king's part in the plot (40–70). Biancifiore is restored to favor and her savior returns to Montoro, still not revealing his identity, but assuring Biancifiore of Florio's enduring love (71–76, end of book 2).

Visits of thanksgiving for Biancifiore's salvation are paid to the temples of the gods, and by chance Diana's shrine is overlooked. Florio, returning to Montoro, grows increasingly despondent, and he reveals his suffering to his host, the duke of Montoro. The latter, with the aid of Ascalion, attempts to distract Florio by sending two very tempting maidens to visit him. So comely and seductive are they that Florio might indeed have succumbed had it not been for the intervention of Love, who reminds him of the faith he owes Biancifiore. He then comes to himself and reproaches the girls for their wanton behavior (1–11). Meanwhile, Biancifiore is subjected to a somewhat similar trial.

A young stranger named Fileno has recently come to court. He knows nothing of Florio and, falling immediately in love with Biancifiore, he is encouraged in his courtship by the king and queen. Simply to please the queen, Biancifiore gives him her veil to wear in a tournament. Fileno distinguishes himself in the jousting and shortly after has occasion to visit Montoro. He meets Florio and tells him of his love for Biancifiore, suggests that it is reciprocated, and offers the veil as evidence (12–17). Florio, deeply shaken, writes Biancifiore a long letter, accusing her of fickleness. She replies at once that she loves only him. This reassures him briefly but then Diana, who has been biding her time, persuades Jealousy to come down and attack Florio. Florio resolves to return to Marmorina and, if necessary, kill Fileno (18–27). Diana, feeling somewhat guilty, brings another supernatural body, Sleep, and its attendant, Dreams, to warn Fileno. In his vision he sees Florio about to kill him; waking, he is told by a friend that there may be some truth in the prophecy. Fileno, apprised for the first time of Florio's relation to Biancifiore, decides to flee (28–32).

Fileno wanders around Italy as far south as Naples, then comes back to Tuscany, and, in a small grove near Certaldo, settles down to lament the injustice of love and the waywardness of women. He is joined by another young man who assures him that his experiences are not unusual and tells a circumstantial tale of his own betrayal. He urges Fileno to cease his lamentations and come away with him, but Fileno refuses (33–36).

Meanwhile, Florio, finding that Fileno has fled, is much comforted and returns to Montoro. But Diana tries again. In the guise of a huntress, even as she appeared to Aeneas, she intercepts King Felice and warns him that his son's life is at stake unless the affair with Biancifiore is broken off. The king returns and tells the queen he is determined to kill Biancifiore with his own hands. The queen, however, dissuades him, suggesting that instead they sell her to some merchants who will take her to the East. The merchants are delighted to get such a prize and with her one serving woman, Glorizia, Biancifiore is carried off. Her lamentations move even her captors to sympathy. She prays to both Venus and Diana and her prayers are heard (37–51). The two goddesses meet; Diana declares herself sufficiently avenged and both deities appear before Biancifiore to assure her that she shall yet enjoy the embraces of her Florio, although some time must pass. The merchant ship touches at Sicily, Rhodes, and finally Alexandria where Biancifiore is sold to the admiral of the king of Babylonia who plans to give her to his sovereign and, meanwhile, has imprisoned her in the Arab Tower (52–56). King Felice, back in Marmorina, gives it out that Biancifiore has died and causes another body to be put in her tomb. Florio is sent for; he is so overcome with despair that he is about to kill himself, but the queen breaks down and reveals the whole story. After reproaching his parents Florio announces his determination to go in search of Biancifiore. His mother gives him a magic ring that has the effect of making the wearer attractive to others and affords protection, also, against fire and flood. Ascalion and a small retinue of young knights accompany him. He tells them that henceforth he shall be known as Filocolo, which, transposing the elements, he says, means "Labor of Love."[11] And under that new name he sets forth on his quest (57–71, end of book 3).

Filocolo, as we must now call him, and his faithful band wander through Italy making their way eventually toward Pisa. Chance brings them to a resting place near Certaldo, which turns out to be exactly the spot where we had left Fileno. Filocolo offers sacrifice to Jove and is rewarded by the god's assurance that his adventure will be successful. Then, attracted by a sparkling fountain, he approaches to drink of it when, marvelously, the water speaks. It is the voice of Fileno, who has been metamorphosed into a fountain. He, not knowing Filocolo is Florio, tells the story of his frustrated love. Filocolo assures him that Florio has forgiven him (1–4). He then presses on with his entourage and they take ship at Pisa, heading for Sicily. But a fearful storm arises and they are grounded in Naples where, as the storm does not abate, they remain for five months as guests of a friend of the faithful Ascalion, companion of Filocolo through all his adventures. Here, Filocolo has a strange vision of birds, all with somewhat arcane allegorical significance but seeming to refer to Boccaccio's unhappy love affair, possibly with Fiammetta (5–13).

After the vision, as they go to visit the tomb of Virgil, the group falls in with a group of wellborn young people. A young woman almost as beautiful as Biancifiore invites them to join the party; she is Fiammetta. Filocolo also makes the acquaintance of a comely young man called Caleon (clearly Boccaccio himself); from him Filocolo learns that Fiammetta is the daughter of the king of Naples. Filocolo tells his story. Then they all go to a pleasant grove where Fiammetta proposes a session dealing with love questions, each member of the party to set a problem for the verdict of the party leader. It is suggested that Ascalion be "king" but he defers to Fiammetta, who assumes the queenship, accepting with a graceful speech, containing Dantean echoes. The Questions of Love are then propounded as follows (14–18).

Question 1 is proposed by Filocolo and begins with a short narrative. A young woman, asked to indicate which of two suitors she prefers, replies by taking the garland worn by one of the young men and putting it on her own head. Her own garland she gives to the other. Whom then does she love more? Fiammetta declares it is the second youth, sure that the essence of love lies in giving. She overrules the objection that lovers like to wear some token of the beloved; this may be true when the token is given but not when it is taken. We take from people we do not love; we give to those whom we love (19–22). [As in all the other questions, the proponent argues against Fiammetta's verdict, she defines it with further arguments, and her decision is accepted.]

Question 2. A young man named Longanio tells of two sisters. One suffers because her lover, whose love she has enjoyed, has been banished and she will not see him again. The other sister suffers because her love is unreciprocated. Which then is unhappier? Fiammetta says it is certainly the first; for the second there is always hope (23–26).

Question 3 is proposed by a young woman named Cara. Of three suitors, one strong, one generous and courteous, and one wise, which shall she choose? Fiammetta rules for the third (27–30).

Question 4 begins with the most substantial narrative of the series, related by Menedon. An ardent lover of a married woman, faithful to her husband, is told by the woman that she will love him when spring flowers bloom in winter. At great expense he brings in a magician who causes the miracle to happen. The woman is greatly distressed but tells her husband she must keep her word. He agrees. Moved by her plight, the lover absolves her. The magician, when he hears of the outcome, refuses his fee. Which is the most generous? Fiammetta says the husband, for he has been willing to give up his honor than which there is nothing more precious (31–34).

Question 5. Clonico reveals that he loves a lady but the love is not returned. He has a friend who has all the delights of love from his lady, but he is tormented by jealousy. Which is in the unhappier state? Fiammetta says the second of the two; there is no remedy for the torments of jealousy (35–38).

Question 6 is proposed by a young lady whose name is not given. She tells of two girls that love her brother. One runs to him and embraces him; the other hangs back in shyness. Which one truly loves him? Fiammetta replies that it is the shy one; love is always timid (39–42).

Question 7. Caleon asks a philosophical-practical question: is love really a good thing? Fiammetta says no, assuming he means the kind of love between the sexes. For there are three kinds of love: the unselfish "honest" love of virtue, the love "out of delight," and the love that can only be called utilitarian. The second kind, the traditional love of romance, is basically selfish and destructive. She says this with regret (43–46).

Question 8 is asked by a lady named Paola. It is simply whether a young man should love someone of higher rank or greater wealth than he is or someone of lower degree. The answer is, choose the higher. One should always look up (47–50).

Question 9 is asked by Ferramonte di Montoro, one of Filocolo's train. He asks whether it is better to love a maiden, a married woman, or a widow. Fiammetta says the widow is best. Ferramonte points out that the maiden is more eager and Fiammetta says that of course if it is a matter of marriage the maiden is best, but for an *affaire,* the widow is to be preferred. They concur on disapproving of the choice of a married woman. That would be wrong—and besides, the married woman is too eager (51–54).

Question 10. Ascalion tells the story of a lady whose fate depends on an ordeal between her defender and her accuser. Her defender arrives too late to fight for her. Her "accuser" pretends to fight against her cause but allows himself to be beaten and so saves her. Of these two, which should the lady take as her true lover? Fiammetta says the first because his intention was good and he was prepared to risk his life whereas the second was only pretending. Ascalion demurs that the second showed more wit, but Fiammetta answers that cleverness must not be confused with virtue (55–58).

Question 11. Graziosa asks whether it is happier for a lover to see his beloved or to dream about her. Fiammetta says he who dreams is the happier and enlarges on the advantages of dreams (59–62).

Question 12. Parmenione tells of a young man who plans to possess his lady through the offices of an old crone, But before he can enjoy his success, the girl's kinsmen catch him. As a punishment, they give him the choice of death or the alternative of sleeping with the girl and the old crone in alternating years. Since he doesn't want to die, he takes the alternative. The question is, which one should he begin with? Fiammetta says by all means with the girl. The future is always unsure (63–66).

Question 13. Messalino tells the story of a knight deeply in love with a married woman who is faithful to her husband. She falls ill and is buried for dead. But going to her tomb, the lover finds her still alive. He takes care of her and brings her back to health, and then restores her to her husband who is overjoyed. The question is: which is greater, the joy of the husband, or the nobility of the lover? Fiammetta unhesitatingly rules for the latter (67–70).

The day has worn on during the course of the storytelling and now Fiammetta breaks up the party, leading Filocolo off. He tours the environs of Naples, and on the day before his departure he has yet another allegorical dream in which he sees seven ladies in a boat (clearly signifying the seven virtues). He then embarks with his entourage to continue the search for Biancifiore (71–74).

Filocolo sails to Sicily, where he meets Sisife, kinsman of the merchants who have carried off Biancifiore. Sisife tells him that they have taken her to Rhodes and from there to Alexandria. Filocolo goes on to Rhodes, where he meets Bellisano, an old friend of Lelio, Biancifiore's father, who joins Filocolo's train as they go on to Alexandria. There they are entertained by Dario, a friend of Bellisano; he tells them that Biancifiore has been bought by the admiral and is being held prisoner in a nearby tower, awaiting the arrival of the sultan to whom she will be given as a part of his tribute (75–84). The only way of approach lies in making a friend of the tower's guardian, the ferocious Sadoc, and after some inner debate as to whether love is worth the risks it entails, Filocolo decides on that course of action. He makes a friend of Sadoc by allowing the latter to beat him at chess; he then reveals the purpose of his mission. Sadoc arranges to have Filocolo hidden in a basket of roses, annually delivered to the captive maidens in the tower.

The scheme works and Filocolo and Biancifiore are at last united. They perform their own marriage ceremony, the statue of Cupid presiding, and Biancifiore's ring is used in the service (85–121). After two nights of bliss, however, the lovers are surprised by the admiral. He has them bound and brought down from the tower in a humiliating fashion. He gives orders for a fire to be prepared. As the lovers are led to the flames, each one grieving for the sad fate of the other, Filocolo recalls the magic ring given him by his mother that warranted protection against fire. In addition to this resource the lovers have also the assistance of two powerful gods. Venus comes to their aid, creating a thick smoke screen around them so that the admiral's men cannot approach, and Mars summons Ascalion and the other members of Filocolo's band to come to their rescue (122–138). A battle ensues in which the admiral is worsted. He sues for peace and when he hears the story of the lovers, he realizes that he is actually Filocolo's uncle; his sister being none other than the wife of Felice and mother of Florio-Filocolo (139–151). He offers lavish hospitality and advises a public marriage ceremony, to which the lovers happily consent. All parties are reconciled and after days of festivities and thanksgiving to the gods, Filocolo and Biancifiore prepare to return to Marmorina (152–165, end of book 4).

Filocolo's parents, meanwhile, are in a state of desperate uncertainty. Filocolo, after a ten months' sojourn in Alexandria, begins the return journey, taking sorrowful leave of his newfound friend, the admiral. Their return route leads Filocolo and his party to Rhodes, where they leave Bellisano, and thence to Sicily, where they again see Sisife, pleased to hear of the happy outcome of Filocolo's quest, and on to Naples, where Filocolo leaves his ships and, sending on a party to advise his father of his safe return, settles down for a lengthy visit in the city he remembers so well (1–4). Here it befalls him, while hunting, to wound a tree with an arrow, and the tree speaks, revealing that it is the metamorphosed Idalogo, whom Venus has changed into a tree. Idalogo tells in detail the story of his life up to the point where his suffering at the hands of a faithless woman had led Venus to take pity on him [it is clear that under the veil Idalogo is Boccaccio himself] (5–8). At the end of his story he tells Filocolo that the lady who was cruel to him has been turned into stone, and he bids Filocolo to seek her out.

Guided by some peasant girls, Filocolo and Biancifiore find the fountain with its marble shaft and three trees standing about it; they learn that the stone and the trees were once women whose pride in their own beauty and power had provoked the gods, and each tells her story at some length. Approving the justice of their punishment, Filocolo asks mercy for Idalogo and the heartless Aleera, now changed into marble (9–28). Filocolo then encounters Caleon, who tells him that Fiammetta has deserted him. He takes Caleon with him as he resumes his homeward journey, going through Capua, Sulmona, l'Aquila, and on to the area of Fiesole. Here, Filocolo remembers the encounter with Fileno and turns aside to revisit him. He now reveals that he is Florio and is prepared to forgive Fileno for his love of Biancifiore; Fileno, thus pardoned, is restored to human shape and joins Filocolo's party (29–37). At this point their progress is interrupted by a battle between two groups of rustics, the Caloni and the Cireti, standing respectively for fugitives from Fiesole and Florence. Filocolo persuades them to make peace and build a new city that they both can share; it is Certaldo (38–43).

Glorizia suggests to Biancifiore that a visit to Rome would be appropriate, since they are now so near the city of her birth, wherein her kinsmen still dwell in numbers. Biancifiore demurs, lest she retard Filocolo's return to his anxious parents. But in a vision, the City of Rome appears to her and invites her to come; Biancifiore proposes the visit to Filocolo, who gladly consents. He makes Caleon the lord of Certaldo and the party moves on to Rome, entering as simple pilgrims and not revealing their regal identities. But Ascalion is recognized by an uncle of Biancifiore, Mennilio. The latter offers hospitality to all the party and they reluctantly accept, still not disclosing their names (44–50). Ascalion does, however, reveal to Filocolo the relationship of his host; Filocolo wants to leave, but Ascalion persuades him to stay on for a short time. Meanwhile, Filocolo continues his walks in Rome; accompanied by Menedon, he visits San Giovanni Laterano and meets the monk Ilario, a descendant of a noble Athenian family and seemingly in charge of the basilica. On learning that Filocolo is a pagan, Ilario is moved to convert him. He tells him the story of the Christian faith from the creation of Adam through the Crucifixion, and Filocolo is converted. In turn, he converts all his companions (51–61).

Ilario, learning Filocolo's story, persuades Mennilio that he should forgive the killing of his brother, Lelio, many years ago, and thus assured that there will be no danger of a vendetta, Filocolo prepares to disclose his true identity to his host. First, he withdraws with all his party some distance outside of Rome and when a message comes from Ilario assuring him of Mennilio's goodwill, he returns in regal splendor, accompanied by his train, which includes not only Biancifiore, but also little Lelio, who has been born to the couple some six months before. Great are the surprise and delight when Mennilio recognizes the prince as the guest he has been entertaining. All are formally baptized Christians (62–71). Filocolo lingers some time in Rome, giving Glorizia an opportunity to renew contact with her family. The festive atmosphere is marred by the death of Ascalion, greatly mourned by Filocolo, who then decides to press on to Marmorina, taking Ilario and Mennilio with him (72–77).

He sends messengers ahead to advise his father of his coming and also to reveal his intention of Christianizing his countrymen. Felice is not pleased by Filocolo's desertion of the old gods, who, after all, so frequently came to his aid in times of need. However, the king is visited in a dream by the One Who Can Do All Things and threatened with dire punishment if he stands in the way of Filocolo's resolution. Accordingly, on his son's arrival, the old king is converted and the new gospel is spread among his subjects (78–82). Filocolo is now at the apex of his life; he has his Biancifiore, his son, Lelio, and his newfound faith as well as the company of his parents to whom he narrates in detail the many adventures he has had since they parted.

He resolves to complete the pilgrimage undertaken years ago by his father-in-law and they all depart for Spain, Felice stopping at Córdoba and Filocolo and Biancifiore pressing on toward Galicia (83–87). En route, they come upon the battlefield where Lelio was surprised and slain many years ago. They feel obliged to give decent burial to the remains, but are uncertain as to how to distinguish the human bones from those of animals. Biancifiore's father appears to his daughter in a vision and tells her that the Christian bones will be colored red, and indicates, too, where his own body can be found, and returning to the battlefield, Filocolo's party collect the Christian bones and send them to Rome for proper burial. Julia is taken from her tomb so that she also may be buried with her husband in the Holy City. The pilgrimage to Santiago is then completed and the two spouses return to Rome (88–91).

Shortly after arrival there, Filocolo has a message from his mother; his father is dying. He hastens to Córdoba in time to get not only his father's blessing, but lengthy instructions on the avoidance of sin and the pursuit of virtue. Filocolo is then crowned and after him his queen Biancifiore (92–95). After festivities and tournaments his friends take their leave, and Ilario returns to Rome, where "in the Greek tongue" he writes down the adventures of Filocolo and Biancifiore.[12] Here, Boccaccio takes leave of his "little book," which has been "a pleasing labor for many years." He sends it to the most beautiful and worthy lady whose name it bears on its forehead (i.e., Fiammetta). He does not recommend it to the "outstanding wits and robust minds" to whom Virgil would appeal, nor to the lofty intellects that would delight in Lucan, Statius, Ovid, or Dante (whose verses his little book must follow with reverence). Rather the one charge of the little book will be to please the lady for whom it is written, and persuade her to be content with one lover. He bids his book: "Let your excuse for the use of the vulgar tongue be the command she laid upon the author" (96–97).

As the foregoing considerably abridged summary indicates, the story is long and digressive. No doubt even our résumé will seem to be somewhat lengthy; it may, however, not be without its uses to the English-speaking reader. For not only is there no English translation of the *Filocolo* (although the very popular French version by Adrien Sevin in 1542 led Henry Grantham in 1567 to excerpt and translate the "Thirteen Most Pleasant and Delectable Questions" [chapters 19–70 of book 4]),[13] there is not even a good summary of its contents. Even the most well-disposed biographers, such as Hutton and Chubb, seem to find the tale too wearisome to follow. One may sympathize with them; yet, the work is an important artifact in the history of Western literature and, quite apart from its historical significance, not without its merits.

First of all, the genesis of the work calls for our attention. In the opening passage Boccaccio tells us of his meeting with Fiammetta, whom he identifies openly as the illegitimate child of Robert of Naples, Maria d'Aquino; he tells how in the course of a conversation they fell to recalling the moving story of Florio and Biancifiore, which was current at the time. Fiammetta, says Boccaccio, suggested that it would be a laudable enterprise to ennoble the tale by giving it a worthy written form, and her devoted lover felt obliged to undertake the task. As we have seen, modern criticism will not allow us to believe in Fiammetta, so perhaps one must take the circumstantial account of her inspiration *cum grano salis*. But it is not impossible that some fair lady expressed such a wish. Furthermore, even if there were no such charming *primum mobile*, the little story would still indicate that the author's intention is to write a book to please the fair sex—which is exactly what he will tell us about his motivation in undertaking the *Decameron*. Taking the opening statement with the conclusion, the message is clear; Boccaccio is writing not for the learned or the serious-minded, he is writing for a class that reads for pleasure, made up largely, if not exclusively, of women. And when he speaks of ennobling the tale, it is clear, too, that he has in mind the aristocracy. In which regard it may be noted—here in distinction from the *Decameron*—that, broadly speaking, all of the characters who have parts to play in the *Filocolo* are rich and noble. The peasantry that appears before us brawling in the last book is an exception—and it is seen as gross and ridiculous.

No doubt it is Boccaccio's purpose to "ennoble" the tale that explains, also, the presence of so much evidence of the young author's reading of the classics. As one might expect, Ovid is all-pervasive, but there are recognizable echoes of Virgil, Statius, Lucan, and most of the Latin authors that circulated in the late Middle Ages. If the sources of the main narrative are in a sense "popular," and, as we have seen, Boccaccio drew apparently on two Old French versions of the tale as well as an Italian rhymed version in somewhat vulgar style, yet the aura of the classical tradition and the music of the high style are ever with us. Nor should the indebtedness to Dante be overlooked. Not only does the episode of the arboreal Idalogo remind us of Pier delle Vigne (as well as of Polydorus), but the prose is sprinkled with phrases clearly derived from an intensive reading of the *Vita nuova*, to say nothing of the *Comedy*.

The work is interesting, too, for what it reveals of the Boccaccian narrative strategy. To be sure, from beginning to end it is the story of Florio and Biancifiore, but formally it is quite easily divisible into five independent parts. Mario Marti compares the work to a loosely assembled pile of blocks, lying beside or on top of one another.[14] It has been remarked by many critics that the story properly ends with the joyous and triumphant union of the faithful lovers at the end of book 4 and that the last book is an unnecessary and rather tedious supplement. But, for that matter, one could also say that book 1 is autonomous. If it is a preface to the main plot and a necessary one, for the material it supplies regarding the origins of the romantic pair, it could also be regarded as the story of Lelio and Julia, which has its beginning, middle, and tragic end set forth in the compass of the narrative. If one liked, one could publish book 1 separately under the title of *The Tragic Tale of Lelio and Julia*.

In this connection the autonomy of the Questions of Love (book 4, chapters 17–72, taking up seventy-four pages of Quaglio's edition) has long been recognized. This engaging interlude has only the most tenuous connection with the main plot; it may fairly be regarded as a novel exercise of Boccaccio's own genius. This is not to say that the concept is entirely original; undoubtedly Boccaccio was familiar with both the old Provençal *partimen*, in which love problems were debated in verse, and the illustrative dialogues set forth in the essay on love of Andreas Capellanus. Boccaccio's "questions," however, differ in two ways from such sources. In the traditional *partimen* the question is merely proposed to a lord or lady; no answer is given, while in Boccaccio's adaptation, as we have seen, Fiammetta does not hesitate to pronounce and defend her verdict. And even more significantly, Boccaccio's questions develop out of narratives, brief, to be sure, but circumstantial.[15]

The "questions" are, at least retrospectively considered, a pilot model for the *Decameron*; the resemblances in detail are striking. There is a presiding officer in both cases: the king or queen of the day in the *Decameron*, Fiammetta in the "questions." Problems are proposed and stories are told by both male and female narrators. And three of the stories that serve as backgrounds for the "questions" are in fact told again in the *Decameron*. But perhaps the most notable of all the similarities is the nature of the frame. The interlude of storytelling is suggested as a way of passing the hot and unpleasant time of day; it is thus a deliberately contrived flight from uncomfortable reality into a world of consoling fantasy. Even as the narrators of the *Decameron* will turn away from the ugly spectacle of the plague and the dangers of contagion, so here their prototypes seek refuge from the rigors of the noonday heat—and perhaps also from the obsessive tension of Filocolo's quest; he seems not at all impatient with the enforced stopover that breaks his arduous journey. Nor is the sequence of "questions" the only foretoken of the masterpiece to come. Nicolas James Perella rightly perceives that the *Filocolo* presents "a theme that Boccaccio was to treat with predilection and consummate art in later works such as the *Ninfale fiesolano* and several tales of the *Decameron*: the natural or instinctive love that attracts two young people of the opposite sex and the persistence of their love against the obstacle erected by an unsympathetic law or by class-conscious relatives concerned with preserving the distinction created by social and economic position."[16]

The *Filocolo* commands our interest, too, for the autobiographical information—or misinformation—that the young author provides. We have noted his intrusions *in propria persona* at the beginning and end of the romance. Nor are these his only interventions. Caleon, whom Filocolo meets in Naples (book 4, chapter 16), tells of his passion for Fiammetta in a way that suggests the author's own infatuation, disclosing, among other matters, that Maria is her real name. But the most arresting—and teasingly suggestive—Boccaccio *in maschera* is the tree-bound Idalogo of book 5, from whom Filocolo's unfortunately misdirected arrow calls forth lamentation—and therewith a pitiful and circumstantial autobiography.

For Idalogo (whose name signifies "wood-speaker"), thus unintentionally bruised, is more than willing, as was Dante's Pier delle Vigne before him, to tell his shocked and embarrassed listeners all about himself. He relates that years ago, from his home on a little hill standing in a part of Italy known as Tuscia, there came into the white kingdom of Franconarcos a shepherd named Eucomos, skilled not only in the care of sheep, but also in the playing of his rustic pipe. So sweet was his music and so persuasive his speech that he succeeded in seducing the fair Gannai, daughter of Franconarcos, leading her to believe she was truly his wife. Of their union two children were born, Idalogo himself being one. Shortly afterward, the fickle Eucomos abandoned the princess, returning to his homeland where he took another mate, named Garemirta, who also bore him children. Idalogo (apparently forgetting his twin of whom we hear nothing more) attempted to follow his father but was turned away from the paternal door by "two ferocious bears." He then came into "these woods" (Naples and its environs) to carry on the work he was prepared for and there he met a wise shepherd, Calmeta, who instructed him in the science of astronomy. As a result of this study, Idalogo abandoned his previous occupation and prepared "to follow Pallas." His studies were sometimes interrupted by the seasonal appearance of fair ladies in the grove wherein he was dwelling. Successively from the flock (although he has called them ladies, Idalogo now speaks of them as birds) he detached a dove, a blackbird, a parrot, and finally a pheasant, the enchantment of which was irresistible. Encouraged by her invitation, he pursued and captured her and for some time was happy in her company. But then, alas, exemplifying the faithlessness of her kind, she abandoned him for another. Thus betrayed, Idalogo concludes, he wandered through the woods in despair until Venus, out of pity for his restlessness, turned him into a tree.

The story is clearly meant to suggest a hidden meaning and such words as Tuscia (Tuscany) and Garemirta (an anagram for Margarita —a variant spelling of Margherita—Boccaccio's stepmother) are easy clues. With these the reader can work out the author's "biography." His father in the exercise of his craft (business) came to France where he seduced the daughter of the king (Gannai would seem to be an anagram for Gianna or *gallice* Jeanne) who bore him twins, one of whom is the speaker, *ipse* Boccaccio. The son followed his father to Italy where he was turned away by his hostile stepmother and step-brother (the bears); he went to Naples where he practiced his vocation (commerce); subsequently he abandoned business for learning and poetry (Pallas). He had a number of love affairs of no great significance and finally a grand passion for Fiammetta, who betrayed him.

The tale of Idalogo is the most detailed of all the veiled accounts of the youthful years of our poet-novelist. It is supported by allusions in other minor works, as we shall have occasion to note. But, as we remarked in chapter 2, the pillars of this attractive structure have no external support; both the French mother and the Angevin princess have eluded the detection of the most conscientious biographers and archivists. On the other hand, the blueprint, as it were, corresponds in schematic fashion to the truth: an illegitimate son of a Tuscan merchant did indeed come to Naples, practice his trade, study astronomy, turn to the study of letters, and have a number of love affairs. We may fairly see, in the narrative of Idalogo (and the hints given by similar sugges-tive figures in other products of the poet as well as in the avowals of the author himself), a kind of fanciful re-creation of his early years, *Dichtung*, to be sure, but with a substratum of *Wahrheit*. In writing such romances as the *Filocolo*, the author is concurrently rewriting his own romance: a dream sequence, not strictly factual yet carrying the substance of real incidents and sentimental motifs truly experienced by the dreamer.

Leaving aside for the moment the question of credibility and the quotient of factual truth, the recurrent presence of the author in his own inventions has its significance as a determinant of the nature of his aesthetic practice. These personal mooring lines anchor his work to his own time, place, and identity, thus bringing, one may say, a new kind of narrative sophistication into the art of fiction. So, too, the successive scenes of action are clearly identified, particularly the various pilgrimages around Italy are carefully charted. Perhaps it is this approach as much as anything else that justifies Branca in calling the *Filocolo* "our first modern novel"—a scholarly verdict which, as we have noted, is in accord with that of the impressionistic Chubb fifty years ago. For Salvatore Battaglia the romance marks "the baptism of the [prose] narrative in Italy and in Europe."[17] Such tributes may justify our lingering a moment to comment on the measure of the author's achievement and on the impact of the romance itself.

Its failings are all too apparent: the digressions are annoying, the lengthy speeches and the self-conscious parading of classical erudition, the want of discipline are aesthetic blemishes. There are troublesome contradictions in the narrative. Why is little Julia recognized as of noble stock at the time of her birth but subsequently regarded as base-born, once she has engaged Florio's affections? What gods must we—or does the author—believe in: the Christian God who motivates the journey to Compostela or the reliable Olympian platoon—Venus, Mars, and Diana—who, as it were, take over almost immediately and recurrently intervene in the action? Indeed today's reader is likely to sympathize with old King Felice when he fails to understand why his son, so long and loyally protected by the old gods must, at the end of the journey, so readily abandon them. Yet, with all its flaws, the story has authentic appeal. Digressions to the contrary notwithstanding, there is a story line and it is faithfully followed and developed. The plot gives us stirring action and real suspense. Many descriptive passages arouse our admiration. Critics have noted the two erotic scenes: the near seduction of the hero by a pair of brazen lasses in book 3 and the highly charged account of the two lovers in the tower in book 4, as exemplifying Boccaccio's effectiveness in an area close to his heart. The golden room in which Biancifiore is imprisoned is a tour de force of luxuriant description that anticipates a certain sensual exuberance normally associated with the Renaissance, conveying the character of Filocolo as well as the suggestion of exotic oriental splendor.

Conceding that the tale is primarily one of incident and adventure, it must also be remarked that characterization is not entirely lacking —at least in the presentation of the protagonist. Muscetta[18] rightly observes that Florio's course is not simply a chivalrous quest, but from the beginning a kind of educational experience. Our hero, at first an obsessed adolescent, becomes a shrewd leader of men and eventually a kind of *pater patriae*; we can see in the sequence of events an Aucassin gradually metamorphosed into an Aeneas or a Charlemagne, aware of his social and dynastic responsibilities. Nor should we overlook the fact that from the beginning this servant of love is tenaciously virtuous; he resists the seductive damsels sent to tempt him and he will not possess his long-sought love until he has ceremonially married her. He wants not a paramour, but a wife. Indeed a strong moralizing current runs through the whole narrative in spite of some sensual scenes. "Love for pleasure" is specifically castigated by Fiammetta in the seventh of the Questions of Love. The *Filocolo* is probably the best argument in all Boccaccio's canon for Robert Hollander's thesis of a moralizing Boccaccio.[19]

Critics have been, in the main, rather harsh in their verdicts of the work. "The narrative is complicated and the relation very long, drawn out, and tiresome," says Edward Hutton,[20] and he probably voices the general opinion of readers if not antiquarian scholars. It is true that Boccaccio's lengthy sentences, full of subordinate clauses, overburdened with rhetorical ornament, and pretentiously classical with due regard for the patterns of the cursus, make for laborious reading. In justice to the author's style, we should remember that the cultured medieval reader, like the medieval traveler, was less interested in getting quickly to his destination than in savoring the pleasures of the journey. Paradoxically perhaps, in medieval literature narrative moves at a faster pace in poetry than in prose; more "art" was applied—and expected—in a sentence of the high style than in a sonnet. Indeed, Sapegno suggests that we should regard the prose of the *Filocolo* as poetry—even if faulty poetry.[21]

With all its shortcomings and deficiencies, the *Filocolo* yet left an honorable legacy. Ernest Hatch Wilkins reminds us that "elements of Boccaccio's Infernal Council (Book I, chapter 9) were borrowed by Sannazaro, Vida, and Tasso; and Tasso found treasures elsewhere in the *Filocolo* as well, Chaucer derived his *Franklin's Tale* mainly from one of the Thirteen Questions, and made incidental use of material from the *Filocolo* in the opening lines of the Prologue to the *Canterbury Tales*, in the *Troilus*, and in the *Legend of Good Women*. Milton's Infernal Council is indebted, ultimately, to Boccaccio; and Keats re-created the union of Florio and Biancifiore in *The Eve of Saint Agnes*. [22] Beyond this catalog of specific influences, the *Filocolo* may also claim to be the primitive forerunner of a type of narrative designed for a long and prosperous career in European letters. In this connection the lighthearted quip of an Italian critic a century ago may be illuminating. It was made apropos of an inconsistency we have mentioned: how is it that Felice and his queen so readily forget the noble origins of Biancifiore, of which indeed, had their own memories been faulty, the faithful Ascalion might well have reminded them, for he is present from the beginning to the end of the action and even serves as a link between Florio and his illustrious Roman in-laws? Why does he not speak? "Because," said Bonaventura Zumbini, "Florio and Biancifiore were a little in the position of Enzo and Lucia of the *Promessi sposi;* if they had been able to get married at the beginning, there would have been no story."[23]

This casual paralleling of two tales of anguished lovers is strikingly illuminating with regard to the nature and originality of the *Filocolo*. Basically it is the archetypal story of the Quest, episodic, discursive, anchored to reality by an occasional naturalistic detail, but mostly by authenticity of simple passion. As far as the quest motif is concerned, one may trace the substance of the *Filocolo* to the legend of Cupid and Psyche, supposedly the remote source of the medieval romance. In wider terms, the quest is the pattern of the *Odyssey* and the *Aeneid*. Clothed in prose, brought from legend to sometimes coarse realism, fleshed out by commentary or digression, this sturdy vehicle will travel far over the roads of Europe, shrewdly and variously directed by such gifted drivers as Cervantes or Sterne or Manzoni. We need not further document this viable and vigorous genre, but we may note that the *Filocolo* is, in the literature of the West, at the head of the line. Later artists will exploit the potential it holds for naturalistic detail, satire, commentary, or quasi-philosophical lucubration—some of which are actually present and all of which exist *in posse* in the first prose novel of our tradition.

ext to the *Decameron*, the *Filostrato* is the best known and most widely read of all Boccaccio's works. Unquestionably, it owes this distinction in large part to its international resonance; Chaucer, who ascribed the tale to one Lollius,[1] based his version of the tale on the Italian work and the theme was later treated by Shakespeare and Dryden, among others. We have also had a twentieth-century version in Christopher Morley's *The Trojan Horse*. And even admitting, as Boccaccio himself does, that the scheme of the narrative goes back to an Old French source, the line of descent, so far as the English writers are concerned, begins with the *Filostrato*, "Love's Victim," as Boccaccio's synthetic Greek is meant to signify. But, quite aside from its honorable role as progenitor of a line of worthy descendants, Boccaccio's work has many merits of its own; the tale of the hapless Trojan prince transcends the medieval mannerism of its presentation and remains readable today. The story line is direct and unencumbered by digressions, pretentious allegory, or the furniture of irrelevant scholarship. The characterization is sharp and convincing and the psychology of the actors in the drama rings true. Both the significance of the work and its chronological place in the canon provide critics and literary historians with substance for meditation and in some cases controversy. We shall be able to discuss such matters if we have before us an outline of the action.

The poetic tale of Troiolo, son of Priam of Troy, is preceded by a brief introduction in prose, addressed to a lady, the object of the poet's affections, now far from him.[2] Boccaccio begins by a reference to a question of love that has often been discussed in his circle (an allusion reminiscent of the Questions of Love in book 4 of the *Filocolo*), that is, whether it is best for a lover to see his lady or to speak of her or to dream of her. He had always defended the last option, the author confesses, for it seemed to him that dreaming of his beloved would give him freedom to imagine her as responsive and affectionate. But now that his lady has left the city and betaken herself to Sannio, he realizes that he was wrong, for he has found it a torment to live without the sight of her. Save for concern for her honor, he would follow her to Sannio. Instead, to find some alleviation of his grief, he has cast about for a poetic theme dealing with an abandoned lover, so that he might express his own feelings under a veil, and he has chosen to tell the story of Troiolo and Criseida. He tells his lady that in the anguish of the forsaken Trojan prince she may see the figure of the author, and in the charming aspects of Criseida she may see herself: the other elements of the story are not relevant to their case, but are simply parts of the ancient tale he is retelling. He concludes with renewed expression of his devotion and a plea to his dear one to speed her return.

The poem, written in ottava rima, begins with an invocation, addressed not to Jove or the Muses, but to the poet's lady, the sole source of his inspiration; should his words win praise, he tells her "thine be the honor and mine the labor." The poet also asks lovers to hearken to his verse and to pray to Love for him (1–6). As the story begins, war is being waged around the walls of Troy and the Trojan priest and seer, Calchas, foresees that the victory must fall to the Greeks. He leaves the city secretly and is enthusiastically received in the Greek camp; he has left behind him his daughter, Criseida, a widow and "angelic to look upon." She appeals to Hector, who promises her that her father's defection will not be held against her, and she continues to live quietly in Troy (7–15).

Spring comes and the Trojans gather in the Palladium to worship Pallas. Criseida attends the rites as does the young prince, Troiolo, son of Priam and brother of Hector. He enjoys the spectacle, noting the manifestations of love among the young men and, smilingly, congratulates himself, for he has known the anguish love can bring, but has now recovered from its wounds and feels himself invulnerable. But at this very moment his eye falls on Criseida, and he is immediately smitten (16–31). He reveals his condition to none, but goes about the city, hoping for a sight of his lady, and love grows in his heart. He takes almost no further interest in the war, although when he does engage in battle, love gives him unusual strength. But gradually his passion wears him down, and he becomes pale and drawn. Criseida seems not even to notice him. At length, Troiolo prays to Love to either help him or send him death (32–57, end of part 1).

One day, as the love-stricken prince languishes in his chamber, his friend, Pandaro, comes upon him and solicitously asks what is the reason for his forlorn state. After some hesitation Troiolo reveals that he is the victim of love. Pandaro offers to help his friend, confessing that he, too, has had sad experiences in love's service. He asks who it is that Troiolo loves; the latter is reluctant to say, for Criseida is a cousin of Pandaro. But when Pandaro swears that even were she his sister he would be willing to help his friend, Troiolo reveals that it is Criseida. Pandaro congratulates the prince on his choice; his cousin, he says, is beautiful and charming, her only fault being that she is "more virtuous than other ladies." But he will help persuade her to accept Troiolo; so long as the relationship is kept secret, every lover has the right to follow his desires. Pandaro is sure that Criseida, too, has desires, for, he avers, all women do and are restrained from revealing them only by fear of shame. So again, he warns that discretion is necessary. He undertakes to approach Criseida on his friend's behalf; Troiolo has little hope, but Pandaro assures him that he is well supplied with "love-kindling words." And Troiolo consenting to his intervention, Pandaro goes to visit Criseida (1–34).

The interview between Pandaro and his winsome cousin, cast in the form of a dialogue all but stagelike in nature and rich in psychological undertones, displays Boccaccio's art at its best. The conversation is an interplay between two very worldly and astute personalities.

Pandaro begins with laughter and the casual banter appropriate between kinsmen. He then eyes Criseida sharply and remarks that she is looking extraordinarily well, adding that she has more to be thankful for than any other fair lady. When she asks the reason for this cryptic statement, Pandaro replies that he has heard that a very fine young man has found her beauty so pleasing as to be almost undone by it. Criseida blushes; such a man, she says, must have little to take up his time, for she has never known anything like that to happen before. Pandaro asks her to put jesting aside; has she not in fact taken notice of her suitor? No, Criseida replies; it is true that one man passes frequently by and gazes at her door, but she knows nothing of him. Pandaro says that the man he speaks of is not a man "not known at all." "Who is it then?" asks Criseida. Her cousin replies in general terms; it is a young man possessed of all good qualities, valiant, high-spirited, and noble; Criseida should take advantage of her good fortune. Indignantly, the widow replies: what man has any claim on her love unless he first marry her? But she still wants to know who he is. On learning that it is Prince Troiolo, she turns pale and can scarcely restrain her tears. She reproaches Pandaro for his intervention; no doubt Troiolo is great and brave and any lady could be happy with him, but she has no thought of love, for she is still in mourning for her husband. She admits that if she could love anyone it would be Troiolo, but it is known that his fancies come and go. Let him find another lady and leave her to her virtuous life. Rebuffed, Pandaro rises to leave. But he assures Criseida that he has recommended Troiolo to her as he would to a sister or a daughter; the prince is truly worthy of her and she may count on his fidelity. He reminds her, too, that though she is now young and fair, old age or death will in time take away her beauty. This remark causes Criseida to reconsider. She asks how Pandaro came to learn of the prince's state and Pandaro relates his interview with Troiolo, stressing the love torments the prince is undergoing. Criseida yields; she is not cruel, she says, and she is willing to see Troiolo provided he will be discreet and see that no shame come to either of them (35–66).

Left alone, Criseida soliloquizes, rationalizing her acceptance of Troiolo. She is solitary, a widow, and young. Why should she not love? "I know not a single lady in this land without a lover," she says. She should make the most of her youth, and Troiolo is of noble birth and acceptable in every way. A lover is better than a husband, too, since he requires no surrender of liberty; besides, there is a special pleasure in secret joys. Yet, doubts return. Love affairs often lead to jealousy and sadness. Troiolo may tire of her. And it will be difficult to keep their *affaire* concealed; she might easily lose her good name. So for a long time she debates with herself. Pandaro, meanwhile, reports the accomplishment of his mission to Troiolo, who is greatly cheered. The next time he passes by Criseida's window she responds to his glances. With this satisfaction, desire grows. At the suggestion of Pandaro, Troiolo writes his lady, pleading for her pity. Her reply is ambiguous, she admits that she loves him and would be pleased to make him happy, but she has her good name to think of. Further letters are exchanged, and ultimately Pandaro intervenes again. Timidly, reluctantly, and yet willingly, Criseida consents to receive a visit from Troiolo, fixing a time when she will be alone in her house (67–143, end of part 2).

After a brief invocation to his lady, Boccaccio resumes his narrative with the return of Pandaro to the waiting prince. He assures his friend that he may soon expect to hold Criseida in his arms and, reminding him that for his sake he has made himself a go-between and risked the good name of a kinswoman, he again stresses the necessity of secrecy. The overjoyed Troiolo swears he will be discreet; his gratitude to Pandaro is so great that he professes himself willing to perform a like office on his behalf should his friend fancy Polyxena (Troiolo's sister) or even the fair Helen herself (3–18). Finally, the right day comes; Pandaro alerts Criseida and sends for Troiolo, who has gone off on war business. Troiolo returns that night and waits outside Criseida's door until she comes to greet him, carrying a torch. The lovers embrace and then repair to Criseida's chamber where they enjoy the full delights of love. The author celebrates their rapture and remarks that no miser who puts riches above love can ever know such happiness (19–38).

As a proclamation of Boccaccio's commitment, his own words may be cited here:

O sweet and long desired night of Love,
What were thou to that pair of happy lovers?
If I were given all the skill and art
possessed by all the poets of the past;

yet by my pen it could not be described.
Let him who has been favored as were they
by courtesy of love, imagine it.
And in some measure he will know their joy (35).
. . . .
Now may those wretched misers, ever wont
to criticize whoever falls in love
and does not, as they do, devote himself,
to money grubbing, by fair means or foul,
consider if that wealth they hold so dear
has ever given them such joy as Love
can in a single moment grant to one
whom friendly fortune has conjoined with him (38).

At dawn the lovers part, planning to meet again. The next morning
Pandaro, calling on his friend, is embraced by him. As Troiolo expresses his gratitude, Pandaro again mentions the need for secrecy
(39–60). The lovers meet again; Troiolo is now in ecstasy and sings
to Pandaro a somewhat lengthy hymn to Venus "who moves all
nature, gods and men" and has given him such bliss. He asks to be made
worthy of his lady and that she may always love him (61–89). So, as
the *affaire* prospers, Troiolo becomes more valiant in battle. During the
truces he takes part in hunting and knightly diversions; he is affable
and courteous with all, envying none. Such are the effects of requited
love. But his happiness is destined to last but a short time, thanks to
jealous Fortune (90–94, end of part 3).

Meanwhile, the war rages. A sally of Hector is repulsed and the
Greeks capture many Trojan leaders. Calchas, reminding the Greeks of
his services, asks to be permitted to offer one of the Trojan captives
in exchange for his daughter. The Greeks consent and offer to exchange
Antenor for Criseida. The Trojans hold counsel and discuss the offer;
Troiolo is present and is greatly distressed as he cannot question the
exchange without revealing his relationship with Criseida. When the
decision is made to accept the Greek offer, the prince swoons. Recovering, he says nothing to his concerned kinsmen, but seeks the solitude
of his chamber (1–22).

Here, the author interrupts his narrative to tell his lady that now that he is to sing of sad things, he will not need her aid; his own unhappy and abandoned condition will be sufficient inspiration. He hopes that if the tale comes to her ears she will return to him at once (23–25). The tale goes on to describe the despair of Troiolo; he throws himself on his bed, beats his head against the wall, incoherently cursing the gods and himself. He rails against Fortune, who has robbed him of the most precious thing in his life; he could more readily have borne the loss of Hector or Priam or even the fall of Troy. The loss of Criseida will mean death for him—and the blow came all unexpectedly. Would that Calchas had died the day he deserted Troy! Finally, the prince falls into a sleep of exhaustion (26–41). Arising, he sends for Pandaro, who also weeps on hearing the bad news. But he tries to comfort Troiolo by reminding him that, after all, he has enjoyed Criseida's love. If she must go, well, there are other women available. But Troiolo will not be solaced; he vows he will always love only Criseida, nor does he find satisfaction in recalling past joys that will come no more. He asks only for death (42–62). Pandaro suggests that Troiolo abduct Criseida, following the example of Paris. Troiolo, however, feels that such an act would cost Criseida her good name, to which Pandaro replies that Helen has done very well without her good name, and that he is sure Criseida would consent. Fortune favors the bold, he affirms. But Troiolo wants first to be sure that Criseida would agree. Pandaro promises to arrange a meeting (63–77).

The news has also reached Criseida. A number of women come to call on her; some congratulate her on the prospect of rejoining her father, some express their sorrow at her leaving, and others hope that in the Greek camp she may be able to arrange terms of peace. Criseida listens to them all, distracted and upset. When they leave she throws herself on her bed, wondering desperately how she will live without Troiolo or he without her. She curses her father; she is being punished for his sins. Her lamentations are interrupted by the entrance of Pandaro (78–95).

Pandaro describes the anguish of Troiolo and he and Criseida weep together. Finally her cousin bids her to compose herself and prepare to receive her stricken love; he then returns to Troiolo and tells him Criseida wants him (96–113). When Troiolo comes, the lovers exchange tears and kisses. Criseida faints, and Troiolo, believing her dead, is about to kill himself when she revives. After more tears and embraces, Criseida says she can see no choice; she must go to the Grecian camp. She bids her lover not to despair, there will be occasions when she can return. Besides, the war may end at any time and then she can come back to Troy. Her father, she says, is avaricious and she will find ways of making it profitable for him to let her return. But the prince is not reassured; he thinks Calchas may well choose to keep his daughter with him and perhaps even find a Greek husband for her. He proposes that they flee together. To this suggestion Criseida objects that flight would disgrace both of them; Troiolo would be called a deserter and her name would be ruined. And she adds that there is a special joy in secret love that perishes when a liaison becomes public. She advises him to follow her plan and wait for a change in Fortune. She promises to return in ten days; she is sure she can devise some way of doing so. Meanwhile, she asks Troiolo to be patient and ever faithful to her. For if he were to love another, she would kill herself. Troiolo assures her that he could never love another; he loves her not for her beauty nor gentle birth nor wealth, but for her noble ways and disdain of all base things. So, at dawn, the lovers reluctantly part (114–167, end of part 4).

The Greek warrior, Diomede, comes to claim Criseida and she is surrendered to him. Troiolo accompanies them as far as the outer ramparts; as he turns away, he implores her to return again lest he die. Diomede, smitten himself by Criseida's charms, notes the distress of the prince. Criseida, silent and subdued, is welcomed by her father (1–14). Retiring to his chamber, Troiolo grieves all day and all night, reproaching himself for allowing Criseida to leave. In the morning he summons Pandaro, who tries to solace him, reminding him that others, too, have suffered similar anguish. He points out that Criseida has promised to return in ten days; to make the time pass, he suggests they leave the city for a while. Accordingly, the two friends visit Sarpedon, who lives some four miles outside of Troy. They are cordially welcomed and entertained with song and music, hunting, banquets, and the company of fair and noble ladies (15–42). But Troiolo can find no joy; after five days he returns to the city and wanders about Troy, revisiting all the scenes associated with Criseida, even the gate where they parted. He composes a song of reproach to Love. Pandaro is his constant companion, ever trying to cheer him (43–71, end of part 5).

In the Greek camp Criseida mourns, disconsolate, with memories of Troiolo ever in her heart. But on the fourth day of her residence in the camp, Diomede calls upon her. He tells her that he has observed her sadness and suspects that love may be its cause. But love for a Trojan, he says, is wasted; the Greeks are destined to win the war and the Trojans will be annihilated. It was for that reason that Calchas, counseled by Diomede himself, had his daughter brought out of the city. She must forget the Trojans who, Diomede asserts, are a boorish folk when compared to the Greeks, among whom Criseida will find someone worthy of her love. He adds that he himself is of royal stock and he concludes by asking Criseida to accept him as her vassal (1–25). In reply, Criseida denies that the Greeks are superior to the Trojans, protests that she has loved no man since the death of her husband; then she adds that if the Greeks win she may listen more favorably to Diomede. Well content, the Greek takes his leave. His handsome appearance has impressed Criseida, she is no longer so painfully tormented by thoughts of Troiolo, and she makes no effort to keep her promise to return (26–34, end of part 6).

On the tenth day after Criseida's departure, Troiolo and Pandaro go to the gate to meet her. They wait all day and far into the night and, as she fails to appear, Troiolo continues to make excuses for her. For six days after the promised day he goes back to the gate, but Criseida never comes. At length, worn out by longing and jealousy, he retires to solitude, seeing no one, weeping all day long, slowly pining away, desirous only of death (1–20). Priam and Hector are deeply concerned; they ask what ails him and he tells them it is a pain in his heart. One night, the prince has a dream in which he sees a wild boar tear the heart out of Criseida, who does not complain but seems to enjoy the operation. Waking, he tells Pandaro of the dream; the boar, he is sure, stands for Diomede, whose ancestor slew the boar of Calidon. In his despair, Troiolo sizes a knife, and only the intervention of Pandaro saves him from suicide (21–36). Pandaro then reproaches his friend for his reaction to an idle dream that may have many interpretations. And he adds: if Criseida has been faithless, Troiolo would do better to revenge himself on her than to commit suicide; let him die, if he must, fighting the Greeks. Troiolo asks Pandaro's forgiveness and asks how he may learn whether or not Criseida has been false. Pandaro suggests writing to her. Troiolo eagerly complies; in a long letter to Criseida, he confesses his doubts about her but protests his own enduring love. Above all he begs her to return, since he can find no joy in life without her (37–75). But when no answer comes from Criseida, Troiolo becomes so enfeebled that he takes to his bed.

His brother, Deifobo, calls on him. He overhears Troiolo in his delirium murmur the name Criseida and thus discovers the prince's secret. He urges Troiolo to go forth and fight the Greeks and the suggestion seems to invigorate the dejected prince. When Deifobo reveals to his kinsmen the truth about his brother, the ladies of the house, including Hecuba, Polyxena, Helen, and Cassandra, visit him "with melodies and singers" and Troiolo is somewhat solaced by their company (76–85). Cassandra reproaches her brother for allowing himself to pine away for love not of a noble lady, but of "the daughter of a wicked priest." Troiolo denies that it is Criseida whom he loves; how would he have let her leave Troy if he had loved her? But if it were she, why would she be unworthy? For Criseida is not only beautiful; she is truly noble, since nobility is not a matter of birth, but of the soul. And he adds that Criseida possesses all the virtues; she is chaste, modest, courteous, and prudent. She would be fit to sit upon a throne, unlike Cassandra, he says, calling his sister a "silly and conceited woman." He bids her begone, and she slinks away as the other women commend Troiolo's words (86–103). At last comes a letter from Criseida, assuring him of her love, making excuses for her failure to return, but repeating her promise to do so, though giving no date. Troiolo is sufficiently revived to renew his combats with the Greeks, in which he distinguishes himself (104–106, end of part 7).

Hector is slain and Troiolo grieves for him, yet even grief cannot dislodge Criseida from his heart. He writes her often and sends Pandaro to visit her during the truces. She answers his letters with fair words and empty promises. Troiolo feels increasingly sure that she has another lover. He soon has reason to confirm his suspicions. Deifobo returns from battle bearing spoils taken from the wounded Diomede; among them is a brooch that Troiolo recognizes as one he had given his lady when they parted. He now knows that he rightly interpreted his dream (1–10). To Pandaro he pours out his grief and resentment, calling down Jove's curse on the faithless woman and vowing to slay Diomede. Pandaro, moved to tears, also condemns Criseida. He regrets now that he ever brought the two lovers together, although he had acted only for the prince's pleasure. He, too, prays the gods to punish his guilty cousin (11–24). Troiolo and Diomede meet several times on the battlefield and exchange thrusts, but neither one triumphs. Finally, Troiolo is slain by Achilles. "Such was the end of the vain hope of Troiolo in base Criseida." The author bids young men be careful in the choice of their loves, for many young women are vain and fickle, and particularly those who have noble ancestors. He asks that prayers be offered to Love on behalf of young Troiolo (25–33, end of part 8).

The author sends his book to his lady, asking it to commend him to her and to tell her of his sad state and beg her either to return or bid his soul leave his body, for without her, death is better than life. But his book should approach his lady only in the company of Love, otherwise it may be ill received.

ONE of the peripheral problems connected with the *Filostrato* is the date of its composition. This is not easy to resolve. Since the story is set in the Homeric era it contains no allusions to events or persons in the poet's own times. The only basis we have for hazarding an opinion on the date of the work (aside from the intuitions—often brilliant but *au fond* always conjectural—of various scholars as touching matters of style and prosody) is the information furnished in the foreword, wherein the author speaks of composing the work during the absence of his lady who has betaken herself to Sannio. Until recently, it has been generally assumed that the lady in question was Fiammetta or, postulating the fleshly existence of such a charmer, Maria d'Aquino, whom the poet encourages us to see disguised under that inflammatory soubriquet. Assuming that she was indeed the absent sweetheart for whom her lover wrote this cautionary tale, scholars have seen Criseida as a kind of warning example held up to her and her role in the narrative as indicative of the young author's uneasy suspicion that Fiammetta and Criseida may have much in common.

The chief point of debate among critics centered on whether the poems had been composed before or after the lover had enjoyed Fiammetta's "full favors." Recently, however, a new interpretation of the foreword, advanced by Vittore Branca,[3] suggests that the absent lady is not Fiammetta, and this thesis would oblige us to revise the dating of the work. In the introduction to his edition of the poem, the Italian author, recapitulating his earlier studies, asserts that we have to deal here not with Fiammetta but rather with a predecessor on the youthful Boccaccio's *via amoris*. Branca's most effective argument is that there is no mention of Fiammetta either in the *proemio* or at the end of the poem, or indeed anywhere in the course of the narrative. And since that fiery *senhal* appears in all other youthful works from the *Filocolo* to the *Elegy of Madonna Fiammetta*, Branca deduces that, along with *Diana's Hunt*, the *Filostrato* owes its inspiration to a lady who ruled the poet's heart before Fiammetta appeared on the horizon, or at least before Boccaccio's Muse recognized her as sole queen. Further, Branca notes that the *proemio* is addressed to one Filomena, and in the course of his dedication the poet speaks of his lady's name as "full of grace," which in the Middle Ages was thought to be the significance of Giovanna. Branca notes, too, that the *Filostrato* lacks the *richesse* of erudition and classical allusions that characterize the other youthful works, beginning with the *Filocolo*; he therefore believes the *Filostrato* was written before the *Filocolo* by a Boccaccio "barely in his twenties"—possibly in 1335.

Branca's arguments are cogent, but some doubts must linger. Many of the details of the enamorment of the young Troiolo, the first meeting in a temple, the young lover deeming himself already a veteran of love's wars and thus ill prepared for the *coup de foudre*, the costume of Criseida, white veil and dark dress, are found likewise in the *Filocolo*. Insofar as these statements are autobiographical must we then assume two ladies, both met under similar topographical and psychological circumstances and dressed in similar costumes? On the other hand, if we refuse to see any truly autobiographical element in the early romances but merely a stylized blending of *Dichtung und Wahrheit*, the use of a different *senhal* may not be especially significant. After all, as we shall see, Fiammetta is called "Lucia" at one point in the *Amorosa visione*. And as far as the absence of erudite paraphernalia is concerned, the same may surely be said of the *Ninfale fiesolano*, which indeed in certain humble "family scenes" and to some degree in the almost adolescent simplicity of the protagonist shows some affinity with the *Filocolo*. Yet that poem is commonly counted the last of Boccaccio's youthful works, immediately preceding the *Decameron*, and its simple story line is considered an evidence of maturity.

One cannot but suspect that if the *Filostrato* had no *proemio* many readers would be inclined to put it rather late in the chronological sequence, as indeed Muscetta does, holding it probable that the poem was composed "in the autumn and winter of 1340, even later than the first part at least of the *Teseida.*"[4] A certain sharpness of design, a simplicity of structure, and a sophisticated skill in characterization by means of dialogue that is, for the times, surprisingly economical, all seem to indicate a more practiced craftsman than the author of the *Filocolo*. In all those respects the *Filostrato,* whatever be the chronology, is a more accomplished work of art than the *Filocolo,* and, one may add, superior, from a twentieth-century point of view, to Chaucer's version of the tale, which has, to be sure, its own beauties, but is in places intolerably prolix.[5] In any event, the sad story of Troiolo, in view of the substance and manner, must be placed among the Neapolitan works; it clearly precedes the infatuation for erotic allegory that will characterize such enterprises as the *Comedy of the Florentine Nymphs* and the *Amorous Vision.*

For the *Filostrato* is firmly fixed in the tradition of courtly love, of which rapturous dedication, adultery, and elitism are the recognizable hallmarks. The setting and the names of the characters are, to be sure, taken from an older source, not essentially courtly at all, the *Roman de Troye* of the late twelfth-century Benoît de Sainte-Maure, in turn drawing on an older Latin work, both of which were concerned with matters more martial than erotic.[6] The indebtedness, avowed by Boccaccio himself, has been fully documented by scholars. But Boccaccio's alterations are much more significant than his borrowings. In the Old French poem the affair of the lover is a mere episode, introduced, it would seem, to relieve the monotony of the battle scenes, which are the principal concern of Benoît. In his *roman* the story begins with the departure of Criseida for the Grecian camp and focuses chiefly on her compliant seduction by Diomede. Neither the preliminary wooing nor the anguish of Troiolo after his lady's desertion come into the tale. As for the first of these significant additions, Boccaccio may have found some suggestions in another subplot of Benoît—the wooing of Polyxena by Achilles. For the anguish of Troiolo he could turn to a long tradition as well as, not impossibly, his own experiences. (We may call into question every *fact* he sets before us with regard to his youthful love affairs, but there is no reason why we should doubt that the emotional responses of his protagonists have a solid "autobiographical" base.) One may concede, too, that the lovers' names, the offstage battle noises (though rarely heard in the course of the story) are essential furnishings. But the elements that give vitality to Boccaccio's narrative and determine its nature are his own creation, having their source either in the conventions of the love cult or in his own stylized autobiography, itself a product of that cult. Troiolo has the single-minded dedication of Florio and his love affair follows the pattern of those of Caleon or Idalogo or of Ibrida in the later *Amorous Vision*. But there are aspects of the *Filostrato* that give the story more weight and that make it aesthetically more meaningful and more convincing than the colorful accounts of the exaltations and miseries of cognate characters in his other romances.

At first sight the profile of the narrative seems easily recognizable; it suggests the conventional medieval treatment of love in the high style. The protagonists are noble and the love that binds them is obsessive, illicit, and secret. The story progresses through the familiar stages from the *coup de foudre* to its foredoomed end in death—at least for Troiolo. A medieval genre presented in classical costumes, one might say. But the tale of the Trojan pair has one distinctive feature that sets it apart from the archetypal love stories of the Middle Ages, such as those of Lancelot and Guinevere, Tristram and Iseult, or

Francesca and her inarticulate Paolo. Criseida is not a wife, but a widow. This distinction somewhat alters the nature of the narrative and is bound to make a difference in our assessment of the heroine. The great love stories of the Middle Ages were adulterous, and if one may say that this characteristic had become a convention, it was also a convention explained or justified by a realistic social fact: the lady had a husband. Hence the need for secrecy and hence, too, the inevitable exaltation, approved by Andreas Capellanus, of love freely given (i.e., to the lover) over love yielded under constraint of law. The impediment to the course of true love between Lancelot and Guinevere had its source in no romantic option of the lovers but in the existence of Arthur, and from this circumstance came all the anguish and eventually the tragedy of the lovers.

But looking at the situation in which Troiolo and Criseida find themselves and accepting at face value their repeated protestations of total commitment, there is no logical reason why they should not have married. Certainly, to put it prosaically, Troiolo would have been a fine "catch" for Criseida; she in turn—as the hero affirms himself when taxed by Cassandra—would have been quite eligible as a princely consort. Their love is illicit, but not adulterous, and for that reason, not truly tragic. Nor can we say that the young Boccaccio is simply following an accepted convention, overlooking or forgetting the realistic element from which the convention derives. On this point Criseida's reasoning, when she is first approached by Pandaro, is most illuminating. Her unabashed soliloquy reveals that she recognizes her sexual needs and is eager to satisfy them, and likewise that she is not prepared to pay the price of being subject to a lawful spouse. She wants "love"—if that is what it is—but she wants freedom, too. She is in fact a pragmatic hedonist. To be sure, she is anxious to protect her good name; hence her insistence on secrecy, but this requirement springs from a desire to conform with the rules of society—there is no vengeful husband in the background. Once she is assured that the relationship will be scrupulously concealed, she is quite prepared to accept Troiolo and, for all her tears on leaving Troy, Diomede as well. Such a calculating intelligence deprives her of any claim to the tragic status of an Iseult; indeed, it removes the whole story from the realm of tragedy and makes of it a realistic account of a relationship between a calculating sensualist on the one hand and an irrational romantic on the other. For Troiolo, although at the beginning fully in accord with Criseida's notion, by the end of the affair is sincerely sorry that he did not do all in his power to keep her; he regrets the missed opportunity to carry her off, whatever scandal might have ensued, and it is quite clear that even the obnoxious bondage of marriage would not have been repugnant to him. Thus, one may fairly say, that if under the Greek trappings we have a medieval romance, that romance in its turn clothes a pattern that is not truly medieval at all; it is one that has served the social novelists of later centuries including our own and one that we can meet again in such "neorealists" as our contemporary Moravia. It is a novel of today.

In this connection we may profitably examine the character of Pandaro. His name is of Greek origin, but the Pandaro of Homer is an archer and not an attorney-at-love. Probably, Boccaccio chose the name without reference to the Homeric original but rather to the significance of the name itself. For him, Pandaro would contain the roots "pan" (everything, all) and "dar" (to give), signifying "one who would give all to a friend." (Thanks to Chaucer's transmission Boccaccio added a word to the English language; strangely enough, "pandaro" is not a common noun in Italian—perhaps because the Italian language had already other words to characterize such "good friends.")

Aside from his name, the role of Pandaro in the liaison is something new, too; critics casting around for "sources" have suggested Gallehault of the Lancelot story, Governail of the Tristram legend, and a few minor characters of the *Filocolo*, assuming that work predates the *Filostrato*; but in fact none of them has a part at all commensurate with that played by Criseida's obliging cousin. It is probably not his role as a go-between that Boccaccio would stress; he seems rather to be set before us as the image of the perfect friend. He is not simply interested in bringing the young prince to his cousin's bed; he consoles Troiolo through every stage of his passion, walks with him, listens to him— at times one cannot but feel sympathy for him in that role—and goes to battle with him. He is a loyal companion and a friendly counselor. Set against the irrational motivations of the prince, the advice of

Pandaro often seems cynical, but it is born of common sense and a laudable desire to help his friend toward happiness or, if need be, to resignation. It is true that he makes light of the difficulties of the conquest of Criseida (or any woman for that matter) and in his persuasion of the young widow he reveals a certain disillusioned realism (hardly disconcerting to Criseida, who understands him perfectly), but when the lovers must part, it is he who suggests they might do better to flee Troy together; in this crisis it is the "romantic" Troiolo who hesitates, fearing public opinion. Pandaro reminds Troiolo that there are other women in the world to replace his lost love, yet it is Pandaro, too, who is willing to carry messages to the Greek camp, well knowing that they serve no purpose. It is he who prevents Troiolo from killing himself, and it is he who listens for hours to the varied outpourings of rapture or rancor from the lips of his obsessed friend. His own words, by contrast, are usually as brief and to the point as they are sensible and sympathetic. If we were to see the principal characters of the *Filostrato* as allegories of human attitudes, we should have to see Pandaro as occupying the middle ground between the calculating Criseida and the impassioned Troiolo—the middle ground, that is, of shrewd, tolerant, and withal benevolent common sense. The author of the *Filostrato* saw himself portrayed in the title role. The author of the *Decameron* is adumbrated in Pandaro.

The *Filostrato* is no less contemporary, or eternal, in the techniques of its exposition than in the nature of its substance. The characters are consistently revealed not by intrusive statements of the author, but by their own words. It is notable that of the seven hundred octaves spent in telling the tale, more than half are *spoken* by the various actors. Some passages, such as the enraptured effusions of Troiolo or his "hymn to Venus," are a little lengthy for our twentieth-century taste, but the dialogues between Pandaro and his cousin and very often between the amiable go-between and the prince are economical and realistic. And in all cases they serve to define very clearly the personalities involved. Catherine Carswell defines accurately, I think, if somewhat rapturously, the nature of Boccaccio's accomplishment. For her, the *Filostrato* is "a splendid invention, quick moving and full-rigged, bearing a cargo of reality in its rough-hewn hold. It is a heroic epic in which the figures are unheroic men and women, an exaltation of love and life above riches, a novel in verse that can soar and plunge."[7] It is no matter for surprise that Shakespeare found the tale suited to his talents.

CHAPTER 6

THE TESEIDA OF THE NUPTIALS OF EMILIA

 he *Teseida* ("Story of Theseus"), Boccaccio's only attempt at the epic—or what he thought was epic —was composed, in the opinion of its most recent editor,[1] during the years between 1339 and 1341. Granting these dates to be reasonably accurate, it follows that the poem was conceived and probably begun in Naples and finished only after the young author had returned to his native Tuscany. Of the aesthetic correlatives of this topographical displacement we shall have more to say later. The dedicatory letter in prose, addressed to Fiammetta, makes it clear that the Neapolitan charmer still reigns in the poet's heart; it reveals, as well, that she has now turned away from him, leaving him only bittersweet memories of that "cruel woman." Yet in his misery the poet still recalls that she was wont to take pleasure in tales of love; this version of a story of that nature he has ventured to present in "latino volgare e per rima" in the hope that it may win back her affections. At the very least, if she will but accept it, he will find consolation in the thought that something of his may reach those delicate hands to which he himself may not hope to return. The letter contains as well a summary of the plot of the story, intended, no doubt, to secure his lady's attention or possibly to facilitate her reading. For further clarification, the poet adds an ample number of glosses, chiefly intended to explain the frequent mythological references contained in the work. We have Boccaccio's own autograph version of the poem, complete with glosses.

The narrative begins with an account of the campaign of Theseus, prince of Athens, against the Amazons. He conquers their queen, Hippolyta, makes her his wife and brings her back to Athens; she is accompanied by her younger sister, Emilia (book 1, 138 stanzas). In Athens Theseus hears of the civil war raging in Thebes, caused by the tyrannical conduct of Creon. He intervenes in the war, overthrows Creon, and brings to Athens as prisoners two youthful noblemen, called Palemone and Arcita, partisans of the defeated Creon (book 2, 99 stanzas).

It happens that the prison cell assigned to the two young noblemen looks out on a garden where Emilia likes to stroll. Both young men observe her and fall at once in love with her. At this point a friend of Theseus, Peritoo, visits the prince and persuades him to free Arcita from imprisonment. Theseus stipulates that Arcita must leave Athens and promise never to return. Arcita accepts his freedom, although with a heavy heart, since banishment signifies that he will no longer be able to see Emilia. Nor does Palemone long enjoy the contemplation of her graces, for winter comes on and she no longer walks in the garden (book 3, 85 stanzas).

Arcita rashly returns to Athens; he assumes the name Penteo and takes service in the household of Theseus, who does not recognize him. Emilia does, however, but she does not indicate her recognition to Arcita, or to anyone else. Arcita falls into the habit of retiring to a secluded grove where he can freely bemoan his unhappy situation and express his love for Emilia (book 4, 92 stanzas). One day he is overheard by Panfilo, the valet of Palemone. Panfilo immediately informs his master of Arcita's presence in the court; he also arranges Palemone's escape from confinement. The latter, armed, goes at once to the grove where Arcita is wont to repair; there he finds his friend sleeping. He wakes him and persuades him that they must fight a duel to determine which of them may court Emilia. Arcita is reluctant to fight a friend but Palemone gives him no choice. They joust; Arcita unhorses Palemone but allows him to recover himself and renew the combat.

At this point, Emilia comes upon them; she immediately informs Theseus (both she and the prince had come into the woods with a hunting party). Theseus is at first angry, but ultimately he relents, for he knows how irresistible the power of Love can be. He had planned, he says, to marry Emilia to his cousin, Achates, but the young man had died. Now he is willing to give her to whichever of the two rivals may prevail in a tournament. A formalized combat is agreed upon; each of the rivals will choose a hundred partisans; Theseus will preside over the tournament. The winner will have Emilia and the loser will abide by whatever decision she may choose to take concerning him. All then return to Athens, and Theseus frees both youths and restores them to their titles and estates (book 5, 105 stanzas).

Fortune, in her treatment of the young Theban princes, had shown the full extent of her power. Now, restored to their estates, they live for a while in friendly harmony, giving lavish hospitality and entertainment to their Athenian friends. But, meanwhile, they provide themselves with new armor and look forward eagerly to the day of decision. From all corners of the world, and out of classical history and legend, heroic figures pour into Athens to take part in the tournament: kings such as Lycurgus and Peleus, heroes such as Ulysses and Diomede, even the heavenly twins, Castor and Pollux. All are given a royal welcome by Theseus and his household. When they see Emilia, they can understand why the rivals are ready to fight for her (book 6, 71 stanzas).

As the day draws near, Theseus speaks in the great theater that is to be the scene of combat, addressing the throng. He is amazed that so many have come to take part in this battle between two young men immoderately inflamed by love. He points out that it is not greed for land or inheritance that motivates them nor yet revenge, but love alone, for which reason he would have the duel fought without hatred. He forbids the use of the lance—the most lethal of weapons—permitting only swords, maces, or war axes. The visitors are to choose whichever side appeals to them; the tournament is to be thought of not as a war, but as a game in honor of Mars. All applaud the words of Theseus and each noble visitor chooses his side; as it happens, the division is even and the sides equally matched. Theseus then leads the warriors to his palace where in all harmony they help each other with their preparations for battle.

The day before the combat, Arcita goes to the temple of Mars and prays for victory, and Palemone to the temple of Venus to pray that he may win Emilia. The prayers of both princes make their way to the dwellings of the respective gods; both are assured that they will have what they asked for. Emilia prays to Diana; she asks only to be left alone and for peace between the rivals. If she must fall to either of the two suitors, she asks Diana to give her to the one who loves her more; she, herself, finds them equally attractive. She asks for an indication of which one will win her. Diana's choir appears and tells Emilia she is fated to be the bride of one of the rivals; Diana will indicate her destiny if Emilia will but look at the altar. She does so and sees two flames on the altar; one goes out and then flares up again, and the other becomes sulphurous and crackles. Emilia does not understand the significance of what she has seen.

The day of the battle comes. The princes arrange their forces and go to meet Theseus in his palace. He leads them to the temple of Mars, where he offers sacrifices and then knights both the young princes. They make their way to the theater of combat; they cannot see Emilia and each feels a little chill in his heart as he hears the trumpets blare and the clamor of the spectators. The arena of combat is described: it is lofty, sheathed in marble, and has more than five hundred tiers. It measures not less than a mile around; the field in the middle is round and vast; there are gates on the east and the west with no other way of entrance. It had been used for gladiatorial combats in the past. On this day it is thronged with visitors and townspeople. Old Aegeus is present, as is Theseus with Hippolyta and Emilia.

Arcita and Palemone make their ceremonial entrances at opposite gates, accompanied by their teams. Arcita looks like a "proud Libyan lion," and Palemone enters as might a "furious and bristling boar." Arcita, seeing Emilia, utters a plea, praising her beauty and asking for her favor and her prayers on his behalf. Palemone silently echoes his rival's words. Then the trumpet sounds. Theseus descends to the arena and reminds the combatants of the conditions of battle. He adds that those taken must fight no more but may remain to watch; anyone who leaves the theater may not return. The victor is to have the lady and the loser to abide by the understanding already reached. The trumpet sounds again. Arcita makes a speech to his men, reminding them that they have the favor of Mars, that it was Palemone who brought on the combat, that they are all of glorious inheritance and engaged in combat with worthy foemen, and so on. Finally, he prays that no ill befall them. Palemone, too, exhorts his followers, although his words are not quoted. And both sides wait for the third blast of the trumpet, which will signal the beginning of the combat (book 7, 145 stanzas).

The combat rages with many vicissitudes and many acts of prowess; the sides are evenly matched. Emilia, looking on, is moved to deplore the workings of Fortune and Love, which have brought about such strife. Gradually, the ranks are thinned and the remaining warriors become exhausted; many withdraw to rest. While Arcita is slackening in his ardor, Mars comes to him in the semblance of Theseus and upbraids him. Arcita renews his efforts and is rewarded. Palemone is bitten by a horse; Arcita frees him and disarms him. Seeing him victorious and knowing she is now destined for him, Emilia finally gives her heart to Arcita; she prays for a speedy end to the combat and for the safety of Arcita. And with the loss of their leader Palemone's followers are soon defeated and captured (book 8, 131 stanzas).

Mars and Venus have watched the duel from above. When Arcita triumphs, Venus points out to Mars that the wish of his votary has been fulfilled, for he is victorious; now it is her turn. Mars consents and Venus summons Erinyes from the lower world. The serpent-dressed goddess comes forth from Hell to the arena of combat. She frightens Arcita's horse, which rears and falls on its rider, crushing his chest. Emilia is horrified. All come to the side of the wounded Arcita, including Emilia who is "too chaste to know how to console him." Palemone, too, grieves for his stricken kinsman, but even more for himself as the loser in the duel. Finally recovering the power of speech, Arcita asks Theseus who is victor. Theseus assures him that he is and may now claim Emilia, and he encourages the wounded prince to think he will live to enjoy her. Emilia, too, consoles him, calling him "husband." Arcita, propped on a chariot, makes a triumphal procession, ending in the palace of Theseus. The defeated followers of Palemone also come to the palace.

Theseus congratulates them on their valor; Arcita orders that all the captives be freed. Palemone asks Emilia what she would do with him, hoping that she will sentence him to death. But she gives him not only his freedom but many rich gifts, and she hopes he will find among the many beautiful women of Greece someone to take her place. He thanks her but vows he will never love anyone but her. Arcita is then married to Emilia, but the day of their nuptials is postponed until Arcita can recover his health (book 9, 83 stanzas). The warriors bury their dead; Theseus learns that Arcita's wound is indeed fatal. And as the latter gradually loses strength, he bids Emilia to marry Palemone when he has gone. She tearfully replies that she would rather remain a virgin. If Theseus must marry her off, let him give her to one of his enemies since love of her brings ill fortune; Palemone does not deserve such a fate. She then gives him her last kisses, promising she will never kiss another man. Arcita prays to Mercury, asking not to be sent to Hades, but to dwell in the Elysian Fields. He mourns his unhappy lot and dies with his gaze fixed on Emilia (book 10, 133 stanzas).

As the soul of Arcita, now well content to have left this poor mortal life behind, looks down from Heaven, a stately funeral is prepared for his body. Palemone builds a shrine for him and games are held in his honor (book 11, 91 stanzas). The visiting heroes take their leave. Theseus persuades the reluctant Emilia to marry Palemone; their nuptials are celebrated with great splendor and Emilia has never looked more beautiful. She goes to Palemone a virgin; he possesses her seven times on their wedding night. In the last three stanzas Boccaccio takes leave of his book, pointing out that it is the first to sing of Mars "in the vernacular of Latium." He compares its progress to a ship's voyage, guided by the Great Bear of his inspiration [i.e., Fiammetta] (book 12, 83 stanzas).

Two valedictory sonnets are attached to the poem. In the first, the author requests the Muses to present his work to the lady for whom it was composed and to invite her to give it a title. In the second sonnet the Muses reply, reassuring the poet that they have presented his verses to the lady and reporting that she was moved to sigh as she read them in solitude and bade that they be entitled the *Teseida of the Nuptials of Emilia*. The Muses are confident of the fame the poem will achieve in ages to come.

The last stanzas of the poem may serve as a point of departure for comment on the nature of the work, for they are a clear indication of what Boccaccio had in mind. When he says that he is the first to use the vernacular to sing of "trials sustained in warfare," noting that his predecessors have employed it only for "onesto parlare" (moral questions) or "amatory verse," he is clearly alluding to the three sectors of proper poetic cultivation as laid down by Dante in the *De vulgari eloquentia*.[2] Boccaccio's master there enumerates the "capital matters which ought to be treated of supremely" as "safety, love and virtue," to be treated in terms of "things most important with respect to them" such as prowess in arms, the fire of love, and the direction of the will. And for all of these topics Dante cites Provençal poets who have treated each of them, but among Italians, he can cite only Cino da Pistoia on love and "Cino's friend" (by which he means himself) on righteousness. No Italian poet, he avers, has yet written supremely on the theme of arms. In composing the *Teseida,* Boccaccio intends to repair this deficiency. Strictly speaking, he is not meeting precisely the requirement that Dante had in mind, for Dante is here thinking of lyric and not narrative poetry as is clearly indicated by his choice of examples: his Provençal war champion is Bertran de Born, who wrote only short lyrics, *cansos* or *sirventes.* But Boccaccio evidently believes that an epic is called for. The *Teseida* (the title itself is significant, formed on the pattern of *Aeneid, Thebaid, Iliad,* and the like) was meant to be an epic, the first in the vulgar tongue of Italy. And his model is not the battle songs of Bertran but the classical epic, particularly the *Thebaid* of Statius.

Epics, if they are to follow the style of the ancients, must have heroes of godlike dimensions, plenty of action and bloodshed, a persistent motivating element (revenge, the founding of a nation, conquest), and they must be set forth in a high style. It is interesting to note that a year earlier—or possibly in the same year—than Boccaccio, in all likelihood, conceived his notion, Francis Petrarch, too, was planning an epic, but Petrarch did not consider the vernacular a worthy vehicle for such a work. Of the two, one must say that Petrarch was the more successful. Whether the *Africa* be an "authentic" epic or not, it is at least not anything else; the *Teseida,* on the other hand, is a hybrid, no true epic at all but with pretentious epic trappings that strain and distort the simple love romance that it might have been.

As for the *Filocolo* and the *Filostrato*, so too for the *Teseida* the author affirms his work is written to please his beloved. And as he had indicated in the foreword to the tale of Troiolo that up to a certain point the heroine bears some resemblance to his lady, so here he remarks in the dedicatory letter that certain passages between Emilia and one of the rival lovers (he will not say which) may recall to the fair Fiammetta "things said and done by me to you and by you to me."[3] In none of the three confessional prefaces does Boccaccio claim that the tale he is about to tell is original with him; he avows he is merely retelling old stories, refraining, however, from identifying the older writers and thus providing joyous sport for his commentators over the centuries. As to the specific sources of the *Teseida*, they are numerous and varied. The story of Theseus and Hippolyta is from classical legend, the Theban expedition of Theseus and many other incidents are from the *Thebaid* of Statius; there are echoes, too, of Lucan and Virgil. However, the plot of the rival lovers is not classical at all. Muscetta affirms that with regard to this story the treatment is new but the theme goes back to the Byzantine romance of Diogenes Akritas,[4] and Boccaccio's allusion in book 1, stanza 2 to a story not yet mentioned by a Latin author strongly suggests some kind of Byzantine precursor, living on perhaps in oral tradition (the young Boccaccio knew no Greek). But many incidents and descriptive passages betray the author's indebtedness to Old French medieval romances, as well as to the *Roman de Thebes* (itself a reworking of Statius), the *Châtelain de Coucy,* and the like. The *Teseida* likewise contains echoes of current *cantari* and, of course, reminiscences of Dante.[5]

Boccaccio was by taste and temperament ill adapted to the role either of "war poet" or creator of epics. In the great epics, as in war itself, the role of a woman is secondary or irrelevant. Whatever may happen on the plains of Troy, if Mars, in the field of letters, ever confronts Venus he is sure to lose. And, surveying the canon of Boccaccio's works, one cannot fail to note that all of them—even the misogynistic *Corbaccio*—center on women; the ladies are, as he readily confesses in the *Decameron*, his lasting inspiration, and even, one might say, his obsession. Limentani, in the foreword to his edition of the *Teseida*,[6] speaks of the contamination of sources and motifs that is characteristic of Boccaccio's early compositions; insofar as the *Teseida* is concerned, the true "contamination" has its roots in the author's appreciation of the sensual charms of the fair sex and of the irresistible power of sexual love.

To be sure, the architect labors manfully to give his structure the appropriately dignified, which is to say classical, embellishments. Following the style of presentation of the Latin epics in the Middle Ages, in which each book was preceded by a brief summary, Boccaccio introduces the action of his books by a summarizing sonnet. Scrupulously, too, his work is divided into twelve books, even as the *Aeneid* and the *Thebaid*. The champions who come to take part in the climactic tournament are all legendary heroes—there is no anachronistic "contamination" in this sector. And, as in the classical epic, the gods participate, holding councils on Olympus and even intervening in the combat, taking appropriate disguises. There are eloquent speeches, hand-to-hand encounters, funeral games.

Lest the action itself fail to convince us, Boccaccio provides plentiful glosses, explaining mythological references of one sort or another. This editorial enterprise is worthy of some attention; there are cases where the glosses, notably those on the prayers to Mars and Venus in book 7, become extended compositions in themselves. The glosses, in truth, are so lavish and learned as to permit us to see in their collective effect an adumbration of the *Genealogie deorum gentilium*, a first flight, as it were, of Boccaccio the encyclopedist. These footnotes, too, enable the author to make explicit the allegory—another element that the medieval reader found in the classical epic and that, apparently, Boccaccio felt was not sufficiently brought out in his narrative. Let the gloss on the house of Mars serve as an example. Stanzas 30–40 of book 7 describe this dwelling, whither the personified prayer of Arcita found its way. "It is set," the author tells us, "in the Thracian fields, under wintry skies, harried by continuous tempests" (30); it stands "in a barren forest of rugged beeches, gnarled and rough" (31); it is built all of steel with gates of iron; reinforced with adamant; Arcita's prayer sees issuing from the gate "mad Impulses," "blind Sin," "Wrath, Fear, Discord" and the like (33–34). All of which is meticulously glossed by the author. On stanza 30 alone he has this to say:

In this part the author describes the house of Mars, concerning which many things must be considered minutely by whoever wants to set them forth in order. However, since it is very superficially touched on hereafter, we shall go over it with a summary explanation. And so that the exposition may be more readily understood, the author says he intends to show four things here. The first is the kind of place where the house of Mars is situated; the second is how the house of Mars is constructed; the third is who is in the house of Mars; the fourth is with what the house of Mars is adorned. I say, therefore, first of all, that the house of Mars is in Thrace, in cold and cloudy places, full of water, wind and ice, wild and thronged with fruitless trees; and in shady places, unfriendly to the sun and full of confusion.

For an understanding of this, it should be remarked that in every man there are two principal appetites. One of these is called the concupiscible appetite, whereby man desires and rejoices to have the things which, according to his judgment—whether it be rational or corrupt—are delightful and pleasing. The other is called the irascible appetite, whereby a man is troubled if delightful things are taken away or impeded, or when they cannot be had. This irascible appetite is found very readily in men of much blood, because blood of its nature is hot, and hot things readily burst into flame on any small provocation. So it happens that men of much blood become angry easily although some, by very strong effort of reason, restrain and conceal their anger.

Since men in cold regions have more blood than elsewhere, the author here puts the temple of Mars, that is to say this irascible appetite, in Thrace, which is a province lying under the north wind and very cold, where men, having much blood, are more fierce, bellicose, and wrathful. Cloudy, he says, is in order to show that anger dims the counsel of reason, which he signifies later on by the ray of the sun, stating that the house of Mars turns it away. By the ice he means the coldness of spirit of a man in wrath, who, overcome by this fire of anger, becomes cruel and harsh and without charity. He says, likewise, that the house of Mars is in a forest, which signifies the covert schemes of mischief that angry men often hatch. And by the barrenness of the forest he indicates the effects of wrath which not only rob men of the fruits of their labors, but ruin them as well. And so in such a forest there is neither shepherd nor beast because the man of wrath cannot rule either himself nor others. So the dwelling of Mars is in such a place as has been briefly shown.[7]

This is but the beginning of the gloss; it may suffice to indicate the nature of the scaffolding of erudition that the author felt necessary to support his edifice.

The Italian critic, Crescini, attributed the first two books to Boccaccio's own creation and found the rest derivative of earlier medieval chivalresque material.[8] Perhaps, for the sake of Boccaccio's avowed purpose, it is regrettable that he did not stick to the theme of Theseus and the subjection of the Amazons, a topic susceptible of expansion into any number of books. For Theseus has a true claim to epic stature; he is warlike, heroic, wreathed in an aura of legendary majesty, and he does not languish over Hippolyta. He defeats her on the field of battle, marries her by force, and makes her a docile wife. And it is the attraction for war and the cause of justice, not love or lust, that moves him to intervene in Thebes, justifying his démarche with the words of Dante's Ulysses, inciting his crew to venture into the unknown for the sake of knowledge and virtue (this is not the only reference to Dante in the *Teseida*, but it is the most effective and, in its place, appropriate). But Theseus is the central figure only in the first two books, and little does he suspect that the shy Emilia, whom he brings back from his campaign against the Amazons, will soon displace him in the direction of the action. To be sure, he reappears at frequent intervals and has a kind of presidential role, but he is no longer a principal of the story.

As touching the last six books, we may recall our remarks on the sources of their theme. Such motifs as love, rivalry, exile for love, assumed names, and the like are, as Limentani remarks, common enough in medieval romances, although the formula as it appears in the *Teseida* may fairly claim to be novel. It is possible that the author thought of the central theme, the war between kinsmen, as a kind of updated version of the mortal combat between Eteocles and Polyneices; the Theban connection would justify such a hypothesis.[9] But in any case, beginning with book 3 we are no longer in a world that is even pseudoclassical. The double title given the work is indicative of its hybrid nature; the *Teseida of the Nuptials of Emilia.* The *Teseida* is soon behind us and we move into a world of medieval romance where women are not only passing fair but transcendentally important; where love conquers all, including the sacred bonds of kinship and friendship.

Sporadically at least, there are indications of the author's intent to give his love story a moralizing message. The glosses on the temples of Mars and Venus, analyzed at some length by Hollander,[10] disclose a didactic purpose clothed, as was the medieval way, in allegory. Perhaps under the influence of these glosses, Bernadette Marie McCoy, the translator of the work, sees the epic "becoming a kind of morality play," adding that "fundamentally philosophical and Boethean, the *Teseida* illustrates the trend toward didactic seriousness during the transition from Boccaccio's Neapolitan to his Florentine period." For her, "clearly the movement of the poet's thought is away from the glamor of aulic romance to the somber mysteries of a man's war within himself."[11] This is well said, particularly if we bear in mind the glosses on the temples. And it is true that the nature of the allegory, as well perhaps as the name of the heroine, as we shall see, are tokens of a topographical-conceptual shift from Neapolitan romance to Tuscan intellectualism.

But the case for hidden meanings and psychological probings in the "epic" can be overstated. A very substantial number of the stanzas are charged with "aulic glamor" and man's war within himself takes second place to the scenes of combat on the battlefield. Without denying allegorical and moralizing suggestions, one may define the *Teseida*, like its predecessors, as basically a tale of lovers, as its fruits make clear. Most critics find the work chiefly interesting as the original begetter of a genre destined to spring into full flower in the Renaissance, exemplified by Boiardo and Ariosto, wherein the skeins of love and war, knightly deeds and the enchantments of fair ladies are woven together in polished octaves.[12]

If the narrative of the *Teseida* does not hold the reader's interest as

compellingly as the *Innamorato* or the *Furioso* (Wilkins did not hesitate
to call it "tedious"[13] and De Sanctis found the style "wordy, weak and
ordinary"[14]), it is only in part because it is long drawn out, and slow
paced (a total of over 9,000 lines of which far too many are given to
meticulous description or rhetorical expansion); a more serious flaw is
the pallid characterization of the major figures of the tale. They lack
the humanizing complexities of Troiolo and Criseida; they are somehow even less memorable than Florio and Biancifiore, of whom they
are kin. We can almost sympathize with Emilia, who can find nothing
to choose between her two admirers until the tournament is nearly
over. Looking closely to be sure, we can see that Arcita is consistently
nobler; he is reluctant to fight his friend for he feels some loyalty to
the claims of friendship and his is the ultimate magnanimity when he
bestows Emilia on his rival ere he takes leave of this world. Palemone
is of coarser fiber; it is his passion for Emilia that brings on the duel.
His prayer to Venus is not for victory, but for possession of Emilia
under any conditions. If there is any lesson in his ultimate triumph,
it is a sad one. It would seem to be a justification of sexual passion over
all other sentiments and indeed all other virtues. But the differences
between the two kinsmen are not sharply brought out and in fact their
shared obsession overrides their differences, lending them similar profiles of rather uninteresting simplicity. Both young heroes are in fact
essentially passive, manipulated in the grand strategy of the plot by
their dominant, erotic infatuation and in its tactical details by the
actions of the supporting cast: Peritoo liberates Arcita; Panfilo plans
Palemone's escape; Theseus arranges their combat; and Mars, Venus,
and Fortune make the ultimate decisions.

Even more acceptant and colorless, to be sure, is Emilia, the focus
of the rivals' desires. There is assuredly no epic quotient in this docile
creature, nor even the stuff of a heroine of the medieval love story.
She is no Iseult; she is a recognizable cousin perhaps of Biancifiore,
but unlike Filocolo's faithful princess, she feels no stirring of recip-
rocating passion in her own heart. The first mention of her describes
her as "picciolina" and we are reminded that she is not yet fifteen
when she is married. Perhaps in naturalistic terms it is hardly surprising that she is not ready for love. (Biancifiore was, but she had the

advantage of meeting Filocolo while yet in the cradle.) Emilia has no preference between her ardent suitors; before the great tourna-ment, her prayer to Diana indicates that she would choose to remain a maiden if she might, and after Arcita's death she is reluctant to espouse Palemone. One may suspect that the seven penetrations of Palemone on his bridal night, indicative more of machismo than rapturous love, brought less pleasure than pain to his child-bride; we are told that he arose the following morning fresh as a rose, but we hear nothing of Emilia's state of mind.

Emilia is meant rather to be contemplated than enjoyed. And not contemplated, as the ladies of the *dolce stil nuovo* were, with resultant idealistic inspiration in the heart of the beholder, for the desire the Amazon princess arouses is not sublimated into any mystical impulse; it remains simply sensual. Perhaps Emilia's finest hour is when she first appears before the enraptured gaze of the imprisoned young noblemen, walking barefoot and clad only in her shift, weaving garlands for herself and singing love ballads. She is not unaware of the eyes that follow her, "artless" though she be. One may even say that she exhibits a certain girlish coquetry, dressing herself with increasing care as she repeats her appearances, singing in her pleasing and clear voice when-ever she thinks she could be overheard. But Boccaccio is careful to assure us that she is not moved by love but merely by that vanity that dwells in every woman's heart (3.30). Nature and not her own will dictates her movements. The picture of Emilia in the garden is cer-tainly one of the most charming Boccaccian moments in the course of the story, at once sensual and delicate, seductive and innocent.

Indeed, Emilia's role is essentially pictorial and, we may add, no heroine of Boccaccio was better equipped to sit for an attractive portrait. As she goes to Palemone's bed, we are given an exhaustive catalog of her charms, covering eleven lingering stanzas (12.53–63). She is tall, we are told, and stands "properly erect"; her hair is long and golden. Her brow is wide and smooth. Her eyebrows are black and her eyes brown (the brown-eyed, golden-haired combination will be the ideal of the Renaissance; inherited by Angelica, it will drive Orlando to madness). Her nose is finely chiseled; her cheeks "roses and lilies." She has a small mouth and chin, the latter dimpled; her neck is full and long, set on sloping shoulders, her bosom "somewhat raised," with firm, round breasts. Her arms are well rounded, her hands long, her fingers slender. She is wide ("grossa") in the hips; her feet are tiny. Her costume is of such nature as to make an inventory of her charms between hip and foot regrettably impossible, but Boccaccio suspects that had they been visible his powers would not have been adequate to describe them. All these treasures are hers ere she has reached the age of fifteen; the author, however, thinks it likely that she had grown more than girls usually do in that short period of time. To be sure, all of these attributes are more or less conventional, but in the gallery of Boccaccio's charmers there is none more scrupulously depicted. We all but step out of Letters into Art as we look upon her; Botticelli could scarcely do more for us.

Her name calls for comment; it has received much attention from modern critics. Palemone's bride is the first Emilia to appear in any work of Boccaccio, nor is the name found in any of the numerous sources of the epic. It is certainly not a Greek name, as might properly be borne by the sister of Hippolyta. Nor is it a Neapolitan name, nor a name out of medieval romance; it is originally of Roman stamp and was in Boccaccio's time current in Tuscany. Wherever "Emilia" came from, it may be said of her creator that, as the song has it, once he had found her he never let her go; the name reappears in the *Comedy of the Florentine Nymphs*, the *Amorous Vision*, and the *Decameron*. Since the Emilia of the *Comedy* seems to stand for the Florentine Emiliana de' Tornaquinci, some scholars have postulated a *tendre* for the lady on Boccaccio's part, deducing that it is she who is remembered in the various works.[15] Branca is cool to that suggestion, regarding an Emilia of flesh and blood as no more credible than a living Fiammetta;[16] he does concede that it is a Tuscan name. As far as the Emilia of the *Teseida* is concerned the conjecture of Billanovich[17] that would see in it a Latinized version of the Greek αἰμυλία, signifying "mildness," would not be inappropriate. It may well be that this northern name is a token of the author's move from Naples to Florence and a proclamation of his allegiance to a Tuscan tradition. The somewhat heavier tone and the nature of the allegorical passages would be like signals of the conversion from simple romantic fantasy to something more intellectual, from aristocratic diversion to a kind of bourgeois sobriety and more serious "scholarship," verging, as we have remarked, on the encyclopedic in the *Teseida*. But perhaps one can make too much of this argument, plausible though it be. It is undeniable that allegory of a Dantean stamp intrudes into the epic (and will dominate the *Comedy of the Florentine Nymphs* and the *Amorous Vision*). Yet *Diana's Hunt* was an allegory, too (albeit less pretentious), and if the learned element with its stock of classical mythology and its pedantic glosses is prominent in the epic, it should not be forgotten that there was already a good deal of classical lore in the *Filocolo*. It is not so much an abandonment of the old recipe as an alteration of the proportion of the ingredients, which is not to deny the significance of the alteration.

But to return to the portrait of Emilia; it may yield a clue to the proper—or at least more sympathetic—appreciation of the poem. For if the *Teseida* lacks both the high gravity of the epic and the pace of a good narrative (even the *Filocolo* is a better story), it yet possesses an engaging pictorial aspect. The ottava lends itself admirably to a depiction of set pieces, as Poliziano's *Stanzas* will demonstrate. It should not surprise us that Boccaccio's set pieces are all of a traditional sort nor should it inhibit our admiration of them. The already trite background of the "sweet season" is effectively sketched in stanza 3 of book 2:

> In the sweet season when the sky makes fair with grass and flowers, the valleys and the hills, clothing anew the plants and trees with fresh and verdant branches where birds rest and sing their lays of love and maidens blithe and gay most keenly feel the flames of Venus burn. It was then that Theseus, in the thrall of love, stood in a garden thinking of his dear.

The parade of heroes eager to take part in the great joust passes in a succession of illuminated vignettes; particularly graphic among them is the figure of the young prince, Nestor, in silverplated steel and golden armor, mounted on a great black horse and carrying a mace. If Emilia evokes Botticelli, the procession of young warriors, brilliantly clad and glowing with martial vigor, will send our fancy on to Benozzo Gozzoli. The theme of the *Teseida* is medieval; its image transports us to the Renaissance.

We may fairly assume that Boccaccio gave some thought to the choice of metrical medium for his venture into the lofty ranges of the epic. For a singer of his times and traditions, the alternatives were two: triple rhyme or ottava rima. The assonantal laisses of the medieval *chansons de geste* had become archaic before Italian literature was born, nor has assonance of itself ever held much appeal for the Italian ear. One may say much the same for the octosyllabic couplet, employed so dextrously by Chrétien de Troyes and Marie de France, although in this case Boccaccio might have found a worthy Italian predecessor in Brunetto Latini's *Tesoretto*. Blank verse, which would seem an obvious choice of a poet of today, would never even have occurred to a fourteenth-century writer, to whom rhyme was an essential requirement for any kind of engagement with the Muses. Dante, in his *De vulgari eloquentia*, wherein, as noted, Boccaccio had found his challenge, had decreed that the hendecasyllable was the measure best suited for expositions of matters of dignity and importance. But only Dante had dared to use terza rima for long and sustained narrative. Boccaccio had employed it—and if somewhat crudely, by no means ineffectively—in following *Diana's Hunt*; subsequently, save for his Dantean allegories, he wisely abandoned it. The octave was the medium for the popular *cantari* or ballads of adventure and romance current in Italy; it had an easy-going discipline, permitting a certain rambling looseness of style, yet, as Boccaccio sensed, it was also potentially adaptable to elegant expression in the hands of a skilled craftsman. If we accept the general opinion among scholars that the *Filostrato* preceded the *Teseida* by some years, our poet had already had his apprenticeship in the composition and manipulation of these compliant stanzas. His return to them for his epic had far-reaching results, establishing, as it did, the appropriateness of the pattern for substance far above the "popular" matter of its origins.

In the *Teseida* there is considerable variation in the grace and fluidity of the octaves and in the author's ability to link them. Granting that the polished deftness and grace they are to display in the hands of Ariosto and Tasso are rare in the pages of the *Teseida*, they are yet so competently and pleasingly deployed as to encourage imitation and to become, via Boiardo, the effective tools of the aforementioned cinquecento masters. The octave, first certified, as it were, by Boccaccio, has served the Muses well down to our own day, and has shown itself adaptable to alien dress, as, among other examples, our own *Don Juan* will suavely testify.

Not only for its manner but also for its matter, the *Teseida* was a seminal and influential work. If the reader of today finds it inflated, discursive, and not very persuasive, we must yet concede that the tale suited very well the tastes of its own times. Chaucer found it sufficiently appealing to imitate it in his Knight's Tale, and it holds its charm down to the age of Dryden.[18] Lord Theseus comes back in *Midsummer Night's Dream* to assume again the presidential role so well played in the *Teseida*. Although the players change from classical to Carolingian costumes, more of the Boccaccian formula than the octave alone is perceptible in the chivalrous romances of the Renaissance, which in turn leave their mark on Spenser. In surveying the progeny of this ambitious creation, it is but proper to remember, too, that it may fairly be called an original work. Various ingredients, as we have noted, may be traced to one source or another, but the mixture is Boccaccio's own invention.

CHAPTER 7

THE COMEDY OF THE
FLORENTINE NYMPHS

hatever the critic's verdict may be with regard to the aesthetic merits of Boccaccio's early works, they supply collectively ample evidence of the vigor and versatility of his creative genius. Hardly had he finished his erudite and substantial epic before he turned his hand to yet another ambitious confection, the *Comedy of the Florentine Nymphs*, sometimes called the *Nymph Song of Ameto* or simply the *Ameto*. Scholars concur in assigning the composition of the work to the years 1341–1342;[1] it is therefore the first of Boccaccio's works conceived and brought to birth in Tuscany. The author was still a young man—not yet thirty—and, as a Tuscan resident, still recently naturalized (or renaturalized); he had been scarcely a year back in his native region. As we noted in chapter 2 and as the autobiographical allusions at the end of the work reveal, these were years of difficult adjustment. Just how, or indeed if, Boccaccio was employed during that period we do not know; what is clear is that he was unhappy with the pattern of his life and seeking for some sense of direction. Perhaps the same may be said of his Muse, ever ready to embark on new adventures and ever eager to take advantage of new winds of inspiration. In the *Comedy of the Florentine Nymphs* they bear the author and his reader, if his patience suffices, on a voyage of daring conceptual exploration. An outline of the narrative will provide a helpful chart.

Others may sing of great things, the author begins modestly, but he is content merely to sing of Love. To be sure, Love is a great Lord, inspiring gods and men alike. Boccaccio proposes to sing of him in a voice proper to his own humble station, not as a poet but simply as a lover, writing for lovers (1; prose). He begins with an invocation to Cytherea, Cupid, and his own gentle lady, "an angelic figure" (2; verse: 91 lines).

He then opens his narrative telling how Ameto[2] the wanderer (*vagabondo*) used to pass his time in the woods under Fiesole, where the Mugnone meets the Arno. One day, resting after the hunt, he hears a lovely song in the distance. Following the music he finds a number of youthful huntresses refreshing themselves in the stream. Their dogs attack him but the nymphs invite him to tarry. He readily obeys and one of them, called Lia,[3] sings a song (3; prose) in which she reveals that she was born of the union of Cesifo, a river-god, and a nymph; she states that she is beautiful and fond of the chase; those who follow her, she promises, will be rewarded (4; verse: 67 lines). Ameto, ravished by the beauty of the nymphs, wonders whether he is worthy of their company. He bathes in the stream and spends all day with the nymphs (5; prose). Thenceforth, he hunts daily with them, helping to catch their game (6; prose). Winter comes and Ameto is left alone. He prepares his hunting and fishing equipment; with the return of spring Lia reappears and Ameto hunts regularly with her. One day he fails to find her. He sits down to wait for her (7; prose), and as he waits he sings a song in which he speaks of her beauty, begs her to rejoin him, and enumerates the simple gifts he has for her (8; verse: 109 lines).

Lia does not return and Ameto goes home disconsolate. However, with the sun entering Taurus, the great annual festival in honor of Venus comes around [perhaps May Day is meant; Taurus reigns from April 21 to May 21]. Lia and Ameto attend the ceremonies in her temple, after which the youth follows the nymph to a grove where they are joined by two other nymphs, one wearing purple,[4] the other wearing red (*porporino*). Their charms are warmly described by the author (9; prose). The sound of a shepherd's pipe is heard; when the shepherd, Teogapen (Love of God), appears, the nymphs ask him to sing for them (10; prose). His song praises the powers of Love; it is a civilizing influence, and if we follow it it can lead us to Heaven,

ridding us of our vices (11; verse: 79 lines). At the end of Teogapen's
song, Lia welcomes another pair of nymphs whose pulchritude is
rapturously described. One is dressed in scarlet (*sanguigno*) and the
other in green (12; prose). For the group, two shepherds, Alcesto[5] and
Acaten, arrange a musical debate; Teogapen will accompany them on
his pipe (13; prose).

In alternating stanzas each singer pleads his case. Alcesto affirms that
he pastures his flock on the hills; Acaten defends the plain. Alcesto
admits his sheep must climb higher, but they drink purer water. Acaten
claims his flock is more numerous (14; verse: 127 lines, of which
Alcesto, who opens and closes the debate, has 73). The nymphs award
the prize to Alcesto. Two more nymphs join the group; one in white,
the other in pink (*rosato*). Their physical assets are glowingly cataloged.
Ameto is moved to song (15; prose); he proclaims his devotion to love
and to the nymphs and prays that they may be forever united (16; verse:
82 lines).

Lia proposes a plan for beguiling the hot hours of the day;[6] she
suggests that each nymph tell the story of her love and follow her
account with a hymn to her favorite deity. All agree and laughingly
put Ameto in the middle of the circle with the office of calling on each
speaker. He begins with the one on his right, dressed in *rosato*, called
Mopsa (17; prose).

In Athens, Mopsa relates, Mars once begot a daughter on a nymph;
from her descended Mopsa's father, named after the family's service "in
place of the eagle" (i.e., as vicars of the emperor). She is first put to
the service of Pallas (i.e., wisdom, which is to say studies or learning),
and then married to a man who follows Vertunno (the god of the
fields) whose name is Nerone. Such clues enable us to identify Mopsa
with Lottiera di Odoalda dei Visdomini della Tosa, married to Nerone
Nigi di Dietisalvi; she is mentioned also in the *Amorosa visione*[7] (43.
79–84). In the allegory she signifies prudence. Mopsa tells us that she
was not happy with her husband. One day as she walked on the shore
she saw a young man drifting in a boat; she was greatly attracted to
him. She bade him come to her; he at first refused but when she
displayed her legs and her breasts, he came to shore. He reciprocated
her love and put aside his former boorishness, becoming courteous and

articulate (he is called Affron—i.e., witless). Mopsa will ever be grateful to Venus (18; prose), but her hymn is addressed to Pallas (19; verse:
40 lines). Ameto is enchanted by Mopsa's story and he envies Affron.
He calls on the next nymph, Emilia, dressed in scarlet (*sanguigno*) (20;
prose).

Emilia states her father was born on the shores of Alfeo (i.e., Arno
in Boccaccio's mythology); he was originally poor but became rich and
acquired noble customs. Her mother was from Corito (Fiesole). After
the death of her father, when she was a mere babe, Emilia entered the
service of Diana (i.e., the convent), then, at her mother's bidding, she
married a young man "of an appealing name." [Various clues make
it possible to identify Emilia with Emiliana de' Tornaquinci, married
to Giovanni di Nello. In the allegory she stands for Justice.]8 She was
not happy in her marriage, remaining at heart still faithful to Diana.

She had a vision one day of Venus, who entered her heart. Some
time later, as she was hunting in a grove, she had another vision; this
time of Minerva and a companion in the skies above, attempting to
force their entrance into Heaven. She could hear their song (21; prose)
in which, singing together, they proclaimed their power to do more
than the Titans and the Giants of old and to displace the gods. (Clearly
it is the voice of Pride [22; verse: 46 lines]). When Emilia, looking
down, saw Venus bending over a wounded youth, the goddess told her
that the youth had abandoned her to follow Pride. Emilia tended the
youth and revived him. He apologized to Venus and the goddess,
forgiving him, bade him henceforth to follow Emilia. At Emilia's
request the youth, whose name is Ibrida (Hybrid), then told her the
story of his life. He is a descendant of the Trojans who founded Paris;
his mother was of good family, married to a knight. On his death, she
had been seduced by a plebeian man of no standing who came from
Certaldo; he (Ibrida) was born of their union.9 His father, abandoning
his mother, then married a woman of his own country, leaving Ibrida's
mother to die. The gods brought death and reverses to the second
family of the faithless father; meanwhile, Ibrida, dedicating himself to
Venus, became an accomplished poet. It was his pride in this achievement that had brought him down. He concludes his story, thanking
Emilia for saving him. In return, she asks only his allegiance in the

service of love (23; prose). Emilia then sings a hymn to Diana-Astrea, celebrating Justice (24; verse: 42 lines). Ameto is moved by the story; he wishes he could be like Ibrida. He then calls on the third nymph, dressed in purple (25; prose).

This is Adiona. She relates that she was born in Cyprus; her father was a nobleman who turned to commerce; she was given in marriage to one Pacifico. [The usual clues indicate that Adiona may be identified as Alionora or Dianora di Niccolò de' Gianfigliazzi, who was married to Pacino Peruzzi, Prior of Florence, 1336–1337. She will reappear in the *Amorosa visione;* "Adiona," in Boccaccio's Greek, signifies the opposite of "dissolute" Dioneo; she stands here for Temperance.] She became, she says, a worshiper of Pomena (goddess of fruits) and describes in detail the marvelous garden that the goddess showed her. Pomena instructed her votary in horticulture and told her of her own birth in the Golden Age and the conditions of that happy time. One day it happened that Adiona met Venus in the garden; the goddess bade her to fall in love and gave her an enchanted kiss. Soon afterward she met Dioneo; a handsome youth, but gluttonous, indolent, and indifferent to her charms. He is the son of Bacchus and Ceres; he regrets that he, too, is not immortal. Adiona promises him immortality and he then follows her; she teaches him the arts of agriculture and they become very happy together (26; prose). She then sings a hymn to Pomena in praise of moderation (27; verse: 40 lines).

Ameto has been listening with most of his attention fixed on the physical charms of the nymphs. At the conclusion of Adiona's song he recovers himself and bids the nymph in white to tell her story (28; prose). She states that her father was from Sicily. On his return from Florence to his home he had found a girl in the Gargano whose parents had taken refuge there [possibly being Ghibelline exiles; this nymph, Acrimonia, probably stands for the real, if not clearly identified, *bella lombarda*,[10] also mentioned in the *Amorosa visione*; allegorically: Fortitude]. She describes herself as the fairest of nine sisters. She had prayed to Bellona (goddess of war) to help her father; her prayers had been granted, so she became a follower of that goddess. At the age of sixteen she was married to someone unworthy of her, a Sicilian who took her from his native island—following a route described in detail—to

Rome. There she had many wooers but resisted them all, though her friends urged her to be indulgent. On her return to Sicily, she again aroused universal admiration among the males and envy among the women. However, a young man named Apaten (i.e., apathy), a relation of Mopsa,[11] pursued her ardently and asked Venus to help him. The goddess responded; she temporarily blinded Acrimonia and told her she must love Apaten, since for her sake he had put aside his boorish ways. Acrimonia could but yield. She has now learned to love Apaten and continues her inspirational work of improving his character and making him worthy of her beauty (29; prose). She then sings a hymn in honor of Bellona (30; verse: 43 lines).

Listening to her story, Ameto again waxes ecstatic, grateful for the privilege of looking upon such lovely creatures; even Paris, he recalls, had only three such objects of contemplation. Ameto's only regret is that his nymphs are clothed; even so, he finds it hard to keep his mind from bold thoughts. He begs Apollo to lengthen the daylight hours and afford him more time for gazing on these lovely beings. He then calls on the nymph clad in *vermiglio* (crimson) to tell her story (31; prose).

She is Agapes; in veiled circumlocution, she states that her ancestors, sprung from Achaia, were originally masons and later became usurers. Her father married a girl of the wealthy Strozzi clan. [Scholars have not been able to identify the living woman under the mask of Agapes, clearly standing for Charity in the allegory]. In due course she herself was married to an old man; she describes with loathing his appearance and his disgusting and ineffectual comportment in the marriage bed. In despair, she came to Venus' temple and besought the goddess to find her an acceptable young lover. Even before her prayer was concluded, it seemed to her (in truth or in a dream, she could not say) that she was borne aloft in a gleaming chariot, drawn by white doves, and set down upon the summit of the Cytherean mountain. Here the goddess, in all her beauty, appeared; Agapes repeated her prayer and Venus assured her it would be granted. The goddess then led her to Cupid, who was tempering his arrows in a stream. Venus, bidding her son depart, invited Agapes to bathe with her in the clear water. Here the goddess embraced the girl and told her that Cupid had been dispatched to bring to her the lover she had prayed for. Presently a pale and timid youth appeared on the bank of the stream; Agapes, dressing hastily, came forth to meet him. Venus presented him as Apyros (i.e., "without fire"; cold), saying he lacked but the fire of love to be perfect and charges Agapes to inflame him. At this point, Agapes says, the vision faded and she found herself back in the temple; standing near her was the pale youth of her dream. She gave him an encouraging glance; he responded, and now by virtue of their repeated embraces he has lost his pallor and has taken on a color deeper than cochineal. Agapes affirms she will ever be faithful to Venus (32; prose). She sings a hymn to the goddess, from whose mountain, she says, two flames come forth, one ascending straight to heaven and the other bending down to earth where it inspires men to seek higher things, freeing us all from fear of death (33; verse: 43 lines).

Ameto meditates on the iniquity of Fortune in giving such a delicious young girl to an old husband. He wishes he had been her spouse; assuredly, he would have known how to make her happy. How sad it is, he reflects, when the time of youth is blighted by poverty. He mentally puts himself in the place of Apyros and imagines the delights of the nymph's hidden charms. He then turns to the green-clad nymph and asks to hear her story (34; prose).

The sixth nymph begins her rather lengthy narrative with a description of the foundation of Naples, of which she is a native. Her mother was of French origin, a noblewoman in the court of King Robert; as to her father, the nymph cannot be sure. It may have been the king himself. Her mother's lawful husband was a gentleman of the House of Aquino, but during a festival at the court, she had caught the fancy of the king, who had subsequently seduced her, but, since she had on the same day enjoyed the attentions of her husband, the green-clad damsel is not certain which of the two was her father. [This, of course, is Fiammetta; allegorically Hope.] She goes on to say that both her mother and her putative father died when she was young. She had been sent to a convent and might have taken the vows, but a rich young man, favored by the king's intervention, made her his bride; since she did not love him, she told herself that she remained true to Vesta, even in marriage. However, one night, while her husband was absent and

she lay alone in her bed, she awoke from an uneasy sleep to find herself
in the arms of an impassioned young man whose voice she seemed to
recognize. She pushed him aside, brought candles to the bedside and
found his face, too, was familiar. Then she told him that women are
not to be taken by force, but she would listen to his defense and then
decide on what to do.

She then gives us, at second hand, the young man's story, thus
offering as it were to the marveling reader a tale within a tale within
a tale. He told her, she reports, that he was born in France, even as
her mother, and that in early adolescence he had come to Naples from
Etruria. On entering the city, he had had a vision of a beautiful girl,
dressed in green, who kissed him and welcomed him to the city where
he would find happiness. Subsequently, he had become enamored of
a nymph called Pampinea, leaving her later for the fairer Abrotonia,
who in her turn had deserted him. He had then abjured the service of
love. But in a vision, both girls had appeared to mock him; they told
him he was destined to love again and in a successive vision they
returned to show him the image of the one destined to rule his heart.
She was dressed in green and the narrator recognized in her the girl
who had greeted him at the city gate six years earlier. On awakening,
he determined to seek out this rare creature, but sixteen months passed
before he encountered her; it was in the Church of San Lorenzo on
Holy Saturday. She was dressed in somber clothing so that he was not
quite sure of her identification, but returning the next day to the
temple, he found her wearing green and had no further doubts. Since
then, he said, he has followed her everywhere, serving her faithfully
and he vowed eternal devotion, suggesting that she cannot have been
unaware of his pursuit. He concluded his story by drawing a knife and
threatening to kill himself unless his love is reciprocated. While the
young woman yet hesitated, she says, Venus appeared and bade her to
yield. Whereupon the twain exchanged vows of fidelity and ever since,
says the nymph, disclosing that her lover, Caleone, likes to call her
Fiammetta, she has been a faithful votary of Venus (35). She then sings
a song in praise of Ariadne's crown and its inspiration for great classical
figures such as Fabricius and Scipio. If mortals but kept their minds
fixed on that crown, they would never fall prey to despair. Fiammetta

proclaims her confidence in winning it and so rising to eternal glory (36; verse: 58 lines).

Ameto has listened with his usual attention, recalling to his memory all the beauties of Naples; he envies Caleone and admires his gesture, as wise as it was bold. He then turns to Lia, dressed in gold, finding her more beautiful than ever and guiltily regretting that he has been sometimes distracted by the charms of the other nymphs. He calls on her to tell her story (37; prose). Lia's contribution, the longest of all, begins with a summary of the history of Florence by the Theban prince, Achimenide, to the present. [Her phraseology, incidentally, reveals that the scene of Ameto's adventures is near Florence.] She concludes by disclosing that she is of the Regaletti family of that city;[12] she has been twice married, her first husband having died. She had always been devoted to Cybele, the mother of the gods, she states, but suddenly, she knew not why, she felt herself consumed by the fires of Venus. She avows her love for Ameto, whom she describes as born of a mother of the noble house of the Nerli,[13] although his father was a plebeian. Illuminated by her (Lia), he has overcome his mental blindness and is now prepared to follow precious things for which she, too, is grateful to Venus (38; prose). She then sings the longest hymn of all, in which she proclaims what she has learned from Cybele [here standing either for Theology or, more specifically, the Church]. Cybele has, in fact, taught her the Christian doctrine, of which the main tenets (the Trinity, the Incarnation, the Redemption, and so on) are explicitly set forth. She looks forward to immortality with her adored Cybele (39; verse: 94 lines). [Lia's song is patently derived from Dante's words in *Paradiso* 24.[14]]

The nymphs now prepare to depart, but they pause to look at a combat in the sky between seven pure white swans and seven storks. The swans triumph and, forthwith, a column of fire descends from Heaven, leaving a train of many colors like a rainbow, from which a sweet voice is presently heard raised in song (40; prose). The voice is that of the Triune God, promising eternal happiness to those who will heed it and bidding the band of nymphs not to be alarmed by its manifestation here (41; verse: 19 lines). Ameto then realizes that the light is not the Venus whom fools call a goddess, but the saintly Venus from whom just and sacred love descends to mortals. He sees the nymphs looking into the light and waxing in beauty—especially Agapes and Lia—as they gaze. He, too, looks into the flame and seems to see, as one might see a glowing coal amidst surrounding fire, the outline of a body that throws forth countless sparks. But his eyes cannot take in the Divine Visage (42; prose), wherefore the Light of Venus, speaking again, in words that echo St. Bernard's prayer for Dante in canto 33 of the *Paradiso*, bids the nymphs to clear Ameto's sight so that he may see its beauties and thus be able to tell others of them (43; verse: 16 lines).

Thus bidden, the nymphs rush upon Ameto as he stands in dazed contemplation of the Light that is the Heavenly Venus. Lia strips off his garments and bathes him in the stream; she then turns him over to Fiammetta, who leads him back to his previous position, confronting Venus. Mopsa dries his eyes, clearing away their previous cloudiness; Emilia directs his vision to Venus; Acrimonia further strengthens his sight; Adonia clothes him with new garments and Agapes, breathing upon him, inspires him with new ardor. He then looks on the holy face with such wonder as Jason's comrades gazed upon their leader when he became a plowman. He begs the Muses to give him strength to tell of the divine beauties he is now contemplating. As he gazes, he sees our human effigy, ever changing in form but always beautiful. He prays then directly to the Triune deity, asking that he may preserve until death his devotion to the nymphs who have led him to this vision. He receives the answer: "Put your hope in us and do well and your desires will draw near." The "goddess" then returns to heaven with her light and the nymphs surround Ameto and break into song (44; prose).[15] In their song they congratulate Ameto on his privileged experience and they reveal that they are truly goddesses, whose mission is to illuminate the world. If Ameto will but remain loyal to them, they will watch over him and bring him at last to Paradise (45; verse: 49 lines).

His vision strengthened and his understanding deepened, Ameto perceives the true nature of the nymphs, at first more pleasing to the eye than the intellect, but now more delightful to the latter. He now understands, too, the real meaning of their stories and what their various lovers signified; he is ashamed of the lustful thoughts he had earlier entertained as he looked upon their charms. He is grateful for the final vision (46; prose). He then sings his song of gratitude to the divine Light, one essence in three persons that rules the world, and to the nymphs, whom he mentions by name. He prays that his words, which may lead others to a true appreciation of the nymphs, may be preserved and that the pages on which they are written may be put to no mean use (47; verse: 70 lines).

As night comes on, birds give way to bats and cicadas to crickets and the party breaks up; Ameto returns to his home (48; prose). The author now speaks; he has been a witness of the events of this memorable day; he envies Ameto's good fortune. As for himself, he must return to a dark and gloomy house where the harsh and horrible sight of a "cold, crude and stingy old man" constantly oppresses him. He is prepared for death, which indeed he invokes night and day (49; verse: 100 lines). He dedicates his book to his Maecenas, Niccolò de Bartolo del Buono of Florence.[16] Whatever faults the work may have, he says, are the result not of malice, but of ignorance; let it be examined and corrected by the Church of Rome or wise men or Niccolò himself (50; prose).

We have remarked that the *Comedy of the Florentine Nymphs* reveals, as did the *Teseida*, the ambitious groping of a young author still seeking his proper direction, or to put it another way, the restlessness of a fertile Muse in quest of ever more challenging forms of expression. Looking at the elaborate design with an eye to its technique, the reader must be impressed by the meticulous care with which the versatile young artist applies his colors to create a novel effect even though the result is not quite as admirable as the ingenuity displayed. A *richesse* of narrative is interwoven with no less luxuriant allegory; unhappily, these vigorous elements may be said rather to confront than to complement each other.

Allegory, it is clear, is the principal quarry of the author. In this sense, we may see much more patently than in the case of the *Teseida* the passage from Neapolitan romance to Tuscan theological symbolism. The shadow of Dante, visible to be sure in some degree in everything Boccaccio wrote, at least of creative nature, here follows us at every step and infiltrates the very fiber of the work. The title is evidently a declaration of intent; the work is to be a *Comedy* like Dante's own and in Dante's understanding of the word; that is to say, proceeding from an unhappy or at least ambiguous beginning to a happy and triumphant conclusion. It has a central "pilgrim," too—the author's alter ego—although it must be granted he is rather static in contrast to Dante's ambulant wayfarer. The mixture of prose and verse imitates, deliberately we may believe, the pattern of the *Vita nuova*,[17] nor is the dramatic appearance of Lia basically unlike the entrance of Beatrice into Dante's life. The theological symbolism is straight from the *Paradiso* and the climactic vision is a recasting of the last cantos of the *Divine Comedy*; indeed, here the substance of the poetic passages (inevitably in terza rima, the verse pattern of Dante's poem, which is used consistently in the *Comedy of the Nymphs*) so closely parallels the words of the Master as to verge on plagiarism. The figural reference to Jason, the plowman, is taken directly from *Paradiso* 2; it is only the most patent and arresting of many specific "borrowings" that could be enumerated. And not only are the *Vita nuova* and the *Divine Comedy* well remembered in the story of Ameto; we find as well, in the rhymed debate of the shepherds in chapter 4, an act of homage to the "Virgilian" eclogues exchanged between the exiled Dante and his admirer, Giovanni del Virgilio.[18]

In keeping with the practice of his revered mentor, Boccaccio is not content to offer his readers simply one allegory; his *Comedy* is a kind of arabesque of allegories. The alluring nymphs are endowed with three identities; aside from being, on the literal level, fair creatures of the woodlands with classical names, they also stand for living Florentine ladies and for the cardinal and Christian virtues as well. We may not doubt that the rustic Ameto is Boccaccio himself, *ipse auctor*, nor, moreover, if his ultimate vision is to have any significance, that he is also, as was Dante the pilgrim, a symbol of Everyman. Subsidiary or peripheral allegories are also provided in abundance. The debate between the shepherds is an allegory of man's choice; the vision of the sky battle between swans and storks, thrown in somewhat gratuitously at the end of the story, is a capsule psychomachia; and the autobiography of each of the seductive nymphs contains its own hidden meaning, or meanings. It is right, for example, that Lia (Faith) should be the daughter of a river-god, for the way to Christian faith lies through the immersion of baptism; it is proper, as well as sensually appealing, that Venus (Divine Love) should embrace Agapes (Charity) in the stream wherein Cupid tempers his arrows.

One may say, too, that the narrative exuberance of the *Comedy of the Nymphs* is in keeping with the author's model. Even as Dante's *Comedy* is a narrative containing within it many narratives, so it is with Boccaccio's work. And even more copiously than Dante he reinforces his fiction with historical material, drawing, as did his master, on classical sources and contemporary chronicles as he chose. The detailed histories of Naples and Florence, in truth somewhat irrelevant to the adventures of the nymphs who linger on them with pedantic prolixity, are evidence of Boccaccio's antiquarian and scholarly interest (as well as further exemplifying the foliation of story on story), and the *Divine Comedy* affords ample proof that such matters were appealing to Dante as well.

Yet, in spite of the saturation of the *Comedy of the Nymphs* in Dantean sources, it is unmistakably a product of Boccaccio's own genius. Conceding its novelty in form and in avowed purpose, we cannot fail to recognize its kinship to its predecessors, the older daughters, as it were, of the author's Muse. The basic allegory of the refining effect of sexual love on the uncouth, but happily malleable young male, was the theme of *Diana's Hunt* and will live on in the *Decameron*. [19] In the *Ameto*, it is elevated to the theological level and this is admittedly an important distinction; for all that, young Ameto and his supporting chorus of nymphs have had their trial run in the earlier work, likewise cast in terza rima. There, too, the votaries of Diana were masks for living women who were at the same time Good Influences, if not Virtues. Of the narrative pattern, Sansovino remarked centuries ago that it is a kind of preliminary sketch of the *Decameron*, being a series of short tales framed by a fictitious background; but looking at it objectively, one can see that it resembles more closely the design already employed in the episode of the Questions of Love set forth in the *Filocolo*; there, as in the *Ameto*, there was but one day of storytelling and one program director. The prose section of the work,

too, marks a return to the world of the *Filocolo*; romantic plots set forth
in ornate, self-conscious style, admittedly more disciplined than that
of the earlier romance and somewhat more briskly paced. Nor is the
antiquarian encyclopedic strain, notable in the *Teseida*, missing.

The intrusion of the author into his own creation is likewise in line
with his standard practice. Aside from his obvious identification with
Ameto, Boccaccio appears twice in the *Comedy of the Nymphs*: as Ibrida,
beloved of Emilia, and again as Fiammetta's Caleone; in the case of
the latter pair, even the names made their initial appearance in the
Filocolo. So again we hear the tale of a youth born of a French lady
of high degree and a plebeian father, of the coming of that youth to
Naples, of the *coup de foudre* in the Church of San Lorenzo on that
unforgettable Holy Saturday. There are some piquant embellishments
in this new version, notably the bedroom scene with Fiammetta (a
lively bit of narrative, worthy of the *Decameron* in pace and style);
there are also some revisions in the details of the "autobiographical"
account. Caleone's mother is merely of French origin; she is of good
social standing but not a princess as she was in the *Filocolo*. Such
inconsistencies, as we have remarked, tend to undermine the belief of
scholars in the existence of any French mother. The fact that Ibrida is
as recognizable a mask as Caleone for the young Boccaccio would seem
to indicate that Emilia, here associated with the former and whose
name had already been glorified in the *Teseida*, had come to share a
place in the author's affections as privileged as that of Fiammetta. Yet,
for Ameto himself, it is Lia who fulfills the role that Dante assigned
to his Beatrice—yet a third charmer, one asks?—or must we here think
only of the allegory? For it is right that Faith should open our eyes
to the attractions of other virtues and lead us eventually to salvation.
There is once more a reference to the author's unhappy domestic
situation; this time it is the harsh and stingy father rather than the
"cruel bears" who drives him almost to suicide. In any event, much
old wine is poured into this new and curiously shaped bottle.

Of this marriage of narrative and allegory, intended by the author
to be a union of equal parties, one may say that it is formally and
technically quite successful. It has, unhappily, a fatal flaw in spirit.
While it does not take much imagination on the part of a reader to

realize, when he finds himself confronted by seven female creatures, each dressed in a different color, that he must prepare himself, sympathetically or otherwise, for allegory, he cannot fail to be distracted by the obsessive depiction of the sensual assets of these fair images, cataloged with intoxicated and, in truth, unseemly enthusiasm. The lady of the troubadours, high born, courteous, and discerning, might very well fulfill her function of refining and ennobling the gross manners of her attendant cavalier; the *donna angelicata* of the *dolce stil nuovo* with her lucent eyes and soul-stirring smile, could fairly claim the right to lead her discreet lover to Paradise (more easily, of course, once she had safely arrived there herself). But when we have been encouraged to linger long and greedily on golden hair, sloping shoulders, graceful necks, rounded breasts, tapering fingers, and similar delectable items, and even invited to speculate on the yet more luscious delights of the "hidden parts," it is very hard to readjust our vision and perceive that these tempting creatures, all of whom confess to illicit liaisons, are after all Prudence, Temperance, Justice, Fortitude, and their Christian sisters.

Hauvette puts it with Gallic eloquence: "La disparité absolue, paradoxale entre le signe employé et la chose signifiée atteint ici les confins du grotesque; il faudrait peu de chose pour que le récit versât dans une indécente bouffonnerie." ("The absolute, paradoxical disparity between the symbol employed and the intended meaning here verges on the grotesque; the tale comes close to being an indecent charade.")[20] For Rocco Montano "the allegorical veil becomes a pretext for profane descriptions and tales";[21] a verdict perhaps a little too harsh, for we may be tolerably sure that for Boccaccio, his allegory was something more than a pretext. Whatever his intentions may have been, the resultant *frattura*, as Quaglio calls it, is ruinous alike to the naturalism and symbolism of the work. Where Dante had fused these elements, Boccaccio estranges them. Yet, there is an episode in Dante's poem that may have given Boccaccio some warrant for his scandalous undressing of the virtues. In *Purgatorio* 28, as Dante's enraptured gaze encounters Matelda across the stream of Lethe, the classical references (to the rape of Proserpine, the love-wounded Venus, and the impassioned Leander) used to describe his response create an erotic aura somewhat at odds with the presentation of personified prelapsarian innocence. Indeed, this scene would fit nicely into the *Comedy of the Nymphs*; for a moment Dante the pilgrim is an Ameto *avant la lettre*. Of course, Dante the poet knows where to stop; we hear nothing of Matelda's rounded breasts or shapely limbs. But it is not unreasonable to assume that this scene made its impression on Boccaccio.

Of this destructive conflict between the means and the end, the medieval reader, familiar with the more sensitive tactical approach of Dante and his school, dedicated to the achievement of a similar didactic purpose, must have been well aware. A twentieth-century reader must find other, if perhaps minor, flaws in the *Comedy of the Nymphs*. For one thing, the narrative *richesse* is more apparent than real. Each of the seven nymphs tells her own story and of course there are differences in detail. But in pattern it is the same story seven times told. The school of criticism today, which specializes in reducing narrative to a series of algebraic formulas, would find one formula suited to describe all of the stories. The digressions, too, are distracting. And the prose style, as for the *Filocolo*, mannered and labored, often to the point of obscurity, full of circumlocutions and rhetorical embellishments, makes the reading of the work anything but a pleasure. As in the case of the *Filocolo*, we must remember that Boccaccio simply followed the practice of his day, in which prose was not so much meant for unobtrusive and efficient exposition as to display the writer's rhetorical skill. If this elaborated, sophisticated, and laborious manner were still held in high esteem, we should have to admire the author's accomplishment in the *Comedy*; but, for better or for worse, we have lost our taste for such obviously contrived and self-conscious elegance.

Perhaps in conclusion it is only fair to remember that although the work in toto may not appeal to us, it is not without incidental charms. As in all of his works, Boccaccio manages to produce some fine pictorial effects: Mopsa on the shore tempting Affron to approach her (chapter 18), Pomona and Adiona in the flourishing garden (chapter 27), Venus and Agapes bathing in the stream (chapter 32), to mention only a few. If circumlocution and digression make the reading difficult, there are passages where the narrative takes over and the pace quickens, arousing our interest. And in spite of the Dantean influence and the echoes of the author's own earlier works, the *Comedy* is original in the sense that nothing quite like it had been attempted before. Within the frame of reference of Boccaccio's own words, we can see, retrospectively as it were, a movement toward the *Decameron*, certainly in design and to some degree in content. And, like all the so-called minor works of this versatile genius, the *Comedy* will leave its legacy. The pastoral mode that, via Sannazaro, comes to full flower in the Renaissance—and not only in Italy—follows on the traces of Ameto and his winsome and articulate, if somewhat ambiguous, chorus of nymphs.

CHAPTER 8

L'AMOROSA VISIONE—
THE VISION OF LOVE

he *Amorosa visione (The Vision of Love)* follows immediately on the heels of the *Comedy of the Florentine Nymphs*. It can hardly have been composed later than 1343, for in canto 41 of the poem, among the bevy of contemporary beauties, the author includes Margherita of Taranto, wife of Walter of Brienne, the duke of Athens; since that inept tyrant was cast out of Florence in disgrace in July of 1343, it seems unlikely that his wife would have been the object of laudatory comment after that date. The *Vision* also contains references to the *Comedy of the Nymphs*, indicating that the latter work preceded it. We may safely think of 1342-early 1343 as the time of composition of this elaborate and original exercise.[1]

The most celebrated—one might almost say notorious—feature of the *Vision*, although nonfunctional and purely ornamental, is the built-in acrostic, probably the most ambitious in this genre of cabalistic virtuosity. The *Vision* is written in terza rima and the initial letters of the terzine spell out words that in turn compose two *sonetti caudati* (sonnets "with tails") and one which is not only *caudato* but also *rinterzato* (i.e., with insertion of seven-syllable lines rhyming with the hendecasyllables). For the first sonnet, the rhyme scheme is *ABBA ABBA CDC DCD EFE;* for the second *ABBA ABBA CDE CDE ED* and for the elaborate third *AaBBbA AaBBbA CDdC DCcD EeEfF.* The ornate patterns give the reader fair warning of the nature of the poem they introduce. In these sonnets Boccaccio proclaims his devotion to his "Fiamma, through whom his heart is warm" and also weaves in his signature, Giovanni di Boccaccio di Certaldo. Lest we should overlook his ingenuity, the author supplies an introductory note call-ing our attention to the device.

Like its immediate predecessor, the *Vision* is an allegory and an allegory heavily saturated with erudition. The predominant influence is Dante, but Ovid lends a helping hand and many passages reveal an indebtedness to other classical writers and to Old French literature, chiefly the *Roman de la Rose.* Like its predecessor, too, the *Vision* is carefully and ingeniously contrived with all but mathematical meticu-lousness; most of the cantos, for example, are of the same length, having eighty-eight lines (twenty-nine tercets with a closing line to rhyme with the middle line of the last tercet). But the *Vision* differs from the *Comedy* in design and structure, and its allegorical message is more personal and less conventional (and much more puzzling) than the one borne by the nymphs and their worshiping swain. It may be helpful if, in the discussion of this curious composition, we break our summary from time to time with commentary.

The poet begins by addressing his lady; he intends to tell her, he says, of what love revealed to him in a vision. For it befell that one day as he was thinking of her, sleep came upon him, bringing a dream in which he seemed to be walking upon a deserted plain. In his uneasy confusion a lady appeared before him; she carried a scepter in one hand and an apple in the other. She offered to lead him to felicity. He followed her and they came to a noble castle.[2] The gateway was somber but the lady assured the poet that it was the way to their ascent and with measured step, as the lady suggested, they entered the castle (1).

It is perhaps not surprising that where Dante looked to Virgil for his initial guidance, Boccaccio should prefer a woman. A principal puzzle of the *Vision* is the identification of this solicitous and fre-quently frustrated lady. Branca lists the various interpretations that have been offered:[3] Virtue, Faith, Reason, Fortitude, the Heavenly Venus (recently revived by Muscetta,[4] and appealing to Hollander), even the Virgin Mary. He abstains from offering any specific designa-tion himself but is content to see the guide as standing simply for "the aspiration to virtue that is in every soul."[5] It is difficult to understand why any of the above-mentioned figures should have so little influence on our dreamer and even more difficult to comprehend why any of them should defer to Fiammetta, who in terms of the story can hardly "stand for" anything more than sexual delight.

In his heart the poet here invokes the "lofty intelligence that moves the third sphere and all the others"; he prays to be given the lyric virtue of Orpheus so that what he has to say may be pleasing to hear. Following his guide, he tells us, he came to a wall in which there were two gates; one very narrow and dark, the other broad and inviting beyond which he could hear sound of revelry. The lady urges him to enter the narrow gate, over which an inscription promises eternal peace.[6] She assures him that although it seems dark it will lead to bright illumination (2). But the dreamer would first see what lies beyond the wider gate, the inscription over which promises abundant earthly glory and also the joys of love. He reminds his guide that it is proper for a man to have experience of all things, short of wickedness; the true good will be the more highly esteemed after savoring the false. While his guide still attempts to dissuade him, two young men—one clad in white, the other in red—come forth from the wide gate; they urge him to enter it with them; the narrow one can be left for his old age.[7] The Lady once more warns him but since the poet stands by his choice, she follows him and the youthful pair go through the broad gate (3).

Inside, the four pilgrims find themselves in a great hall, gleaming with gold and bright colors that only Giotto could have rivaled. Looking first at the wall in front of him, the dreamer sees a woman dressed in purple with a scepter in her right hand, a book in her left (Wisdom; specifically Philosophy). Sitting in a green meadow, she is flanked by seven ladies who appear to be singing; at their feet sits a great throng. To the right of the lady sits Aristotle and the dreamer enumerates no fewer than thirty other men of wisdom, ranging from Socrates to Boethius and including, in addition to all the well-known Greek and Roman philosophers, the Saracens Averroës and Avicenna. The dreamer then turns to the wall on his left (4) where he finds another group portrayed; their eyes are fixed on the seven attendants of the Lady rather than on the Lady Philosophy herself. The identification of the handmaidens with the seven liberal arts is made clear by the roll call of their admirers; Virgil is first among them, followed by a roster of poets and, in a separate category, historians, led by Livy. The dreamer notes that the Lady is putting a laurel crown on the head of one of the figures; his guide tells him that it is Dante Alighieri who is being so honored.

We may interrupt the narrative here to remark that Dante has well earned this tribute from his disciple. For more patently than in any other work of our poet, the hand of the master is evident—both in the general design and in many of the ancillary details of this new enterprise of Boccaccio's adventurous Muse. Like Dante, Giovanni is a wanderer in the wasteland when the vision begins; he finds, even as Dante did, a guide coming from nowhere who offers to lead him on the right path. The portal through which he enters bears an inscription as did the gates of the *Inferno* and throngs of ancient sages and poets —though enumerated in tedious abundance, contrasting unfavorably to Dante's selective tact—are or could be residents of Dante's Limbo. Boccaccio's vision, too, is set forth in the measure of the master, terza rima. It is true that the dreamer does not accept the guidance offered him with the docility of his predecessor, and of this significant detail we shall have more to say. But the pattern of the first five cantos at least is of such a nature that we might well think of ourselves as embarking on a second *Divina Commedia*. All of which is, no doubt, within the author's intention; what better model could a poet follow than that of one singled out by Lady Philosophy herself as the most glorious of all poets, including even the revered ancients?

It is to be noted that this is the first such elevation of Dante to supreme rank recorded in the history of Dante criticism; it is a verdict that honors both master and disciple. Passionate worshiper of the classics as he was, Boccaccio did not allow his judgment here to be swayed by the glamor of antiquity. Among the poets over whom Dante triumphs are such venerable Latin champions as Ovid, Virgil, Lucan, and Horace and such Greek stalwarts as Pindar, Euripides, and Homer himself. A twentieth-century critic might put Homer above Dante (and perhaps Boccaccio would have, had he then been able to read the Greek bard), but for the rest, Boccaccio's verdict would stand unchallenged today. It is not likely, however, that the Master would have approved of his admirer's choice of paths. Any Christian would have or should have spontaneously chosen the straight and narrow way of eternal life instead of the wide and easy road of worldly pleasures. It is true that in the *Convivio*—and later in the *Monarchia*—Dante had spoken of the two beatitudes, one attainable in this life, while conceding the superiority of the other. But given such a choice as our dreamer faces, he would certainly not have entered the worldly gate. Whether from the *Convivio* or elsewhere the dreamer found warrant for his choice, it is certainly a perverse one for a man of the Middle Ages. To be sure, this is an *Amorous* and not a *Divine Vision*; for a poet young and in love, Heaven could wait. The dreamer's choice here goes far to justify De Sanctis's definition of the *Vision* as a parody of the *Divine Comedy*.

The dreamer expresses his joy at seeing the honor paid his master to whom he readily admits his indebtedness. His guide then bids him look at the second wall, on which he sees Glory depicted; she is riding, regal and resplendent, in a chariot followed by a long train of heroes (6). The catalog is lengthy; it will run to some 150 names before concluding in the middle of canto 12. First come the founders of nations such as Janus, Electra, and Dardanus, then the heroes of ancient Troy. (Hector is described as "bello e gentil nell'aspetto a vedere," a line echoing Dante's description of Manfred) and on to great captains such as Alexander and Darius (7) and heroes of the Old Testament—Solomon, Samson, and others—closely pursued by figures of the Theban legend, then more Greeks and Trojans with a special group of figures from the *Aeneid.* Next in line is a group of particular interest to our dreamer; it is composed of illustrious heroines of whom a dozen are named, beginning with Helen and ending with Deianira. Penthesilea is singled out for lengthy praise (8) and Dido, sympathetically portrayed, is given no fewer than twelve lines. Then follow the Roman kings and the heroes (and some villains) of the Republic (9). Hannibal (six lines) and other figures of the Punic Wars come next, followed by Octavian, Pompey, and Mark Antony (accompanied by Cleopatra, to whose death scene fourteen lines are assigned).[8]

The end of the parade shows some chronological confusion: Scipio Africanus is followed by Trajan, and the catalog ends somewhat incon-

sistently with three Roman matrons—Martia, Julia, and Calpurnia
(10). Next come the knights of the Round Table, including Percival
(unknown apparently to Dante). Guinevere is given twelve lines, as
are Tristram and Iseult. Charlemagne and his paladins are not overlooked, although only Roland is identified.[9] Godfrey of Bouillon,
Robert Guiscard, and the Swabians, Frederick II and Barbarossa (both
described as "haughty") are seen pressing hotly after the chariot of
Glory (11); then come Charles of Anjou "laying about him with his
sword," Manfred, Corradino, and "many others," says the dreamer,
whom he omits because he does not care to linger "on the foolish
matter of romances"—an odd remark from the narrator of the *Filocolo*.

His guide presses him to turn his glance to the third wall where
Wealth, gold-clad and gold-crowned, is portrayed, surrounded by
crowds picking away at her treasures. The dreamer expresses contempt
for the intense greed exhibited by this folk; among them he recognizes
some who seem to be repentant, but their remorse comes too late (12).
Among the traditional examples of the avaricious whom the poet can
identify are Midas, Crassus, Pygmalion, and the like; he recognizes,
also, a closer contemporary, Azzolino da Romano (another echo of
Dante) (13). A vast number of new "Pharisees" (i.e., avaricious clergy),
unnamed, as they are in Dante's treatment of them, swell the throng;
they preach poverty but never turn their eyes from the treasure. Robert
of Sicily is there, too, represented as concealing his hoarded wealth,
and, looking closely at one of the grubbing figures, the dreamer
recognizes "one who had freely, cheerfully, and benignly brought him
up as his son and whom he is happy to call his father." In which
connection the dreamer admits that if wealth could be achieved with
honor he would choose to be rich himself, for only the wealthy are
esteemed and respected. He then turns to the wall dedicated to al-
mighty Love (14).

Although the encyclopedic register of names is so copious as to
benumb the reader, the critic may properly remark upon another aspect
of these animated catalogs. For the lists are not merely recited by the
poet; they are figures *seen* and, as the vision progresses, they are or seem
to be figures seen in action; the Swabians hurrying, Philip hoarding,
Boccaccino grubbing, and the like. For the topos of the illustrated wall,

if we may call it that, there is classical warrant in the scenes depicted
in Dido's palace that so deeply moved the heart of the shipwrecked
Trojan, and if we extend the concept to include the pictorial surface
we have the example of Arachne's web, provided by Ovid (whose
presence is scarcely less persistent than Dante's in Giovanni's vision),
and before that the shield of Achilles. The cinematic bas-reliefs on the
first terrace of the *Purgatorio* must also surely have been in Boccaccio's
mind. A supplementary inspiration here may have been, too, not
literary but iconographic. Boccaccio's age is also the age of Giotto,
whose frescoes were to be seen in Padua, Florence, and in Boccaccio's
time, Naples.[10] Indeed the allusion to Giotto in canto 3 speaks for itself.

But whatever and however numerous the inspirations may have
been, Boccaccio's elaboration of the concept is notable. One may
reasonably suggest that in the succession of murals we have enumerated
we may see a progression from the static "painted wall" to the presentation of "triumphs" wherein the object of the vision is not a surface
but the evocation of a parade of allegorical and historical figures. The
medieval zenith of this genre is represented by Petrarch's *Triumphs* and
Petrarch found his inspiration, it would seem, in the *Visione*.[11] To be
sure, there is a Dantean example of this kind of artifact, too; the
symbolic procession at the conclusion of the *Purgatorio* may be regarded as the first "triumph" in Italian literature, but it remained for
Boccaccio to elaborate and exploit the pattern, giving it central significance, one might say thus "selling" it to his enchanted successors.

To the panel of Love, Boccaccio dedicates, as might be expected,
much more space than to any other of his categories of worldly
"goods." Fifteen of the poem's fifty cantos are devoted to the realm
of the tender passion. Indeed, the poet openly avows his intention of
lingering in this attractive sector. It opens with—inevitably—yet
another springtime garden wherein a great lord is seen seated on two
eagles with two lions at his feet. He has wings and he holds in his hands
arrows of gold and lead. At his side sits a lovely lady, managing to
look at once like an angel and like Venus (15). Speaking, she identifies
herself as a heaven-sent servant of Love, always obedient to her lord.
The dreamer regards her with rapture and hopes to learn her name, but
it is not revealed to him at this time.

He then raises his eyes aloft and sees Jove take the shape of a bull and abduct Europa; then, as a shower of gold descends, seduce Danaë (16); the stories of Io, Callisto, Leda (17), Semele, Asteria, Latona, Antiope, and Alcmena follow (18). The story of Alcmena, from a medieval source, is notable for its comic tone; indeed, many of the legends of the wayward king of the gods are retold with a kind of emancipated brio. Jove's amorous exploits are succeeded by the more notorious affairs of the lesser gods, Mars, Apollo, Neptune (19), Bacchus, Pallas, and Pluto. Then comes the pathetic tale of Pyramus and Thisbe (given forty lines; 20). The lengthy lamentations of Hypsipyle and Medea, abandoned by Jason, have a canto to themselves (21) after which comes the Athenian cycle of Theseus, beginning with Ariadne and ending with Hippolytus; the perverted passions of Pasiphaë, Myrrha, Narcissus, Cephalus, and Procris are recounted (22), followed by the legend of Orpheus and Eurydice. Both Deidamia (23) and Briseis lament at some length their desertion by Achilles who, in his turn, comes on stage to grieve for Polyxena. Next come Hero and Leander, the ill-fated and unpatriotic Scylla (24), Alpheus and Arethusa, Aegisthus, Canace and Marcareus, Byblis (whose protestations cover forty-three lines), Phyllis, Meleager and Atalanta, and Acontius and Cydippe (25), after which we move to the entrapment of Hercules by Iole; the abandoned Deianira in her reproaches manages to enumerate all of the labors of the hero (26). The judgment of Paris is next presented, with the subsequent abduction of Helen and desertion of Oenone. After a brief allusion to the tale of Iphis and Ianthe, the poet passes to Laodamia and Penelope (27); to the story of Dido, set forth with deep sympathy, an entire canto (28) is dedicated and carries over thirty lines into the next one. The roll call concludes with a few nonclassical evocations: Florio and Biancifiore, Lancelot and Tristram (both of whom we had already encountered in the mural of Glory). At the end of his catalog the dreamer looks again at the handmaiden of Love and concludes with thirty-five lines in praise of her and the works of her master (29).

It is sad to be obliged to acknowledge that the Kingdom of Love, the most spacious and dearest to the heart of the author of all the divisions of this transient world, is the most laborious to traverse—

certainly for a reader of today and probably even for the poet's contemporaries. There are simply too many names, nor is the range of amorous experiences and attitudes sufficiently varied; monotony is inevitable. Rather than a *pinacoteca* of attractive evocations, as they are no doubt meant to be, these cantos are for the most part nothing more than a census of conventional exempla supplied by industrious research. It is to be remarked that in this section Ovid has replaced Dante as the poet's primary source; one finds passages that seem in fact simply transcriptions either from the *Metamorphoses* or the *Heroides*, both of which it is not hard to imagine Boccaccio held propped before him as he wrote.

Some details are worthy of observation as indicative of the author's interests. Of all the notes that Love can sound, it is the pathetic chord that Boccaccio finds most appealing; more lines are assigned to the laments of forsaken damsels than to any other product or manifestation of the divine passion. In truth, the figure of the betrayed and abandoned lover is one of Boccaccio's most persistent obsessions; in the *Filostrato* it is the young male whose anguish is piteously portrayed; in the *Elegy of Madonna Fiammetta*, as we shall see, the deserted woman will be given extensive treatment. And to be sure, such figures are appropriate to Boccaccio's talents; he is at heart a sentimentalist, a romantic whose emotional self-indulgence verges on the morbid. The ultimate expression of his taste will emerge in the depiction of the exasperatingly patient Griselda. Nor is there anything to criticize in the selection of such a theme. But in the *Amorosa visione* the surfeit of exempla moves us not to compassion, but to boredom. Dante was wisely content to give us but one Francesca, but in the cantos we have been summarizing the reader encounters an unending sequence of wailing and reproachful females. We could weep for Dido or Deidamia or Thisbe, if we could look upon any one of them alone. But as they pass by us in plaintive succession, it becomes increasingly more difficult to be moved by their laments. One weeping woman may well stir our hearts; a parade of tearful heroines can only breed indifference and tedium. The most charitable observation a critic can make is that, in this part of the *Vision*, it is Boccaccio the scholar who displaces the artist; as for the glosses of the *Teseida*, so for these cantos one may say that their substance is a kind of preliminary draft of the learned compilations that will take up most of the author's later years. Looking at them in this light we may willingly recognize their importance in literary history; but, taken collectively at least, although there is life and empathy in such episodes as that of Dido, these cantos may claim no true citizenship in the world of art.

Exalted by the vision of such glorious lovers, the dreamer suggests to his guide that his choice of entering the wider door has been justified. But she replies that all these fine sights are but ephemeral and not to be confused with the eternal Good. She invites him to follow her and observe the operations of Fortune (30). Accordingly, the party of four enters yet another vast hall, full of lively—and moving—pictures. Fortune herself is depicted seated on a chariot, drawn by spotted horses; she is ugly to look upon, her tangled hair falls before her face. Blind and deaf to all entreaties, she moves on without rest, incessantly spinning her wheel on which the dreamer seems to see human figures rising and falling. He tells his guide that he recognizes the lady; she is indeed his worst enemy. But his guide smiles and tells him that all the gifts of Fortune are transitory and false (31). Men seek from Fortune, she says, such gifts as wealth, honors, power, nobility of blood, and happiness in love; if such things are not given them, they blame Fortune. But all such prizes have their price. The guide cites the worries that go with wealth, the responsibilities of power, the permanent uneasiness of mind of those in eminence. Furthermore, Fortune's gifts, she adds, regularly lead to vice and corruption (32). Particularly silly, the guide states, are those who look to Fortune for the gift of nobility. For true nobility has nothing to do with "gentle blood" but derives from Virtue alone (a thesis that readers of Dante's *Convivio* will find familiar). Therefore, a wise man will spurn Fortune's gifts, aware of the dangers that they bear.

The guide then shows Giovanni the fate of various nations and individuals whom Fortune first favored and then betrayed: Thebes and Troy; Agamemnon, Turnus, Xerxes, Atamanthas (34), Alexander, Arachne, Darius, Niobe, Icarus, Carthage, Fiesole, Marius (35); the examples of Dionysius of Syracuse and Pompey are treated at length (36). The downfall of Caesar and Nero, then Ovid's fall from grace are cited. The dreamer avows himself convinced; he is now persuaded of the vanity of human things and is ready to go back and follow his guide through the narrow door that he had at first spurned. She gladly leads him toward it, but by another route, not retracing their steps. Following her, the dreamer espies an opening on his left and through it he sees a beautiful garden—yet another, the reader will note. He and his young comrades (who are still with us) wish to look inside; the guide strongly protests against this second excursus from the *via diritta* (37).

Since the basic allegory of the *Vision* is the portrayal of human experience on earth, it is to be expected that a consideration of Fortune should be set forth at some length. The mysterious operations of that capricious goddess fascinate us even in the sophisticated, not to say skeptical, times in which we now live, as the wide popularity of the "science" of astrology demonstrates. In an effort to understand what lies behind blind chance, if it is blind, or to anticipate the workings of a hidden power—is it a power with a plan?—that defies all rational calculation, mankind has resorted to all kinds of hypotheses and invented more than one "science" of prediction. In the Middle Ages, deeply religious and darkly superstitious, the study of Fortune's role could not fail to engage the attention of men of intellectual bent or pretensions: scholars, churchmen, or poets. Perhaps the crucial question was whether Fortune should be seen as some kind of authorized agent of divinity—God's providence in operation—or as a supreme power, irresponsible and sinister. Dante's answer, given in the sixth canto of the *Inferno*, was clear on this point. For Dante, Fortune was an angel of God, delegated to assure the proper distribution of earthly goods in accordance with the divine will although "oltre la diffension del senno umano," which is to say, beyond the power of men to control or even to comprehend.

Boccaccio's Fortune seems more ambivalent. She is presented in a most unattractive guise, having in it nothing of the angelic. She is as ugly as she is inexorable and the poet does not hesitate to call her his worst enemy. Yet the roll call of exempla in cantos 34, 35, and 36 presents figures traditionally associated with presumption and overweening rapacity, thus casting Fortune in the role not so much of

capricious distributor as that of avenger, and all men of faith know
in Whose hands vengeance lies. Some color of Dante's Serene Arbiter
thus blends with Boccaccio's conception, which contains elements less
orthodox and even obscurantist. It is significant that this potent goddess, unlike the other personifications of the determinants of mortal
life: Wealth, Power, Glory, has an entire room dedicated to her. Of
course, this has to be so; otherwise, we should have had to find room
for her on each of the four walls of the first Great Hall, since she has
her part to play in all human endeavor, whatever be the dominant
motivation or the goals sought. By giving her a room of her own,
Boccaccio stresses her importance and endows her with her own special
and ominous identity. Unfortunately, this approach also creates an
aesthetic flaw; it leads to repetition of material previously employed
in the decoration of the walls of the first hall; the stuff of Thebes, Troy,
and Carthage is plundered again, thus placing an unreasonable demand
on the patience of the reader who has heard all about them already and
is by now glutted with catalogs. Perhaps the dreamer is, too; he seems
to indicate as much by his avowal of willingness to follow his guide
and see what lies beyond the narrow gate that he had first ignored.

The dreamer, over the protests of his guide, who yet follows him,
enters the garden. There, as he moves with measured stride,[12] looking
about him he beholds a wondrous fountain. A large quadrilateral base,
porporino in color supports a round bowl of purple hue; from the center
of the bowl rises a column as brightly shining as if it were made of
diamond, crowned by a golden capital. On top of the capital stand
three nude female figures facing outward. One—of dark tint—
through a smiling face sheds tears that fall into the basin; from the
breast of the second, who is red as fire, water gushes forth; the third,
pure white, has a stream cascading from her head. At each angle of the
supporting quadrilateral stands a feminine figure: one dressed in multicolored garments, another (who has three faces) all in white, a third
seems to be clad in iron, and the fourth glows like an emerald (38).

Looking close, the dreamer sees that the streams cast by the three
fountain figures remain separate and pour forth through different
apertures. The stream from the white figure flows eastward, issuing
through the head of a lion and irrigates the garden, keeping it in bloom

through all the seasons of the year; that flowing from the red figure issues through a bull's head and runs southward; it, too, irrigates the garden but only in the appropriate season of the year; the tears of the dark woman come forth through a wolf's head and meander aimlessly through a region that bears neither flower nor fruit. Spontaneously, our hero moves to follow the course of the stream that issues from the bull's head; vainly does his guide suggest that he would do better to follow the course of that which pours from the lion's mouth.

As we have seen elsewhere, it is Boccaccio's style to tell a story within a story and to pile allegory upon allegory. It might seem that the subject of love had already received adequate treatment in the fifteen cantos dedicated above to its splendors and miseries. Love has enjoyed its long, and exhaustive, triumph; are not this fair garden and the ornate fountain something of a redundancy? In the author's intention, at least, such an objection would not be justified. For when we move into the Garden of Love, we are not merely moving into another allegory, but into another kind of allegory. Broadly speaking, the allegories we have seen heretofore were generalized concepts fortified by historical allusion; the fountain with its statues and its streams presents an allegory of philosophical and theological implications and at the same time and by the same token an allegory of more personal relevance, confessional in nature. With these concluding cantos the vision moves to a deeper level, as the all but Byzantine elaboration is meant to suggest. To state the matter a little simplistically: the fountain presents a psychological allegory and leads us into the world of the dreamer's own experience.

The individual features of the symbolic fountain require some explanation; their interpretation is not always easy.[13] A plausible reading of the three female figures from whom the waters flow would see them as corresponding to the three kinds of love defined by Fiammetta in the *Filocolo*. Reigning over the session devoted to the Questions of Love in that romance, the queen of the group had laid down that:

> There are three states of love. The first is called "amore onesto" [we may translate "onesto" here by its English cognate "honest" if we bear in mind that it carries overtones also of "decent" and "chaste"]; this the

good, right, and royal love which all should regularly welcome. The second is called "amore per diletto" ["love for pleasure"] and it is that sort to which we [i.e., Fiammetta and her companions] are subject. This is our god. The third is "amore per utilità" ["love for expediency"; "calculating love"]; the world holds more of this than of any other kind. This sort of love is involved with Fortune; so long as Fortune lasts, it will endure and likewise it will vanish when Fortune does. This love is the destroyer of many good things and, properly speaking, should be called hate rather than love.

So the white lady, signifying the first mode, may be seen as Divine Love or Charity, the red figure as sexual love, and the dark woman who weeps through her smile as false love. With such an interpretation the associated details are consistent. Pouring out through the mouth of the lion, the king of beasts, and flowing toward the east, whence came our Faith, the waters of charity ensure eternal fertility, defying the alternations of the seasons. Through the jaws of the lustful and fecundating bull—the sign of the flowering springtime and the reign of Flora—and flowing toward the warm and passionate south, issues a stream no less nourishing to growing things but only within the limits prescribed by nature. From the rapacious wolf pours a stream that, like fickle Fortune, follows a course of unpredictable meanderings, producing in the area it laves no growth of any kind but rather bleak sterility. As in the *Filocolo,* Fiammetta had conceded that the second kind of love was the sort most cherished by the youthful group for whom she speaks, so here it is the second stream that the dreamer chooses to follow, despite his guide's exhortations.

If the fountain signifies love in action—or the operations of love —it would seem likely that the pediment on which it stands should symbolize the stage of love *in posse* or at least in preparation; specifically the attributes or dispositions that the aspirant love must possess, conditions, in the language of the *dolce stil nuovo*, that shape "the gentle heart" and make of it, as Guinizelli and Dante had suggested, the proper and unique abode of love. Vittore Branca, accepting this reading,[14] feels that further specification of the symbolism of the ladies would be hazardous; Crescini, to whom we owe the interpretation of the ladies who make up the fountain itself, does not hesitate to suggest that the four figures of the pediment may be seen as "love, the perception necessary to love, the strength to endure the trials of love, and hope that strengthens the lover's heart." It is a reading that has the virtue of consistency. In any case, it is interesting to note that the stonework of this remarkable edifice has been quarried in varying proportions, from Christian tradition, the love cult of the troubadours (as codified by Andreas Capellanus) and the "sweet new style" of Dante's school (the darker elements reveal the somber veining of Guido Cavalcanti's "Donna mi prega"). The red stream will lead us into the ambivalent sector of the ecstasy and the agony of sexual love —and into the autobiographical revelations that bring the vision to its conclusion.

Following the course of the red brooklet, the dreamer's eye lights on a band of fair ladies; he tells his guide he is going to approach them; she may join him or await his return. She chooses to wait. He presses on with his young companions, "not knowing whether he was doing well or ill." A description of the beautiful vernal landscape follows; we are told, too, that we are midway through the Ram [even as Chaucer at the start of his pilgrimage] and that it is the fourth hour of the day (i.e., 10:00 A.M.) (40). The first lady the dreamer recognizes —so beautiful that he at first thinks she is a goddess—is the "bella lombarda" (probably the lady, unidentified by scholars, whom we first met playing the leading role in *Diana's Hunt*). She sings an enchanting song but the dreamer's companions urge him to move on; he then encounters a series of aristocratic contemporary ladies: Agnes of Périgord, daughter of Charles II of Naples; an unidentified Florentine "nymph"; Lia (who civilized Ameto); Margherita, wife of Walter of Brienne, for eleven months tyrant of Florence; and other beauties who pass by unnamed. The dreamer's rapture at the sight of so much loveliness is so great as to cause him almost "to lose his free will" (41). A second group of fair women includes the duchess of Calabria (later to become Queen Joan), an unidentified Neapolitan princess, Andrea Acciaiuoli (sister of Boccaccio's powerful, if unreliable, friend) and Dalfina di Barasso—all described in singularly cumbersome circumlocutions, as Boccaccio gropes for the elegant style suitable for such patrician presentations. Passing to yet a third bevy, the poet sees Eleonora of Aragon and beside her his own Fiammetta; the latter is here described as of the same stock that produced the great Dominican, Thomas Aquinas, done to death, Boccaccio affirms (following Dante), by Charles of Anjou, and we learn here, too, that her first name is Mary. This group also includes the noblewoman Margherita d'Asino, Lottiera della Tosa (the Mopsa of the *Comedy of the Florentine Nymphs*) (43), Isabella d'Ibelin (another Angevin lady), Alionora de' Gianfigliazzi (whom we met under the mask of Adiona in the story of Ameto), Giovanna, countess of Squillace, and the lady who played the part of Emilia in the *Comedy*. Others are there, too, but the poet cannot name them, for he finds his attention entirely absorbed in the contemplation of Fiammetta. His rapturous gaze lasts twenty-four days. At last she speaks, bidding him accept her sovereignty and promise eternal fidelity to her, which he is quick to do.

The roll call of contemporary patrician dames is reminiscent of the enumeration of the huntresses in *Diana's Hunt*. It is notable that in this register—autobiographical in nature—Neapolitan and Tuscan beauties alike find place. Boccaccio is here paying tribute to the high society that he has been privileged to frequent—or at least to observe—in the travels of his youth. The details concerning Fiammetta match, in general outline, what we have heard about her in the poet's earlier romances: she is a lady of the court (a peer, it would seem, of Eleanor of Aragon, the natural daughter of Frederick III of Sicily), and she is of the celebrated House of Aquino. It is true that nothing is said here of her quasi-royal birth, nor of her French mother. If such discrepancies open the road to skepticism with regard to the truth of the author's account of his *amours* and even with regard to the very existence of his "little flame," it may also be reasonably argued that the reiterated presentation of the general pattern might—for readers disposed to faith rather than doubt—serve as evidence of at least a kernel of veracity. Strict correspondence of all the versions might in fact be seen as indicative of the fictitious rather than factual. The reader is free to choose.

Fiammetta then opens the dreamer's breast and inscribes her name upon his heart; she links him to her with a slender chain running from her breast to his little finger. Ever since then, the dreamer avers, he has thought only of her, taking the good with the bad as love may decree, but never despairing of his ultimate reward (45). In this happy servitude he remains for another 135 days. Then, suddenly, he sees himself lying in the garden, his garments cast aside and his lady in his arms. Fiammetta asks him how he came to be there and he answers that it was through the guidance of a lady who is waiting for him outside the garden. Fiammetta bids him go and find her, assuring him that his guide will lead him on the right path. She bids him to obey the guide unless the lady commands him to forget her.[15] She dismisses him affectionately (46) and forthwith he hastens back through the garden, not seeing any of the fair ones he so much admired earlier, for he is intent on finding his guide. She would have him at first follow her and then return for Fiammetta. But the dreamer insists that they go back at once to his beloved, pointing out that it is only noon and plenty of time is left for resuming the journey. He swears that after rejoining Fiammetta he will do anything the guide bids him, except forsake his beloved.

Now eager to meet Fiammetta, the guide consents and they return to where the latter awaits them (47). The ladies meet; the guide calls Fiammetta her sister and urges the dreamer to follow his beloved, for she has been sent from Heaven. She then bids Fiammetta to lead her lover aright and tells the pair that they must never part. She suggests they linger a while in the garden before she leads them upward. Dancing and picking flowers, the lovers move off; they enter an enclosed bower, leaving their guide outside (48). The dreamer reflects that the enclosure seems made for the fulfillment of his desires and he senses that Fiammetta is willing to yield. She has dropped into slumber but the dreamer awakens her with a kiss. At first she demurs, then, though fearful lest the guide return, shows herself wholeheartedly ready ("tutta disposta") to yield. So intense is the dreamer's joy that his dream breaks and his Amorous Vision fades away.[16] The garden has vanished, the hero is alone; he would have died of grief save for his hope of some day returning "in perfect essence" (49). Looking back, he perceives his guide (who, oddly, seems to have survived the dream of which she was a part); she invites him to follow her—not back to the garden but in another direction that will bring him to perfect bliss. The narrative ends here, "just when the allegory should have reached its fulfillment and its *raison d'être*," Sapegno comments.[17] Is it possible that the *Vision* is an unfinished poem? Perhaps we should ponder the implications of the fact that it has exactly half the number of cantos as the *Divine Comedy*. Yet it hardly seems likely that Boccaccio ever intended to give us another fifty cantos; certainly the completion of the acrostic assures us that the *Vision* is not "broken off" in the normal sense of the phrase.

The author brings his work to a conclusion with an address to Fiammetta. He asks her to read and if need be emend his *Vision*; it was written only for her. He speaks of it as so many "parolette" ("simple words") composed artlessly for love alone. He also asks his lady to dissipate any envy that may attach to his work; she is his only desire and he will be forever faithful to her (50).

The allegory of the last cantos is complex and occasionally ambiguous. Insofar as its autobiographical facet is concerned, we may remark that Boccaccio's account of the length of his love service—135 days plus the 24 days of rapturous expectancy mentioned in canto 44—matches at least approximately the experiential chronology, affirmed in preceding works; the first encounter with Fiammetta took place in late March or early April and the time of her surrender (occasioned by the daring gesture of Caleone as recounted in the *Comedy of the Florentine Nymphs*) came under the sign of Scorpio. To be sure, the count does not come out precisely equal and scholars have resorted to various hypotheses, not quite satisfactory, to explain the discrepancy. Even so, and conceding with Branca that the mathematical precision of the *Vision* has a touch of the "surrealistic,"[18] the correspondence is accurate enough for poetic purposes. If in terms of the *Vision* itself it seems a little odd that Lady Virtue has been kept waiting outside the garden 159 days, by one count, while by another only two hours (from ten o'clock to noon) make up the interval, we can but observe that in dreams time has its own adaptability.

Leaving aside the strictly autobiographical aspect of the culminating vision, Branca has pertinently remarked[19] that the successive phases of the dreamer's passion are in harmony with the "grades" or "degrees" through which, according to the authoritative Andreas Capellanus, the true lover must pass, which is to say through acceptance, to willing and ever-hopeful servitude, on to the enjoyment of certain intimate privileges, and ultimately to the culmination of possession. Branca is right, I think, in seeing in the erotic play of canto 46 merely the third stage; fulfillment comes only in the climactic embrace of canto 49.

What is much less clear is the significance of the relationship between Lady Virtue and Fiammetta. Branca argues that in putting Love before Virtue (for it is the guide who must come to Fiammetta) and in seeing in his lady his true and angelic leader to the better life, Boccaccio is not only following Guinizelli, who mistook his lady for a resident of Heaven and passed his vision on to Dante, but is also in full accord with Christian doctrine, reflecting, in Branca's words, "the Christian intellectual position which prescribes love as the necessary origin and life-giving element of every virtue."[20] One cannot but wonder, however, if the austere Christian theologians had in mind quite the same kind of love as is symbolized by the appetizing Fiammetta. And even within the allegory, there are a few false notes. It is true—and in accordance with Branca's thesis—that Lady Virtue, once she has seen Fiammetta, greets her as a sister and gives the dreamer into her charge. She even goes so far as to say that Fiammetta was sent down from Heaven to guide her lover on the right road. Yet we cannot fail to remark that when the dreamer and his lady approach the culmination of their joy, Lady Virtue has been left out of sight; it would seem deliberately evaded. Can Love have no need of Virtue? Possibly only in dreams, for the dreamer's enjoyment is brief and transitory and the text is not quite explicit even with regard to its completeness. Certainly when he awakens it is Virtue who takes him in hand again and proposes to lead him through the narrow way into eternal felicity; for this second and truly holy pilgrimage she—not Fiammetta—will guide him, in spite of her apparent abdication in canto 48. Does the Angelic Woman then truly lead us to Heaven or only, at best, to an earthly facsimile thereof? There is in fact an unresolved dichotomy running through the allegory; one cannot but remember that when (in canto 40) the dreamer chose to leave his mentor and enter Love's garden he was not sure whether he was doing well or ill.

By making his original choice, the self-willed explorer ignored not only the counsel of his guide but also the example of his master, Dante. One cannot easily imagine the questing pilgrim of the *Comedy* turning away from the path suggested by Virgil and much less straying from Beatrice to explore appealing byways. Boccaccio's choice here—and the confession that accompanies it—give us the most illuminating "autobiographical information" in the *Vision*. One may see in his action a kind of dramatization of Petrarch's pathetic statement, "I know the best and cling to the worst," but there is no regret attached to Boccaccio's exercise of his option. In this sense, the *Vision* is the most revealing of all the minor works as touching the aims of his Muse. He is telling us, in effect, that while he does not doubt for a minute the supremacy of things eternal, his interest is centered on the glamorous if transient glories of this world. "The record of a non-conversion," Hollander calls the *Vision*.[21] It is notable that the author ends his narrative before even so much as crossing the sill of the straight and narrow way that leads to salvation. The *Vision* thus prepares us in its way for the emancipated and hedonistic view of life that colors much of the *Decameron*.

This connection, if it be admitted, is one of the few facets of the *Vision* that make it worth the effort of reading. It cannot be called a masterpiece; in the perspective of Italian letters, it hardly looms large; Momigliano's *Storia della letteratura italiana* dismisses the poem in one casual sentence and Flora's exhaustive five-volume survey gives it only a brief paragraph. The overall critical verdict is disparaging; Scaglione speaks of the poem's "obvious and miserable failure, logical and aesthetic."[22] And even Vittore Branca, the dedicated and meticulous editor of the *Vision*, calls it "a most mediocre poem."[23] Its faults will be apparent through a mere scanning of the summary furnished above. With regard to the numerous catalogs, it must be conceded that in many places they are enlivened by sharp, descriptive phrases and occasional empathetic vignettes; even so, the remorseless parade of erudition taxes a reader's endurance. The allegory, the most distracting to be contrived, even in an age of allegories, is by turns obvious to the point of banality and irritatingly obscure. Insofar as it is decipherable, it seems to be perverse and subversive of conventional medieval values.

The main narrative is halting and rather frail; the *Vision* is not as good a "story" as the *Filocolo* or the *Filostrato* or even the creaking *Teseida*, and it lacks the *richesse* of the subsidiary tales that contribute some lively pages to the *Comedy of the Nymphs*. Only in the depiction of the protagonist will some (though by no means all) readers find a certain appeal; the dreamer's unshakable zeal to learn all he can of the world we live in and his stubborn exaltation of his flesh and blood lady over all temptations to turn to higher things has its undeniable attraction.

Yet for all its faults, from the point of view of literary history the *Vision* cannot be overlooked. The succession of historical-allegorical murals had, as we have noted, its effects on Petrarch; certain motifs will be picked up by writers of the Renaissance. For Boccaccio specialists in particular the work is fascinating for its foreshadowing of later works. Muscetta rightly calls it a "vivaio" (nursery of seedlings) destined to flourish in the Boccaccian grove.[24] In the catalogs of illustrious names, both the *De casibus* and the *De mulieribus claris* are adumbrated and to some extent the *Genealogie* as well. The plaintive chorus of abandoned women will receive sharper focus in the *Elegy of Madonna Fiammetta*, and the legendary love affair of Jove and Calisto (one of the many fables recalled in cantos 17 and 18) contains the germ of the *Nymph Song of Fiesole*.

CHAPTER 9

THE ELEGY OF MADONNA FIAMMETTA

 he *Elegy of Madonna Fiammetta*, sometimes called simply *Fiammetta*, was written, at least according to the calculations of recent scholars, in the period 1343–1344.[1] Accepting that dating, we can only marvel at the gulf that separates the character of the work from the nature and style of its immediate predecessors in the Boccaccian canon. We have here no allegorical mosaic in Dantean terza rima, no seductive nymphs whose rosy flesh and tempting limbs are draped in vestments of ethical symbolism; here is no romanticized would-be classical epic. Instead the scene is contemporary society, the protagonist an upper-class woman of that society, calling for our comprehension and compassion, needing no allegorical interpretation. Branca, sharpening the verdict of Carducci a century ago, calls the *Fiammetta* the first modern psychological-realistic novel.[2] Boccaccio himself is well aware of his change of course; he tells the "enamored ladies" to whom the book is dedicated (as the *Decameron* will be) that they will find its pages innocent of "Greek fables embellished with falsehoods" and "Trojan battlefields befouled with blood" —certainly palinodic words for the author of the *Filostrato* and the *Teseida*. We may remark, too, that in accordance with the realistic nature of the time and place, Fiammetta's pathetic story is set forth in prose.

We do not know enough about the details of Boccaccio's life nor the literary influences to which he may have been exposed to explain

just why his Muse led him into a new path at this point in his career.[3]
If the assumed dates are correct the work was composed not long after
the fall of the duke of Athens, followed by a period of civic unrest
in Florence. The people, regarding the Bardi as accomplices of the
despot, burned and plundered the palace of that family, with which
Boccaccio had long been associated. Perhaps in such tumultuous times
further exercises in allegory seemed irrelevant. No doubt the unsettled
political situation in Florence rekindled the nostalgia for Naples that
always glowed in our poet's heart; there is a notable passage in chapter
2 of *Fiammetta* in which life in the city of the Arno is compared
unfavorably with the ordered felicity that reigned in the Angevin
capital. Possibly the genesis of the work is primarily literary, inspired
by the author's reading of Seneca.

As for the prose, Branca, largely on the evidence of a Latin translation that Boccaccio made of an explorer's description of the Canaries,
deduces a new appreciation of the brisk, factual style in the writings
of travelers, merchants, and the like.[4] The influence of Dante's *Convivio*
is also perceptible;[5] incidentally, the designation "elegy" is Dantean;
according to Dante (*De vulgari eloquentia* 2.4–6) it is a recognized
narrative style, applicable to a pathetic substance. Or perhaps we may
see in *Fiammetta* another instance, whatever be its origins, of the taste
for novelty, characteristic of the author's persistent experimentalism.
To a degree, every successive title of Boccaccio has an element of
novelty in its conception; all of his works are "different." But the
difference in *Fiammetta* is, in certain respects, more marked than in any
of its predecessors. But let Fiammetta, who tells her own story, speak
for herself. (A first-person confessional account from the lips of a
woman is in itself something of a novelty in the Middle Ages; no doubt
Fiammetta is following the example—though with greater prolixity
—of some of the bruised heroines of Ovid's *Heroides*.)

She begins by defining her social status; she was born, she tells us,
to noble parents and under what appeared to be a bountiful and benign
fortune.[6] She was reared by a "reverent and sage matron from whom
she learned every good quality." She also grew increasingly beautiful
and confesses to the satisfaction she got from hearing her praises
spoken. She had many suitors and she chose for her husband "a most

complete and perfect gentleman" with whom she lived for some time in conjugal happiness. Had it not been for the work of Fortune, using love as a weapon, she would have continued to live a happy life.

A disturbing dream, in which she suffers the venomous bite of a serpent and sees the sun blotted out and the earth grow dark around her, is a presage of her fate. The vision's dire prediction is soon fulfilled. For the next morning Fiammetta goes to attend divine service where, after enjoying as usual the glances of admiration that are bestowed upon her, by chance her eyes light upon a gentleman leaning against a column; he is young, handsome, and becomingly dressed. She looks at him repeatedly; finally, their glances meet and from that moment she is forever lost. Wearing her finest apparel she seeks every occasion to see him again; they meet in various social gatherings but he is always discreet and reserved in his speech; she meanwhile burns more intensely every day with amorous desire. Her old nurse suspects something is wrong and soon learns the truth. She implores Fiammetta to resist Love's temptations, warning her of the social dangers and the unhappiness certain to follow if she yields. But Fiammetta can only say that she is powerless against Love. The nurse reproaches her for taking such an attitude; Love, she says, is ever in wait for the wealthy and the wellborn; it is an indulgence of the rich and its excesses are never found among the poor. But her words only anger Fiammetta, who declares that she is now such a servant of Love that she must have her lover or die.

Yet even so, Fiammetta tells us, she might have heeded her nurse had it not been that Venus herself appeared before her, lecturing her on her duty to love and reminding her of love's triumphs even over the gods. Animals, birds, indeed all living things, the goddess says, must obey love. Nor, she continues, should Fiammetta feel any shame; the examples of thousands of noble ladies before her would excuse her. Nor should fidelity to her husband stand in her way, for love takes no account of marriage and in fact most husbands have their own love affairs, and men should not be privileged over women in these matters. Fiammetta, convinced, promises to obey Venus and asks the goddess to reward her, whereupon Venus shows Fiammetta the image of her lover and assures her that he is worthy.

Fiammetta then sets out to kindle the flame within her lover's heart; he responds but shows himself discreet. He makes friends with all of Fiammetta's circle and cultivates her husband in particular. Fiammetta tells us of the secret language of words and gestures employed by her lover and herself; they invent the names Fiammetta and Panfilo in order to speak of each other more freely. Fiammetta employs a trusted maid to carry messages between them. Finally they come together; although she affects reluctance, her surrender is a great joy to her. So their relationship begins, carried on in secret and not without frequent fears; yet Fiammetta finds it a source of great happiness that endures "many months and days" (chapter 1).

Meanwhile, "cruel Fortune was preparing a malicious poison" for the enamored woman. It happens one night, as the lovers lie in Fiammetta's bed, that she hears Panfilo groan in his sleep. On being awakened he confesses that his heart has sorely troubled him because he must soon leave his love; he has been summoned home by his father, now an old man. Shaken, Fiammetta objects and argues that his father does not need the love and presence of Panfilo as much as she does. Probably, she says, if the old man realized the strength of their love he would not want his son to return. She goes so far as to say that since his father is old and probably not well, it is doing him no favor to prolong his life. If the visit of his son could cure him that would be all very well, but since it cannot avail, it is pointless; while on the other hand, the absence of Panfilo would mean her own death. She adds that there can be no doubt of the fact that Panfilo would be much happier remaining in Naples, a city more pleasing, more opulent, and much better administered than his native town. But Panfilo insists he must leave; he could hardly use their illegitimate and indeed hidden relationship to justify his failure to obey his father. He assures her, however, that he will be away only three or four months. Fiammetta then asks him to delay his departure, pointing out that it is a bad season to travel, with storms and heavy rains and snow on the hills. But Panfilo replies that the sooner he leaves the sooner he will return; one must risk the weather as one risks all the hazards of travel. He swears he will never love anyone but Fiammetta and he swears also that he will return within four months. So her lover takes his leave; at the moment of departure,

Fiammetta swoons in his arms and learns the details of his leave-taking
only from her maid, from whom she hears that Panfilo, departing, had
hit his foot on the doorsill; this seems to Fiammetta an evil augury
(chapter 2).

Fiammetta describes the successive phases of worry and anguish
ensuing on her lover's departure. She is at first reassured by letters
telling of his safe arrival, then she begins to fear that he may be so,
happy at home that he will think of her with resentment for having
delayed his return; she feels jealousy, too, of the women in his native
city. She finds some comfort in frequenting the circles where Panfilo
was known; though she does not dare to ask about him, she occasionally hears reports of him, some saying they expect him soon to return.
But the days pass. Fiammetta watches throughout the night, gazing at
the moon, thinking that Panfilo must be doing likewise. Sometimes she
attempts to find distraction by having her attendants tell stories and
telling some herself; she prefers fantastic and merry tales. Often she
makes believe Panfilo is with her and holds imaginary conversations
with him. She dreams of him frequently, sometimes of his return,
sometimes of his death. As the time of his return draws near, she
becomes more cheerful, goes more readily into society, and pays more
attention to her dress and appearance, rehearsing the moment of reunion (chapter 3). But the time comes and passes and there is no word
of Panfilo. Fiammetta is tormented by anxieties; perhaps his father has
detained him, perhaps he has suffered some accident on the return
journey. And, concurrently, she is tormented by jealousy, recalling the
well-known fickleness of men. She is resolved, however, to remain
faithful (chapter 4).

A merchant, a compatriot of Panfilo, comes to Naples and, as he is
showing his wares to a group of ladies of which Fiammetta is one, one
of the gentlewomen inquires about Panfilo. The merchant replies that
he has married. Fiammetta conceals her shock at this news; she remarks
that the lady asking the question seems in some dismay. Retiring to
her chamber, Fiammetta feels she has been doubly deceived; not only
has Panfilo taken a wife, but he had been unfaithful to her even in
Naples. In a long tirade, she reproaches her absent lover for his faithlessness, pleads her own loyalty, calls on the gods to punish her false

lover, and curses his new marriage. Yet for all that she longs for his return and soon falls to making excuses for him. His father may have forced him to marry; as for the Neapolitan lady, she may have revealed her love for Panfilo, but that does not necessarily mean that she was loved in return.

So Fiammetta lives on in misery and anxiety. Her only refuge is sleep, but her dreams are painful; she begs Venus to release her from bondage. Her husband cannot but remark her condition although unsuspecting of its cause. Solicitously, he suggests a visit to the seashore with all its delights, including the healthful baths. Fiammetta at first demurs lest in her absence Panfilo might return, but finally she consents. At the seashore she tries to take part in all the diversions: fishing, hunting, bathing, and merrymaking, but she is haunted by the memory of Panfilo recalled to her by the scene. Grown shrewd, she can now detect among her companions the signs of their happy amours and this increases her melancholy. Friends begin to notice her altered state; some think she is ill, others suspect a love affair, but so well has Fiammetta covered her passion that the suspicion dies. It hurts her to hear others say that her beauty has gone, even though without Panfilo it is meaningless to her. She berates Fortune for her cruelty; recalling the happy circumstances of her birth, her high position, and her wealth, she accuses Fortune of spoiling everything.[7] Particularly she resents Fortune's intrusion into Love's domain; had Fortune bereft her merely of her wealth, that would have been a different matter. Yet Fiammetta is prepared to forgive Fortune if she will but bring Panfilo back to her.

Returning to her account of social life Fiammetta describes the parties and festivals of spring and summer seasons with particular attention to the tournaments engaged in by the young men. Consideration of the diversions of the aristocracy and their luxury leads Fiammetta, who without her lover can no longer enjoy them, to meditate on the wholesome purity of the simple life; she passes to an encomium of the Golden Age, which knew neither wealth nor war nor "dissolute love." She is reproached by her friends for letting her beauty fade and neglecting her dress; since she cannot disclose the real reason, her answer, expressing disdain for such vanities, brings her a reputation for saintly asceticism. In this she takes no pleasure, but prays again either for the return of Panfilo or for the release of death (chapter 5).

A full year has passed since the lovers' parting. A servant of Fiammetta, returning from Panfilo's city, reports that he is not married (the lady seen entering his house amid nuptial festivities was not his wife but his new stepmother) but that he is enamored of a very fair lady of that city who reciprocates his love. Hearing such tidings, Fiammetta retires to her chamber where she swoons. She utters long and bitter reproaches to the absent Panfilo, ending with the hope that his new love will betray him as he has betrayed his faithful Fiammetta. So great is her grief that she wakes her husband with her sobs as they lie in bed. He asks her why she is so disturbed and she replies that the ghost of her brother, violently slain and unavenged, has appeared to her. Her husband comforts her as best he can and inwardly she reproaches herself for her infidelity to her spouse, a better man in every way than her lover, but, she reflects, it is human nature to scorn what one has and prize what one cannot have.

As her melancholy becomes deeper her old servant admonishes her, pointing out that she has been brought to this state by following passion rather than reason. The nurse suggests that Fiammetta should put aside all further thought of Panfilo (she may rejoice that at least her honor is safe since their relationship was secret) and resume her normal life as if Panfilo never existed. This Fiammetta cannot do. She breaks into a bitter invective against her unknown rival, "the damned adulteress"; she would like to be borne off to where the false pair dwell so that she might scratch her rival's face and destroy her body "with greedy teeth." The nurse cautions her not to reveal herself by such injudicious outcries; her husband might hear her. Fiammetta answers that she would be pleased to suffer the punishment she well deserves from her husband. The nurse replies at some length; she reminds Fiammetta that her love was of her own willful choosing; without her consent Love could never have overcome her. If then of her own free will she has delivered herself to Panfilo she must be prepared to submit to his treatment of her. The deceits of wooers are well known, she adds, nor is there any law to punish them, as various classical examples attest. Indeed, her rival may by now have been deceived even as Fiammetta was herself. Or, if she has in fact captured Panfilo with her wiles, then Fiammetta can do the same with another man; such are the ways of love. If Fiammetta insists on being a slave of love she had best take a new lover at once; there are plenty of available and willing gentlemen. Again she cites classical examples of such action on the part of jilted women. Finally, she advises Fiammetta to accept her loss philosophically, to continue to conceal her infidelity from her husband, and to live henceforth "with virtue and hope," accepting cheerfully what Fortune brings since it cannot be altered—but sometimes when things are at their worst Fortune brings a change for the better.

Fiammetta is not persuaded by this good counsel; her days grow sadder and she falls to planning suicide. She considers various methods and decides that she will throw herself from the top of one of her castle's towers. But, the decision made, reaction sets in and she postpones the deed, persuading herself that after all Panfilo may yet return. And if he does, she can either win him back to her or cause him pain by her suicide. Yet this resolution also falters and one night, taking advantage of her nurse's absence, Fiammetta leaves her chamber and makes her way toward the top of the tower. But her robe becomes entangled in a broken railing; she is detected by her nurse and brought back forcibly to her chamber. The nurse lectures her on the folly of suicide, pointing out that it is surely the last way to win back her lover. After this attempt Fiammetta is carefully guarded; she abandons the notion of suicide and instead decides to make a pilgrimage that would take her through Panfilo's city. Her husband approves of the plan but suggests waiting for a more convenient time. Meanwhile, Fiammetta turns to sorcerers and witches, but although they promise much, they can do nothing (chapter 6).

The months pass and spring returns, but amid all the flowering of nature and gaiety of youth, Fiammetta remains withdrawn and unconsoled. And Fortune prepares yet another stroke. For as Fiammetta sits in her lonely misery the nurse breaks in with the joyous news that Panfilo is about to return; this she has learned from a fellow countryman of the truant lover, met by chance as he landed from his ship. He knew Panfilo and has given assurance that he will return in a matter of days. Fiammetta can hardly believe the good news but finally, putting doubt aside, she attends to her dress and her person and notes that her beauty, ravaged by months of grief, is beginning to return. In fact, this improvement is commented on by her family and friends. Now, in her new elation, she blames herself for her doubts; the rumors she has heard about her lover's behavior were probably idle gossip. She should never have lost faith in him; no doubt he has delayed his return simply to test her fidelity. She resolves that he will never learn of her suspicions. She dreams rapturously of their coming reunion. As the day draws near she begins to watch the street for a sight of him; often she thinks she sees him but he does not appear. On the day his return is expected, she dresses in her best finery and can hardly restrain herself from going to the port to meet his ship. But the truth is that there has been a mistake and the Panfilo who arrives is not her Panfilo. So sharp is her disappointment that Fiammetta swoons and has to be carried off to bed. So the old train of life returns, with increased wretchedness. She longs more than ever for death and lives only for the faint hope of the pilgrimage she has planned (chapter 7).

At this point the narrative, as such, ends. Fiammetta compares her sufferings with the pains of various heroines of antiquity (drawn mostly from Ovid) and proves to her own satisfaction that she has suffered more cruelly than any of them, from Byblis to Hecuba, from Myrrha to Dido; and more bitterly, too, she adds, than any of the hapless heroines of the chivalrous romances, such as Iseult. She concludes by assuring her intended audience of gentle ladies that her anguish has been greater than her pen could portray; she will now no further trouble her readers. She prays now only for the return or the death of Panfilo (chapter 8).

Taking leave of her book, Fiammetta sends it forth to the eyes of "enamored ladies." She bids her book not to be ashamed of its lack of beauty or adornment or even its ruffled leaves or blotched and blurred pages; such a condition becomes the content and may serve to arouse compassion in its readers. Perhaps her story may also stand as a warning against the guileful deceits practiced by men. If Fortune should bring the book into the hands of some woman so lucky in love as to laugh at the author's sorrows, let her bethink herself of the inconsistencies of that very Fortune. To readers who show compassion, the book is to beg for their prayers on Fiammetta's behalf. But whoever the lady may be who reads its pages, Fiammetta hopes that she will be happy in her love—except, of course, if the book should fall into the hands of her rival. In that case the book should strive to touch her conscience and persuade her to restore Panfilo. Fiammetta bids her book to shun the eyes of men; if by chance it should reach Panfilo, however, then he should read it—only if it can persuade him to come back to its author. And finally, should any lady be moved to complain of the poor composition of the work, she should call to mind the circumstances of the writer and be moved to admiration rather than disparagement. Fiammetta is tolerably sure that her book will be safe from the attacks of envy; should she be wrong, well, it will be only another evil stroke of Fortune, insignificant when compared to those she has already suffered. She bids her book live on as an example to other women and as a reminder of its afflicted author (chapter 9).

The outline of the plot enables us to assess the quality and extent of the novelty of the work as compared with its predecessors. One may say, to be sure, that the figure of the abandoned woman is a traditional theme; an all but archetypal image. We have but to recall Boccaccio's own extensive gallery of such forlorn females, set forth at rather extensive length in the *Amorosa visione*. Dido is the classical example in both senses of the word, and in the pages of the *Elegy* itself there are many passages that reveal the author's fruitful perusal of Ovid's *Heroides*, notably the sad tale of Phyllis and Demophoön. Seneca, too, is patently perceptible in the machinery of the action and in the role of the nurse.[8] But in the depiction of the deserted Neapolitan lady of fashion the classics are not simply transcribed nor even imitated but rather utilized quite naturally and properly to add a kind of eternal dimension to a contemporary account. Fiammetta is a woman of her own time and place and her own localized and defined situation. In spite of her egocentric introspection, the context of her world is not ignored. The descriptions, though brief, of the parties and festivities and social mores of the time give the narrative an authenticity of texture that owes nothing to the classics—indeed is hardly classical at all.

To the contrary, so clearly marked are the realistic coordinates that

it has long been suspected that the *Elegy* is "autobiographical"—
though with a difference. For assuming, as until recently most readers
of the *Elegy* have assumed, that there was a real Fiammetta who first
loved and then jilted the young poet, what we find in the *Elegy* may
readily be seen as a reedition of that true story with the roles reversed;
"a mirror-image projection" of the author's own experience and a kind
of wishful revision of the intolerable truth, even a kind of revenge for
a heartless dismissal. Luigi Russo calls it "a *Filostrato* turned upside
down."⁹ It is impossible to say how much truth there is in this view
of the *Elegy;* it is plausible enough if we believe in the truth of the
earlier accounts of the romance, from the introduction of the *Filocolo*
to the conclusion of the *Amorosa visione,* or even if we believe in the
more or less consistent fictionalized "truth" about the author's Neapolitan involvement as set forth in his earlier works. We do not, for all
the efforts of recent scholars, have evidence firm enough either to
accept or deny the autobiographical thesis. It is perhaps easier to refute
the intention of "revenge," at least if we see it as indicative of rancor
or resentment. Fiammetta is portrayed certainly without illusion but
never without compassion. We may remark, too, on the autobiographical side, that she is also portrayed without the romantic halo of royal
birth; the Fiammetta of the *Elegy* is a lady of good family and wealthy
connections but she is no princess—nor is Panfilo anything more than
a merchant's son. The *coup de foudre* needs no support from the courtly
tradition; to be sure, it takes place in church, but there is no circumstantially portentous description of time and place. The whole affair proceeds without the medieval embellishments deriving either from
Dante's *Vita nuova* or the doctrines of Andreas Capellanus that had
characterized earlier versions.

It is, in fact, this programmatically unsentimental treatment of a
sentimental pattern that gives the *Elegy* its novel character. Fiammetta
is the slave of love but she is at the same time a very perceptive observer
and a lucid analyst of her malady. Her recurrent hopes, in which she
cannot quite believe, her surrenders to despair that are never quite final,
her tirades, her self-reproaches, indulgences in self-pity, all such
manifestations of her state are not at all romanticized but have about
them the ring of truth, as convincing, to put it in terms of our own

day, as the confessions of an alcoholic or a drug addict. Why is it, she asks herself, waking in the night beside her affectionate husband, that her heart must be set on another man, in every way inferior to her legitimate spouse? She cannot say—but she cannot change either, and in this hopeless awareness of her weakness there is eternal human anguish. If the *Elegy* looks back to Seneca, it also looks forward to Moravia.

The Great God of Love himself is stripped of his finery, if not his authority, in this disillusioned novel. Fiammetta's nurse realistically sees this love (the grand passion of Iseult, Guinevere, Tristram, and for the most part young Giovanni Boccaccio himself) as no ineluctable celestial force but as a game played by the idle rich who have the time for such diversions. The poor who have their living to earn know nothing of it. Such games, she implies, need not be taken too seriously, and, as we have noted, she suggests later on in the story that if Fiammetta must have a lover, there are plenty available among the young gentlemen of Naples; it is foolish to waste time sighing for the treacherous Panfilo. It is in fact the nurse who incarnates the underlying intent of the author and who is, in herself, the clearest indication of the new direction of Boccaccio's interest. One cannot, strictly speaking, say that the nurse is of the working class; she is an affiliate, as it were, of the opulent family that she serves. She seems to have some classical education herself and is capable of sententious reflections on Fortune in the style of a philosopher. But *au fond* she is of the people and her presence in the story, particularly in combination with the prominence assigned to her, is significant. She is the first representative of her class to have a speaking part assigned to her in all the works of Boccaccio we have so far studied. (Pandaro, the counselor of Troiolo, has much the same pragmatically acceptant philosophy but he is of the upper level of society.) The nurse points the way to the democratic realism that will characterize the dominant chord of the *Decameron*.

The prose of the *Elegy* also shows a significant development. No doubt to a reader today it would still seem somewhat over-rhetorical and self-conscious; the sentences are long and the word order, following Latin patterns, would seem to us stilted. Fiammetta, who comes close to losing her mind, never loses her gift for sophisticated exposition structured with art—and perhaps a certain complacence. But if we compare this to the prose of *Filocolo*, elaborate and dense, or to that of the *Comedy of the Florentine Nymphs*, where the virtuosity of the author gives every period an all but labyrinthine complexity, the style of the *Elegy* will seem relatively straightforward and clear.[10] In manner as well as mood the *Elegy* points the way to Boccaccio's masterpiece: Russo calls it "the romance poetically closest to the *Decameron*.[11] It is significant that the distraught Fiammetta, seeking relief from her torments, likes to hear stories told—and participates herself in the exchange. Boccaccio will be thinking of her as he prepares his hundred tales.

CHAPTER 10

THE NYMPH SONG
OF FIESOLE

he *Nymph Song of Fiesole*, which through the years has enjoyed universal critical approval for its graceful charm, has for some time been the subject of debate among scholars with respect both to its attribution and its dating. Only one manuscript—and that a late one—attributes the poem to Boccaccio.[1] Furthermore, uniquely among the youthful works (and very uncharacteristically), the *Nymph Song* provides no overt autobiographical peg (such as an allusion to Fiammetta or the author's own circumstances) that would support definitive attribution. Critics today, although some with reservations, concur in accepting Boccaccio's authorship if only, as Muscetta remarks,[2] because it would be hard to think of any contemporary likely to have produced such a work. And if we are willing to assume that the poem is indeed Boccaccio's, we can then recognize in a few details a certain kinship with earlier fruits of the author's genius.

As to the dating, we have remarked elsewhere that the precise chronology óf the early works is impossible to determine. For years critical consensus had seen the *Nymph Song* as the last in the series of pre-*Decameron* works, dated circa 1346. This hypothesis has recently been challenged by P. G. Ricci, who would see the "poemetto" as a product of the Neapolitan experimental years, adducing as evidence the "popular" style of the octaves in which the poet narrates his idyll.[3] Armando Balduino, the most recent editor of the *Nymph Song*, discusses at some length the validity of Ricci's notion; he concludes by confessing that for him the later (traditional) date assigned to the work still seems preferable.[4] His strongest argument, and one that must appeal to the average reader, innocent of the subtleties of purely stylistic criticism, lies in the *mise-en-scène* of the poem. It has a Florentine (or Fiesolan) background; it tells the story of two rivers familiar to every Florentine; the little idyll may be seen in some sense as a patriotic glorification of the author's homeland. It is hard to see how such a theme and such a setting could have been expected to find a response in the circle of Neapolitan courtiers for whom the *Filocolo*, the *Caccia di Diana*, and the *Filostrato* were clearly intended.

The story line, like that of the *Elegy of Madonna Fiammetta*, is simple and uncomplicated, unbroken by subplots or erudite digressions. The action takes place in the golden age of prehistory when the slopes of Fiesole were inhabited by bands of virginal nymphs, all devotees of Diana. One day, as the goddess is holding council with her followers by a spring, now known as Fonte Aquelli, a young shepherd, Africo, "age twenty or a little less," chances to pass by and catch a glimpse of the winsome troop. One nymph in particular seizes his attention, and he falls immediately in love with her. She is about fifteen years old; she has curling blond tresses and Africo overhears one of her companions calling her "Mensola." When the nymphs depart Africo makes his way home, disconsolate; he has lost his heart to the maiden whom he may never see again. He retires to his little room without speaking to his aged parents and passes a sleepless night (1–41).

So for some time he languishes, but at last one night Venus, accompanied by Cupid, appears to him in a vision. Reproaching him for his lethargy, she bids him go forth and seek his beloved; at her command, Cupid pierces Africo's breast with an arrow that fixes his burning desire forever. He goes to look for Mensola and finds three nymphs bathing in a stream; they run off in fright, telling him nothing of Mensola; once more Africo comes home, where he finds his worried father awaiting him (42–72). Pressed by his father, Girafone, to explain his long absence, Africo says that he has been pursuing a doe over the hills. Girafone, suspecting the truth, bids his son beware, for the doe is assuredly the property of Diana; he relates that his own father,

Mugnone, had loved a nymph of Diana and had pursued and violated her; the goddess had caught him in the act and had slain both the nymph and her ravisher with one arrow. The stream by which Mugnone fell now bears his name. Africo promises he will abandon the search (73–97).

But he goes forth the following day and this time he comes upon Mensola. She takes flight at sight of him; he follows, imploring her to stay. She turns to hurl a javelin at him but even as she throws it their eyes meet and she cries out a warning. The javelin misses its mark; Africo, cheered by the implications of the nymph's cry of warning, continues his search for her but again in vain. Once more he returns disconsolate to his home (98–131). Hearing his lamentations, his mother, Alimena, comes to comfort him; he tells her he has had a bad fall and asks to be left alone. In his despair Africo calls on Venus to help him or on Death to release him. Alimena prepares a medicinal bath; Girafone repeatedly asks his son to reveal what ails him. For four days the youth pines, losing his color and inveighing against the cruelty of the nymph. The sight of his haggard features mirrored in a fountain distresses him; he compares his lot with the enjoyment of love that he observes in the flocks and the birds. He decides to sacrifice a lamb to Venus. The sacrificial lamb, cut in two parts, miraculously arises reintegrated in the fire; a clear token that Venus has heard Africo's prayer (132–193).

And, indeed, that night she appears to him again. She counsels him to clothe himself in female apparel and go forth disguised as a nymph. This trick will enable him to approach Mensola and Venus promises to aid him in his wooing. [Jove disguised himself as Diana to approach Callisto (see note 6 below); so, too, Achilles took advantage of the feminine garb in which his mother had clothed him to seduce Deidamia. But in Boccaccio's narrative, the scheme develops naturally out of the situation; the reader is hardly aware of sources unless he goes purposefully looking for them. In no other work of Boccaccio does the scholar so unobtrusively collaborate with the creative writer.] Africo steals a gown from his mother, provides himself with bow and arrows, and once more goes in search of Mensola. He finds her and her band engaged in hunting down a wild boar. Africo joins in the hunt and kills the boar; Mensola commends his skill. Africo also takes part in the nymphs' archery practice; Venus disposes that his arrow and Mensola's always hit closest to the mark; this, too, encourages Mensola's cordiality to him (194–222).

After their exercise the nymphs enjoy a simple meal, roasting the boar and other game, "prepared with neither spice nor sauce," over an open fire in a cavern. They drink from wooden cups water mixed with herbs and honey. Afterward all make their way to the mountain, Mensola still in the company of the disguised Africo. On reaching a stream all the nymphs undress and bathe. Africo waits until all are in the water, then he, too, strips and prepares to join them, thus revealing his sex. The nymphs flee in panic; Africo is, however, able to seize Mensola. She defends herself vigorously, but his strength prevails and at last, in the phrase of the author, "Sir Mace wins Mount Fig and enters the castle." [It is probably the description of Mensola's violation and later that of the second passionate coupling that leads Wilkins to comment: "If it were not for the execrably bad taste of a very few stanzas, the *Ninfale* would be one of the most charming of all idylls."[5] But the almost brutal portrayal of the lovemaking is an integral part of the ingenuous naturalism, capable of being both tender and coarse, that is at the root of "the simplicity and strength of the emotions"— in Wilkins's own admiring phrase—characteristic of the poem.]

In her despair the ravished nymph attempts to throw herself on her spear, but Africo prevents her and carries her off in a swoon to a grove. Thinking her dead, he is about to kill himself, but the nymph revives. Africo then tells her of his long-enduring love for her, asks pardon for his violence, and begs her to love him (223–277). Mensola forgives him but, still grieving for her lost virginity, refuses his invitation to go with him to his home. She promises to live and even to reciprocate his love. She assures him that she will come often to this spot to meet him but now she bids him leave her. Africo begs her to let him enjoy her embraces once more and reluctantly she consents, all unaware of the consequences of "love's couplings," and conceives a son. Night comes on and the lovers part; Africo puts on his man's garments again and makes his way back to his parents, who have been anxiously waiting for him. Mensola, meanwhile, goes her lonely way, terrified of the vengeance of Diana; she recalls the fate of Callisto[6] and the punishment accorded to the nymph violated by Mugnone (278–340).

The next day Africo hastens to the rendezvous but Mensola does not appear; although she now loves him, the fear of Diana has made her resolve never to see him again. After more than a month passes, Africo can no longer bear his torment; making his way to the side of the stream where he had taken Mensola, he bids farewell to his parents, charges the stream henceforth to bear his name, and impales himself on his spear (341–361). As the stream flows by Girafone's cottage, he notices its red hue; following upstream, he comes upon the body of his son. He brings it back to the stricken mother. Lamenting their loss, the grieving parents bury the ashes of their son on the bank of the stream that is now known by his name (362–372). Mensola rejoins the band of nymphs and resumes her old life, though she often thinks sadly and tenderly of Africo. She hopes that Diana will not learn of her defilement but after three months have passed, observing changes in her body, she consults an old nymph, Sinidecchia, and learns from her that she is pregnant. Sinidecchia, moved by the young nymph's innocence, promises to help her. She bids her remain in hiding until her delivery; Mensola obeys and is undetected by the other nymphs; she now regrets she did not keep her promise to meet Africo again; she looks for him, but in vain (373–400).

Diana comes back to visit her troupe and at the same time Mensola is delivered of her baby, assisted by the goddess of childbirth. Diana finds her playing with her child by the side of the river and, realizing that Mensola has lost her chastity, the goddess causes her to dissolve in the river, which ever since has been called after her, the Mensola. Diana takes the child to Sinidecchia; the latter, in turn, having learned from Mensola the name of her ravisher, takes it to Africo's parents. They are delighted to have the handsome boy, whom they called Pruneo (for he was found by Diana among the brambles), and they carefully bring him up to manhood (401–435).

Now, concluding the story, the author tells us that when Pruneo reached his eighteenth year, the legendary Atalante came to Tuscany and founded Fiesole. The nymphs were dispersed or forced to marry. Atalante took Girafone into his city and made Pruneo first his servant and then his seneschal. Pruneo, having achieved renown and begotten ten sons, died in old age, mourned by all (436–453). The narrative properly ends here with Boccaccio supplying a summary of Villani's history of Florence from its founding by the Romans to its reconstruction by Charlemagne after Totila had razed it to the ground (454–464). In an epilogue the author states that he has now fulfilled the command laid upon him by the one who had bestowed upon him the talent necessary to write his verses, that is Love, "whose servant I have always been and always wish to be" (465–466). He praises the power of Love and he prays that no ignorant or churlish person be allowed to read his book, which is intended for "the virtuous, the kindly and the meek." In the last stanzas Love accepts the book and assures the author that it will be kept from those who have never been Love's servants (467–473).

Critics have unanimously admired the simple but engaging narrative and the unpretentious and economical presentation of Boccaccio's pastoral idyll, "essentially a novella in form" as its twentieth-century translator Daniel Donno remarks.[7] If we may see a memory of Ameto (see chapter 7) in Africo's first encounter with the nymphs and a kind of generic affinity with *Diana's Hunt* in the background, yet the *Nymph Song* differs sharply from such works in its freedom from allegorical superstructure, enigmatic autobiographical allusions, and ponderous erudition. The story moves along at a good pace, events follow a logical sequence, descriptive passages are brief and effective; the work attests to a discipline heretofore wanting in the products of Boccaccio's pen. Momigliano rightly calls the *Nymph Song* the most homogeneous of the minor works;[8] from this point of view it is an improvement even over the *Elegy of Madonna Fiammetta*. As we read it today we may perhaps think Africo's groanings for love are a little prolonged, but such was the fashion of the times and, compared to Troiolo and Fiammetta, Africo seems almost laconic. It is true, too, if we look for faults in the construction of the poem, that the last stanzas move from the central narrative to an irrelevant capsule history of early Florence. But this is a slight blemish and indeed the Florentine postscript may be seen as an expression of the writer's pride in his Tuscan origins, a natural avowal if we think of the work as composed at a time when Boccaccio had come to accept Tuscany as his homeland.

The simplicity of the plot is matched by a matter-of-fact, almost "country style" treatment of descriptive detail. Diana is surrounded by no Olympian aura; Venus, even in the visions, speaks with an unaffected familiarity; Lucina, summoned from above to serve as midwife, does her duty as she might in any Italian hamlet and departs with no halo of divinity about her. The language of the poem and the tone of the dialogues are consistently simple, not to say "popular," as a number of critics have remarked. The unpolished, at times almost careless, composition of the ottava rima in which the poem is written resembles that of the *cantari* or ballads of street singers,[9] which likewise would blend legendary substance with popular realism, and suggests that Boccaccio had in mind an audience not of aristocrats or intellectuals, but of middle-class readers able to savor with a certain sophistication the charm of the narrative and the naturalism of its characters. A century later Boccaccio will find an appreciative listener in Lorenzo de' Medici, whose *Ambra* will carry on the message of the *Nymph Song* and bring it into the mainstream of the Renaissance pastoral.[10]

An appealing feature of the story is the realistic yet tender depiction of family relationships. The *Ninfale* is the most "familial" of Boccaccio's works. The solicitude of Africo's parents for their troubled boy is portrayed with warm and pervasive empathy and the joy of the old folks when the baby Pruneo is brought to them is as touching as it is convincingly described.[11] The *Filostrato,* as we observed, also had its moments of pleasantly naturalistic evocations of family life, but the sketches of little Pruneo either playing with his mother or delighting his doting grandparents are not found elsewhere in the earlier works. If there is an autobiographical source for such scenes, it may lie in the author's observation of his half brother, born about the same time as the idyll was composed (assuming the traditional dating is right);[12] it may even be of more intimate nature, as Hauvette suggested,[13] for it seems at least possible that 1346 was the year of the birth of one of Boccaccio's own illegitimate children. Whatever their inspiration, these appealing vignettes lend a special charm to the narrative. Mensola, too, with her innocent virginity, her fear-ridden pregnancy, and her conversion to joyous motherhood, seems drawn from life. Sapegno

is captivated by this unaffected girl-mother. "The figure of Mensola,"
he writes, "so new, so different from the coquettish Criseida and the
impassioned Fiammetta, resembling perhaps Biancifiore in the *Filocolo*
(but how much more alive!), offers to the poetry of Boccaccio a new
motif: motherhood," and accepted, as he goes on to say, not as a duty
or a responsibility but almost as a kind of novel and delightful game;
he quotes the account of the child's birth (stanzas 404–406):[14]

And so, one day, while hiding in her place,
all of a sudden Mensola began
to feel through all her body piercing pains.
The Goddess, then, of childbirth she invoked,
and a small infant boy was quickly born.
Lucina raised the baby from the ground,
tenderly placed him in her arms, and said,
"He will be great, some day," and so she fled.

Mensola's pains had been too fierce and vast,
too fierce and vast for a sweet, simple girl
who'd never been through such a deed before.
But when she saw that she had given birth
to such a lovely babe, her pains were gone.
As best she could, she made a tiny dress
for him at once, then suckled him at breast,
and kissed him, kissed him, unaware of rest.

Her baby was so darling and so dear,
so fair his face, he seemed a wonder new.
Curly and golden was his silken hair:
he was the perfect image of his sire.
Oh, look at him but once, and there you see
Africo in his eyes and in his brows.
So like his dad was he in every feature,
Mensola loved the more her newborn creature.

So much already did she love her child
she could not keep her gaze away from him.
Oh, not to lose a moment of her bliss,

she was unwilling to present her babe
even to Sinidecchia. Sweet illusion!
Africo seemed to be right there with her,
and so she played with him and, smiling glad,
with tender hand caressed his tiny head.[15]

In truth, the *Nymph Song* is *au fond,* not so much an idyll of the
Golden Age as a warm and only slightly idealized story of honest
country folk and adolescent love. Its directness and its tolerant empathy
prepare us for the *Decameron.* Erich Auerbach shrewdly remarks: "It
is in the intermediate idyllic style that [Boccaccio] wrote the last and
by far the most beautiful of his youthful works, the *Ninfale fiesolano*;
and the intermediate style serves, too, for the great book of the hundred
novelle."[16] In no other work of our author is matter wed more happily
to manner.

It must, however, be admitted that the *Nymph Song* would be a
better poem had it ended with the adoption of Pruneo by his grandparents. Hauvette defines the last forty ottave as a clumsy historical
appendix to an idyll;[17] Hollander, too, concedes these verses are
"hardly great literature, or even very good Boccaccio" although he
argues that the moral antithesis between the impassioned and egocentric Africo and the admirably disciplined Pruneo (who marries, has ten
children, and becomes a pillar of the establishment) is a significant part
of the author's intention.[18] Undeniably there is something palinodic in
the life and miracles of Pruneo (which would, however, hardly justify
the lengthy digest of Villani) yet this model of propriety owes his
being to a moment of unsanctioned and intemperate passion. Boccaccio's moralizing is always a little ambiguous. And whatever ethical
purpose we may see in the appendix, it will seem to most readers a
false note, a *stonatura.* Remembering the *Nymph Song*, our minds will
go back to the integrity of youthful passion, wherein, to quote Tusiani,
"sex is synonymous with innocence,"[19] and the evocative pastoral
setting, deftly and winningly woven. It is enough.

CHAPTER 11

THE CORBACCIO

he *Nymph Song*, as we have noted, in the general
opinion of scholars, was followed by the *Decameron*
approximately four years later. It will be convenient, however, to complete our discussion of the
minor creative works of our author with some
remarks on the *Corbaccio*, written well after the
Decameron; it is chronologically the last of Boccaccio's creative works
and, save for the items dealing with Dante, the last of his works written
in the vernacular. As in so many other cases, the exact date to be
assigned to the composition of this brief but pungent fantasy (it runs
to about seventy-five octavo pages) is uncertain and has recently
become a matter of some controversy. If we may identify the protagonist of the tale with its author, we may assume the work was composed
about 1355, for in the course of the narrative, the protagonist is defined
as being some forty years out of swaddling clothes at the time of the
vision he is permitted to have and to report. In this case the *Corbaccio*
would be the product of the years shortly after the completion of the
Decameron. Recently, Giorgio Padoan has suggested that a date a
decade later should be postulated;[1] his notion has not met with general
approval, however, and P. G. Ricci, whose edition of the work appeared in 1965, rejects it.[2] Anthony K. Cassell, whose translation of the
work into English (1975) is accompanied by a useful introduction and
copious notes, finds the earlier date "more plausible,"[3] and I think with
good reason. Not only is the reference to "forty years out of swaddling

clothes" too pointed to overlook, but the texture of the prose and the vigor of the exposition seem closely akin to what we find in the *Decameron*— there is, further, a thematic link between the two works, of which we shall have more to say. But whichever date we choose to accept, the *Corbaccio* is the last excursus into the field of fiction on the part of our inventive author.

Perhaps even more puzzling than the date is the meaning of the title of the work; some scholars have taken the word as borrowed from the Spanish *corbacho*, signifying "scourge," which is quite appropriate to the tone of the content, as we shall see; others see it as meaning "dirty crow," intended as a designation of the unhappy and anonymous woman who is the target of the author's vituperative attacks. The latter meaning is accepted, and convincingly defended, by Cassell.[4]

The narrative is prefaced by a very brief *proemium*, of a pious solemnity that is in sharp contrast to the worldly affability of the foreword to the *Decameron*. Anyone who is silent about benefits received, the author asserts, is thankless and ungrateful. For his part, he intends to reveal in the following "humble treatise" a special grace granted him by the Virgin, who interceded for him. The treatise will manifest his gratitude and it may very well also prove beneficial to others. The author hopes that God will so direct his hand that the work may redound to the honor and glory of His Holy Name and therewith be of use and consolation to its readers. This is the author's sole reason for writing it.

The tale is told by a protagonist who does not identify himself either by name or nation. He begins by telling the reader of the deep depression into which he fell after being rejected by his lady. He was indeed close to doing away with himself and was restrained only by the thought that such an act would probably please his faithless charmer. Drying his tears, he tells us, he went forth to find solace in the company of friends. After which, much restored, he returned to his chamber and retired to rest. And in his sleep, Fortune sent him a vision that he will share with us.

In his dream he seems to find himself standing on a beautiful path in a countryside he could not identify. The path lures him on and he follows it eagerly but, as he progresses, pleasant grass gives way to thorns and brambles and the way becomes rough. At a certain point, looking back, he can see a dense fog coming up; it soon envelops him in impenetrable darkness. By the time the fog has thinned night has come on and, looking about him, the wayfarer (we shall henceforth call him *A,* since he chooses to be anonymous) can see about him a wild and savage landscape and on his terrified ears fall the roars and growlings of what must be savage beasts. Unable to move, *A* can only deplore his ill-judged entrance into the wasteland and call upon God for help.

The aura of the *selva selvaggia* of the *Inferno* is perceptible in this passage and Marga Cottino-Jones feels, too, that "the whole vision of the labyrinth of love seems to set off remarkable suggestions of Dante's sestina 'Al poco giorno e al gran cerchio d'ombra,' one of the *canzoni pietrose* ["stony odes"] centered on sexual imagery."[5] For what it is worth we may observe that the image of a woodland, first seductive and then menacing, is found in one of Petrarch's letters (*Sen.* 4.5) and with overt allegorical intention. "At first the wood which images this life of ours," he says, "is attractive, but the deeper you penetrate, the more thorny and tangled the jungle becomes." Of course, as Curtius notes, "straying in a wood is a motif of the French romance of chivalry"[6]—and probably ultimately folkloristic; one has only to re- call the tale of Hansel and Gretel where, as here, the forest is first seductive and then dangerous.

As if in answer to his prayer, looking toward the east, *A* sees coming toward him a solitary man, tall, gaunt, rather forbidding in appearance, and wearing a cloak of glowing vermilion. *A* observes the stranger's approach with fear, but as he draws nearer, *A* notes that his aspect is gentle and also vaguely familiar. While he is trying to recall the stranger's name, the latter addresses him by his own and asks how he came to be in such a wild place. *A* replies that he has been led astray by "the false pleasure of transient things"; he begs the stranger to help him find his way out of the woods. The stranger replies that *A*'s presence in the forest is indeed evidence of mad distraction; had he but considered the nature of those eyes by whose light (once so dear to the stranger himself) he had first entered upon the path, he would not have presumed to ask for help. (A somewhat tortuous way of identifying himself as the husband of the woman who had driven *A* to distraction.) But, the red-cloaked figure continues, since he has been banished from mortal life, wrath has given way to charity and he is disposed to help *A*.

On learning that he is addressing a ghost, *A* is seized with terror; only the paralysis of fright prevents him from running off. But the ghost smiles and reiterates his desire to be helpful. He cannot, he says, lead *A* out of the woods at once, for the place where he now finds himself is easy to enter but difficult to leave; one must first learn fortitude and wisdom. Since he cannot immediately depart, *A* requests permission to ask a few questions of his spectral friend. First, he would know the nature of the place and who it was that dispatched the ghost to his rescue. The ghost replies that the place is variously styled, "the Labyrinth of Love," "the Pigsty of Venus," and "the Valley of Sighs and Woes" (all signifying the sad captivity into which lovers fall). The ghost adds that he himself does not dwell there, for it is a place meant only for the living; his own abode is "harsher but less dangerous." Harsher because of its torments; for example his bright cloak is woven not of cloth but of fire. He is condemned to dwell there because of two sins in his lifetime: his greed for money and the unbecoming tolerance with which he endured his wife's excesses. Yet the place in which he dwells (clearly Purgatory) is less dangerous than the wood because all the inhabitants of his region are sure of ultimate salvation. And as to who sent him: he has come at God's command. This favor has been vouchsafed to *A* because of the contrition he has always shown for his sins and his devotion to the Virgin Mary, who has intervened for him.

After expressing his gratitude and his hope that the Virgin may yet lead him to eternal life, *A* asks if this gloomy valley is reserved only for those who have been banished from the Court of Love. With pity for *A*'s ignorance, the ghost replies that this *is* the Court of Love, though it were better called a labyrinth, since it is not easy to find a way out. He adds that the growls that troubled *A* during the night were emitted by the ensnared lovers, whose utterances sound like bestial noises to the ears of sensible men. The ghost says that *A* should have recognized the place for what it was since this was by no means his first visit. Abashed, *A* admits the charge; his only excuse is that he was so terrified that he did not realize where he was. The ghost then suggests that they sit down and converse until light comes to guide them. Their conversation should be frank and open, he says, nor should *A* be embarrassed because the woman of his obsession is the ghost's widow. *A* points out that since she was a widow before he met her, he has done the ghost no wrong.

A then describes his first meeting with the lady. A friend had described her to him as being uniquely attractive, generous, sensible, eloquent, charming, and ready to admire masculine prowess. So *A*'s desire to see her had been aroused. He made his way to a place where he hoped to find her and recognized her at once, although she was dressed very simply in black with a white wimple. As he observed her walking and talking with her friends, his admiration grew. He wrote her a letter discreetly expressing his devotion and received a somewhat ambiguous reply. He noted that the style and language hardly justified his friend's opinion of the lady's eloquence; even so, with undiminished ardor, he wrote her again, and this time there was no reply. But what caused *A*'s distress was his learning that the woman had shown his letter to her lover, one Absalom, and together they had mocked him. Absalom, further, had spread the story abroad, thus making *A* a laughing-stock for the public. Finally, he had seen the woman pointing him out with derision as her would-be lover. It was this that had embittered him and driven him into a state of suicidal despair.

The ghost then announces his intention to speak at some length "for the sake of your salvation and perhaps another's." He will speak first of *A* himself, then of the object of his infatuation, and finally of the underlying causes of his wretched state. He begins by reproving *A* for letting himself be entrapped. For, he says, *A* is "now some forty years out of swaddling clothes" and the pursuit of love is unseemly for a mature man; it is, like dancing, jousting, and such things, suitable only to youth. In the second place, he notes that *A* had always been a man devoted to study; he had always scorned commerce and "more zealously than his father would have wished" had dedicated himself to scholarship and poetry. And his studies should have taught him the truth about love and about himself. For, as wise men should know, love is a passion that blinds the spirit, warps the intellect, robs one of memory, and wastes both health and wealth; it is "a thing without reason or order" and "the vice of unhealthy minds." History proves all this. Yet there are wretched mortals like A who think of it as a god and even pray to it.

His studies, too, the ghost continues, should have taught A the true nature of woman, "an imperfect creature, abominable to speak of." On this topic the ghost discourses at length. With picturesque, vigorous, and frequently coarse illustration, he demonstrates that women are dirty and bent on seducing men with the aid of tricks and cosmetics; they are likewise vain, greedy, contentious, irritable, fickle, false, and interminably garrulous. And they pass on their arts and deceits to their daughters. They like to point out in their pride that the Virgin was a woman, but, says the ghost, the Virgin is unique and only a mere handful of women follow her example. Man, God's direct creation, is a superior being; indeed, "the lowest man in the world, provided he has not lost the good of the intellect, is worth more than any woman, held, temporarily, to excel all other women." A's studies should have taught him as much and should further have taught him respect for himself as a scholar. He should have sought out not public places but solitary spots more suitable for thought; the Muses would have provided far more fitting company and consolation than womankind. "For," he adds, "the Muses will neither desert you nor deride you . . . they will not ask you to consider how many coals are needed to boil a skein of coarse flax, whether Viterbo linen is finer than that of Romagna, whether the baker's wife keeps the oven too hot or if the maid has given the dough enough time to rise. They won't tell you what Mrs. So-and-So and Mrs. Such-and-Such did last night or how many Our Fathers they said during the sermon; they won't ask you whether a dress should be worn with new accessories or be left as it is. They won't ask you for money to buy cosmetics, powder jars or skin creams." He concludes by warning A to be careful lest the Muses banish him since he turns so readily to women.

The ghost now moves to specific comment on his sometime wife and the source of A's present anguish. He had married her, he says, after the death of his first wife with whom he had been "less unhappy." The woman, too, had been married before and so came to him already well skilled in wifely wiles. She entered his house with the meekness of a dove but soon changed into a serpent. She tyrannized over the household; when crossed she would remind him of her family's nobility (concerning which the ghost seems to have some doubts). She spent lavishly and tried to get her hands on all the money that came into the family. Indeed, says the ghost, ironically, in her way, she displayed all the virtues A's friend found in her. She made herself "attractive" by eating and drinking copiously (to make herself "plump-cheeked and big-bottomed" as fashion required) and by spending hours and treasures on cosmetics, coiffures, and the like. She was never happy unless she was the center of attention; she expected every man's eye to follow her. Such were the praiseworthy habits mentioned by A's friend. She took not one but many lovers and was not reluctant to spend money (her husband's money, of course) on go-betweens or lavish presents for her lovers—such was her "generosity." And courteous she was, too, if by that we mean that she never said no to a lover; only God's providence saved A from being readily accepted, says the ghost. Her "wisdom" had nothing to do with theology, law, or politics; with respect to such matters she was as indifferent as she was ignorant, but she was "wise" in the wisdom esteemed by her circle— in the techniques of manipulating love affairs. Yes, and it is true that she admired men of prowess; but for her prowess had no application to the battlefield, it was of the kind displayed in the bedroom. Nor is it surprising that she should praise "eloquence" and admire "great speakers" since her own tongue was never still and she was always ready to tell anyone what was going on in the world, "whether Queen Joan slept last night with the King" or what the Florentines were planning for their city (which wouldn't be too hard considering none of the counselors can keep a secret) nor would she allow anyone to argue with any statement she made.

The ghost pauses in his analysis here to explain that the coarse and strong language he is now preparing to use is unavoidable. Doctors are often obliged to prescribe foul remedies for a serious illness and there is no sickness more in need of purging than that of love. With this apology he launches on a description of his former wife's physical characteristics, lingering at some length on the items of female anatomy normally concealed from view and with a scurrilous relish that John A. Symonds found "disgusting."[7] Nor would one have to be a Victorian to concur. Here and elsewhere the violence of the diatribe is so outrageous as to verge on burlesque, lending plausibility to the ingenious thesis of J. P. Barricelli, who argues that in this work Boccaccio is satirizing misogyny no less than womankind.[8] And indeed it is true, as he points out, that if the woman of the story is an object of contempt, neither the dreamer nor the ghost, objectively considered, is much to be admired; rather than wisdom, their discourse bespeaks the rancor of the rejected. Within the terms of the *Corbaccio* itself Barricelli's argument is appealing; less so if taken with consideration of the works that precede and follow it.

Finally, the ghost concludes, so great was the misery the woman caused him to suffer that it brought him to his death. Once the woman found herself a widow, she laid hands on her husband's estate, robbing his other heirs of their due. She also made a great show of grief and left his house to take up her residence in a little cottage near a church, ostensibly for pious reasons but actually to facilitate her lecherous projects; she knew, too, that should all else fail, she would have the friars, "notorious consolers of widows," readily available. She uses the church as a "baited trap" to ensnare young men. She does little praying but much reading of French romances: Tristram, Lancelot, Fleur and Blanchefleur. Recently, in addition to her other conquests, she has taken Absalom for her lover—poor fool, did he but know it, he has been cuckolded himself [one suspects, by the ghost before he became such].

In conclusion the ghost reveals that he is very familiar with the woman's shabby treatment of *A.* He discloses that it is sometimes permitted souls in his condition to revisit their old homes. On one such visit he had found his widow lying in bed with her lover; he had seen her get up and fetch *A*'s letter, had heard the pair deride its writer, and had seen Absalom composing the woman's answer. But the ghost points out that *A* had only himself to blame if he was foolish enough to put any trust in women. Furthermore, he adds sharply, *A* himself was hardly in good faith; if he truly believed the woman was modest and virtuous, he would never have hoped to win her; his hopes were based on an assumption of her weakness. But, after all, it is well for him that he did not win her; she would have brought him neither health nor wealth but only evil. In fact, A had more to offer her than she had for him. For he is, first of all, a man and therefore her superior; he is as handsome as she is (even though she paints and adorns herself while he rarely even washes his face); she is "ahead of him" only in being his senior. And as for the nobility she vaunts, it is not true nobility, the source of which is in virtue alone, but false nobility based on family pride and wealth, all of it earned by violence and rapine.

A has listened with bowed head and remorseful heart. He thanks the ghost for his edifying discourse but he adds that his own state is worse than before, for he now realizes the enormity of his sin and despairs of forgiveness. But the ghost reassures him that God's mercy is infinite and, furthermore, A's sin sprang not from malice but ignorance. He suggests that A may make amends by completely reversing his line of conduct; henceforth, he should not love but instead hate the woman's beauty and attraction, and love only the salvation of her soul. He should no longer seek her out but, on the contrary, avoid her. Finally, the ghost suggests that A write about the woman and expose her deceitfulness and wickedness; his talent for writing is well known and such a work could serve a useful purpose. It could warn others of the woman's evil ways and it could humble her, thus leading to her salvation. A vows that he will write such a work if he is granted the time; he will so vituperate the woman's baseness that she will wish she had never seen him.

A then asks why the ghost was chosen to rescue him from the labyrinth; the latter answers that any soul in Purgatory would be eager to help and many were more competent than he. But he was chosen for the office probably because his connection with the woman would assure A's shame in his presence and consequently his willingness to listen; furthermore, his experience supplied him with details known only to him. A asks what he can do for the ghost; the answer is merely to give alms and have masses offered for him. The ghost then points out a light rising in the east and says the time for parting has come.

The light advances, forming a luminous path stretching before the pair. They follow it and ascend a lofty mountain; looking back, *A* can see how dark and dismal the valley truly is. The ghost says that *A* is now free to leave and as *A* turns to thank him, his rescuer vanishes and simultaneously the dream ends.

Waking, bathed in a sweat, *A* goes to tell his friends of his vision. All agree with him in his interpretation and he firmly decides to give up his infatuation for the woman. In a few days he is completely recovered; he then resolves so to chastise her with words that she will never again "show a letter sent to her without remembering my letter and my name with pain and shame." In a brief "conclusion" Boccaccio charges his book to be useful, especially to young men who set out unguided through unsafe places, trusting too much in themselves. His book is to eschew evil women, especially the one who has been the cause of its composition; she would ill receive it. She is, however, "to be pricked by the sharpest goad you carry with you and God grant it may wound her swiftly and fearlessly."

Such is the substance of this atrabilious cautionary tale, a strange account indeed to hear from the lips of one who in the *Decameron* had openly and aggressively avowed his admiration for womankind. So marked is the change of direction that some scholars in recent years have labored to depersonalize the narrative, as it were; that is, to revise the traditional view that the theme of the *Corbaccio* is autobiographical and born of the author's disillusioning experience at the hands of a frivolous woman. It is argued that the *A* of the story is not so much Giovanni Boccaccio as a kind of Everyman, and that the *Corbaccio* is a literary exercise, another in the long list of misogynistic tracts current in the Middle Ages. Proponents of this theory have no difficulty in pointing out that much of the invective is made up of more or less direct quotation from Juvenal and a half a dozen medieval authorities of antifeminist bias.[9] Yet even granting that many of the spices are borrowed, one cannot but wonder why a writer would go to the trouble of preparing such a sauce unless he had some good reason for it. If the arguments are borrowed, the emotion need not be so—nor does it seem to be—and if the sentiments are personal, it seems most likely that they were motivated by personal experience.

We may well see in the *Corbaccio*, as P. G. Ricci does, a product of the "great psychological crisis" the author suffered about the time of his forty-fifth birthday, a crisis to which contributed, in no small degree, "the mortification suffered in matters of love, when he, a citizen to be honored and respected, saw himself pointed out as an object of ridicule."[10] And indeed the internal evidence, taken at face value, strongly supports the "autobiographical" interpretation. The anonymous protagonist is described as being about forty-five years of age, as one who has won fame as a writer and has previously sung of love, and as a man who from his birth has consistently despised commerce and wooed the Muses. If "Everyman" is not Giovanni Boccaccio, the resemblance is certainly striking. It is, tangentially, interesting to note how closely the details of the narrative parallel those of the seventh story of the eighth day of the *Decameron*. There, too, a scholar is mocked by a woman, who shares his letter with another lover. Save for a more moderate tone, it is the same story and it has an intensity of commitment that cannot fail to suggest "autobiographical" inspiration. The reader is certainly encouraged to believe that Boccaccio was in fact deeply wounded by an unappreciative woman —and one hard to forget.

Many elements of the design of the *Corbaccio* are familiar to us; one may say the work clearly bears the author's trademark. As in a number of the other works, we have here, too, a story within a story. The pattern of a vision is hardly new either; aside from being a standard medieval formula it recalls specifically the *Amorosa visione* and is also, like that work, charged with echoes of the *Divine Comedy*; the lonely and frightened wayfarer, the dark wood, the appearance of the ghostly comforter, the light of salvation at the end of the journey, and various minor echoes in the phraseology and *mise-en-scène*. The long monologue of the ghost is distantly related to the confessions of Caleon in the *Filocolo*. In which connection it is interesting to note the palinodic verdict on the romance of Florio and Biancifiore, the first source of the young Boccaccio's narrative inspiration, is here viewed with contempt. In the matter of style there is much to commend in the *Corbaccio*; the manner is at times a little prolix and discursive, but in general is marked by a vivacity that suggests the rhythm and fiber of the *Decameron*. Sallies of pure—or almost pure—humor are not lacking; here, for example, is one of the weaknesses of womankind illustrated with comic effectiveness:

> So that they may appear loving to those for whom in fact they care little, each one will spend the night berating her husband: "yes, indeed I can see how much you love me—why, I'd be blind if I didn't notice there is someone much dearer to you than I am. Do you think me a fool? Don't you think I know whom you're in love with and go chasing after and talk with every day? I do, all right; I have better spies than you think. Poor me! A long time I've been in this house and not since the first time have you ever said 'welcome, my love' when I have joined you in bed. But by God's Holy Cross I vow I'll treat you as you are treating me. I'm skinny, am I? And not so pretty as you-know-who? Well, you know what I mean; to one who kisses two mouths one must stink. No—stay away from me; so help me God, you'll not touch me. Go chasing after those you deserve; you certainly don't deserve me. Go and show yourself for what you are. You'll get what's coming to you. Remember you didn't pick me out of the mud. When I think of the men and the kind of men who would have taken me without a dowry and counted themselves lucky! And to you I actually gave money!"[11]

It is in the buoyant naturalism of such passages that the kinship of the *Corbaccio* and Boccaccio's masterpiece is readily perceptible; save for the remorseless savagery of its antifeminism, the *Corbaccio* might have fitted very well into the hundred tales; in fact, the passage quoted above is cut of the same cloth with which the emancipated wife of Ricciardo di Chinzica cloaks her waywardness (Day 2, Story 10). Yet it is to be stressed that the difference is significant: for the enterprising Bartolomea of the *Decameron* the reader feels and is meant to feel sympathy, albeit tinged with amusement; for the false and guileful woman of the *Corbaccio* only distaste and disgust are elicited. Granting that womanhood is occasionally criticized and even castigated in the course of the *Decameron*'s copious and variegated pages, yet the dominant chord of the work is anything but misogynistic. The like may be said of every other product of the lady-loving author; if occasionally, in the minor theme, as it were, we are warned of the deceits of unworthy women, yet the faith in true love—and therewith in a loyal woman—never wavers. The *Corbaccio*, on the other hand, might well be entitled *De contemptu mulierum*. The repudiation of love is pointed up, no doubt intentionally, by the palinodic confrontation of Muses and women; in the *Decameron* the author had expressly stated his preference for the latter. Now, bringing them once more into rivalry, he opts for the Muses. The change of attitude will be permanent, too; we shall have no further works singing the praises of the fair sex from this *quondam* devotee of Venus.

If it is true, as Boccaccio's contemporary Ludovico Bartoli (who set the *Corbaccio* into ottava rima) assures us, that the author later came to regard his work with scorn[12] this argues no repudiation of the negative attitude toward love and womankind. (For that matter, the repentant Boccaccio would have, in the season of pious renunciation, also consigned the *Decameron* to the flames.) In fact, the works yet to come seem to testify to a kind of wearied indifference to love, ladies, and romance. It is in this sense that the *Corbaccio* may be the most significantly "autobiographical" of all Boccaccio's works; under the veil of the narrative a kind of conversion seems to be avowed. As Marga Cottino-Jones remarks: "What had been in the *Decameron* and in Boccaccio's earlier works a wholehearted admiration for natural love and spontaneous physical attraction, becomes in the *Corbaccio* a stern condemnation of love. . . . The natural human values, cherished and enjoyed in the *Decameron,* are here abandoned in favor of a totally absorbing commitment to spiritual and intellectual perfection."[13]

Perhaps the positive "commitment" is not quite as obvious as the repudiation side of the medal, but however we may define it a change of course is clearly indicated. The reader may well contemplate the new Boccaccio with a little sadness. For the "commitment to spiritual and intellectual perfection," in sober truth, will not lead the reformed servant of love to the composition of deeply moving confessional or religious works but only to the compilation of encyclopedias. Recognizing the scholarly merits of the *De casibus*, the *Genealogie*, and *De mulieribus claris* and the service they performed for generations to come, one may deplore their cost: the extinction of the joyous, creative spirit. Never again will the genius of the artist, love-inspired, create for us a Troiolo or a Fiammetta or a Mensola.

Finally, we may remark that this little work, although lively and robust in its own right (however much of its substance may be derivative) has failed to have—unlike so many other products of its creator —any notable influence on subsequent letters. For one thing, although antifeminism is a recurrent motif in the world of letters, the misogynistic tirade as such has never become a recognized genre; romance and gallantry had a much stronger appeal during the centuries that immediately followed Boccaccio's time. For another thing, well, articulate, and erudite woman-haters had either their own experiences or other and older models to turn to. Succeeding generations had much to learn from the *Filostrato* and the *Teseida*; invective, happily for us, is not widely cultivated by creative writers—and embittered scholars always have Juvenal.

CHAPTER 12

RHYMES

n 1364, as we have noted in chapter 2, Boccaccio, in an excess of repentance for the waywardness of his early years, consigned to the flames the lyrical compositions of his youth. It is possible to question the efficacy of this pious gesture since many of his verses had long been in circulation and had been copied and preserved in manuscripts not in the author's possession. Nor did his new austerity prevent him from returning to court the lyric muse in later life, although it must be admitted that the substance of the rhymes written in old age is different from that of the youthful lines and no longer hymns the praises of Lord Love. How many items are lost to us forever through the austere decision of their composer we shall never know. Perhaps not so very many. But the author's impetuous action created a serious problem for his editors. In the years since the death of the poet, scholars and men of letters have collected as best they could the items that escaped the flames, piecing together from manuscripts and old anthologies the fragments of the doomed *Canzoniere*. Two editions of the *Rhymes* have appeared in the twentieth century, the first by Aldo Francesco Massèra[1] and the second by Vittore Branca.[2] Massèra lists 126 compositions as certainly attributable to Boccaccio (Branca definitely rejects two of these and has strong reservations about three others); he prints another 19 of doubtful attribution (to this section Branca adds a dozen more that he believes have an equally good claim to legitimacy).

Massèra's arrangement of the poems follows what he believes to be the correct chronological sequence; his disposition of the verses has in general some support from tradition. Although Branca, out of respect for the tradition and having in mind the convenience of scholars, reproduces Massèra's order in his edition, he pointedly affirms that his predecessor's arrangement follows an ideal but arbitrary biography of the poet and "represents the acme of the biographical mania"[3] of the old school of Boccaccian criticism. Yet Branca refrains from suggesting his own arrangement; he considers his edition still tentative and leaves the improved ordering to the scholar yet to come who will give us the definitive edition. Branca is right when he remarks that Boccaccio had never given any indication of an intention to bring his scattered verses into an organic unity (in marked contrast to the procedure of his master Petrarch) but rather had meant them to be read as individual compositions. Indeed, Massèra is of the same opinion but feels bound to seek for chronological order. It is hardly his fault if such an order suggests a planned *canzoniere*; indeed, an editor is bound to look for some systematic method of presenting his subject's verses. And if Massèra's disposition is "arbitrary" it is still valuable to the student and the reader; until we have more information on dates of composition and more certainty in the matter of authenticity, an "ideal" biography provides a useful pattern for a consideration of the lyrics.

Let us begin with the group regarded as authentic. Of these, 113 in Massèra's edition are sonnets (Branca is unwilling to accept 2 of them), another 3 are sonnets "tailed" with a rhyming couplet (Branca attributes one of these to Petrarch), and one is a one-line fragment that may or may not be part of a sonnet. The collection further contains 4 *ballate*, 2 madrigals (short verse forms of fixed patterns), a *sirventese* (a "catalog" in verse) in terza rima, another composition in terza rima (not accepted as authentic by Branca), and the first stanza of a sestina.

The first sixty-nine items compose the "Fiammetta section." In number 6, her name is mentioned and it seems reasonable to assume, given the close association of motifs, biographical or fictional, that the same seductive lady is the subject of all of these poems. Perhaps the very first sonnet is an exception; one may agree that this "charming fantasy," as an older critic describes it,[4] portraying a kind of pastoral allegory, indicates a maturity of technique that would suggest it should come later in the sequence. But certainly beginning with sonnet 2, wherein the poet describes the occasion of his enamorment in Petrarchan style, the trajectory suggested seems plausible. The first eighteen numbers are charged with the idealism associated with Dante's followers of the *dolce stil nuovo*; the lady is an "angiolella" in sonnet 2 and an "angela o ninfa o dea" in sonnet 4. Echoes of Dante and Petrarch are, not surprisingly, frequent[5] (some manuscripts, in fact, attribute sonnet 2 to Petrarch). In sonnet 9 both masters are present; the tone of the poem is Dantean while the lady it sings of has the "golden, curling tresses" of Laura.

Themes and motifs common to all practitioners of "courtly love" are to be found in these presumably early efforts: the heavenly beauty of the lady, her elevating charm, the awesome power of Love and its ennobling virtue, the willing submission of the lover; in sum, the attitudes recommended by Andreas Capellanus and assumed by love poets of the preceding generations. It is fair to say, however, that if the thematic substance of these verses is hardly novel and stylistic and verbal echoes of Dante and Petrarch abound, yet there are details of individuality if not originality. There are a number of sonnets celebrating Fiammetta's beautiful voice and we find, too, a subcluster depicting the lady against a marine background, suggestive of the scenery of the *Elegy of Madonna Fiammetta*; for that matter, the reminiscences of Dante and Petrarch are matched by phrases and descriptive items that call to mind Boccaccio's own works, notably the *Elegy*, the *Amorosa visione*, and *Diana's Hunt*.

The idealistic tone is maintained consistently through sonnet 18, which might have been written by an authentic disciple of the "sweet new style." Indeed, the first quatrain

> When I look on you, lady fair and dear
> I feel a sweetness pouring through my eyes
> of virtue such that I cannot but feel
> it drives all bitter passion from the heart

would not be out of place in the *Vita nuova*. But in the last line for the first time the poet dares ask for something—only, to be sure, to be allowed to bring pleasure to such a rare creature—but as Massèra points out, "desire is becoming materialized,"[6] and in the following sonnet he begs her for "a sigh," that is to say, her *compassio*. After this Laura is no longer identifiable with Beatrice. In number 34 the poet begins to have a premonition of misery, and the theme of unsatisfied desire and its concomitant torments is dominant through the next thirty sonnets, some of them given a realistic color by references to the corrupting Neapolitan background or by chronological allusions—in number 47 he speaks of having wasted five years in love service—and all of them charged with reminiscences of Petrarch, either in concept or language or both. In number 36 the lady has become the poet's "enemy," and in number 50 the lover enumerates the various ways he could put an end to himself.

With number 55 a new stage begins; the poet accepts all his suffering and rejoices because the lady has at last given him her "saluto" and hope of something more. In number 58 he senses what by number 59 he has learned: that a lover should never despair. "Love has now changed my sighs to song," he proclaims. He is sad once more in the little sequence of 60 through 62 because Fiammetta has gone to Baia and he may not accompany her, but in 63 he, too, is permitted entrance into that earthly paradise and celebrates it with a joyous sonnet. (His song is introduced by a catalog of mountains that takes up all the first eight lines; all the great peaks of history are compared unfavorably with Misenus, the background hill of Baia. The device may be an imitation of Petrarch's similar river catalog [*Rhymes* 148]; but Boccaccio's list certainly adumbrates the "scholarly" *De montibus* of his later years.) In number 65 he is again uneasy, fearing that the air of Baia may corrupt his lady, and in numbers 66 through 68 he speaks of the pain he feels when he is obliged to take leave of her. Massèra would associate these verses with the departure of Boccaccio from Naples for Florence in 1340. But for the kind of appendix of three sonnets of which we shall speak presently, the verses would seem to close out the Fiammetta cycle.

Certainly 69, the *sirventese* in terza rima, marks a break. In this exercise, running to seventy lines, the poet sings the charms of a dozen fair ladies, all of Florentine families. It is a kind of pocket version of *Diana's Hunt*, although the allegory is not really developed. It may well have been written with the same purpose in mind as that which must have, at least in part, motivated the *Hunt*; that is, to assert poetically the writer's familiarity with the aristocratic circles, the "right people" as it were, of a new environment. A number of the ladies of the *sirventese* appear again (or is it concurrently?—one cannot date the poem with precision) in the *Ameto* and the *Amorosa visione*. Assuredly, Naples is behind us. The *sirventese*, incidentally, is followed by a graceful *ballata* (of the same stamp as the poems that will round out the days of the *Decameron*) in which the ladies sing of their devotion to all-powerful Love.

One may perhaps speculate about Massèra's placing of the *sirventese*. Ideally, one feels, it should follow and not precede the three successive items (as Massèra prints them) in which the poet records an unhappy experience in Baia; in succession he curses the town, his own eyes for the sights they have seen, and Love itself. According to Massèra, "this trio of embittered reproaches—clearly a sub-sequence, since all the sonnets refer to the same disillusioning incident—may be thought of as composed in 1343 or 1344,"[7] on the occasion of the poet's return to Naples, when, presumably, he found Fiammetta playing him false. There is, however, no firm evidence for such a return, nor for that matter does it seem likely that Boccaccio's intense passion for Fiammetta would still be burning so brightly after his awestruck contemplation of the bevy of Florentine beauties enumerated in the *sirventese*. They would seem much more appropriate as recording the last stage in the infatuation of the young poet for the beguiling siren of his youth. (To be sure, he will return to "Fiammetta," but she will be no longer the living woman but a figure of idealized memory.)

Number 80, a sonnet, introduces a new current. In tones so suggestive of Petrarch's that the poem has been by some scholars attributed to his master, Boccaccio sadly comments on his age—he is now thirty-five—and the wasted years behind him. Yet he avows he cannot shake off the shackles of Love. But now it is no longer love of Fiammetta, as the following nine sonnets make clear, but for another woman, apparently a widow. It is not unreasonable to see in this charmer, who brings her lover no joy but only frustration, the mature seductress of the *Corbaccio*. Sonnet 89, in fact, echoes the virulent misogynism of that acidulous work, asserting that there is no madness as great as that of a man who voluntarily subjects himself to a woman. Perhaps it is the melancholy born of such love despair that is responsible for the cycle of poems 92–95, in which the poet, in tones reminiscent of Dante, deplores the social condition of the contemporary world, wherein justice, virtue, and the cult of letters may no longer thrive.

In number 96 he dedicates himself to Phoebus as the only guiding light left to him—which is to say that only the cult of poetry can console us for the sorry state of things. Sonnets 97–106 may be seen as composing the section "in morte di Fiammetta." In this sequence, which, again, clearly follows the Petrarchan design and yet seems to refer to a personal experience, Boccaccio has first a premonition of his lady's death and then a series in which he sees her in Heaven, now reconciled and affectionately disposed toward her follower. Particularly close to Petrarch's example is sonnet 101, wherein Fiammetta urges her liege man to look upward and aspire to join her.

Number 106 is interesting for its realistic allusion to the obesity with which Boccaccio was afflicted in his later years: "It seems to me, as my thoughts wander, that I have lost that heaviness which weighs me down and have even as a bird, raised myself to Heaven." In number 108 he regrets, rather touchingly and with his characteristic modesty, that his art never merited the award of the laurel—thus disclosing to us that he would have welcomed a formal coronation. Visions of the sanctified lady give way to more generalized reflections on the poet's wasted years and the fragility of mortal things (numbers 109–113) and the cycle closes with a half a dozen items of purely religious nature. In 114 the poet bids his soul turn to God; in 115 he asks for Christ's mercy; in 116 he prays that God may prepare him for eternal life and concludes—as did Petrarch—with a somewhat lengthy appeal to the Virgin (numbers 117–119). If this group of poems is in a sense conventional, reflecting not only Petrarch but the whole medieval tradition, yet the tone of personal commitment is unmistakable: this sequence contains the most moving verses of Boccaccio's whole *canzoniere*.

Ideally, the *Rhymes* should end with the prayers to the Virgin; had
Boccaccio edited his scattered items, we may be reasonably sure they
would have so concluded. In Massèra's edition, however, they are
followed by six "occasional" sonnets of the poet's old age: two rather
coarsely rebuking an unnamed critic, three in which he apologizes to
another unidentified carper who had accused him of vulgarizing
Dante's *Comedy* by expounding it to the masses (Boccaccio humbly
admits he was driven to give his lectures partly by poverty; he is now
glad he has abandoned them), and, climactically, a sonnet on the death
of Petrarch. This last is the best known of all Boccaccio's lyrics and
deservedly so. It bears quotation here:

> To that fair kingdom, O my gentle lord,
> Whither all souls aspire in God's grace
> You have ascended, rising from this base
> And sinful world to win your fair reward
> (Which here you oft and ardently implored)
> And now may look upon your Laura's face.
> There my Fiammetta also has her place
> In sight of Him by seraphim adored.
> Sennuccio, Cino, Dante—these for aye
> Are of your company and in peace untold
> You penetrate to depths we may not chart.
> If in this erring life you loved me, pray
> Raise me up with you where I may behold
> Her who first kindled love within my heart.[8]

Of the twenty-nine poems that Massèra hesitates to assign with
certainty to Boccaccio, Branca defines only seventeen as "probably"
written by our poet. We have noted that Branca adds another eleven
poems to this ambiguous group; however, when he comes to analyze his
additions, he finds only one in the category of probably authentic
attributions. We may learn something of the manner and matter of these
tentative items if we note that of the total of forty-one poems, no fewer
than twenty-four are, in one manuscript or another, attributed to
Petrarch. Their substance is woven of the same threads as the authen-
ticated numbers, ranging from the idealistic rapture of love's first stages

to the palinodic appeal to the Virgin. Indeed, number 41, Branca's last candidate for consideration, is a poem in terza rima addressed to the Virgin, which some authorities have assigned to Dante.

Looking at Boccaccio's modest and unplanned *canzoniere*, we may remark, first of all, that the motifs and attitudes it displays are conventional. If we find reminiscences of Dante and Petrarch, it may not always be a matter of direct imitation, although of course the purely verbal echoes are hardly fortuitous. The ecstatic idealization of the beloved, her supernatural endowments, the awesome power of love, the joy and pain of total dedication, the uneasy moments of self-questioning, the ultimate turning to Heaven—these topics recur not only in Dante and Petrarch, but in varying degree and with slightly differing emphasis in the lyrics of the *dolce stil nuovo*, the Sicilians before them, and the Provençal troubadours at the head of the line—to say nothing of Ovid.[9] Of course, Dante and Petrarch poured new wine into these old bottles. If we look for something distinctive if not entirely novel in the contribution of the last of the triumvirate, we shall find it perhaps in a slightly sharper realism, a more immediate response to the moment. It is a difference of degree only, but it is possible to say that in the score of sonnets or verse most typically Boccaccian we find a more intense focus on the experience and less of a tendency to universalize the emotion. In this sense the lyrics typical of Boccaccio's genius are "autobiographical," even if the autobiography is romanticized. The sonnets of the Baia sequence, for example, depict a scene of sharp reality; the sonnets in service of the *Corbaccio* widow, if we may so designate her, have a mordancy suggestive of an experience still raw and not yet seen in perspective, and of course truly "occasional" are the sonnets on the Dante lectures and, most of all, the lines cited above on the death of Petrarch.

Formally, too, Boccaccio's verse is in harmony with the lyric tradition that nourished it. We have seen that the great majority of poems attributed to him are sonnets. It is worth noting that, so far as we know, he never attempted the high style of the *canzone* as exemplified by Dante and carried on by Petrarch. Such compositions call for a philosophical, all but scholastic, elaboration that was foreign to our poet's nature. In matters of imagery and rhetorical devices we find

Boccaccio mining the same ground as his masters': the ship imagery, the bittersweet juxtaposition of springtime and unrequited love, the dialogues with Love itself—such themes are found in Boccaccio's *canzoniere* as well as those of his predecessors. So, too, the abundance of classical allusions—perhaps line for line more frequently in Boccaccio than in Petrarch. An occasional display of virtuosity in the rhyming, contrived antitheses, and the like—these glittering ornaments are also legacies that our poet does not despise. The "category" sonnets are notable; numbers 63, 86, and 88 all dedicate their first eight lines to lists—respectively of mountains, remedies, and mortal dangers. This is a rather high percentage of encyclopedic sonnets in a relatively small *canzoniere*. Here, as we have observed apropos of number 88, it is hard to be sure whether Boccaccio is imitating Petrarch or following his own native taste. Indeed, in this connection it is only right to remark once more that if the echoes of Dante and Petrarch are numerous in his collection of lyrics, no less abundant are the passages that show an affinity with his own works, notably, but not exclusively, the *Elegy of Madonna Fiammetta*, the *Amorosa visione*, and the *Corbaccio*.

In the canon of Boccaccio's works his *Rhymes* do not occupy a very high place. The reasons for their relatively low rating are not hard to determine. First of all, they are truly—as Petrarch's were not, although he disingenuously so designated them—*rerum vulgarium fragmenta*, mere fragments of vernacular verse. Their author never troubled to collect them or edit them and since his time they have been largely ignored by scholars and critics, save for a few items that are or seem to be of "autobiographical" interest.[10] So they have until quite recently been unable to make a collective impact. Furthermore, they have been, one might say, doubly overshadowed. In its genre the *Canzoniere* of Petrarch simply dominates the field and has had a magnetic attraction that has dimmed—for most generations—even the lyric production of Dante.

The Renaissance, too, brought forth *canzonieri* more appealing and much more brightly polished than the offerings of our poet; one has only to think of Lorenzo and Michelangelo, to say nothing of Boiardo, Ariosto, and Tasso. The *Rhymes* have been likewise overshadowed by their author's other works, many of which, as we have had occasion to note, were innovative and seminal. The restless, experimental spirit of Boccaccio is readily recognizable not only in the *Decameron*, but also in the *Filostrato*, the *Teseida*, the *Ninfale fiesolano*, indeed to some degree in all his works in the vernacular. The *Rhymes*, on the other hand, show our author laboring in a familiar, well-tilled field. As a result critics and literary historians have tended to ignore, or at best to disparage, the *Rhymes*. Wilkins, for one, dismisses them as having "little individual character"[11]; Sapegno, although he applauds the grace of the opening sonnet and finds some emotional depth in the verses of the poet's later years, yet calls the *Rhymes* "literary exercise and nothing more."[12]

For a more sympathetic and perhaps more perceptive comment, we must look to De Sanctis (although his verdict is not entirely flattering). He writes: "Even in the *Rime* we find the new man fighting with the old form. They have the same repertory as before, of love, sighs, repentances, supplications to God and the Madonna; but the lovely idealism is gone from it. Behind the forms is a different content, badly suited to them. In name, woman is still an angel—but what an angel! Here we have the charming coquettish woman of ordinary life, and the distracted lover profanely sighing in the Platonic, traditional manner, or leaving his angel in the lurch and discoursing on death and fate and railing against women."[13] This observation shows that the great critic read the *Rhymes* with one eye on the *Decameron*, for it would be easy to find, among the *Rhymes*, some that refute his general statements. Just the same, he does give Boccaccio credit for a certain emancipation from tradition, if not outright originality.

In conclusion, without praising these lyrics beyond their due, it seems fair to say that if they lack the polished grace of Petrarch's verse (as does every other *canzoniere* in recorded history) and the loftiness of Dante's Muse, yet the most characteristic of them do have a kind of realistic and honest immersion in the moment that sets them apart from the offerings of Boccaccio's titanic predecessors. Rosario Ferreri's comment that the verses reveal the author's "inherent need for concreteness"[14] defines this distinctive aspect of Boccaccio's lyrics, creations of a sharp-eyed storyteller rather than an enraptured dreamer.

CHAPTER 13

THE LIFE OF DANTE AND THE LECTURES ON THE COMEDY

occaccio's deep interest in Dante's work," Giorgio Petrocchi writes, "is attested by a series of items: first of all the three copies of Dante's poem made by him (in the Chigian, Riccardian and Toledan manuscripts), the 'arguments' in *terza rima* and the rubrics in prose, a letter of 1372 to Jacopo Pizzinga, a poem on Dante's *Comedy* addressed to Petrarch; but this interest is documented in a form more complex and concrete in two special works: *The Life of Dante* and the *Commentary* (or *Lectures on Dante's Comedy*)."[1] Although there is a considerable interval of time between the dates of composition of these works and a notable difference in their form if not their intention (for both are meant to glorify the master), it will be appropriate to consider them together. Both are products of the post-*Decameron* Boccaccio and both were written in the vernacular—in distinction from the other "scholarly" products of the author's later years.

The first, in chronological order and certainly in appeal for the average reader, is a biographical-critical monograph on the author of the *Comedy*. It is known under various titles. Commonly it is spoken of as "Boccaccio's *Life of Dante*"; in the course of his commentary on the *Comedy* the author himself refers to it as a "little treatise *(trattatello)* in praise of Dante Alighieri," but the title preceding the text of the work (and so the correct title as P. G. Ricci, the most recent editor, reminds us) is *De origine, vita, studiis et moribus viri clarissimi Dantis*

Aligerii Florentini poete illustris, et de operibus compositis ab eodem (On the Origin, Life, Studies and Habits of the Most famous Dante Alighieri the Florentine, the Illustrious Poet, and on the Works Composed by Him). [2] If this is a rather pretentious title for a somewhat slim book (it runs to about sixty-five octavo pages in the longest of its versions), yet it must be granted that all the items enumerated are at least touched upon in the course of the work. Given the title, one might have expected the treatise to be written in Latin; it was, however, meant to accompany a selection of Dante's vernacular verse and, in harmony with the master's theory as set forth in the *Convivio* (1.5) affirming that a Latin commentary on a vernacular text would be inappropriate, Italian seemed the fitting vehicle. The Latin title lends a certain dignity to the essay and bears witness to the reverent seriousness with which the writer approached his lofty subject.

The genesis of the treatise goes back, in concept at least, to the youthful Neapolitan season, when Boccaccio's spontaneous admiration for his great compatriot was intensified by conversations with Cino da Pistoia and possibly Sennuccio del Bene (later a neighbor in the early Florentine years). Ricci would assign the actual composition of the first draft to the period between 1351 and 1355, the years, as he puts it, "of the most intense activity of Boccaccio's life."[3] They were also the years, as we observed in speaking of the *Corbaccio*, of a change of focus in his literary ambitions. He had recently finished the *Decameron* and was already at work on his great scholarly compilations in Latin, under the guidance, or at least following the direction, of Petrarch. With such works the *Trattatello* has something in common, for it too is a work, in intention at least, "scholarly" rather than creative, but readers will have no trouble finding in it passages and attitudes that echo the manner of the *Decameron*—and the *Corbaccio*, too, for that matter.

A study of the *Trattatello* is complicated by somewhat unusual textual problems. There are successive and varying versions of the work. We have the first draft in Boccaccio's own hand, bearing the above-cited title. Then there is a *compendio* or better, two versions of a *compendio*: the first (also in the author's hand) somewhat shorter than the first "edition," and the second, once more expanded. The relationship between these versions is scrupulously analyzed by Ricci, whose findings we summarize here.[4] The date of the final draft is as yet uncertain and controversial. It was commonly believed to be contemporaneous or nearly so with the preparation of the public lectures on the *Commedia* that Boccaccio gave in 1373; Ricci, however, largely on the evidence of Boccaccio's handwriting, believes that it was more likely the work of the "anni Certaldesi" ("years in Certaldo"), the early 1360s, when Boccaccio had retired from public life to his country home. We may note that although the substance of the *Trattatello* assembles materials collected at first hand by the biographer, yet the design and approach indicate that, as in the case of much of Boccaccio's writing, the author is following a model, in this case the *Life of Virgil* by Donatus.

In reviewing the content of the little treatise we shall follow the first version, leaving for subsequent comment the major points of difference between this version and the so-called *compendio*.[5] Our summary follows Ricci's text, indicating his numeration of paragraphs.

The *Trattatello* opens with a lengthy tirade against Florence, which instead of following the examples of great cities of the past, always grateful to their leading citizens, sent into exile her most illustrious son. To atone for such ingratitude, Boccaccio, a Florentine himself, will attempt to honor the great poet not by a monument but by the use of letters, "poor though his may be for such a lofty enterprise." He will use a humble and "light" style, he says, for he is incapable of anything better, and will write in the Florentine idiom in which Dante's great works were composed. He will set forth things that Dante was too modest to say of himself and he will discuss the works of the poet. Boccaccio hopes that his book will be of such a nature as to brighten rather than obscure the name of Dante; he will gladly accept correction for anything said amiss: against such dangers he invokes the aid of "Him who drew that other to his vision."

After a rapid survey of the rise and vicissitudes of Florence from its foundation by Rome to its rebuilding by Charlemagne, Boccaccio speaks of Dante's origins. The poet is descended, he says, from the Roman nobleman, Eliseo de' Frangipani, established in Florence at the time of Charlemagne. The crusader Cacciaguida of this stock, took to

wife a lady of the Aldighieri of Ferrara, she gave the name Aldighieri
to one of her sons and such was his virtue that his descendants took
his name as their surname, shortening it to Alighieri (11–17).[6]

Before Dante's birth his mother had a dream in which she saw her
son, nourished by the berries of the laurel, grow up swiftly to become
a shepherd. As he strove to seize the foliage of the laurel tree, she saw
him fall—and then rise again in the shape of a peacock.[7] On his birth
his parents concurred in naming him appropriately "Dante" ("the
Giver"). "This was that Dante granted to our age through God's special
grace. This was that Dante who was first to open the way for the return
of the Muses, long exiled from Italy. By him the glory of the Florentine speech is displayed, by him every grace of the vernacular is
regulated by proper numbers, and we may say truly that through him
poetry, long dead, has been restored to life. Considering such matters,
we may see clearly that he could have borne no other name than
Dante" (17–19).

This "singular glory of Italy" was born in 1265; from earliest
childhood he was drawn to the study of the poets, whom he perceived
to be no mere storytellers but teachers of truth. He soon became
familiar with the works of Virgil, Ovid, Horace, and other poets of
stature; he had no interest in the money-making studies to which
everyone turns nowadays. His zeal for learning took him first to
Bologna and later, toward the beginning of his old age,[8] to Paris
(20–27).

A life dedicated to study requires solitude and detachment. But
Dante throughout his whole life was compelled to suffer many distrac-
tions: the fierce and unbearable passion of love, a wife, domestic and
public cares, exile and poverty. Of these Boccaccio will speak *seriatim*.
He begins with Dante's first encounter with Beatrice. The episode has
all the idyllic flavor of a scene from one of Boccaccio's own romances
and may well bear quoting. "In the season," we are told,

> "when the sweetness of Heaven once more clothes the earth in its
> adornments, making it all smiling with the variety of flowers among
> the verdant leaves, it was the custom of the men and women of our
> city to assemble in their own districts and hold festivals. Among the

rest, one Folco Portinari, a man highly esteemed by his fellow citizens, had invited his neighbors to a feast in his house on the first of May. Among the neighbors was the Alighieri we have mentioned and with him (as boys are wont to accompany their fathers, especially to places of festivity) was Dante, at that time nearing the end of his ninth year. There were many boys and girls of his age present and with them Dante fell to sporting and playing, so far as the compass of his years permitted. Among the throng of children was a daughter of Folco, Bice—although the poet would always call her by the full form of her name, Beatrice. She was eight years old, winsome in her girlish way, with pleasing and courteous manners, more sober and modest in word and gesture than her age would call for. Her features were delicate and harmoniously disposed, not only beautiful but full of such innocent charm that many thought of her as a little angel. Such as I here depict her—or perhaps fairer—she appeared before the eyes of Dante on this festive occasion—not, I suppose, for the first time, but for the first time with power to make him fall in love. He, child that he was, took her fair visage into his heart with such affection that never henceforth, as long as he lived, did it leave him. Indeed, as childhood passed, that love grew. It was a chaste love, free of licentious desire. And such a love, though some might argue, in view of the beauty of the lines addressed to Beatrice, that it was an inspiration to his art, must surely have been an obstacle to the pursuit of his studies and the development of his genius" (28–38).[9]

In her twenty-fourth year Beatrice died and Dante was for a time inconsolable. His parents, out of concern for his condition, arranged a marriage for him. But the remedy was worse than the ill it was meant to cure. A married man has no opportunity for the solitude, study, and meditation that are essential to a scholar. For a wife's demands give a man no peace and life with such a suspicious creature is trying. And in a digression, the tone of which recalls a similar passage in the *Corbaccio* (not surprisingly since in both cases the source is St. Jerome, echoing Theophrastus), Boccaccio enlarges on the vanity of women, the cost of satisfying their desires, the obligations entailed by marriage, and so on. He admits that he has no evidence that Dante's marriage was an unhappy one but he notes that when the poet went into exile he did not take his wife with him nor did he even allow her to join him. Marriage, Boccaccio concludes, is not a bad thing for all men, but philosophers should leave the institution to rich men and lords and workers and find their own pleasure in philosophy, the best of spouses (39–59).

Domestic cares were followed by political cares. Moved by desire to bring peace to the warring factions of Florence, Dante sought public office; his reward was unmerited exile. His example serves to show how much trust can be put in the people and how unwise is the philosopher who participates in civic affairs (60–71). In the years of exile, Dante wandered from court to court in Italy and finally made his way to Paris where he devoted himself to study. But when Henry VII invaded Italy, Dante joined him; on the failure of the imperial enterprise he withdrew to Romagna where Guido Novello da Polenta, lord of Ravenna, sheltered him until his death (72–81).

Considering then, Boccaccio continues, the obstacles to study that Dante had to contend with: love, marriage, political involvement, exile, and poverty, we must marvel at his accomplishments. Had he but been granted greater scope and more leisure he would have been "as a god on earth." In his last years in Ravenna he trained many scholars in poetry, particularly in the vernacular of which he was the first champion. In September, 1321, on the feast of Santa Croce (September 14) Dante died. Guido gave him an honorable funeral and proposed to have a monument erected for him, inviting various poets to send in their tributes to be carved on the tomb. But Guido lost his estate and died in exile before he could have the tomb built. Of the tributes offered, Boccaccio quotes that written by Giovanni del Virgilio (82–91).

After another invective against Florence, proud of her rich merchants, artisans, and petty aristocracy, but harsh and ungrateful toward her great bard, Boccaccio proceeds to a description of the poet, physical and moral. This passage provides us with the best sketch we have of Dante's appearance, and Ricci comments[10] that many details must have come to Boccaccio from people who had seen the poet. The poet was, says his biographer, "of middle height[11]; and when he had reached maturity he went somewhat bowed, his gait grave and gentle, and ever clad in most seemly apparel, in such garb as befitted his ripe years. His face was long, his nose aquiline, and his eyes rather large than small; his jaws big and the underlip protruding beyond the upper. His complexion was dark, his hair and beard thick, black and curling, and his expression was ever melancholy and thoughtful."[12] The mention of Dante's dark complexion and black beard reminds his biographer of the incident in Verona where a simple woman cited such features as evidence that the poet could go to Hell and return.

The great poet, Boccaccio assures us, was temperate in food and drink, given to long vigils, and rarely spoke save when addressed; yet on the proper occasions he was capable of great eloquence. In his youth he was much given to music and was on intimate terms with the best singers and musicians of his day.[13] He was a faithful subject of love, which inspired him to attain the preeminence he held in vernacular verse. He was fond of solitude and even in company he was frequently so withdrawn in thought that he would not answer questions put to him until he had finished his meditation. His gift for concentration was illustrated by his reading a book in the streets of Siena while all the tumult of a noisy tournament went on about him. He had a remarkable memory. He desired honor and glory—perhaps more eagerly than was proper to one of his character; it may be that for that reason he particularly esteemed poetry. For it is true that philosophy is the noblest study of all, but it can be appreciated only by a few, and there are many famous philosophers—while, on the other hand, poetry can be enjoyed by all, and great poets are few. So, hoping to win the laurel crown, Dante dedicated himself to poetry—and he would have won the crown, had he been willing to accept it anywhere but in Florence (92–126).

Poetry, Boccaccio tells us, embarking on another and significant digression, had its inception in primitive man's first intimations of divinity. And as with the growth of the cult of the divine, the gods were honored with works of art, sculpture, painting, and the like, of the same nature were the first poems, set forth in measured rhythmical patterns. Later, kings and heroes were similarly honored. So poetry was in a sense theology and gentile poets, even as Scripture does, set forth great truths under a veil of adornment. The subject matter of the

gentile poets and that of Scripture are not the same—they are even
"adverse," for Scripture reveals divine truth. Yet the methods are the
same and the poets reveal their own kind of truth. So, for example,
in Hercules being transformed into a god and Lycaon into a wolf we
may see under the veil of the fables the moral truth that good deeds
are rewarded and wicked deeds punished. And similar "poetic fiction"
may be observed in the vision of Daniel and elsewhere in the Old
Testament and in the marvelous fantasies of the Apocalypse in the
New. To rebuke poets for the use of fables is to rebuke Scripture, too.
Further, the obscurity of poetic language is justified by the demonstra-
ble fact that whatever we gain through toil is sweeter to our taste than
what we receive without effort. So the poets wisely surround "the
hidden fruit" with the "verdure and the bark" of their eloquence.
Therefore, when the subject is the same, Poetry may be equated with
Theology. Did not Christ himself make use of allegory? And we have,
too, the authority of Aristotle who called poets "the first theologians"
(127–155).

Turning now to the significance of the laurel, Boccaccio refers to
Solon's prescription for a well-governed state: it should have ways of
rewarding its good citizens and punishing the bad ones. For that reason
crowns of laurel were in antiquity regularly awarded to poets and
generals of distinction.[14] The laurel was chosen in part, no doubt,
because of its association with Apollo, but also because of its three
significant properties: its leaves never lose their verdancy, the tree has
never been known to be struck by lightning, and it is always fragrant.
It is not surprising that Dante should desire to win such a crown
(156–162).

Continuing with his assessment of Dante's character, Boccaccio
notes that the poet was a very proud man. He cites in evidence Dante's
refusal to return to Florence under conditions that he deemed humiliating[15] and his celebrated remark on the occasion when, in an emergency,
the Florentine council considered sending an emissary to the pope: "If
I go, who stays? If I stay, who goes?" Dante was also an intemperate
partisan. (Boccaccio here speaks of the Guelph and Ghibelline parties,
but states that he does not know the origin of the names and says
nothing of their different compositions and programs.) Dante, he says,

was first a Guelph, but, exiled by his party, became such a fierce Ghibelline that it was said of him that he would have stoned any woman or child who spoke against the party. Boccaccio is sorry to be obliged to reveal Dante's shortcomings; he must do so, however, in the interest of truth; his honesty will assure that the good he has to say of his subject will be believed. With this apology he discloses that Dante, throughout his whole lifetime, was lecherous, a natural vice to be sure but certainly not praiseworthy. Still, who could blame Dante? "Not I, certainly," says Boccaccio, who reminds us of other great figures who had succumbed to the "vicious attraction of womankind" through the course of history; Jove himself was a victim and Adam, and even Solomon, the wisest of kings.

Boccaccio then moves to a systematic catalog of Dante's works, lest the poet fail to receive due credit for his compositions or lest the work of another be falsely attributed to him. The *Vita nuova*, he notes, was composed in Dante's twenty-sixth year; it is a "marvelously beautiful" work, although in his later years Dante was ashamed of having written it.[16] "Some years" after the *Vita nuova* Dante conceived the notion of writing the *Comedy*; its purpose would be to reprove the wicked, honor the good, and win glory for himself. He chose poetry as his vehicle and embarked on the work in his thirty-fifth year.[17] And on the *Comedy*, among many vicissitudes and while concurrently composing other works, the poet labored the rest of his life. He had finished only seven cantos when he was driven to exile, leaving his work behind him. Fortunately these cantos came into the hands of Dino Lambertuccio, who sent them to the Marchese Moroello Malespina, in whose court Dante was living, and at the bidding of the Marchese Dante resumed his work.[18] He could attend to it only sporadically; it was his custom when he had finished half a dozen cantos to send them to Cane della Scala, lord of Verona. At the time of the poet's death the last thirteen cantos of the *Paradiso* were still missing. Dante's son, Jacopo, was granted a vision of his father who appeared to him in a dream and showed him where the missing cantos might be found.[19] Dante originally had intended to write his *Comedy* in Latin,[20] Boccaccio affirms, quoting the opening lines, but then had chosen the vernacular out of a desire to make his work useful to all men and not the literati alone;

many princes and men of prominence can no longer read Latin and even the study of Virgil has been neglected. "Some maintain" that the three divisions of the epic were dedicated respectively to Uguccione della Faggiuola, lord of Pisa, the Marchese Moroello Malespina and Frederick III of Sicily; others say that the whole work was dedicated to Cane della Scala[21]; Boccaccio has no opinion of his own on the matter (163–194).

Passing to the *Monarchia*, after summarizing Dante's arguments, Boccaccio says the treatise was composed on the occasion of Henry VII's descent into Italy; he notes that the book was condemned as heretical and burned some years after its author's death by Cardinal Beltrando, the papal legate in Lombardy. Next, Boccaccio mentions briefly the *Eclogues* sent to Giovanni del Virgilio, the *Convivio* (speculating, as others have since, on the reasons it was not finished), the *De vulgari eloquentia* (composed, says Boccaccio, incorrectly, when Dante was near his death), and the numerous Latin epistles and verses in the vernacular (195–201).

Concluding his study the author modestly states that his account of Dante may be corrected or improved on by others; he has merely done his best. Indeed, if his errors give occasion for others to write about the great poet, he will be content. Before ending his work Boccaccio feels obliged to interpret the dream of Dante's mother, mentioned above. The birth under the laurel would signify the propitious nature of the heavens at that time; the poet becoming a shepherd signifies his "spiritual pastorate" as a teacher of mankind; the peacock is a figure of the *Comedy*, the hundred eyes standing for the hundred cantos, and so on. In fact, the dream is analyzed and interpreted in the same manner —even applying to the peacock the famous four meanings—as will be used in the interpretation of the *Comedy* (202–228).

There are not very great substantial differences between the original *Trattatello* and the *Compendio*. As noted, the first version of the latter work (first, at least, according to Ricci) is tighter and less discursive; the lengthy invective against Florence, for example, is omitted as well as a few other minor digressions not essential to the narrative. Of the lesser changes we may here mention two of interest. Speaking of poetry in the *Compendio*, Boccaccio no longer claims that it is "the same" as theology, but affirms merely that it "resembles" theology. And, in connection with Dante's lustfulness, he adds, immediately after the passage on the death of Beatrice, that the poet was to love other women in the course of his life, specifying a certain "Pargoletta" of Lucca and "a mountain woman" of the Casentino.[22] In general, the tone of the *Compendio* is somewhat more objective and for that reason less spontaneous and—as a literary work—less appealing.

Considered as a biography the *Trattatello* is not entirely satisfactory. It is true that it contains a few items not documented elsewhere, the family name of Beatrice, the visit to Paris, and some precious anecdotes. But there are some surprising gaps—the more puzzling when we consider that Boccaccio had many contacts with individuals who had known Dante: Cina da Pistoia, Sennuccio del Bene, the cousin of Beatrice, and the poet's own daughter. He does not tell us, for example, the name of Dante's mother, whether the poet had brothers or sisters, nor how many children he had, nor even the name of his wife. Dante's early schooling in Florence is mentioned, but no specific school is named; nothing is said of Brunetto Latini, nor for that matter of the circle of *dolce stil nuovo* poets with whom the young Alighieri was intimate. Scholars have also noted factual errors: Dante was affianced by his parents well before the time of Beatrice's death, for example, and, as we have mentioned, Boccaccio's dating of the *De vulgari eloquentia* is incorrect.

It has been remarked that most of the factual information and indeed the comments on Dante's character and customs could all be deduced from a reading of the poet's works. Nor have the original contributions of the biographer always met with universal acceptance. Most *dantisti* nowadays seem ready to believe Beatrice was the daughter of Folco Portinari; on the other hand, the visit to Paris is still a controversial item, and the account of the seven cantos left behind in Florence (though very circumstantially set forth) is seen as more probably a gloss on the opening line of the *Inferno* 8 than as a historical fact. Scholars of an older generation than ours were distressed by Boccaccio's affirmation of Dante's enduring lustfulness. "Had [Boccaccio] independent evidence of it or did he only infer it from the study of Dante's own works?" asks Wicksteed, concluding that the latter alternative is likely.[23] So, too, the gratuitous assumption that Dante's marriage was an unhappy one has disturbed Dante worshipers, and, in fact, Boccaccio grants that such an opinion must be based to a certain extent on negative evidence. Broadly speaking, what the *Trattatello* does for us is to bring together and organize all the facts and inferences that can be drawn from a reading of the works—in the manner, one might say, of the old Provençal *vidas*. In spite of the biographer's commitment to realism, the biography remains an exemplum, rather than a *vita*.

Viewed as a work of criticism, the *Trattatello* is somewhat superficial and erratic. Dante's *opera* are enumerated and praised but with little critical analysis; the brevity of their summaries might make one wonder occasionally how well Boccaccio actually knew them. Yet with all its shortcomings the treatise is of great value and significance as a disclosure of what a near contemporary could see and appreciate in the *Comedy* and its author. In this respect the work is, to be sure, not entirely unique, for the early commentaries on the great poem provide a similar point of reference, but it is especially precious as coming from the pen of a fellow poet and scholar. If in its pages we learn perhaps more about the author than his subject, this is, in this case, hardly to be deplored and is furthermore a remark that could be made about many lives of great men.

The passage on the meaning and purpose of poetry is of particular interest, whether Boccaccio be here speaking for Dante or himself. The defense of the poet's function, motivated in part by the desire to affirm the importance of poetry and the stature of poets against the contempt, disparagement, or indifference often shown the Muse by lawyers, doctors, men of commerce, and sometimes theologians, is a well-argued statement of the medieval aesthetic theory. It is not a theory original with Boccaccio, however. The concept of an underlying "truth" both suggested and concealed by a beautiful veil is basic to many works of the Middle Ages, including the *Divine Comedy*; Petrarch had been very explicit about such matters in his Coronation Speech, his letter to his brother Gherardo (*Fam.* 10.4), and his *Metrical Letter* (2.10; henceforth referred to as *Ep. Met.*), all works known to Boccaccio before the summer of 1351, as Ricci notes.[24] In the ninth book of the *Africa*, too, the whole passage from the definition of poetry to the significance of the laurel closely parallels Boccaccio's argument; we may imagine the subject recurred often in conversations between Boccaccio and his mentor.

Perhaps, when all is said and done (though we may not expect universal concurrence in this view), the principal attraction of the *Trattatello* lies neither in the plausibility of its historical substance nor in its critical pronouncements, but rather in the liveliness of the narrative and the perceptibly joyous commitment of the writer. If we choose for a moment to look upon the *Trattatello* simply as a creative work, we shall find the depiction of scenes and events as pleasing as it is effective. From such a point of view, anecdotes and digressions—the meeting with Beatrice, the comments on marriage and the like—are all appropriate and functional. The author's infectious enthusiasm lends to his pages an attractive and enduring warmth. The prose style, both in pace and color, is not inferior to that of the best pages of the *Decameron*.

In the last years of his life, as we noted in chapter 2, Boccaccio was commissioned by the Commune of Florence to give a series of public lectures explicating the *Divine Comedy*. The *Esposizioni* are the written version of those lectures. Undoubtedly the substance of the manuscripts differs considerably from what the lecturer actually said. Assuredly they contain a good deal of supplementary information, too copious for inclusion in an oral address; it is not unlikely, on the other hand, that some things were said in the lectures that were not subsequently transcribed in the *Esposizioni*. There have not been wanting scholars who believe that much of the commentary as we have it is not Boccaccio's work at all.[25]

The lecturer begins with the traditional medieval *accessus*, or introduction. Boccaccio discusses the significance of the word *comedy*, the form of the poem, and its various meanings; he follows very closely the *Letter to Can Grande* with which he was clearly familiar, although he does not seem to think it was written by Dante. He gives a short summary of the author's life, incidentally not mentioning his Ghibelline sympathies, and refers his hearers to his *Trattatello* for further details. Naturally enough, since Boccaccio was addressing a new and different audience, some items already set forth in the *Trattatello* were repeated in the *accessus*, notably Dante's original intention of composing his poem in Latin and his reasons for ultimately choosing the vernacular. The *accessus* also contains a rather lengthy discussion of the *Inferno* as depicted by classical writers.

The *accessus* is followed by a canto-by-canto analysis of the *Comedy*. In part 1 of each lecture the literal meaning is expounded and in part 2 the commentator discusses the allegorical significance of the canto. Such at least is his general practice, although such divisions do not appear in his discussions of cantos 10, 11, 15, 16, and 17. It is interesting to note that in the twelve cantos where the division is made the exposition of the literal sense takes up about twice as many pages as the explication of the allegory. For canto 1 the space is evenly divided (of necessity the allegory of the forest, the hill, the beasts, and so on calls for lengthy treatment) but in cantos 5 and 12, for example, the disparity is remarkable. In both cases the nature of the content is such as to enable Boccaccio to develop his chief interest, which lies in history, mythology, or even gossip, rather than in allegory. The illustrious lustful in canto 5 require lengthy informational comment (already happily available to the author in his Latin *compendia*) as do the tyrants of canto 10 submerged in the Phlegethon. Throughout the *expositiones* much supplementary erudition from other works of Boccaccio, particularly the *Genealogies of the Pagan Gods*, is brought in.[26] The commentator is well aware of his emphasis: he writes, toward the end of his gloss of canto 1, that not every word in such a work as the *Comedy* is susceptible of allegorical interpretation; indeed many words are simply meant to carry on the narrative and bear perforce only a literal sense. "What has allegory to do with such lines as 'The company of six is reduced to two' (4.148) or 'So I descended into the first circle' (5.1) and many such?" he asks, adding, "yet if such passages are removed, how can the author proceed with the desired order of his demonstration? How otherwise can the passages bearing a second sense be put together?"

In common with most of the early commentators, Boccaccio is ever alert to defend the orthodoxy of his master. The statement on the eternal destiny of the suicides in canto 13, whose bodies will hang from trees even after Judgment Day, is not, Boccaccio assures us, an opinion expressed by the writer himself, any more than is the statement a few lines later that seems to attribute to the pagan god Mars some influence over the destiny of Florence. What the protective commentator would have made of the statement that the soul of a traitor descends directly to Hell, leaving his body behind among the living (33.124–126) or for that matter of the presence of Cato in Purgatory we cannot say, since the *Commentary* breaks off in the middle of the *Inferno*. Boccaccio is also eager to defend Dante's excellence as a stylist; he makes a rather touching defense of the phrase "ed io sol uno" (literally "and I one alone") (2.2) against the charge of "inculcatio" or redundancy. On the other hand, he will occasionally correct his master; in his gloss on *Inferno* 1, "il bello stile che m'ha fatto onore" ("the fair style that has won me honor"), assuming that the honor comes from the composition of the *Comedy,* he accuses Dante of using the preterite for the future and so committing a *solecismo.*

To scholars of the *Comedy*, Boccaccio's *Esposizioni* are precious. Yet in some respects they are disappointing. For one thing they break off at the end of the first lines of canto 17. And while what we have is substantial in bulk (some seven hundred octavo pages) it is not without flaws. Sapegno, speaking for critics in general and certainly for all readers, describes the commentary as "a vast and prolix work, and furthermore very uneven." He adds that overall the book "gives the impression of a provisional collection of material, only partly re-worked with a proper edition in mind, in part left in its primitive state of notes to be developed orally."[27] In this statement, too, his opinion coincides with the general verdict; in his recent edition of the *Esposizioni* Giorgio Padoan speaks of the work as essentially "a collection of filing cards" drawn from Boccaccio's own Latin *compendia* and the works of preceding commentators—all left in an unedited state.[28] So as they come to us the lectures are full of repetitions, inconsistencies, and transcribed pedantry that combine to make tedious reading.

The strength of the *Esposizioni* lies in their excellent linguistic perception and their occasional bits of historical information that we do not find in other commentaries; for example, the story of Francesca's marriage to Gianciotto by proxy and her innocent assumption that Paolo was to be her husband. If this blunts a little Dante's point it also wins our sympathy for Francesca. But is it in fact true? Most critics seem to believe that the romance was an invention of the compassionate author of the *Decameron*, always ready to find excuses for charming if errant ladies. It must be said, too, that among the merits of the *Esposizioni* is an engaging intimacy of approach, an easy unpedagogical lack of pretentiousness; commenting on the famous crux "tra feltro e feltro" ("between felt and felt") (*Inferno* 1.105) Boccaccio tells us candidly that he really doesn't understand what is meant and will content himself with summarizing the interpretations of others.

The course of lectures, offered in the church of Santo Stefano in Badia, began in October of 1373 and may have continued into the following April.[29] Both preparation and exposition must have been difficult for the lecturer, now old, weary, and infirm; and obliged, furthermore, to speak before a mixed public in a room described by a disciple as "inordinata et neglecta" ("poorly maintained and run down").[30] Even so, he might have continued save for the reproaches of an austere pedant who persuaded him that he was debasing Dante by expounding his poem to an audience unworthy of appreciating the master's words. As we have noted (chapter 2, p. 64) Boccaccio took this rebuke to heart and brought his lectures to a close. One may suspect that the unidentified *literatus* may also have been responsible for the lecturer's failure to put his notes in order and prepare a polished version of his *Commentary* (although perhaps it was merely a matter of fatigue and shortness of time; Boccaccio had but a year left to live when he gave up his lectures). In any case, readers of both Dante and Boccaccio will find that unidentified false counselor hard to forgive.

CHAPTER 14

THE GENEALOGIES OF THE PAGAN GODS

n his introduction to *Boccaccio on Poetry* Charles Osgood remarks that Boccaccio would be disappointed by the reputation he enjoys today; the author of the *Decameron,* he adds, had hoped to be remembered as a scholar-humanist rather than as a literary artist.[1] We have noted that as the years passed the novelist and romance writer gave way increasingly to the scholar and humanist; if he did not actually repudiate the works of his youth (this is a somewhat controversial question, at least with regard to the *Decameron*) yet he came to regard them all as items of minor importance, to apologize for rather than to glory in. His major investment was in the *Genealogies of the Gods*, on which he toiled assiduously during the last twenty-five years of his life and which, it is probable, had its beginnings many years before, perhaps in the Neapolitan period.[2] Nowadays the *Genealogies*, save for the last two chapters, is of purely historical interest. We have better compilations of classical deities, and certainly no one would turn to the *Genealogies* for reading pleasure. Boccaccio's contemporaries, however, approved of his aims and appreciated his labors. Villani, his first biographer, mentions only the Latin works by name and among these he gives highest praise to the *Genealogies*, "a pleasant and useful work" and "indispensable" to anyone desiring to understand the allegories of the poets.[3]

The book is dedicated to Hugo, King of Cyprus. In chapter 13 of book 15, Boccaccio addresses the monarch: "You well know, O excellent king, how much I protested and delayed when your officer Donino urged and besought me to grant your request and take up this labor. As the years went by, it happened that your friend and my fellow-townsman, Bechino Bellincioni, on his way from Cyprus, met me at Ravenna. After he expressed in agreeable manner your Highness's kind consideration toward unworthy me, he began with wonderfully urgent importunity to rouse my mind from the drowsiness into which it had fallen over this work: and this he said he did at your command."[4] Osgood believes the meeting with Donino may have taken place in Forlì in 1347; the importunities of Bechino Bellincioni followed three years later.[5] The wording somehow suggests that the notion of taking up this labor had occurred to the young scholar even before the meeting with Donino; perhaps his drowsiness was dispelled as much by the encounter with Petrarch as by the exhortations of Bellincioni. In any event it is clear that in 1350 Boccaccio began his enterprise in earnest. He may have finished a first draft as early as 1360 but he did not allow the work to be copied until 1371 when he yielded to the pleas of a group of Neapolitan friends. Even then he requested that it should not be circulated and there is evidence that he was still working on it in 1374–1375. The king of Cyprus had been seven years in his grave by that time but Boccaccio chooses to address him, in the passages we have quoted, as if he were still alive.

The work is divided into fifteen books, subdivided into chapters. Each book treats of the families of various key gods and goddesses and the books are preceded by genealogical trees. The last two books contain the author's defense of his work—and, incidentally, of poetry.

The broad scope and massive bulk of the *Genealogies* may well justify the author's pride in his accomplishment and also explain the admiration it called forth from contemporary scholars and those of later generations. The thirteen chapters that make up the truly encyclopedic part of the work are broken down into 698 subchapters, each dealing with a special figure of ancient mythology. Since such items also call for frequent mention of associated deities or heroes the total number of names cited is considerably higher. Vincenzo Romano's edition[6] regrettably contains no index of figures mentioned; it does, on the other hand, scrupulously catalog the authorities quoted; in this area too the total is impressive and provides convincing evidence of Boccaccio's voracious reading and scholarly commitment. No fewer than 175 authors are cited as sources, ranging from classical authorities to the writer's own contemporaries. Of the classical writers Virgil is quoted 254 times and there are 209 references to Ovid. Homer is quoted 110 times, an indication that the hospitality accorded to the abrasive Leontius Pilatus was well rewarded. There are over two hundred allusions to a rather mysterious Theodontius, described by Osgood as "an unidentified writer whose works are lost, and whom some have thought fictitious."[7]

Boccaccio's references to his own contemporaries are especially interesting. Needless to say frequent mention is made of Petrarch (although for the most part in the last two books; the apologia, one might say, rather than the compendium itself) and on the last page of the work the author invites his eminent teacher "piously and kindly to remove any errors" he may have inadvertently been guilty of.[8]

He also mentions Dante, for whom he says "praise is superfluous," and Francesco da Barberini, though he quotes him but once. Chapter 6 of book 15[9] is in fact a section that an author today would call "acknowledgments"; aside from the great names we have mentioned Boccaccio expresses his gratitude to Barlaam and Leontius Pilatus, his teachers of Greek, and to "that noble and venerable old man Andalò di Negre of Genova . . . my teacher of astronomy." Such references have enabled Boccaccio's biographers to document the poet's contacts and interests in the youthful Neapolitan period (see our chapter 2); his insistence on calling them back to memory is a tribute to his generous nature. The style of the concluding chapters is notably fresh and lively and occasionally the *novelliere* emerges from the scholarly veil. The paragraph on Dante is a capsule biography, and the comment on Paul of Perugia calls irresistibly for quotation. Of him Boccaccio writes:

Advanced in years, of great and varied learning, he was long the Librarian of the famous king Robert of Sicily and Jerusalem. If there was ever a man possessed of the curiosity of research he was the one. A word from his prince was sufficient to send him hunting through a dozen books of history, fable, or poetry. He thus enjoyed peculiar friendship with Barlaam, and though it could not be based upon common interests in Latin culture, it was a means by which Paul drank deeply of Greek lore. He wrote a huge book which he called *The Collections*; it included much matter on various subjects, but particularly his ingatherings of pagan mythology from Latin authors, together with whatever he could collect on the same subject from the Greeks, probably with Barlaam's help. I shall never hesitate to acknowledge that when still a youngster, long before you [i.e., King Hugo to whom the book is dedicated] drew my mind to this undertaking, I drank deep of that work with more appetite than discretion. Especially did I prefer that part set down under the name Theodontius. But to the very serious inconvenience of this book of mine, I found that his saucy wife Biella, after his death, willfully destroyed this and many other books of Paul's.[10]

Boccaccio's *Genealogies* are not merely catalogs of names with indications of kinship among the immortals. With scholarly tenacity and poetic insight he strives also to explain the significance of his gallery of mythological figures. We may here borrow Sapegno's compact and lucid exposition of the nature of the work.

[The author] proceeds in an orderly and methodical way, calling on the most various works (some of them quite rare and unknown even to scholars of today), and making use as well of what he has picked up from the spoken words of men such as Paul of Perugia and Leontius Pilatus, with scrupulous indications in each case of the source of his information. And if it is possible to point out errors in a work so laboriously compiled in the second half of the 14th century, yet the wonder and admiration with which one contemplates the enormous mass of facts collected and catalogued and of authorities consulted by Boccaccio are fully justified. Moreover he is not content merely to copy and catalogue the contents of the ancient fables; in addition, convinced as he is that under the veil of the literal a deeper truth is concealed, he makes every effort to find it, first of all noting the explanations he has found in classical writers and then, as he says in the "Proemio" where these are lacking or seem to him inadequate, stating his own opinion. Which is to say that he interprets the myths in their literal and historical sense, then in the allegorical or moral sense and finally in a Christian anagogical sense. At times he prefers to insist on an historical explanation (as when he speaks of Jupiter as a wise man, coming from Arcadia, who taught the Athenians to live in civilized fashion, and was subsequently elevated to godhood by them) [book 2, chap. 2]. . . . At other times he offers a naturalistic explanation as in the case of Aurora, daughter of a Titan and Earth, which he sees as the light of dawn which comes from the sun, and "seems as it rises over the eastern horizon, to the observer to come forth from the earth" [book 4, chap. 27]. Again, it suits him to take the myths in an allegorical-moral sense as when in Adonis changed into a flower he sees symbolized "the brevity of mortal beauty, since what is rosy and colorful in the morning becomes languid, pale and wasted with nightfall" [book 2, chap. 23]. In the various cases the choice of the interpretative method seems somewhat arbitrary, and often indeed the various "meanings" are mingled and interwoven with some imprecision.[11]

Hauvette's criticism is sharper; Boccaccio's curiosity, he observes, "was not directed by any fixed method. Faithful to the teachings of scriptural exegesis, of which Dante's work had already offered a curious application to poetry, he recognized in the fables three senses: literal or historical, allegorical or moral, anagogical or Christian. . . . But, although he tended to favor the historical sense, Boccaccio's choice among these three interpretations seems arbitrary—more arbitrary is his way of combining them or superimposing one on another—more or less following his fancy." But the French critic is quick to add that "such are the pardonable gropings of a pioneer—these vacillations must not prevent us from recognizing the lively curiosity and the conscientious zeal manifest in Boccaccio's investigations."[12] Whatever their limitations the *Genealogies* served men of letters throughout Europe for two centuries at least; a translation into French, published in 1498, attests to the enduring prestige of the work beyond the Alps.

Since the informational chapters of the *Genealogies* are not available in English, a specimen of the compiler's method and manner may be included here. Speaking of "Venus, eleventh daughter of Jupiter and mother of Cupid" Boccaccio writes as follows:[13]

As Homer attests, Venus was the daughter of Jupiter and Dione; it is she whom Cicero, in his *De natura deorum*, calls the third daughter. She is said to have been the wife of Vulcan, and they say that she loved Mars and of their mutual infatuation and adultery I have spoken above when discussing Mars. She is also considered to be the mother of Aeneas, and in this connection I spoke of her when I mentioned the wound that she suffered at the hand of Diomedes. I spoke of her also when I told the story of Adonis and how she cherished him when she was accidentally wounded by her son, Cupid. Nor are there lacking those who believe what has been said about her, for we read in Sacred History that she instituted the oldest profession on earth. St. Augustine seems to affirm as much when in his *City of God* he says: "gifts were given her by the Phoenicians for the prostitution of their daughters before they married them off to their husbands." Further, the poet Claudianus speaks of her in his *Praises of Stilicho* where he describes a garden of pleasure and delight, situated, most gracious King, on your island of Cyprus, wherein can readily be found all the sights suggestive of lascivious conduct. For he begins thus: "a large mountain overshadows the Ionian Sea with the cliffs of Cyprus"—and continues with forty-six verses of description that I do not repeat here because the passage is excessively long. Here, too, having described the pleasure garden, he displays how reverently and with what lavish ornament the cult of Venus was exalted, saying "there was Venus, reposing on a glittering throne, casually arranging her tresses while on her right and left hand stood her Italian sisters whom she was refreshing with copious showers of nectar"; with a bite of her ivory white teeth she causes much discord, yet all the while unobtrusively she creates notable harmonies. ... Since in speaking of her charms many things have been said about fictitious assumptions concerning the goddess, it would seem superfluous to repeat them here. There remain to be mentioned only such things as one hesitates to discard. Some people think that this Venus is one and the same with Cypria. I think there were two such goddesses and that our Venus was indeed the daughter of Jupiter and Dione and the wife of Vulcan and that the other one was the daughter of a Syrian and either Venus or Dione and was the wife of Adonis.[14] Those who believe that the two are really one and the same say that she was the daughter of Jupiter and Dione and was wed first to Vulcan and later to Adonis. They hold that because of her exceptional beauty Venus was considered divine by the Cypriots and called a goddess and that, as such, she was honored with religious rites. They assert that there was an altar and a temple dedicated to her at Paphos and that worshipers used to make this altar fragrant with incense and flowers—and nothing more because, for various reasons, sweet-smelling things delight her. They say, too, that when she stood near a man she became inflamed with such an itch that she usually declined the shelter of a brothel and made love right in the open. And to cover the wantonness of her actions they say that she recommended whoredom to the women of Cyprus and instituted among them the practice of making profit by cheapening their bodies. From their practice it followed that even virgins were sent to the beaches to be given to Venus as sacrificial offerings. And further, that from the virgins' intercourse with strangers, Venus appropriated all the payments. Theodontius adds even more, stating that such a sinful practice continued for a long time and not in Cyprus alone but even in Italy where it was imported. This assertion is confirmed by Justin, who says that at one time the practice was prevalent among the Locrians where it was regarded as a votive offering to Venus.

The encyclopedic information that fills up the thirteen books, admirable as it is in scope, has long since been supplemented, corrected, and refined by the labors of generations of scholars who have reworked the field, with increasingly better tools. One would turn to the *Genealogies* today—if at all—not for the authoritative word on any myth or fabulous figure but merely to learn what was known or thought of such matters in the late Middle Ages. But the last two books are of a different nature. As we have seen, book 15 is of great interest for the biographical information it yields, not only with regard to the author's life, but also as touching his use of authorities, living and dead. The fourteenth book likewise has its special character; it is in effect a defense of poetry and while such an apologia is, of course, like the first thirteen books, substance for intellectual historians, it deals with concepts that transcend their times and are of concern to scholars and critics of any generation.[15] This book, like the fifteenth, but to an even greater degree, is given enduring vitality by the ardent commitment of the author. We shall summarize the main points here, making use of Osgood's excellent translation, from which all quotations are taken.[16]

Boccaccio states that, his work now done, he will with God's help defend his enterprise against objections made "of the art and works of poetry." He hopes that the massive bulk of the work (although it is still incomplete) will confirm the king in his opinion that poets are not merely storytellers "but men of great learning endowed with a sort of divine intelligence and skill." Such enemies Boccaccio divides into four categories: the ignorant who denigrate everything, pretentious pedants, jurists who despise poetry because it does not lead to wealth, and "hypocrites" who call poetry useless and poets creators of lewd and absurd tales. Boccaccio is particularly vigorous in his rebuttal to lawyers and hypocrites. To the former he points out that there are higher rewards than wealth; poets even as philosophers look beyond material gain to the second class, to those who dare to quote Plato's dictum that poets should be banished and therefore are dangerous adversaries, he opposes a blunt denial: "poetry is useful," he says; like other studies it is derived from God. He admits however that there are some corrupt poets—but only a small minority (proem through chapter 6).

We may observe here that the battle between the money-making clan and the followers of the Muse is a familiar feature of medieval letters; it is the subject, as we shall see, of one of Boccaccio's eclogues and both in the *Convivio* and the *Comedy* Dante harangues against wealth as a corrupter of virtue. As for the class called "hypocrites," whomever Boccaccio may have had in mind (quite possibly clerics), they are indeed dangerous. For to the pious mentality of the Middle Ages it might quite readily seem that one's intellectual talents should be dedicated not to the irrelevancies of poetry but to the study of divine things. This uneasiness haunted Petrarch and is apparent in the palinodic lines of his last sonnet. The same uneasiness probably accounts, in part at least, for Dante's abandonment of the *Convivio;* the last *cantica* of the *Comedy* is as much theological as poetic (more so, Croce thought).

In chapter 7 Boccaccio offers his definition of poetry; it is, he says, "a sort of fervid and exquisite invention, with fervid expression in speech or writing, of what the mind has invented. It proceeds from the bosom of God." It can create all things. Yet, he goes on to say, fervor of itself is not enough. A poet needs "instruments," i.e., "the precepts of the other liberal arts both moral and natural." He needs a copious vocabulary; he should also observe the monuments and relics of the ancients; he should know the geography "of various lands, seas, rivers and mountains."[17] Other useful assets for one who would woo the muse are quiet places of retirement, peace of mind, desire for worldly glory, and "the ardent period of life." Concluding, he notes that the word "poetry" is from Greek *poëtes*, signifying "exquisite discourse" and that "whatever is composed under a veil and thus exquisitely wrought, is poetry and poetry alone." (Here Boccaccio faithfully echoes Petrarch who expressed the same sentiments in *Africa* 9 and *Ep. Met.* 2.10).

After expressing some uncertainty about the origins of poetry, substantially enlarging on some arguments already set forth in his *Life of Dante* (chapter 8), Boccaccio returns to his defense. The composition of stories, he affirms, is not to be condemned; it is useful, for the meaning of fiction is far from superficial. Fiction is, in fact, a form of discourse that, under the guise of invention, illustrates or proves an idea; as the superficial aspect is removed the meaning of the author becomes clear (a notion, as Osgood reminds us, that probably has its source in Macrobius).[18] He sees four possible combinations of fiction and truth: (1) when the fiction lacks all appearance of truth, as when beasts talk (for example in Aesop's fables); (2) when superficially fiction and truth mingle—as in the fables; this form, he adds, is widely used, sometimes for sublime purposes and sometimes by corrupt poets; (3) when "fiction" is more truly history, as in Virgil and Homer; yet even here the hidden meaning is different; (4) when fiction contains no truth at all—as in old wives' tales. Boccaccio defends all but the last kind by examples from Scripture. He concludes that the power of fiction is such that it pleases the unlearned by its external appearance and exercises the minds of the learned with its hidden truths and thus both are edified and delighted (10). Which is almost literally what Petrarch says in *Ep. Met.* 2.10, lines 8–9; that may well have been in Boccaccio's mind, for by way of illustrating his thesis he refers to the work of that most distinguished Christian gentleman Francis Petrarch: "would he have wasted his time on his *Eclogues* or his *De remediis* if they were stories and nothing more?" Boccaccio's modesty, he adds, prevents him from citing his own eclogues as examples (10).

Still following on Messer Francesco's traces (*De vita solitaria, Invective against Doctors* 4),[19] Boccaccio affirms that poets need solitude for meditation, although this doesn't mean they are antisocial; Dante, for example, was a friend of Frederick of Aragon[20] and the illustrious duke of Verona, "and everyone knows that Francesco Petrarca has been on terms of great intimacy and affection with the Emperor Charles, with John, King of France, with Robert, King of Jerusalem and Sicily and with many an exalted prelate besides" (11).

To the charge that poets are sometimes obscure their apologist retorts: so are philosophers. And often the fault is in the reader rather than the poet. In any case it is not proper for a poet to "rip up his veil" and in fact obscurity encourages study and strengthens the memory (as Petrarch says in his *Invective against Doctors* 3). Good poets are "invariably explicable if approached by a sane mind." To be sure a reader must prepare himself in rhetoric, figures of diction, vocabulary and the like; indeed those who want to appreciate poetry must read, persevere, . . . sit up nights and exert their minds to the utmost (12). Poets are not liars; they do not write to deceive; if their detractors object that their stories are not literally true—well the same may be said of Revelations and St. John is no liar. . . . It cannot be denied that some poets say there are many gods and not one alone. But they don't quite mean that—and if some pagan poets apprehended Christian truth only dimly—well the same could be said of Plato and Aristotle. Again, the charge is that poets celebrate the adulteries of the gods and show them as changing shapes. Boccaccio will not here defend the wickedness of "the common poets" but as for the portrayal of Jove under various forms, Holy Writ does the same with God, the Church, and Mary; such figures have mystic meanings even as with the poets. Again, poets are said to lead their readers into criminal practices. It must be admitted that some have; Ovid perhaps, although probably his young readers would have followed their own desires in any case. But what of Homer, Hesiod, Virgil, Horace, and Juvenal? This type of critic has probably never read these poets. Poets in fact teach righteousness. Nor is it fair to speak of poets as "aping philosophers." Poets *are* philosophers but their meditations are clothed in art and beauty. They were better called apes of Nature for in their "tiny letters" they can make you see storms and seas and skies (13–17).

Boccaccio, conceding that it would be better to study sacred books, yet affirms it is no sin to read poetry. "We cannot at all times follow the same inclination and occasionally some men incline to poetical writers." And why should we not be allowed to read pagan poets if we are permitted to read heretical works and look at paintings of pagan scenes?

The Muses' champion now offers some daring and not entirely convincing refutation of authorities. When Jerome said the songs of poets were the food of devils, Boccaccio simply states that the good saint couldn't possibly have meant *all* poets; after all Fulgentius wrote a book of myths, Augustine often cited Virgil, St. Paul quoted pagan poets, and Jesus spoke in parables in the style of the comic poets. Nor did Plato, certainly, mean to banish all poets: he would never have banished Homer, Virgil, Petrarch Ennius, and others—[21] and inevitably Boccaccio concludes with another brief eulogy of Petrarch who "from his youth has lived celibate and such has been his horror at impure and illicit love that his friends know him for a perfect model of saintly and honorable living" (18–19).

The foregoing will suffice to give a good notion of Boccaccio's concept of poetry. In his view a poet must be what we should call nowadays a dedicated scholar as much as anything else. Poetry requires long training and discipline and even the readers of poems must undergo the proper course of instruction. In effect Boccaccio strives to put poetry in a class with philosophy and even, though somewhat tentatively, with theology. Spontaneity and openness of expression count for little; indeed the first must be moderated and the second, in his theory, would be a definite flaw. Boccaccio was not of course speaking merely for himself. This elitist concept was standard in the Middle Ages; as we have noted, Boccaccio's views often merely echo those of Petrarch who remarked in the aforementioned *Ep. Met.* 2.10 that poets were saying nothing different from what had been said by such wise men as Plato and Aristotle, and Dante (*Par.* 2, 10–11) saves his loftiest verse for the few who have spent years in arduous study.

Clearly poetry is not for the masses and not so much for the heart as
the head. In which connection it is interesting to note that Dante, who
covers in the course of his writings practically all movements and
schools of poetry of his day, never so much as alludes to his contemporary Jacopone da Todi, whose simple, passionate *laudi* can still move
many a reader today. Perhaps, as much as any moral misgivings,
Boccaccio's mature reservations concerning his own *Decameron* were
motivated by his awareness that it had no "veil," no philosophical
significance, and no "poetry."

The first chapters of book 15, as we have noted, are dedicated to
acknowledgments, particularly to the compiler's contemporaries. Having as it were discharged that obligation, the author moves to what
is essentially an apologia for his book as a whole and to a certain extent
for his life and career. These pages are of interest for the opinions
expressed and for the biographical information casually supplied, but
they are more than that; in tone, style, and manner they are pages that
reveal Boccaccio more intimately and more engagingly than any other
passage of his works. One seems to be in the very presence of the old
scholar.

He begins prosaically enough by refuting the possible charge of
citing unknown or unimportant classical authorities. He concedes that
his sources are many and some not well known but they are all valuable
because of their antiquity. He is willing to vouch for the authenticity
of their existence; he has done his duty in bringing such obscure names
to the attention of his readers. "Books cannot of themselves fly from
library shelves into the hands of students; it is the duty of those who
are familiar with them to act as proxies for those who are not."[22] Since
poetry has never had the avid attention of annotators and commentators as Law, Medicine, Theology, Philosophy have had, his copious
authorities are necessary (6).

To the charge that he has been guilty of "gratuitous and ostentatious
quotation of Greek poetry" Boccaccio replies that sometimes he has
found things in Homer that were not to be found elsewhere and
sometimes he has simply chosen to quote directly from him rather than
from a middleman. He admits he has occasionally quoted passages of
poetry for his own pleasure. Against the charge that quotation of

Greek is absurd because today no one reads it, Boccaccio can only say that he is sorry for Latin learning if we can no longer so much as recognize Greek characters. Latin literature would gain much light through an alliance with Greek, nor have the Latin writers yet brought to us all the Greeks have to tell us. Besides, he adds, if he has quoted Greek out of pure ostentation, he has a right to do so. "Did I not receive [Leontius Pilatus] into my house, entertain him for a long time and make the utmost effort personally that he should be appointed professor in Florence?" From him Boccaccio had learned many passages of Homer and he has a right to quote them. "Yet there are swine who fly into a rage at me for mingling Greek verses with Latin—and little glory do I get for my pains."

Another necessary defense is that of the writer's orthodoxy. Some pious people will no doubt reproach him, he says, for saying that pagan poets are theologians, yet Augustine seems to allow that they are at least natural theologians and their writings often deal with divine things. Of course not being Christian they are not sacred theologians. But their theology can be employed in behalf of Christian truth, such a poet could indeed be a sacred theologian, Dante for example. Some good souls too think it improper for Christians to study pagan antiquity lest they be corrupted by it. But, Boccaccio argues, save for few that is most unlikely: in the early days of the Church such anxiety was justifiable "but today . . . the hateful doctrine of paganism has been cast into utter and perpetual darkness." Boys or neophytes might indeed be vulnerable but not a mature Christian firm in his faith. Lest there be any doubt that the definition applies to him Boccaccio launches on a lengthy *credo,* reinforcing the tenets of the Nicene Creed with additional details drawn from Scripture. He is sure that his faith is strong enough to defend him against the lures of paganism, which he seems to equate with sexual attraction.

Some will object, he continues, that he might better have used his time in the study of higher things—in more sacred matters, especially theological studies. He concedes that theology is indeed higher but it is not possible for every man to be a theologian; each man has his own special talent with which he is born and which he is bound to cultivate [the author here follows both Petrarch and Dante]. And his vocation "as experience from my mother's womb has shown, is clearly the study of poetry." For that he was born. His father's efforts to make him a businessman and later a lawyer only resulted in his becoming neither —"and missed being a good poet besides." It is too late for him to turn to sacred studies; since he believes he is called to poetry by God's will: he will stand fast in it.

He moves on next to specific charges against his book, observing that some say that he has been too brief in his accounts; others that he has been too prolix. He concedes there may be some truth in these charges but such was the nature of the work; some items had to be summarized or they would have been out of proportion. Others, he admits, he lingered on "from pure delectation of mind such as occasionally makes the pen of the better writers very generous." Answering the charge that his book was not actually solicited by King Hugo, Boccaccio waxes very indignant. He has proof, he says, of the king's repeated urgings; granted they came through intermediaries; if Boccaccio has been deceived it is their fault. But aside from that he states he didn't need Hugo's invitation; a king nearby would have been glad to accept the dedication. Further, his book needed no dedication, and it is kings who are honored by such offerings and not the writers who make them, as again is proved by the case of Robert of Sicily and Petrarch. Boccaccio concludes with a blanket apology for faults his book may contain and the hope that his eminent teacher, the far-famed Francis Petrarch, will remove any errors in the work.

A unique feature of the *Genealogies* is the series of designs of genealogical trees that illustrates the text. There are thirteen such sketches, one preceding each of the informational chapters; the final chapters call for no such illustrations. These sketches appear in the only extant autograph manuscript; they are meant to supply visual aid to the laborious and scrupulous account of celestial families and septs. If some of them are so luxuriant as to seem as likely to confuse as to clarify, they are noteworthy as giving Boccaccio yet another primacy. According to Wilkins, who finds their antecedents in the "arbor juris of medieval law, the circle and line charts found in historical and biblical MSS, and the Jesse-trees found in biblical MSS and elsewhere, they are the earliest secular genealogical trees properly so called."

"They constitute," he adds, "also the first elaborated series of genealogical charts."[23] In this connection we may remark that Boccaccio's penchant for illustration should not surprise us; the autograph Hamilton manuscript of the *Decameron* contains a number of sketches by his hand, as does the *Zibaldone laurenziano*.[24] It has been said that Boccaccio could have made a living as a copyist; he might have done equally well as an illustrator.

Concurrently with his preparation of the *Genealogies* Boccaccio worked on another compendium, smaller and less demanding, undertaken, so he tells us, as a distraction from the more arduous effort required by the *Genealogies.* He gave to this "jocosus labor" or pastime, as we might paraphrase the Latin, the rather imposing title of *De montibus, silvis, fontibus, lacubus, fluminibus, stagnis seu paldibus, et de nominibus maris liber.* Begun, according to Branca,[25] in the period 1355–1357, and revised and amended up to the last year of the compiler's life, this topographical guide and companion to classical literature (the first of its kind as Mattalia points out)[26] was highly esteemed and widely utilized by men of letters up to the Renaissance.[27] The range is wide and catholic; there is room for "Ararath" as well as Ida and the hill of Fiesole too, "olivetis plenus"; the infernal and fanciful Cocytus is cataloged among the rivers as are the Thames and the Po; Horace's Bandusiae and Petrarch's Sorga are numbered among the fountains.

Although undertaken as a diversion, Boccaccio's geographical dictionary contains an impressive number of items. Some 560 mountains are listed, from Alac ("limpidum seu lubricum") to Ziph ("squallidus vel caligans")—both in Syria. Thirty-six forests, 116 fountains and 90 lakes are identified, and the catalog of rivers (from Arno to Zonus) contains over nine hundred entries. "Swamps and Marshes" has 60 entries and "Names of the seas" (the word is given a broad definition) run to a total of 94. Each classification is preceded by a paragraph of definition and editorial comment.

Boccaccio's manner is relaxed and informal, "chatty," one might say. Most of the entries are brief ("Edon mons Thraciae est," "Oscurus scytharus est fluvius") but when the compiler encounters a name that has a special literary or personal association he enlarges his commentary, sometimes with appealing enthusiasm. The Nile receives very lengthy treatment (almost two hundred lines); we learn, among other things, that it is "totius orbis permaximus fluvius," that its upper reaches border on lands productive of "beluarum immanium: et crocodillorum et hippotamorum et aliorum similium" and further that its waters make women fertile. The Po too is given considerable space. The entry on the Sorga, classed as a *fons*, not a *fluvius*, leads to a panegyric of "that illustrious man and famous poet, my fellow citizen and my mentor," who had found in his refuge in Vaucluse, putting behind him the new Babylon, tranquillity of mind and inspiration for such works as the *Africa*, the *Bucolicum carmen*, the *Metrical Letters*, and most notably the essay on the life of solitude, "a work seemingly of divine rather than human genius." And to most readers of today the most moving remark of all appears in the item on the Arno, which heads the long list of rivers not for alphabetical reasons only but because "it is the river of my native land and above all others familiar to me since my childhood." Tracing the course of the Tuscan stream the writer also suggests, intentionally or otherwise, a link between himself and his master, born on the shores of the same historic river. The work concludes with a modest epilogue in which, yet once more, Petrarch, envisioned in the glory of his coronation, is eulogized.

As in the case of the *Genealogies*, the sophisticated scholarship of more recent encyclopedists has made *De montibus* obsolete; there is no modern edition of the work.[28]

CHAPTER 15

CONCERNING FAMOUS WOMEN

mong all of Boccaccio's Latin *compendia*, composed in the medieval tradition as informational manuals or *summae*, the treatise *Concerning Famous Women* is uniquely attractive to the reader of today; it has purely literary attributes that set it apart from its companion volumes of capsulized erudition. Francis MacManus is undoubtedly right, if somewhat patronizing, when he remarks: "Although the admonitions it contains are tedious, the book of renowned ladies is the least fatiguing of the later works."[1] If it derives patently from the encyclopedic aspirations that occasioned the compilation of the longer and more pretentious (and indubitably more "scholarly") *Genealogies of the Pagan Gods*, its immediate genesis may well lie in the author's desire to follow the example of his master Petrarch, who, as Boccaccio informs us in his preface,[2] was already well launched on his catalog of Famous Men. It was all but inevitable that to the faithful disciple a companion piece, as it were, would seem appropriate.

And of course the substance of the work also bespeaks Boccaccio's abiding interest in the fair sex, so frankly avowed in the *Decameron*. For he remarks (also in his preface) "If men should be praised whenever (with the strength that Nature has given them) they perform great deeds, how much more should women be extolled (almost all of whom are endowed by Nature with tenderness, frail bodies and sluggish minds) if they have acquired a manly spirit and if with keen intelligence they have dared undertake and have accomplished even the most difficult deeds?"[3] Of this somewhat ambiguous view of womankind, which feminists may well regard with a certain suspicion, we shall have more to say later.

Vittorio Zaccaria, the work's most recent editor, noting that its "remote genesis" goes back to the spiritual reorientation in Boccaccio's life occasioned by the meeting with Petrarch in 1350, places the composition of the book in the summer of 1361, after the encounter with Leontius Pilatus, adding that the author continued to make additions and revisions until the eve of his death.[4] It is evident that the work was begun after Boccaccio's "conversion"; the author is no longer the carefree teller of the hundred tales but already the reformed Brother John, pious, sententious, and censorious. Yet here and there as the parade of glittering heroines passes before our eyes the narrative spark glows again and if the pages of this work of serious research lack the brio of the *Decameron* they are nevertheless infused with the author's lively personality. There is nothing arid about these little vignettes.

The work is prefaced by a dedicatory letter to Andrea Acciaiuoli, countess of Altavilla and sister of the seneschal of the Kingdom of Naples from whom Boccaccio had long expected preferment. (The letter obviously predates the ultimately disillusioning visit to Naples in 1362.) It is a somewhat odd dedication. Boccaccio confesses that he had at first planned to offer the work to Queen Joan; he had come to feel, however, he says, that the "half extinguished little spark" ("semisopita favillula") of his effort might be totally obscured by the royal splendor of so great a monarch. Since he dared not aim so high he felt that the next most worthy person would be the countess, in view of her marvelous virtues and many splendid and honorable accomplishments—and besides, he adds, Andrea is from the Greek *andres* signifying "men", as if to suggest that the lady bearing the name should be put on a plane of equality with the worthiest of men. He begs her to read the work attentively and not to be shocked if she occasionally finds lascivious matters mixed with sacred things, as his exposition occasionally required, but rather to persevere and seek the flower under the thorn. He suggests that when she reads of the virtues of pagan women she should blush if she, a Christian woman, does not feel that she too possesses them; let such women serve as examples for her. He bids the countess, too, to be as preeminent in intellectual and moral qualities as she is in beauty, youth, and charm. He cautions her against the use of cosmetics. History does not record what the Lady Andrea made of this prescriptive eulogy.

The letter of dedication is followed by a succinct foreword, in which, as noted, Boccaccio refers to Petrarch's work *On Famous Men*. He says further that when he writes of famous women, he does not necessarily mean "virtuous" women but rather women who have attained renown through any kind of notable action. He admits that, save for Eve, his catalog contains no Hebrew or Christian women; the two categories could not be put side by side, he says, for they did not strive for the same goal and in any case the stories of saintly Christian women have been told repeatedly by pious men, whereas no one as yet has brought out a work dealing specifically with pagan women. [Friar John may be a pillar of orthodoxy now but his heart is still in pagan antiquity; he is not going to give us any saints' lives.] Revealing an intent not only instructive but didactic, the author states that he has decided to include among his sketches "some pleasant invitations to virtue and some sharp barbs intended to put evil to flight."[5] He confesses too that he has somewhat enlarged on the material he found in "ancient sources" (of which he names none).

Of the 106 brief chapters that compose the work, 104 are dedicated to the portrayal of individual women; the 2 others treat, respectively, the wives of the Minyans (notable for their conjugal devotion) and the wives of the Cimbrians, memorable for their collective resolution to preserve their chastity at the cost of their lives. In keeping with the prescription of the preface, the great majority of profiles are drawn from pagan antiquity. The only exceptions are the sketch of Eve— whose claim to fame can hardly be overlooked—and six postclassical figures appearing at the end of the work: Pope Joan, the Empress Irene of Constantinople, Constance, the mother of Frederick II, the widow Camiola (a Tuscan woman married to a Sicilian nobleman), and Queen Joan of Naples to whom Boccaccio had originally intended to dedicate his book. The last half dozen make up a rather puzzling appendage, perhaps we may see in them an example of the syncretistic intent, evident also in Dante's *Comedy,* that was a recurrent aspect of early humanism. The sketch of Queen Joan, attributing to her virtues and achievements that historians have not easily perceived, is a courtly and calculated gesture; the other ladies, at least among Boccaccio's Italian contemporaries, had long been subjects of comment and indeed gossip. However, in the main the roll call is strictly classical, coming down in chronological succession from the Greek and Roman goddesses and mythological figures to the celebrated historical characters of Roman history. Guarino notes that the sources most frequently called upon are Valerius Maximus, Livy, Hyginus, and Tacitus; he enumerates also many others.[6]

In the introduction to his edition Zaccaria argues vigorously that the work is more historical–literary than didactic in purpose.[7] This may well be true; it is impossible to read the mind of the author over the intervening centuries, but unprejudiced readers may find the purpose honored at least as much in the breach as in the observance. It is true, admittedly, that the framework is supplied by history and the order is chronological. Some of the sketches seem to indicate an emancipation from conventional moral rigidity. The prostitute Laena, for example, wins the author's admiration for her loyalty and fortitude; her profession is irrelevant. At times too an almost feminist thesis is adumbrated in the portrayal of women admirable for qualities other than the traditional virtues of modesty, docility, and piety. Perhaps it was the sincere intention of the author to set before us a series of great women of strong personality and capable of high achievement. Yet this attitude is far from consistent; a recurrent didacticism openly avowed in the statement quoted above characterizes the work. These imposing ladies may be truly historical figures but they are also meant, as Guido Guarino says, to be "examples of vice or virtue."[8]

It is not necessarily a matter to be deplored if Clio's serenity is clouded by moralistic concern. The effect in fact is to give to the gallery of illustrious females a humanizing if not truly humanistic dimension. Their compiler becomes their critic and in some sense their creator, providing them with speeches, speculating on their motivations. Often they take on the vivacity of characters in a novel; indeed some of them have stories reminiscent of the characters of the *Decameron*. Guarino notes that the account of Paulina is suggestive of the story of the Venetian woman (day 4, story 2) whose credulous vanity allowed her to believe she was loved by the Archangel Gabriel, and he sees in the falsely canonized Flora a resemblance to the nucleus of the tale of Ciappelletto with which the hundred tales begin.[9] The reader may feel too that in the case of Dido the historian's empathy makes of his subject something more than an exemplum; his defense of the ill-starred queen gives her a life of her own. (This in the teeth of Virgil, as it were, but it should be remembered that Petrarch had a like high opinion of the lady.)[10]

On the euhemeristic principle that obtains frequently also in the *Genealogies*, Boccaccio will not grant to the pagan deities any legitimate claim to divinity. Juno, for example, is not a heaven-born goddess but simply a woman "later made queen of heaven through the fiction of the poets and the senseless generosity of the ancients."[11] So too, Ceres was "a very ancient queen of Sicily;" Minerva, who discovered and invented so many useful arts, was "by antiquity, the dispenser of divinity, made into the goddess of wisdom"; and Venus was simply a woman of such rare beauty that men readily believed her divine. The treatment of Venus in fact exemplifies not only the author's euhemerism but also his naturalistic approach to mythology. "It was known," he writes, "that [Venus'] first husband Vulcan had found her lying with a man-at-arms and this is the basis [of the story] of her adultery with Mars." The same thesis is argued in the sketch of Flora; no goddess of spring at all, Boccaccio assures us, but a prostitute who achieved social position and prestige by her shrewdness and so became honored as a goddess after her death. (If, as we have noted, her paradoxical apotheosis is a kind of parallel to the canonization of Ciappelletto, the moral indignation with which her story is told is in sharp contrast to the easygoing skepticism that colors the account of the Florentine charlatan and may serve to measure the distance the author has been carried by his "conversion.") Other myths are given allegorical interpretations of a more or less realistic nature. Circe, for example, is a personification of the lustfulness of women that changes men into beasts, Iole's domination of Hercules carries a like meaning.

Such interpretations sharpen our perception of the fundamental and irreconcilable contradiction in effect, if not in conscious intention, that *Concerning Famous Women* reveals. Ostensibly the work is a tribute to women and furthermore a recognition, even a celebration, unclouded by considerations of either piety or eroticism, of their worth. For the first time in a medieval work of any substance women are appreciated and admired neither as intercessors nor mistresses but as individual human beings remarkable for their achievements and their personalities. Nor is there any good reason to question the author's sincerity; in the vast majority of the exempla presented his respect for his subject is patent. Yet at the same time a countercurrent, composed of old-fashioned and essentially misogynistic elements, runs through the work. The pious eulogy of chastity, for example, is a recurrent motif, not without a certain undertaste of prurience. Even women, such as Zenobia, who achieved greatly in war and politics, are admired more for their chastity than their exploits. In this area the passage from theoretical pontification to practical prescription is a constant temptation to our reformed Brother John. From the experience of Europa we learn that "it is not good to give girls too much freedom to stroll about and listen to the words of strangers." From the example of the warrior-virgin Camilla the author would hope "the girls of our time might learn what is proper for them in their parents' home, in churches, and in theaters where most onlookers and harsh judges of behavior congregate," and so "not to listen to shameful words, to keep silent and avoid idleness, feasting, elegance, dancing and the company of young men." Still, some measure of parental understanding is advisable; the sad story of Thisbe teaches us that "the ardor of the young should be curbed slowly, lest in our desire to oppose them with sudden impediments we drive them to despair and perdition." Parents are likewise bidden to be cautious about making nuns of their daughters while the girls are "young or ignorant or under coercion." Only when, after proper upbringing, they are mature and fully aware of what they are doing should they be permitted to take the vows—"but I believe there would be very few of these."

This skeptical assessment of female continence clearly illustrates the persistent misogynistic current we have noted. In effect this anthology of famous women demonstrates what women can do—in spite of being women. The view of the fair sex that emerges from the tangential comment on many of the sketches is anything but flattering and, had not the *Corbaccio* prepared us for it, even disconcerting, coming as it does from the pen of the champion of womanhood who so eloquently defended the sex in the pages of his masterpiece. Examples abound. Eve's yielding to the tempter is characteristic of "a woman's fickleness." In his sketch of the Sibyl Amalthea, the author reminds us that men have a greater aptitude "for all things" than women. Admiring the exploits of the Persian Artemisia, "what can we think except that it was an error of Nature to give female sex to a body which had been endowed by God with a magnificent and virile spirit?" The female artist Irene is worthy of special praise because "art is very alien to the mind of a woman"; the gracious generosity of the legendary Busa reminds Boccaccio that in general "women have innate frugality and little generosity." Elsewhere we are told gratuitously that women are "very suspicious creatures," "innately obstinate," "cowardly, accustomed to flee to their husbands' bosom at the slightest noise of a mouse even in full daylight," and that they habitually "lead sluggish lives" —and these are but a few of the *obiter dicta* of this erstwhile *defensor mulierum*. We may conclude by citing one especially revealing passage. In discussing Poppaea, Nero's wife, (who, incidentally, "practiced lasciviousness in private, the universal vice of women") the author ends with the comment that he could have said more against the "excessive softness, the flattery, wantonness and tears which are a woman's certain and deadly poison for the soul of a man who trusts her. But I decided to omit these matters lest I seem to be writing a satire rather than a history."

For a more detailed account of Boccaccio's ambivalent feminism than we offer here, the reader may turn to Guarino's introduction to his translation of the work. His resolution of the matter is perceptive. "As always," he concludes, "Boccaccio moves forward instinctively towards a new era, but his progress is hindered by the *impedimenta* and traditions of a former age."[12] One may readily concur; the clash of tradition and innovation in matters of concept, style, form, and attitude is characteristic of our author. But in no other work are the two faces of his Janus so sharply delineated as they are in *Concerning Famous Women.*

The disparagement of the female is accompanied by a tendency to point out the decadence of the mores of the present in contrast to the decency of the past. Girls, we are told, are no longer properly brought up, the old virtues of moderation and restraint are no longer practiced; it is no wonder that we live nowadays in a woman-dominated world in which men have themselves become womanish. The interweaving of these two threads hardly surprises us: antifeminists are traditionally reactionaries. To the eye of the prophet of doom moral decay and the emancipation of woman go hand in hand. Insofar as Boccaccio's treatise is concerned this is a matter not entirely regrettable; it lends spice to his substance and is at the root of one of the book's most poetic and suggestive passages, ultimately Lucretian but set forth with new vigor and destined to reecho through the Renaissance: well worthy of mention here.

The sketch of Ceres and the arts she is said to have taught the human race leads to an ambivalent assessment of the achievements of civilization as measured against the virtues of the golden age. "Who would regret," Boccaccio inquires rhetorically,[13] "that savage nomads were led out of the woods and into cities? Or that grain from sown seeds refined the human body and strengthened the limbs? Or that the world, once covered with thorns, underbrush, and weeds, was changed into a place of beauty and useful to mankind? Or that so many men's minds were roused from sluggishness to thought? Or that so many new towns, cities, and states were built, giving rise to so many admirable and cherished customs?" Of course these things are "good in themselves." But there is nothing to praise in the fact that men, once satisfied with wild fruit, nuts, and milk of animals were attracted to delicate and unknown foods. No longer satisfied by the laws of nature, sober, modest, and guileless, men became vulnerable to vices long latent and now prepared to come into the open. The land, once held in common by all, was fenced off into fields. The labor of cultivation began and also for the first time "mine" and "thine" came to trouble the peace of old. "From this came poverty and slavery, dissension, hatred, bloody wars and burning envy." This led to navigation, the reciprocal discovery of East and West—and "the softening of the body, the swelling of the belly, display in dress and at the board." The dependence on cultivation, too, signifies misery and starvation when crops fail, and consequently leads to disease, degeneration, and untimely death. "Having pondered such things I scarcely know whether—nay but rather I do know that those golden centuries, primitive and uncivilized though they were, are yet greatly to be preferred to our age of iron and indeed to all other ages."

If one wants to see how far Boccaccio has come since the *Decameron* one has but to compare this passage with the story of Cymon (day 5, story 1), the simple yokel civilized by love. Romantic love, in fact the theme and the inspiration of the younger Boccaccio, is all but banished from the pages of *Famous Women*; it is exalted only in the tender tale of Pyramus and Thisbe—and even there it is accepted with some reservations.

In conclusion, seeking to define the nature of *Concerning Famous Women*, we may well accept the verdict of Daniele Mattalia who calls the book "a compromise between historical erudition and the novella —a pleasing work of learning,"[14] adding only that its avowed purpose, however faulty in fulfillment, gives it a unique status in medieval letters.

The book had a considerable European resonance. Its inspiration seems patent in Chaucer's *Legend of Fair Women*,[15] although direct influence is debatable. Three editions of the work were published before 1500, and at some time between 1534 and 1547 Henry Parker, Lord Morley (the translator of Petrarch's *Triumphs*) translated forty-six of the items into English, although his work had to wait three centuries for publication.[16] His sixteenth-century English lends an appropriate tone to the harrowing story of Pyramus and Thisbe (even in such a tongue did Bottom and Quince recite the tale for the delectation of their betters). We may, by way of illustrating Boccaccio's style and substance, quote Parker's version here.[17] It runs as follows:

> Thisbe of Babylon more by the unhappy fortune that she had in loving Pyramus than by any other notable deed, is put here among the

noble and famous women. Nor of this woman we have no notable knowledge who, by the ancient writers, were her parents. But it is evident that Pyramus and she were nigh neighbors, and their houses joining, the one nigh the other. By which neighborhood having together continual company, and both passing goodly and fair, as they grew in age, so grew their love into extreme burning fire and that by sighs the one declared unto the other. And so they both come into lawful age, where that Thisbe was marriable, her father kept her still at home, to the intent to marry her, wherewith as well Pyramus as she were greatly displeased withal, seeking busily the way how to commune and meet together. At the last they found a clift in the wall, which no man afore had found, at which clift they met together, oft times with sighs and tears and lamentations, in promitting peax, embracing and perpetual love while their lives endured. And so with such enflammings they counseled to run away the next night and how they might beguile them of their fathers house, and who that first escaped, should go to a wood thereby, where was a fair fountain, and not far from thence the grave of King Ninus, and he or she that first came, should tarry the coming of the other. Thisbe, that percase more ardently loved, was the first that deceived her guardians, and with a cloak cast over her head, in the still of the night, all alone got out of her father's house, and, the moon giving light to her way, all hastily went onward and came at the last to the well, trembling for every light noise she heard, and seeing coming to the well a lioness, all afraid, leaving behind her her veil and her cloak, fled into the wood. The lioness, when she had well fed, finding there the cloak and the veil, with her bloody mouth tore it in pieces and after drinking of the well went her way. Pyramus that had tarried somewhat too long leaving his father's house, in the still of the night came into the wood, and finding the cloak and the veil of Thisbe torn and all fouled with bloody spots here and there, thinking that some wild beast had devoured her, filled all the places about him with clamour and cry, accusing himself that he was the cause of the death of that most sweet, loving virgin, and despising for that his life, having his sword about him, took the point there of and thrust it to his heart and so fell down dead in the place. What more? Thisbe, esteeming the lioness to be gone, and fearing lest Pyramus should think she should tarry too long, by that way she went into the wood, she came again to the fountain, and seeing there Pyramus, not all dead, but

CHAPTER 16

THE BUCCOLICUM CARMEN
(PASTORAL SONG)

t some time between 1370 and 1374, Boccaccio sent to his clerical friend, Brother Martino da Signa, the final version of his *Buccolicum carmen*. With the text he enclosed a covering letter,[1] explaining the nature of the genre of pastoral verse known as the eclogue, summarizing the history of the form, and adding an explanatory note on all but the first two of his own sixteen contributions to the genre. The eclogue, he states, began with Theocritus and, among the classical writers, was most successfully cultivated by Virgil. Since the end of the ancient world, he adds, the form has fallen into abeyance and no eclogue worthy of note has been written until recently when Petrarch turned his hand to them; he had elevated their style. Boccaccio states that Virgil had been the first to use the bucolic manner to conceal a meaning "hidden under the bark" although he had not always given a second sense to the names of his interlocutors. Petrarch, however, regularly used names of allegorical significance. With regard to his own compositions Boccaccio says that he has followed Virgil's example, at least to some degree, in that he has not given to "all" his personae a secondary significance.

Our poet's history of the development of the eclogue is somewhat sketchy but it is useful as revealing the sources of his inspiration. And, in fact, essentially his eclogues are Virgilian but the immediate spur to their composition and the resultant color they take on have their origin in a close and admiring study of Petrarch's *Bucolicum carmen*.

Perhaps one should temper the statement by adding "as we now have them." A few of Boccaccio's efforts predate his meeting with Petrarch in 1350; critics have noted that the eclogues written after that date show a more marked influence of the singer of Vaucluse. It seems a little odd that, in his introductory remarks, Boccaccio makes no mention of Dante, of whose pioneering example both he and his master must have been aware.

Since the bucolic form, as Petrarch and Boccaccio employed it, was a vehicle for social commentary and personal confession concealed under a pastoral veil, the inner truth was often difficult for a reader to apprehend. It is for this reason that Boccaccio comments on his compositions for the illumination of Brother Martino, omitting however the first two as too trivial for attention—"nullius enim momenti sunt." His remarks will provide the most convenient as well as the most authoritative basis for our consideration of his eclogues.

The first two, so disparagingly put aside by their author, are "amorous" poems, dealing with the unrequited love of a pair of shepherds; they are entitled respectively "Galla" and "Pampinea." P. G. Ricci notes[2] that the name of the former, as well as the pattern of the eclogue, comes from Virgil's last eclogue, in which Gallus laments his loss of Lycoris. In Boccaccio's verses Galla is the heartless woman and the deserted shepherd is Damone. Ricci believes the eclogue was written shortly after the poet's return from a visit to Naples (1345–1346); he identifies Damone with Boccaccio but is hesitant with regard to the cruel Galla, merely noting that the name of Emiliana de' Tornaquinci has been put forth.[3] The title of the second eclogue, "Pampinea," recalls the name of the somewhat shadowy "inamorata" of Caleone (i.e., Boccaccio) in the *Comedy of the Florentine Nymphs* (see chapter 7) and, of course, likewise the name of the somewhat self-assured young woman who is one of the storytellers in the *Decameron*. Presumably the Palemon of the eclogue, who deplores Pampinea's infidelity, stands for Boccaccio too. It is interesting that this, of all the eclogues, is a simple monologue; of the "interlocutores" mentioned in the title only Palemon speaks. An allusion to the Arno in the last lines makes it clear that the second eclogue, like the first, was composed in Tuscany, probably during the same period as the first.

With the third eclogue we enter a new sector, wherein politics displaces love, and commentary, sometimes acidulous, takes the place of amorous lamentation. "Faunus," the name given to the third eclogue, stands for Francesco degli Ordelaffi, Boccaccio tells us, and the poem deals with the campaign of this ambitious Ghibelline despot as an ally of the Hungarians in their invasion of the Kingdom of Naples in 1347. (For Boccaccio's part in this enterprise see chapter 2.) The fourth eclogue, "Dorus" (derived from Boccaccio's Greek word *doris,* signifying "bitterness"), depicts the sad plight of Louis of Taranto, second husband of Queen Joan, driven from his kingdom by the savage Polyphemus (i.e., Louis of Hungary) and succored by his faithful Pythias (Niccolò Acciaiuoli). Dorus, i.e., Louis of Taranto, who has good cause to feel bitter, describes, with partisan rancor, the brutal actions of his conqueror in the occupation of Naples. The fifth eclogue, "Silva cadens" ("The decaying woods"), deplores the sorry state of the southern kingdom and mourns the death of the great Robert. "In accordance with the pastoral style," Boccaccio comments, "I call the city a wood, since woods are inhabited by beasts as cities are by men, whom, again following the bucolic style, I call sheep, kids and occasionally oxen."[4] The sixth eclogue, "Alceste," takes its name from the Greek words *alce,* meaning virtue, and *aestus,* fervor, and stands for Louis of Taranto; the verses celebrate the triumphant return of the prince to Naples.

Eclogues 4 to 6 make up what might be called the Neapolitan War sequence; eclogues 7 and 9, "Iurgium" ("The Contest") and "Lipis" ("Anxiety"), deal with the uneasy and somewhat shameful (at least in the poet's view) accommodations made between Florence and the Emperor Charles IV in 1355; in the ninth the name "Batracos" (frog) is used to signify "Florentine," "since," Boccaccio avers, "we are overly loquacious and inept in warfare."[5]

The eighth eclogue, coming between such clearly political sorties, is a little puzzling; in effect it is a personal invective directed against one "Midas" (who gives his name to the poem), a man of greed and avarice. W. Leonard Grant, following the general opinion of earlier authorities, identifies Midas with Niccolò Acciaiuoli, adding: "The eclogue describes how an honest shepherd named Pythias has been lured by false promises into Midas's realm but is strongly advised by an old friend to leave while the opportunity is still open to him. These circumstances so closely parallel Boccaccio's invitation to Naples (1361) and his subsequent (1362 and 1363) disillusionment that it is hard not to interpret the poem accordingly."[6] If this be so the eclogue is out of chronological order; more likely it may be associated, as Branca suggests, with an earlier abortive trip to the Angevin capital in 1355, though to be sure, Branca confesses, of this trip "we know little."[7] The reference to the coronation of Zanobi da Strada (which took place in May 1355) suggests very strongly that the eclogue may be of that year and so at least chronologically at home with eclogues 7 and 9. For the rather surprising divergence in the assessments of Acciaiuoli in eclogues 4 and 8 we refer the reader to what has been said of the matter in chapter 2.

Grant sees a clear stylistic distinction between the first six eclogues and those that follow and argues that "Boccaccio began his pastorals under the influence of Dante. But after meeting Petrarch in Florence (1350) he turned from mere pastoral cipher to pastoral cryptogram: eclogues XII–XVI are quite as difficult as anything in Petrarch."[8] His theory may be valid (although not all of the last eight eclogues are unduly cryptic), but a reader more interested in substance than in style may find that a more significant shift comes with the tenth eclogue. From this point on politics ceases to be the chief concern of Boccaccio's shepherds; matters of more enduring significance are pondered: religion and art and the state of the poet's soul.

The title of the tenth eclogue, "Vallis opaca," ("Dark Valley") has clearly intentional Dantean implications; its substance is a dialogue between an unhappy mortal named Dorilus and a revenant called Lycidas, who describes to Dorilus the pains of Hell. It is certainly one of the more enigmatic items in the series; by Lycidas, Boccaccio says, "I intend to signify one who was once a tyrant" (Francesco Corazzini suggests the duke of Athens[9] but the identification is by no means certain) and all we learn of Dorilus is that he is not a king but a *plebeius homo*. Since he is encouraged by his dour and disturbing visitor to forget his poverty and devote himself to the art of poetry, it is not unlikely, as Grant suspects, that Dorilus is the alias of the author himself.[10] Since the identification of the interlocutors is tentative it is not possible to follow with assurance all the allusions in the eclogue. But perhaps this limitation is irrelevant to the main purpose of the poem, which, clearly, is to depict, as colorfully as possible, the eternal misery of the damned. Lycidas takes on the charge with gusto; his report reads (in part) as follows:

Deep in the middle world a grotto lies,
called Trenaros, that Phoebus never sees
and thither are we borne, unhappy wretches,
to whom the gate of Heaven is denied.
Hard by the entrance to this precinct stands
as sentinel an ever watchful hound;
prancing, he welcomes those who enter in,
wagging his tail, but with his teeth he checks
all who would seek to leave the place, unless
his lord bids otherwise. There you may see
forests and meads and lakes and flowing streams.
Mists rising from the marshes and dark clouds
confer a gloomy aspect and the crags
are fouled by dust up-rising from the vale.
There winter and dark and black night forever rule.
A hidden fire burns, fueled not by logs
but by the cunning of the gods. Think not
our dwelling place is like the fertile fields
under Pelorus or the plains of Tyre
nor the rose covered slopes of Lebanon,
nor Tymbrean hills nor set on smiling heights
made fragrant by acanthus boughs nor yet
upon the Po's fair and attractive banks—
nay, rather we inhabit somber heaths
covered with crowsfoot and oppressive yews
and everywhere you look what meets your eye
is nought but briar, thorn and dreary willows
with limbs distorted. The whole wilderness
of tangled boughs casts bleak and dismal shadows
and drips incessantly with sodden rain
while through it sluggishly flow stinking streams

fed from above, with filth and venom charged
to spread pollution. In that place you'll find
no nimble goats nor swiftly coursing deer
for it is overrun with snakes and every pest
of dreadful Lybia, constantly intent
on harrying us with scourgings of their tails
or vicious bites or breath-constricting squeezes.
Your ears are soothed by the seductive notes
of sirens on their sea-girt rocks or songs
of woodland nymphs or warblings of birds,
wafted from verdant branches. But for us
it is quite otherwise: throughout this cavern
lugubrious wails resound while savage boars
gnash angry fangs and ravenous lions fill
the air with roarings. Such dire harmonies
reëcho in our ears without surcease.

    DORILUS: What would you tell me, Lycidas? Could Nature
or any other artisan create
in earth's deep entrails such a fearsome realm?

    LYCIDAS: Why not, in truth? The hand that shaped the stars
and the dark woodlands can make what it will.
But listen further, pray; there is yet worse
to come. Upon a rock King Pluto sits
beside his brooding consort. Both are crowned
with fuscous fronds and clothed in black sheep-hides.
About them throng all mortal maladies:
foul mange and all infections of the herd
and burning fevers and cold winter's chills
and death's own dreadful image. In the midst
of all these horrors—add, too, crawling snakes
and blood-stained scaly things—the shepherd dour
cares not to solace his afflicted flock
with song or lyre nor does he with a reed
caress them gently; rather, climbing high
upon a peak, he blows his mournful horn
to terrify the anxious herd of shades.
With such blasts he arouses frenzied fear
and bids the thorny copses to be burned

so through the clearings bulls may freely charge.
To reckon up the sum of all the groans
his horn engenders you have but to count
the stars that fill the heavens or the grains
of yellow sand that form the ocean's floor.
Then Jove in anger shakes the sky and fills
the woods with ominous rumblings as he casts
his thunderbolts. The clouds collapse and fall
and hail pelts down to shatter every glade,
while furious gales uproot the knotty oaks.

. . . .
Then, calling on the steeds of Diomed
and Geryon's fierce hounds, the savage herdsman
assaults us as we cling to one another
in the dire wasteland, hunted without rest
by Hydras, while his helpers, grim and prompt,
surround the throng, with threats of ill to come.
You would not credit what the herd endures:
he calls on his black bulls and from the heights
he drives these beasts into the lower world
and summons sharp-fanged snakes which he incites,
beating their scaly backs with his rough staff,
its point made sharp by fire, and from the crest
he hurls wolves down into the flaming pit
and often in his rage falls down amongst them.[11]

The eleventh eclogue is entitled "Pantheon" for, Boccaccio explains, "Pan means all and Theon means God and in its verses, from beginning to end divine things are the subject of discussion."[12] The interlocutors, Mirtilis and Glaucus, stand respectively for the Church and St. Peter. The red and green of the myrtle leaf appropriately suggest the persecution suffered by the Church and the hope that characterizes its mission; St. Peter was a fisherman and so, of course, was Glaucus. In the course of the poem the life of Christ is narrated. Every time he is mentioned he is given a different name, ranging from Codrus, the legendary king of Athens, to King Arthur; each name—they number eleven in all—is suited to the action described. Noting that all but two of the soubriquets are taken from Greek mythology, Grant concludes: "The intention of this seems to be to insist that Christ is the sum and more than the sum of all the virtues belonging to the heroes of antiquity."[13] He further remarks that the forty lines describing the Nativity are seminal; later ecloguists would return to the theme and expand it, creating as it were, the subgenre of the Christian pastoral.

"Saphos," signifying Poetry, is the title of the twelfth eclogue. Of the two interlocutors, according to Boccaccio's gloss, Caliopes stands for "pleasing sound" for "it seems that the strength of poetry consists almost entirely in good presentation regulated by poetic measures";[14] "Aristeus is Boccaccio himself, taking his name from one in antiquity" who was eager to become a poet but suffered from a voice impediment up to the time of adolescence. The thesis of the eclogue is that poetry is sacred, and a practitioner of the art, even though he be not a poet of the highest order, is yet a *vates* and worthy of honor. Underlying the argument is a concept of poetry that we should call elitist today.

Poetry is likewise the subject of the thirteenth eclogue, called "Laurea." In form the poem is a contest in song between two shepherds; Daphnis, standing for an unspecified poet, and Stilbon (according to Boccaccio an appellation of Mercury, the god of commerce) representing a certain merchant of Genoa, with whom, the author tells us, he once engaged in a debate similar to the one reported in the eclogue. The name of Critis, the third shepherd, who serves as arbiter in the debate, needs no gloss. He awards the prize to Daphnis, as we might expect. In form this is an eclogue composed with unusual discipline, its interlocutors speak in alternating quatrains, following the pattern of Virgil's third eclogue.

The following two eclogues are notably personal and confessional. Of the fourteenth its author tells us that "it is called Olympia from the greek 'olympus' which in Italian would be 'splendid, lucent and in heaven' and in these lines much is said of the nature of the celestial regions. There are four interlocutors: Silvius, Camalus, Terapon and Olympia. By Silvius I mean myself, since it was in a certain woodland that I first thought of this eclogue. Camalus in Greek signifies feckless, torpid; it illustrates the behavior of a stupid servant. I do not give the meaning of Terapon for I cannot remember it without seeing the book from which I took it along with the others. You know that memory is faulty especially in the old."[15] [Happily, not among commentators; Grant reminds us that it is the Greek word for servant.][16] "By Olympia I mean a little daughter of mine who died at an age in which, according to our belief, those who die become citizens of heaven; in life I called her Violante, in death Olympia or heavenly."[17] This intimate and moving poem, "by all odds the most effective of the collection,"[18] describes a vision in which the poet's daughter appears to him, coming down from Paradise. Flanked by her brothers and sisters, she comforts her father and tells him of her life in Heaven, which she describes in Virgilian and Dantean terms; at the end she assures him that good works will open the way of salvation for him too.

The fifteenth eclogue, no less intimate in nature, presents a dialogue between Phylostropos (from the Greek words *philos*, love, and *tropos*, conversion, according to Boccaccio) and Typhlus, which in Greek means "blind." "By Phylostropos," he continues, "I mean my glorious master Francesco Petrarca, through whose precepts I was often led to turn my mind to things eternal, putting aside enjoyment of things temporal and destined to perish. By Typhlus I mean myself or anyone else blinded by the mist of mortal things."[19] The last gloss is interesting, attempting to give the allegory a universal dimension and perhaps suggesting that all of us may hope for such a conversion as is here attested. In the action of the little drama, Phylostropos, who gives his name to the eclogue, is eventually successful in persuading Typhlus to change his style of life.

The last poem, called "Angelus" (signifying "messenger," or "guide," of the preceding eclogues and offering them to "the friend to whom I send them here")[20] is in effect a dedication of the whole *Buccolicum carmen* to Donato degli Albanzani, an intimate friend of both Boccaccio and Petrarch, and here called "Appenninus, with reference to his dwelling in the hills; Angelus signifies the eclogue itself."

The eclogues, in the form we have them, were composed over the span of years running from 1350 to 1369; 1370, according to Branca, was the year of their "publication and diffusion."[21] Since the influence of Petrarch is pervasive in the *Carmen*, critics inevitably tend to compare it with the eclogues of Boccaccio's mentor. Perhaps this pardonable approach has deprived Boccaccio's verses of some of the acclaim they should have received. Mattalia pronounces a critical verdict shared by the few scholars who have studied the *Carmen* when he affirms that its principal interest for the reader is "documentary."[22] If this be so then it is only fair to add that the documentation is abundant and significant; in the words of Massèra: "The *Carmen* is a collection of autobiographical documents which hold the answers to more than one of the questions with regard to our knowledge of Boccaccio the man and the humanist."[23] The eclogues in fact give us a capsule biography of the poet's inner life and record his major concerns: from the evocation of the romantic infatuations of his youth to the ultimate conversion, taking in on the way due account of his interest in politics—Neapolitan or Florentine—and his passion for poetry and its precious connotations. Through the charade of somewhat misty allegory and farfetched classical allusions the poet speaks to us with consistent and rare sincerity, particularly but not exclusively in the last four eclogues.

It is possible too that a reader of goodwill may find in the *Carmen* some qualities that raise it above the level of the purely documentary. The pastoral fiction is pleasantly and effectively preserved; the dialogues are skillfully composed, the didactic or expositional thrust is on the whole well disciplined. The eclogues are not unduly padded and are of easily readable dimension. The average length is 175 lines; the longest of the series is "Olympia" and, as it is the most moving of all, one could even wish it were longer. There are, too, embedded in the texture of the artfully contrived tapestry, many passages of real eloquence. We may cite the exchange between Florence and the emperor (9), the forceful if somewhat melodramatic depiction of Hell (10) of which we have given a sample, the persuasive account of Petrarch's role in Boccaccio's conversion (15), and—once more and especially—the authentic poetry of the entire fourteenth eclogue. The theme of this poem is very similar to that of the well-known Middle English lyric, "The Pearl." There is no evidence for Boccaccio's influence on the author of "The Pearl," although such a notion is tempting, but the affinity led the English scholar Israel Gollancz to translate Boccaccio's lines. His version conveys very effectively the emotional tone of the original. We may conclude our discussion of the *Carmen* by quoting a few lines from that translation as indicative of the measure of the poet's accomplishment and to counteract the dismal impression made by the recital of Dorilus. Here Olympia tells her father of the joys of Paradise:[24]

Remote, beyond the reach of sickly sheep,
Bright with perpetual light, a mountain rears;
There Phoebus first, from Earth below, ascends;
On topmost peak a wood, with towering palms,
With festal laurels, cedars ever-green,
Peace-loving olive-trees, to Pallas dear.
Who could describe the many flowers? the scents
The zephyrs waft? and who the silvery streams,
Their wondrous waters sprinkling all about,
Meandering here and there with murmurs sweet,
And drawing in their course full many a bough?
Such golden fruit th' Hesperides ne'er saw;
Gold-hued are birds there, and gold-horned goats
And gentle deer; moreover, lambs are there
Whose snowy fleeces gleam with brightest gold;
And oxen, too, and bulls, and fatted cows.
Resplendent all with gold; yea, lions tame,
And griffins tame, their manes with gold all bright.
Golden our sun, and silvern is our moon;
Grander than yours the stars that shine on us.
'Tis ever Spring; no southern gale strikes there;
A joyous calm the place pervades. Earth's mists
And Night, all things that jar, are banished thence.
Death comes not to the flocks, nor ailing Age;
And far are grievous cares, and want, and grief.
Things wished for freely come to all. What more?
The air, so soft, with sweet-toned song resounds.
 . . . .
High, on a grassy mound, in glory sits
Arcesilas,[25] shepherding flocks and worlds.
But, verily, would'st thou His aspect know,
It were in vain: the mind this cannot grasp.

All life is He, too fair, wholly serene;
And in His bosom rests a Lamb, milk-white,
Sweet Sustenance for folk, whereby we live;
Thence comes our weal, and life to those re-born.
And from Them both alike there flames a fire,
Wondrous to trow! To all things spreads that light:
The sad it comforts, purges the mind's eye,
Counsels the wretched, strengthens those that fall,
With sweetest love informs the souls of men.
An aged band of Satyrs, suppliant,
Their hoary locks with rosy chaplets crowned,
Stand there: with lute & song the Lamb they praise.
And then the Purple Order, well revered,
Their temples all engirt with laurel green;
At cross-roads these with pipes the true God sang,
And, strong of soul, they conquered cruel toils.
Then come the Snow-white Host; lilies their brows
Enwreathe. To these is joined our little band,
Thy children fair. The Saffron Order next,
Illustrious, resplendent, with loud voice
Sing praises of the Gods, and serve the King.[26]
'Mong these Asylas[27] sang; how calm his look,
When first the mount received me from the woods!

CHAPTER 17

THE FATES OF
ILLUSTRIOUS MEN

he *De casibus virorum illustrium (The Fates of Illustri-
ous Men)* is a long work divided into nine books
and probably inspired by Petrarch's *De viris illus-
tribus.* The work was written sometime between
1355 and 1360 and, as was Boccaccio's custom, re-
touched during the author's later years.[1] It enumerates the downfalls of famous characters in history—beginning with
Adam and coming down to the sad case of King John of France whose
defeat and capture by the English, "a vile and contemptible race," at
Poitiers in 1356, made a notable impression on Petrarch too. As for his
Decameron, Boccaccio gives a kind of frame to his gallery of melancholy portraits: he imagines himself seated at his desk as these unhappy
and sometimes resentful figures from the past come before him asking
him to hear their sad stories and record them for the benefit of
posterity. The frame here is the familiar "dream pattern," already
employed by our author in the *Vision of Love.* As Louis Brewer Hall
points out in an illuminating introduction to his translation of the
work, the device of the vision, a commonplace of medieval literature,
is here employed with notable originality "to organize the continuity
of the stories"[2]—made, as it were, to serve a quasi-historiographical
purpose.

The thread of history, however, is frequently broken off to make
room for personal commentary. Even as the narrative sequence of the
Decameron is interrupted by the author's interventions, so the parade

of doomed princes is occasionally halted to allow the author an opportunity for appropriate reflections—a technique that adds spice to the sauce and moves the work out of history into a more creative area. At the beginning of book 6, for example, there is a dialogue between the writer and Fortune, who, at first displeased with him, finally relents and assures him that because of his accomplishments Certaldo will be remembered along with the great cities of antiquity, and at the beginning of book 8 Petrarch appears before his disciple to encourage him and urge him to persevere in his quest of eternal fame. The method of presenting his dramatis personae affords the writer an opportunity for critical and moral observations; to some he listens willingly, others he dismisses with impatience and sometimes with a lecture. The work is dedicated to Boccaccio's friend Mainardo Cavalcanti, to whom he rather ingenuously confesses he had thought first of offering his book to some more prominent personage. However, after observing the characters of the pope and the emperor and the shortcomings of the crowned heads of Europe, he avers he found none so worthy of a dedication as Cavalcanti—of humbler than royal station, yet of illustrious family and possessed of a mind fit to appreciate the gift.

Although *De casibus*, in tone and in form, is essentially a medieval work, it has certain features that may be called modern. Hall remarks on Boccaccio's scrupulous checking of sources[3]—a basic practice of today's historians—and some scholars, noting that the author does not merely chronicle events but looks for underlying causes, have seen *Downfalls* as a new departure in historiography.[4] But in fact Boccaccio had discussed sources—and abundantly—in the *Genealogies* and his concern with causes and motivations does not focus on either social or economic matters but consistently on the potential for moralistic interpretation. His principal source, not surprisingly, is Livy, for whom he had, as did Dante and Petrarch, unbounded admiration. Hall affirms that Boccaccio's "popularization of Livy and Roman history contributed vitally to the re-evaluation of the classics that was characteristic of the Renaissance,"[5] and further suggests that the respect for Livy may be at the roots of Boccaccio's praise of patriotism (at the end of book 3 the author intervenes to castigate those who do not love their country) and even sees in the admiring treatment of Attilius Regulus (book 5) a kind of adumbration of the Machiavellian ethic. This may be claiming too much. In any case Livy is by no means Boccaccio's only source; he draws freely on such hallowed authorities as Valerius Maximus, Suetonius, Josephus, Eusebius, and Gregory of Tours among others.[6]

Yet another aspect of the work is called to our attention by Hall, who finds it

> important not only for its contribution to the rebirth of the classics, but also for its contribution to the history of drama. It provides a transition between medieval drama and that of the sixteenth century. The mysteries, miracles and *laudi* all concern themselves with some aspect of the story of mankind—from the fall of Adam, through Christ's redemption of man on the cross, to the Last Judgment. The miracles, of course, were concerned with one of the saints' lives. The very nature of these stories is such that the ultimate resolution had to be in Heaven. This fact underlines all great literature of the Middle Ages, whether the work be *The Divine Comedy* of Dante or Chaucer's *Troilus and Cresida*. In *The Fates of Illustrious Men*, however, the characters are punished here on earth, and this change of setting from Hell to Earth is one of the milestones of literary history.[7]

This statement is subject to some reservations; one can readily call to mind examples of sinners in the *Divine Comedy* who were punished on earth as well as in Heaven, but it is useful as, by implication, demonstrating that Boccaccio's motivation was not that of a historian but a moralist.

However, even though recognizing the merits of the *De casibus* and conceding its quotient of originality, one is bound to admit that a lengthy catalog of miseries and frustrations, beginning with Adam and ending only with the author's contemporaries, makes for monotony; it is hardly surprising that there has been no edition of the work since the seventeenth century.[8] Yet in its own time and down through the Renaissance *De casibus* was very well thought of. Ricci notes that there are no fewer than eighty-three manuscripts of the work and that printed editions through the end of the sixteenth century number twenty-eight. It seems likely that Chaucer's Monk was one of the earlier readers of these edifying pages;[9] the work was widely translated, and from a French version Lydgate drew the substance of his *Fall of Princes*. [10] The date of Lydgate's adaptation (1430–1438) indicates the enduring appeal Boccaccio's moralizing had for succeeding generations. Wright states that "for the men of the fifteenth century Boccaccio was the great moralist, comparable to Boethius and Seneca,"[11] and another scholar reports that "in Spain . . . *De Casibus* and *De Claris Mulieribus* were quoted side by side with the book of Genesis and the works of St. Augustine."[12]

The twentieth-century reader, less interested than his forebears in moral guidance, may yet find the perusal of *Downfalls* at least sporadically worth the effort. The last chapters contain some interesting references to events witnessed or heard of by the author himself. He gives us, for example, a sizable account of Walter of Brienne, the duke of Athens, and he records that his father, Boccaccino, was a witness of the execution of Jacques de Molay, Grand Master of the Templars, in 1314, thus documenting at least one sojourn of Boccaccio *père* in Paris. And aside from such personal reminiscences, the reader, given sufficient patience, may find in the pages of *De casibus* occasional evidence that under the mantle of scholarship and research the natural gifts of the born novelist have not been totally suffocated. As Ricci well says[13] Boccaccio is here trying to conciliate his still vigorous narrative bent with the intent to moralize for the common good and with the use of Latin, the means of expression of a higher nobility (as Petrarch had taught him). In this context the story of Filippa of Catania may be cited; though written in Latin and with moral purpose, its pace and brio would not be out of place in the *Decameron*. It reads as follows:[14]

> In the season of my early youth when I frequented the court of Robert, king of Jerusalem and Sicily, a man well on in years and of notable memory, Marino Bulgaro, native of Ischia and from boyhood skilled in the art of seamanship, together with one Costantino Rocca, a Calabrian as worthy of reverence for his age as for his merits, was wont to review the ancient nobility of the former court and among

other things they would speak of the expedition made by Robert, at that time duke of Calabria, by order of his father King Charles, against Frederick (of Aragon) who was occupying Sicily. And it fell out that while Robert was encamped near Trapani, during a lull in the fighting, Violante, his wife gave birth to a son. And because there were no other women at hand, Filippa, of whom we intend to speak here, was engaged as wet nurse for the duke's son; she was a young woman, to be sure of pleasing appearance and manner, but being very poor was serving as a laundress; she had a few days earlier borne a son to her husband, a simple fisherman. She won the favor of the duchess who on returning to Naples took her along as a servant although her child had died. And Bulgaro and Rocca likewise affirmed that at that time a certain Raimondo Capanni, who was said to be an Ethiopian (nor did his complexion belie the supposition) had been bought from some pirates by Raimondo Capanni, the chief cook of King Charles. The latter, finding his slave very diligent, had him baptized, gave him his own name and surname, freed him, and put him in charge of almost all the operations of the royal kitchen. And not long after, when the master went off to war, the freedman took over all his functions. Soon he began to accumulate property; he bought a house, furnishings, horses, and engaged servants; he went on to win the favor of the king and all the nobles and to amass riches. With the help of his friends he was promoted from charge of the kitchen to the care of the royal vestments. At this point the duchess, anxious to do something for Filippa, who had long served her and who claimed to have been left a widow, gave her in marriage to Raimondo as he seemed to the duchess a most appropriate consort. And to add splendor to the nuptials the brazen Raimondo, forgetting his former condition of slavery, asked to be made a knight. Having achieved such a lofty rank, the Ethiopian cavalier entered the bedchamber of the washerwoman from Catania.

Such things concerning the origin of the nobility—or better the fame—of Filippa I heard from the mouth of the old gentlemen I have mentioned. I shall now speak of things of which I was, in part, a witness. Raimondo, risen from scullion to knight, and further ennobled by his marriage to Filippa da Catania, began to show himself by no means inferior to his fellow soldiers; he carried out the duties given him; he took charge of many things and by his diligence began greatly to increase his personal fortune. As for Filippa, Violante having died and Sancha, wife of Robert, now king, having come to Naples, she served the new queen with great loyalty and assiduity. She was no less attentive to Maria, wife of Charles, King Robert's son; she was in constant attendance on these ladies, obeying their every command, always full of zeal and displaying her mastery in the preparation of various lotions. Thus when Giovanna, daughter of Duke Charles, was born, Filippa, senior in service and by all considered well trained and discreet (being herself now mother of three grown sons by Raimondo), was chosen to be nurse and governess of the little princess. And at the same time Raimondo became majordomo of the queen's court.

Soon afterward Charles and Maria both died and Filippa came to be revered and honored as if she were Giovanna's mother. Raimondo was named court seneschal. How ridiculous is the thought of the Ethiopian, coming from the servants' quarters and bearing the heavy smells of the kitchen, presenting to Robert the homage of protocol, taking precedence over the young nobles, presiding over the court, and dispensing justice to postulants! But so it goes: Fortune raises whom she will. So high had the spouses risen in prestige that two of their sons were created knights and made illustrious marriages; coming into possession of castles, towns, lands of excellent yield, horses, countless servants, fine clothes, and everything in abundance; you would have thought them scions of lofty families rather than sons of an Ethiopian. At length, after Raimondo's death and royal burial, his sons took over the office of their father. When the second son died, a few years later Robert, the third son, put aside his clerical vestments and took up the profession of arms. And in process of time, after the death of the eldest son who left a daughter, Sancha, already quite grown up (who as a girl had been brought up by her grandmother along with Giovanna), Robert, now sole survivor, assumed the office of seneschal as if hereditary through his father and brothers. Having lost her husband and two of her children, Filippa's felicity was somewhat marred; nevertheless, with the passage of the years her splendorous estate grew even brighter. And it came about in this fashion: Giovanna had been given in marriage to Andrea, son of Caroberto, king of Hungary; when Robert died and Sancha had entered a convent, by the evil machinations of some courtiers hostility arose between King Andrea and Queen Giovanna. On which account the barons of the realm who, during Robert's lifetime had sworn fealty to Giovanna, despised Andrea, and Robert from the office of court seneschal was promoted by Giovanna to be grand seneschal of the kingdom of Sicily, and his niece Sancha was given in marriage to Charles, count of Morcone.

Since Filippa had by these associations waxed in prestige, everyone believed that, save for the name, she held the scepter of a queen. But Fortune did not spare her old age. Before that brief time of decrepitude had passed which the exalted woman could look forward to, Fortune with a sudden reversal of things turned so black that the splendors of the past seemed to have been achieved to bring shame rather than honor. Ludovico, king of Hungary, unable to endure the unworthy treatment accorded his brother Andrea by Giovanna and her adherents, through money (and contrary to the intention and the dying wish of Robert) secured the pope's consent to Andrea's coronation as king of Jerusalem and Sicily. Emissaries carrying the pope's mandate had already landed at Gaeta when some barons of the realm, well knowing the harshness of the young prince and no doubt alarmed by the prospect of his well-deserved anger if he should be crowned, and fearing their own predictable punishment, secretly began to employ every means to see that his coronation should not take place and formed a conspiracy against him. Just who these individuals were and what methods they employed to kill the youth is not to our purpose here; we know enough for our narrative: that is that one night, through treachery on the part of the conspirators, in the city of Aversa the prince was called out of his bedchambers and strangled. With the coming of morning the cruel and wicked crime was discovered and the story ran through the city and thence through the whole kingdom, raising a great clamor against those who were responsible. In the first rush to avenge such a crime some young Calabrians who had been attendants on Andrea were seized and amid cruel tortures put to a shameful death. But since they denied their guilt Hugo, count of Avellino, with the assent of all the barons was charged with seeking out the instigators and at his discretion passing judgment on any who were involved in the misdeed. He then, on what basis I could not say, had Roberto Capanni, count of Terlizzi and grand seneschal of the realm of Sicily; Sancha, countess of Morcone; and the old and unhappy Filippa of Catania; along with some others, all thrown into prison. And without delay he had raised on a ship in the harbor in front of Naples a number of poles with sharp nails and there in accordance with the local custom and in the presence of all the people and Filippa he tortured the wretched Sancha and Roberto. It is not known what they confessed; however, judging by what followed it was firmly believed that they were responsible for Andrea's death. So a few days later Roberto, Filippa, and Sancha were bound naked to three separate carts and hauled through the city. A crowd pressed around them from all sides shouting insults while the executioners tore them apart bit by bit with hot pincers and knives until they arrived at the place where the little life left to them was to be ended by fire. The miserable and aged Filippa however could not stand such tortures and reached the pyre already lifeless in the hands of the executioner. She was there quartered; her heart and other organs were removed and hung over one of the gates of Naples—testimony for a long time of savage cruelty, the rest of her body was burned. Sancha was removed from the cart, tied to a stake, and burned alive, as was Roberto. This was not enough for some of the bystanders so that the bodies half burned were taken from the flames; the hearts were taken out and by some, as if in some ghastly sacrificial ritual, were eaten. Then the cadavers were dragged by hooks through the city, contaminated in the sewers and other filthy places, and left, lacerated as they were, exposed and unburied. Such was the end of Filippa, and better had it been for her if she had chosen to sustain her poverty as a washerwoman than wickedly to seek greatness amidst royal luxury and thus, condemned to the flames, achieve her own ruin and the loss of all she had acquired.

Boccaccio concludes his lengthy and portentous survey with a warning to rulers, urging them to live virtuously and to be ever aware of the instability of human affairs and the unpredictable revolutions of Fortune's wheel. Some rulers pondered him well; it is recorded that Philip II of Spain owned no fewer than five manuscripts of the work.[15] Boccaccio would have been pleased to know his book was destined for such honor. In fact we may suspect that *De casibus* gave its author— for two centuries—just the kind of fame he strove to win.

CHAPTER 18

LETTERS AND LESSER
LATIN WORKS

occaccio, unlike Petrarch, never collected his letters; we may fairly assume that he wrote many more than the scant few that have come down to us. The nineteenth-century collection of Francesco Corazzini[1] contained a total of thirty-three items, some of which, however, were dedications to various works of the author rather than true letters. The edition of reference today is that of Aldo Francesco Massèra, containing twenty-four "epistolae."[2] All of these were originally written in Latin but for two of them (number 5, to Niccolò Acciaiuoli and number 12, to Francesco Nelli) the Latin originals have not survived; for these Massèra prints Italian translations made before the Latin texts were lost. Of the letters not originally written in Latin (and therefore omitted by Massèra) three (two in Italian and one in the Neapolitan dialect) have been published in our day by Nicola Bruscoli.[3] Since the appearance of his work (1940) three additional letters have come to light.[4]

Boccaccio—again unlike his revered master—wrote his letters for purposes of communication; he was not especially concerned with composing essays in epistolary form. This is not to say that his letters lack rhetorical adornment or are faulty in style, but rather that their chief appeal lies in the information they supply of historical or autobiographical nature. Great interest naturally attaches to the letters addressed to Petrarch; and those to Zanobi da Strada, Pino de' Rossi and Mainardo Cavalcanti are very personal, and in various ways revealing and moving. We have had occasion to cite them in the preceding pages, as well as the letters that served as introductions or explanations of his works. Although the number is small the nature of the letters, open and unaffectedly sincere, sheds a light on their writer's temperament that is not supplied elsewhere in his works. By way of exemplifying Boccaccio's epistolary manner we shall offer here a translation of the last letter to come from his hand. It is addressed to Francescuolo da Brossano, Petrarch's son-in-law. Although somewhat effusive by our standards and to some degree self-serving, it is yet a moving self-portrait of the weary old scholar, composed as he is about to join his departed master, dated from Certaldo, November 3 (1374).[5]

> Dearest brother: I received on the 19th of October (1374) your sad letter; not recognizing the handwriting, I broke the seal and glanced at the name of the sender; as soon as I saw your name I knew what I would read in the letter: the news of the happy passage of our father and preceptor Francesco Petrarca from this earthly Babylon to the Heavenly Jerusalem—for although none of our friends save you wrote to inform me, I had, to my utmost grief, heard of it from common rumor that was spreading the news abroad. I had wept without surcease for several days—not to mourn his ascent to heaven but rather because I perceived myself wretched and abandoned. Nor is it a matter for surprise; no mortal was more attached to him than I. And, to overlook nothing, I had intended to join you up there in order to pay to your grief and mine the tribute of tears that was due, and with you to raise my lamentations to God and to Heaven and finally to say a last farewell at the tomb of such a father. However, it is now ten months since, while I was in my city giving public readings of Dante's *Comedy,* a sickness, more persistent and bothersome than dangerous, fell upon me. And although for four months exhorted by my friends, I have been following the advice—I won't say of doctors but of charlatans—it has grown continually worse and my digestion has been so strained by potions and fastings, that I have fallen into a state of weakness all but incredible to anyone who has not had a like experience. One has but to look at my face to see the truth of what I say. Poor thing that I am, I would look to you very different from the man you saw in Venice. The skin

hangs from my once sleek body, my color has changed, my vision is clouded, my legs are unsteady, and my hands tremble. Far from climbing the high peaks of the Apennines I was barely able, supported by some friends, to get from Florence to my ancestral town of Certaldo, where, depressed and only half alive, rotting in idleness and uncertain of my state, I remain, awaiting medication and grace from God, who alone can give orders to fevers.

But, to speak no more of myself: seeing and reading your letter I was again overcome, and once more I wept through the night: not, I confess, out of pity for that best of men, for I am certain, as I recall his sober habits, his fastings, vigils and prayers, his innate compassion, and his love of God and his fellow man, that, putting aside the tribulations of this wretched life, he flew into the presence of the eternal Father, there to enjoy forever his God and his eternal glory—nay but rather for me and for his friends abandoned in this stormy world, incessantly shaken and battered as a ship without pilot driven onto the rocks by wind and wave. And as I think on the countless fluctuations of my heart I can easily understand the feelings of you and Tullia, your consort [Petrarch's daughter] and my dear sister whom I held forever in honor; nor do I doubt that you have been stricken by a sorrow more bitter than mine, for the force of grief is truly strong in one who must see what he would not choose to see. But what can we do? If you are as wise as I think you are, you will know that everyone is born to die. Our Sylvanus [Petrarch] has done what all of us, in a short while, must do: he has died in the fullness of years; nay, he did not die; he preceded us and from the seat allotted him among the pious, he now feels compassion for our woes, praying the all-merciful Father that He may give us pilgrims strength to overcome our vices, and that at our end He may grant us a serene departure, pleasing to Him, and lead us, with no impediment of snares set by the Adversary, directly to Him. And, not to be too lengthy, if you will consider such things, you will say those who loved that man of such a great name must not only feel bound to put aside their lamentations but even to feel happy and hopeful of future salvation. I beg you by your fidelity and our friendship, to offer such comfort to Tullia, for women are less strong in enduring such grief and have greater need of help than men. But this I believe you may already have done.

You add that he ended his days in the village of Arquà on the plain of Padua, disposing that in that place his ashes should be left to eternal tranquillity, and that you intend to build to his enduring memory a beautiful and magnificent tomb. Alas, I confess my fault, if it be such: I, a Florentine, envy Arquà, seeing that through the baseness of others rather than any merit of its own, it has been granted the rare felicity of having committed to its custody the body of him whose noble breast was the most acceptable shelter of the Muses and of all Helicon, the most loving sanctuary of philosophy, the richest and most admirable ornament of the liberal arts, and especially with respect to Ciceronian eloquence, as his writings clearly reveal. On this account Arquà, almost unknown even to the Paduans, to say nothing of strangers and inhabitants of faraway nations, will be widely known and its name will rise in prestige throughout the world, even as we in our minds are wont to esteem the hills of Posilippo, though we have not seen them, because at their feet lie the bones of Virgil. It will have the honor accorded to Tomi and the river Fasi, on the far shores of the Black Sea, where lie the bones of Pelignian Naso, or the Smyrna of Homer and other such places, while we value not at all the Hyrcanian crags, fabulous Ethiopia, or the Arcadian streams flowing under a cold sky, since they are not adorned with such titles. I do not doubt that in the future the mariner, coming from the farthest shores of the ocean, laden with riches, as his prow cleaves the waves of the Adriatic, seeing in the distance the proud Euganean peaks, will exclaim to himself and his friends: "There we may behold the hills that preserve within them the ornament of the temple of all learning, Petrarch, sweetest of poets of old, by vote of the Senate, in the mother city, crowned with the triumphal laurel, leaving so many lauded works as shining witnesses of sacred fame." Thither will come perhaps the dark Indian, the fierce Spaniard or Saramatian, moved by admiration for the sacred name, and, gazing on the tomb of such a famous man, all with pious reverence will salute the buried remains, deploring their misfortune that did not permit them to see while living him whom they visit in death. O luckless fatherland, to whom it was not granted to preserve the ashes of such an illustrious son, to whom such rare glory was denied! To be sure, thou art unworthy of such splendor inasmuch as while he lived thou didst take no care to draw him to thee and give him a merited shelter in thy bosom. Thou wouldst have called him to thee had he been an architect of crimes, a forger of treacheries, a guileful champion of avarice, envy, or ingratitude.

Yet, even so, I would that this honor had gone to thee rather than to Arquà. But it has so fallen out in order that the truth of the old saying might be confirmed: "No man is a prophet in his own country." It may be that he avoided it deliberately in order, in his humility, to imitate his master and redeemer Christ, whose will it was to grant the honor of his origin, with respect to his mortal family, to Nazareth rather than Jerusalem,[6] and to have as his mother a poor but holy maiden rather than great and proud queens of those times. So, as it has pleased God, may the renowned name of Arquà long live and may its inhabitants long preserve those precious remains. I approve too the idea of raising a monument to him, for the magnificence of his splendor and the excellence of his works well deserve it. Yet possibly it may be of small importance in the eyes of scholars, for the virtues of the one buried rather than the ornaments of his cadaver are held in regard by those among whom he made himself through his many volumes more luminous than the sun. However, it will be a memorial to the ignorant whose books are paintings and sculptures, and it will be further a stimulus to inquire what kind of man lies therein, what his merits and his glory, and through the answers the renown of the great sage will no doubt be somewhat extended. But it pleases me to call your attention to one thing: illustrious men lie with greater honor in an unknown sepulcher than in one of little beauty. And if you would perceive this, consider how Fortune treated Pompey the Great. I believe she repented of having allowed him to be snatched from mortal things by such an unhappy death, that is, stabbed by the treachery of an Egyptian boy, and therefore she decided that him whom she had made great while alive, she would exhibit as most great in death. And for that reason she forbade that his body—for a day a marvelous plaything of the sea— should be enclosed in a sepulchral urn, in order that it might be rumored that the entire coast from Pelusium to Canopus served as his tomb; and his limbs, which being dispersed and scattered, had not been covered by sand, were covered instead by the starry sky, since they might not conveniently have been enclosed by the marble of Luni or the stone of Paros. Wherefore so great waxed the reverence for the abandoned corpse that the considerate traveler was constantly tormented by the fear of treading with rash foot on the bones of one who so often with arms and empire had trodden upon the necks of kings. If, on the other hand, that hero had chanced to die among his own people, I could hardly believe, in view of the great things achieved by him, that even the great tomb which Artemisia, queen of the Carii, had built of old to her husband Mausoleus near Halicarnassus would have been adequate. So before you begin, ponder what you are about to do.

I cannot in brief compass properly speak of the munificence he displayed toward his friends and me, wherefore for the moment I shall set it aside for a more convenient time, if such is given me, and content myself here with a few words dealing only with me. I had learned indeed through his many favors in times past how much he loved me while he lived and now I see factual proof for he has maintained that affection up to his death, and if, after that leave-taking that we call death, in that better life there is still love between friends, I believe that he loves me and will continue to love me—not that I ever deserved it but because it was his way to cling tenaciously to anyone he had made his own and I was truly his own for more than forty years. And further in order to manifest by deed to the ignorant what he could not in the future hope to do with words and writing, he was moved to number me, as you say, among his heirs, leaving me a large portion of his goods. And by heaven I rejoice and am glad that he did so; I am sorry, however, that it has fallen to me to claim so swiftly and without delay the part of his inheritance assigned to me; I would rather that he had lived and I were without his legacy.

My letter was meant to end here, but a certain concern impels me to add something. I should have been pleased to hear what disposition has been made of that great man's most valuable library, for there are different rumors and suppositions circulating among us. What troubles me most of all is the destiny in store for the books he composed himself and especially that *Africa* of his which I consider a divine work. I should like to know if it still exists and will be preserved or whether it has been consigned to the flames, as he, while living, as you know, often threatened to do, being excessively severe toward his own work. I have heard—I do not know from whom—that some have been given the charge of examining this and other books of his and preserving those that they deem worthy of saving. I am surprised at the ignorance of whoever set up such a committee and I am more alarmed when I think of the rashness and ineptitude of the examiners. For who among mortals will dare with an ill-omened pen to amend what our distinguished master has approved? Not Cicero, were he to return, or Horace or Virgil. Alas, my fear is that the task has been given to lawyers who, because they know the laws and, as they themselves proclaim with their impure mouths, especially those dealing with breadwinning, think they are experts in all matters. I pray God provide that the poems and the other sacred compositions of our poet may not lack for succor. But finally, if the matter must proceed according to their judgment, write me if you have time, and send me every copy that can be sent to those who desire it. Please give me information too about the other works, especially the *Trionfi* which some say have been already burnt with the unanimous consent of those sages. I shall worry about these writings until I hear from you. And with reason, for learning has no more dangerous enemy than the ignorant, and, further, I have long known how many envious and bitter enemies the fame of this preeminent man may claim. Of a surety if they can, they will deface and hide those books and condemn those they do not understand, making every effort to destroy them. You must be vigilant in preventing this, for Italy's men of talent, now and in the future, will be robbed of many useful and helpful things if without due consideration all his books are subjected to the verdict of the ignorant or delivered into the hands of the envious. Further, if it can be done at your convenience, I ardently desire a copy of that quite lengthy letter which was the last he wrote me, wherein I believe he expressed his opinion about the suggestion I had made to him that he give himself some little relaxation from his many assiduous labors;[7] I would like too a copy of the last of my *novelle*[8] which he honored with his writing. He sent me both of these items; according to brother Luigi of the Order of the Hermits they were lost on the way through the carelessness of their bearer. I believe it was the work of those who have charge of presentations; they often filch them and unjustly claim them as their own. I know it will be difficult for you but one must in all confidence disclose one's desires to a friend. Illness prevents me from writing further, and so to come to my last request I beg you to count me as yours, and may you live long in health, dear brother.

I finished writing this letter in Certaldo on November 3d and as you may see, I cannot say I was quick about it; it took me almost three

whole days, save for some intervals of a few hours to restore the
strength of this weary body, to write this brief letter.

Your Giovanni Boccaccio, if he is anything

Massèra's edition of the *Opere latine minori* contains not only the
Buccolicum carmen and the *epistolae* but also the Latin texts of eight
carmina and four compositions in prose. Three of the *carmina* are very
brief; one (number 4) is a one-line defiance of the archbishop of Milan
put in the mouth of the Lion of Florence, another (number 6) is a
four-line "explicit" written by Boccaccio at the end of an edition of
the *Divine Comedy*, while number 8 is the epitaph the poet wrote for
himself (see chapter 2, p. 64).[9] The remaining five are what Petrarch
would have called *epistolae metrice*. Numbers 1 and 2 are addressed to
Checcho di Meletto Rossi with whom Boccaccio was on intimate
terms in the years immediately following his youthful residence in
Naples: number 3 was later largely incorporated into Eclogue 4 of the
Buccolicum carmen; both of those letters are full of political allusions.
Number 3 is addressed to Petrarch; it is consists of forty verses in praise
of Dante and was sent to Petrarch to accompany a copy of the *Divine
Comedy*, presented to Petrarch by his faithful disciple, composed,[10]
Massèra affirms, between the summer of 1351 and May of 1353. Number 5 is a reply to a letter sent to Boccaccio by Zanobi da Strada;
Boccaccio encourages his friend to continue his poetic efforts even
though the times are difficult. Number 7 is the longest of the *carmina*
(180 lines) and was probably written during the last year of the poet's
life.[11] It is addressed to Petrarch's *Africa*, offering the poem hospitality
in Florence; it is really intended to spur Petrarch's editors to the
divulgation of the epic.

Finally, Massèra includes in his volume four *Scripta breviora* in prose;
the first is a short essay on mythological allegory,[12] the last three are
brief biographical sketches of Petrarch, St. Peter Damian, and Livy
(lauded not only as a historian but as a master of prose writing)
respectively. The profile of Petrarch written, according to Massèra,[13]
in 1348–1349 is of particular interest; Boccaccio speaks with unbounded admiration of Petrarch's intellectual gifts and moral rectitude.

Among the master's works the *Africa* comes in for special praise, although Boccaccio confesses that as yet no copies of the epic have circulated. He concedes that Petrarch may have been "molested" by lust but assures us that he was never overcome by it; he suspects that "Laura" is no woman but a symbol of poetic glory. He is impressed by his subject's ability to combine the life of solitude with occasional mingling in the great world and rejoices in his intimacy with the great, notably Robert of Sicily. And perhaps having his own experience in mind, Boccaccio speaks admiringly of Petrarch's tenacious pursuit of the Muse in the face of his father's determination to make him a lawyer. The sketch also contains a physical description of his master. Petrarch, we learn, was tall, with a round face, and complexion neither pale nor swarthy but becomingly between the two. Petrarch in his own *Letter to Posterity* also says his skin is neither pale nor dark, he gives the impression that he was of medium height; it is regrettable that neither he nor his admirer tells us the color of his eyes or hair. One may regret too that Boccaccio did not return to his biographical essay in later years (as he did to so many of his works); we should then have had an account of Messer Francesco's career in full maturity and perhaps have learned more of his circle of friends and of his relations with the Visconti and the doge of Venice. But we can be sure of one thing; had Boccaccio covered the life span of his master until the end, we should never have had a word of criticism. We have but to read the letter to Francescuolo Brossano, previously quoted, to appreciate the depth of the disciple's dedication to his "preceptor."

CHAPTER 19

THE DECAMERON

n view of the unique nature and importance of the *Decameron* it has seemed appropriate to reserve discussion of the masterpiece to our final chapter, in violation of the chronological order we have followed in our survey of Boccaccio's other works. In such an order the *Decameron* has, at least relatively, an easily definable place. It was written, in the opinion of most critics, in the years immediately following the incidence of the Black Death in Florence; 1349–1351 are the years commonly assigned to its composition.[1] One might see it as a kind of watershed between the works of Boccaccio's fancy and those that were the fruit of his scholarly and critical labors. It stands, however, clearly apart from both. As a nineteenth-century critic perceptively wrote: "Between the ambitious poems of his youth and the learned works of his mature years Boccaccio grants himself a moment of relaxation and child-like mischief. He writes the *Decameron* and through approach to reality wins immortality."[2] It is possible to suspect that if we did not know Boccaccio was the author of the work we should not be at all certain that it could be assigned either to the inventive creator of the *Filostrato* and the *Amorosa visione* or to the pedantic compiler of the *Genealogies.*

Since we do know that all of these works are of the same pen it is easy for critics to detect adumbrations (though tenuous) of the *Decameron* in the Neapolitan romances and traces of the creative artist in the *De mulieribus* or the *De casibus.* Two tokens of linkage with the

earlier works are in fact readily apparent in the introductory pages of
the masterpiece. The name given the work is consistent with the
author's penchant for Greek titles. It is likely that in this case the title
was suggested by the *Hexameron* of St. Ambrose, a work of scriptural
exegesis; the suspicion of a parodic intent is fortified when we observe
that the first meeting of the lighthearted band of storytellers takes place
in a church. The subtitle, *Prince Galeotto*, is evocative too. Gallehault
was Lancelot's go-between in the seduction of Guinevere (we may
recall that it was a book that served a similar function in the downfall
of Dante's doomed Francesca) and so suggests a connection with the
courtly romances of Boccaccio's youthful Muse. And, as we shall see,
the names assigned to the frame characters subtly remind us of the
earlier works.

Even so, the differences are greater than the similarities; seen against
the background of the works that preceded and followed it, the
Decameron must seem a marvelous anomaly. Between the idealistic
romantic poet and the sober scrupulous pedant, the realist, disillusioned,
tolerant, sometimes bawdy, intrudes. Between the writer of adventure
stories for the upper classes and the scholar eager to serve the intellectual,
stands the narrator of tales and anecdotes whose public is looking neither
for inspiration nor instruction but simply for diversion.

The scene is neither Troy nor Thebes nor prehistoric Fiesole but the
author's own city (and that of most of his readers), contemporary
Florence. It fell out not long ago, the introduction tells us, that in the
midst of the plague that was devastating Florence with all its attendant
physical miseries and relaxation of normal decencies, ten young people,
three men and seven women, met in Santa Maria Novella and after
some discussion resolved to remove to the country, leaving the horrors
of the city behind them, and amuse themselves as best they could as
members of what one might call a large convivial house party. Seeking
for ways of passing the time they hit upon the device of storytelling.
Each one presides for a day and each one tells a story every day. To
make things a little more challenging, after the first day the king or
queen assigns a topic; to vary the pattern thus established, on the ninth
day no topic is set. One of the young men requests and is given
permission to tell the last tale of each day with license to choose his

own subject. Otherwise the sequence of storytellers is not fixed. After the second day and again after the sixth, the group, displaying the restlessness of affluent youth, moves to a new pleasance; thus the "action" of the storytelling has three settings. All of this background activity develops naturally, one might say spontaneously. But of course the meat of the *Decameron* is not in the manipulation of the cast or the scenery but in the stories told by the talented entertainers.

The tales vary considerably in length although none is very long: some are merely one-page anecdotes; the longest runs to only twenty-seven pages (in Branca's octavo edition),[3] the average length is seven and a half pages. Brevity and some variation combine to avert any likelihood of tedium. The settings of the stories range topographically from England to Cathay, "at sea, in cities, woods, rooms, caves, and deserts";[4] chronologically from legendary times to the contemporary scene. But the extremes are exceptional; no fewer than seventy-nine of the narratives have an Italian background (twenty-nine are set in Florence—a proportion significant enough to assure a Tuscan flavor), and only twenty-five are set in times that can be called ancient or remote.

A survey of the dramatis personae of the *Decameron* discloses a similar pattern of wide scope yet with a centralized core. E. H. Wilkins has eloquently indicated the multiplicity of social classes and vocations represented in the work: "kings, princes, princesses, ministers of state, knights, squires, abbots, abbesses, monks, nuns, priests, soldiers, doctors, lawyers, philosophers, pedants, students, painters, bankers, wine merchants, inn-keepers, millers, bakers, coopers, usurers, troubadours, minstrels, peasants, servants, simpletons, pilgrims, misers, spendthrifts, sharpers, bullies, thieves, pirates, parasites, gluttons, drunkards, gamblers, police, and lovers of all sorts and kinds."[5] The parade undeniably supplies evidence of the author's range of interest and, if we remark that approximately 20 percent of the Decameronians are members of the working or peasant classes, also of a kind of tolerant democracy surprising in one who has hitherto dealt with Trojan and Theban princes. However it must be noted too that the remaining 80 percent of the actors must be defined as of the aristocracy or upper bourgeoisie; it is clear that generally speaking the emancipated *raconteurs* or *racon-*

teuses are primarily interested in the motivations and behavior of their own class, well off and self-confident. About a third of the characters on the crowded stage of Boccaccio's comedy are women. "Further . . . the women, like the clergy, make an impression that more than compensates for their numerical inferiority. Out of the hundred stories there are thirty-two wherein women have a central role and another forty-two in which their part is so significant that without them there would be no story. Dante's *Comedy*, which has a population slightly larger than that of the *Decameron*, contains only a score of women, of which the greater part is composed of *exempla* from antiquity."[6]

Although the proportion of characters actually described as merchants (or merchants' wives) is only about 10 percent, Branca well defines the work as "the epic of the merchant class";[7] the basic bourgeois tone of the Decameronian world is evident both in the nature of the stories told and in the comments of the joyous *brigata*. These wellborn young people on holiday are not looking for self-improvement or philosophical exercise; they are out to have a good time and to amuse themselves and each other. Save for those of the last day, of which we shall say more later, their stories are hardly inspirational or even elevating and only to a slight (and debatable) degree instructive. Thirty-eight of the ninety stories (leaving the tenth day out of the reckoning) are told specifically to elicit mirth and merriment; as Wilkins states, "The *Decameron* is in the main a book of laughter"[8] and all the tales are meant to arouse wonder at the diverting ways of men, women, and Fortune with no obvious straining for moral or metaphysical implication. The medieval virtues of faith, courage, and liberality (again save for the tenth day) are ignored; to be sure stinginess is not admired but neither is incautious prodigality. Military valor is recognized but there is no tale of war for its own sake, nor any true hero-soldier.

What the storytellers consistently admire is the use of one's wits, whether it be in simple verbal interchange, in the operation of some clever plot (even fraud), or used defensively to cope with one's enemies or the unpredictable strokes of Fortune. They are much interested in sex too; of the one hundred tales told 67 percent present situations where a sexual relationship (one cannot always call it love) is central to the action. Motivation is strictly worldly and pragmatic; the roll call of protagonists includes no saintly figure whose thoughts are on eternal things, nor any intellectual of truly scholarly interests, save for one who makes a very brief anecdotal appearance.[9]

Such, in brief, are the dimensions of Boccaccio's pungent and sometimes spicy package. We may now examine it more closely, beginning, as it were, with the wrappings. In an affable *proemio* the author defines the motivation of his storytelling. He recalls that years ago when he had suffered much under the torments of love a friend had come to his aid, consoling him with pleasing discourses. That love has now passed away as all things must but Boccaccio remains grateful for the solace of his friend's words. So he proposes now to offer distraction to others afflicted as he once was; he has in mind particularly women, who, having fewer social activities than men, must find their cares harder to endure. The language of the *proemio* is in the high style, as if to confer dignity on the altruistic intent of the author. The reference to his own love misery, which came about because he had loved a lady of higher station, suggests his devotion to Fiammetta (whether or not she was real) but the terms are too generalized to confirm such a suspicion. Nor do we have any way of knowing what good friend (if any) it was that solaced the young lover in his hour of need. What we do have is a clear statement that his stories are meant to take his readers' minds off their troubles—and nothing more.

The *proemio* is followed by a direct address to "the most charming ladies," apologizing for the fact that his work must have a heavy and unpleasant beginning. They must look upon it as a steep and rough mountain to be climbed in order to enjoy the more beautiful meadow that lies beyond it. And he is obliged to lead the ladies over this rough part because it is a necessary prelude to the pleasant and much longer part that will follow. For it is against the background of the plague in Florence that his young narrators come together.

In the description of the plague of 1348 that follows Boccaccio stresses two aspects of the Black Death, of which critics are in substantial agreement he was a witness[10] (even though, strange as it may seem to a reader today, some of his descriptive passages are translated from the account of Paulus Diaconus of an earlier plague in Lombardy[11]).

He dwells at some length on the realistic details of the pestilence: its symptoms, its onslaught, the ubiquitous corpses, and the crowded churchyards, and makes the further point that the calamity brought in its train a decline of decency, driving many frightened souls to carousing and dissipation and breaking down the traditional modesty between the sexes. "A woman," he tells us, "no matter how refined and well bred, would, if she fell sick, willingly take a man into her service, without regard either to his age or social station, and, should the need arise, expose any part of her body to him as freely as to another woman."[12] This may explain, the author opines, the absence of modesty in the women who survived the plague.

The discipline of normal society disappeared: "In the midst of the affliction and misery that had befallen the city even the revered authority of the laws, divine and human, had all but lapsed and dissolved, for its ministers and agents, dead, sick or deprived of their assistants, could not attend to their duties." For many citizens, he adds, flight seemed the only answer; "they abandoned their city, their houses, their neighborhoods, their belongings and their own flesh and blood to seek a refuge in the country, either in the environs of Florence or elsewhere."[13] Which is precisely the line of action taken by the band of storytellers who meet by chance on a Tuesday morning in the almost deserted church of Santa Maria Novella.

This somewhat forbidding preface to the ladies, then, serves to anchor the *Decameron* to a specific time and place, giving it realistic support, and at the same time to explain if not justify the genesis of the unchaperoned house party of mixed sexes and the emancipated and sometimes downright bawdy nature of some of the tales they tell. This "frame" taken in conjunction with the ten narrators also serves a function at once aesthetic and practical as Bosco observed;[14] the stories by themselves, a mere random collection of items, would have lacked weight and authority and would have seemed merely frivolous and idle. Such a frame may even be said to be traditional in the long history of narrative anthologies; we have but to think of the *Thousand and One Nights* and the *Book of the Seven Sages*, widely known in the Middle Ages.[15] English readers will recall Chaucer's prologue; whether composed under the influence of Boccaccio or not we shall leave Chaucerians to decide. Nor should we forget that Boccaccio himself had used the device of the frame, notably in the question sequence of the *Filocolo* and in the *Comedy of the Florentine Nymphs*.

Of course the frame has a protective function, too, since it is not Boccaccio but rather the ten young people who tell the tales. One may see a kind of chain of disclaimed responsibility since the narrators also are merely reporters; for example what Filippa says (6.7)[16] is a part of Filostrato's report as relayed to the reader by the author, who cannot be held accountable for the veracity of the tale, much less for the opinions expressed by the saucy young matron.

Let us now look more closely at the storytellers as they come before us on that fateful spring morning. None of them is older than twenty-seven and the youngest is not yet eighteen. All of them are intelligent, wellborn, and comely; they are likewise well-mannered, charming, and of modest comportment. Boccaccio assures us that they are real women and not fictional characters; he refrains from giving their names, lest any of them be offended by the things they are said to have told and listened to in the course of the ten days, and lest they incur reproach in view of the stricter standards of propriety that have returned after the plague. However he will call them by names that will approximately describe their qualities. "The first and eldest we shall call Pampinea, the second Fiammetta, the third Filomena, and the fourth Emilia. The fifth we shall name Lauretta, the sixth Neifile, and the last, not without reason, Elissa."[17]

Pampinea's suggestion to abandon the city for the salubrious tranquillity of the country is agreeable to all the young women. Filomena and Elissa comment that the company and guidance of some men would be welcome and, as if on cue, three young men enter the church, all looking for their *innamorate* who are included in the group of seven females. Of the other women, some are related to either one or another of the young men, the youngest of whom is twenty-five years old. In order of presentation they are called Panfilo, Filostrato, and Dioneo.

Individual characterization is sketchy and to an English-speaking reader who approaches the work looking for something like the *Canterbury Tales*, may be a little disconcerting.[18] This is not to say that there is no distinction at all among the personae of the frame.

Pampinea is clearly the "big sister," the "take charge girl," as we might say; it is she who suggests the excursion and she who rules over the first day. If statistical support for her seniority is necessary we may note that she has more wordage assigned to her than any other female, not only in the introduction and in the intervals of the storytelling but in the narration itself. Her narratives take up more pages than those of any other of the girls, although Fiammetta is a close second. Fiammetta too has the distinction of being the only one of the females to whom is accorded a fairly full if rather generalized physical description (4. conclusion), and her name as well as some of her stories would seem to suggest a Neapolitan origin. At the other end of the scale Neifile is clearly the youngest as her name indicates; Elissa seems to rank next in order of youth. Appropriately, they are given the least narrative space. (For what it is worth, we may note that Neifile is thrice given the privilege of starting the day's storytelling—more often than any of the other characters.) The men are somewhat more sharply distinguished. They are, of course, as Hauvette noted,[19] facets of Boccaccio himself in the varied aspects of his love relationships: Panfilo is the successful and happy lover (as he was in the *Elegy of Madonna Fiammetta*), Filostrato "il tradito" who has suffered rejection, and Dioneo the carefree skeptic.[20] On the whole the men are more clearly differentiated than the women in spite of their common autobiographical genesis; Dioneo is certainly the most memorable of all the storytellers; Panfilo seems to be the senior of the trio with his calm assurance and placid temperament (he is given more narrative space than any of the rest), and Filostrato is notable as being the only one of the band who wants to hear sad stories.

All of the male characters are, one might say, named after love; "Filostrato" and "Panfilo" contain the Greek root *philos*, long dear to Boccaccio, and "Dioneo" is ultimately derived from Dione, mother of Venus and sometimes used to signify the goddess of love herself. This nomenclature reinforces the author's own cheerful avowal (in the interval between the third and fourth days) of his devotion to womankind. If we look at the characterization of the young men, taking into consideration the tales they tell, their comments on the narratives of others, and their presumably revealing lyrics, we may agree with

Guido Almansi that "only bawdy Dioneo survives as a real character on close analysis."[21]

To be sure it is Dioneo's racy parade of lively stories that is his chief asset but his role in the frame is almost equally notable; it is he who prompts Pampinea to devise a way of passing the time and it is he who improves on Filomena's notion of a daily topic by requesting permission to tell his story last and to be free to choose his own subject, thus introducing an element of variation into an otherwise predictable pattern. The function of this blithe and spirited rogue, as Filomena thinks of him (1.10), is to underline, as it were, the emancipated tone of the whole enterprise; more than any of the others he seems to be a spokesman for the author (who, for that matter, is quite ready to speak for himself from time to time). Dioneo is also a kind of large-size composite of all the other storytellers, distilling the naturalistic freedom that is found in the narratives of all the young people; outdoing them too, while accepting their program, in the palinodic tenth day. Finally, it is not too much to say that it is to Dioneo's contributions more than to those of any other frame character that the *Decameron* owes its long and enduring popularity. The color of his narratives tinges the whole work; without Alibec and Frate Cipolla and the articulate wife of Ricciardo da Chinzica—to say nothing of the patient Griselda—the *Decameron* would lose much of its savor. It is fair to add that his stories are the most memorable not only for their carefree content but also for their artistry. He has more pages allotted to him than any narrator save Panfilo but, except for Griselda on whom he spends seventeen pages, his stories are all set forth with remarkable economy and, generally speaking, in a brisk style, free of the medieval elaboration and self-conscious rhetoric that frequently creeps into the contributions of his companions—admittedly the content dictates the manner of exposition.

So it must be granted that some distinctions are made. Yet the similarities among the narrators are more marked than the differences. They are all of the same class of society, all of a like age, and in fact interrelated. And such differences as a careful reader may detect in the author's somewhat imprecise allusions are not borne out by the stories they tell. An easy example is Filostrato. As noted, he calls for sad tales and his song at the end of day 4 reveals him as a disappointed and unhappy lover—yet it is he who tells the story of Masetto's harvest of lusty nuns and the tale of the saucy Filippa. Indeed, save for his own contribution to the gloomy cycle he prescribes, none of his stories reveals any element of melancholia. Nor is Fiammetta's penchant for stories from the South consistently followed; two of her tales are distinctively Florentine and three others have no Neapolitan relevance. We may well suspect that it was Boccaccio's intention (quite different from that of Chaucer) to avoid making too sharp definitions of the storytellers. One may believe that in so doing he intended to keep the focus of his readers' attention on the tales themselves; storytelling is his purpose and not the depiction of personalities—certainly not the panoramic exempla of social classes.

Both the numbers of and the names borne by the storytellers suggest if not strict allegory at least symbolic allusions. Three, seven, and ten are magic numbers; they are built into the structure of the *Divine Comedy*; in selecting them Boccaccio must surely have had in mind his master's tactical deployment of them. Their precise significance in the *Decameron* is not easy to determine. Ten is perhaps the easiest; aside from symbolizing perfection, it is functional in the architecture of the work: ten days properly call for ten storytellers, each to be king or queen for a day. Of the many associations of the number seven, theological or otherwise, it seems unlikely that, given the context, the ladies could stand for the Virtues; perhaps the seven liberal arts is a more plausible reading. For the erotic trio of males, Branca can only suggest that it serves to fill out the required ten and adds that it may symbolize the masculine principle.[22]

With the names we are on firmer ground. The names of all the men and four of the women have already appeared more or less prominently in the author's earlier works. Of the three new names, it is generally agreed that Lauretta and Elissa (another name for Dido) are acts of homage to Petrarch and Virgil respectively. In Neifile Muscetta sees a similar gesture to the "sweet new style"—an evocation of the *pargoletta* of Dante's *Rime* 87 and 89.[23] The accumulation of such data enables Branca to conclude that the names of the frame characters are allusions to the various literary traditions that Boccaccio has followed in his previous writing career and perhaps suggest, programmatically, their fusion in his masterpiece.[24]

The dynamics of the frame follow their own natural course. When Pampinea has led her friends to their refuge—a fine palace surrounded by pleasant and verdant grounds some two miles from the city— Dioneo suggests that some kind of structure or program be set up for their leisure. Pampinea, assenting, proposes that during their sojourn each member of the party should be king or queen for a day; the first to be elected and the sequent "rulers" to be appointed by their predecessors. All concur and elect Pampinea as their first queen. She then makes all the necessary household arrangements, delegating various duties to the staff of servants who have accompanied the band, and after a morning of casual diversion—song, dancing, and promenades, followed by a fine meal elegantly served and an hour of repose—the queen assembles the group in a cool glade and suggests they pass the time by telling stories. The choice of subject is to be at the narrator's option. The rest of the band readily concurs and the queen calls on Panfilo to tell the first tale. It should be noted that in the course of her household dispositions Pampinea remarks that they are made to insure that the group may be "happy, orderly and virtuous" and she adds the corollary that none should bring anything but good news from the outside world.

The first three stories told set the tone of the *Decameron*. And the first of all, Panfilo's story of the emancipated Cepperello, is particularly significant; aside from being one of the best of the hundred tales, it has some challenging ambiguities. Called from Florence to Burgundy to assist his business partners, the notary Cepperello, renowned for his lust, mendacity, and irreverence, falls mortally ill. His partners are in terror lest the inevitable deathbed confession, revealing his wickedness, may bring their business into disgrace. Cepperello—whom the French preferred to call Ciappelletto—reassures them. And his solution is as simple as it is shocking. He makes a totally false confession, describing himself as all but saintly, truly penitent for the few trivial failings he can remember, but through this false penance depicting himself as a man of irreproachable character. The innocent priest accepts all this and on Ciappelletto's death speaks of him with such admiration that the sacrilegious reprobate is locally venerated as a saint. Panfilo piously concludes by remarking that it is possible that at the very end the rogue may have shown true contrition, yet judging from what we know, he should properly be damned. This story is well received, particularly by the ladies.

Giovanni Getto, who rightly considers the legend of Ciappelletto "one of the most remarkable stories of the entire collection," defined it as "complex and profound" and "one of the most noteworthy of the whole series."[25] The basic complexity lies no doubt in the sharp contrast between the substance of the tale and the manner of the telling. In a number of ways the content is truly scandalous. There is no more sacrilegious act possible than a false confession *in extremis*, which displays a willful indifference, even a kind of contempt, for the Creator. Further, Ciappelletto's imaginative reconstruction of his own life-style is a parody on the lives of the saints. And, finally, his ultimate canonization casts doubt on the cult of the saints of God. We are bound to ask how many revered shrines are dedicated to frauds and hypocrites —if we but knew the truth. It is a story that, if we were to take it seriously, we should dismiss with disgust and revulsion. But in fact Panfilo tells it with a breezy zest, bringing out the comic aspects of the plot (the false confession of the unscrupulous sinner to the innocent priest is a masterpiece of humorous dialogue) and from the very beginning the total depravity of Ciappelletto is so extravagant as to arouse not so much horror as amusement. Indeed we cannot help admiring his imperturbable effrontery.

It is notable that among the attentive band of listeners the tale aroused "laughter in part." Laughter first of all—and perhaps we should leave it there. But "in part" because other interpretations tease us and will not readily allow themselves to be put aside. Even Ciappelletto has his own ambiguity. Taking his action at face value, if it reveals him as a complete skeptic and liar, it also makes evident one admirable quality: loyalty to his friends; "rather than jeopardise the dominion of Italian bankers in Burgundy, rather than be false to the mercantile ethic, he chooses in full awareness eternal damnation"[26] (assuming he believes in eternal damnation). And, more basically, is his exemplum really inimical to true faith? The contrary is possible. "It is one of the cardinal points in the Christian creed," says Thomas K. Seung, "that God can and does bring good out of evil. [His] use of Ciappelletto's evil designs for a good purpose is eloquent testimony to the omnipotence of His will."[27] And, in fact, such is the pious statement of Panfilo in his introductory remarks—only, with Momigliano, we may suspect a touch of mischief in that virtuous affirmation.[28] One is tempted to concur in the midst of such complexities with the verdict of Croce: "the story affirms nothing and denies nothing."[29] And it is this ambivalent neutrality that makes it a key story for the whole work. If transcendent values are not denied they are certainly not in the forefront of the concerns of the worldly folk of the *Decameron*.

The second story, lightheartedly comic in tone, is much less shocking than the saga of Cepperello but carries a like charge of tolerant skepticism. Neifile tells the tale of Abraham the Jew, a merchant of Paris, besought by his Christian friend, Jehannot de Chevigny, a fellow merchant, to convert to Christianity. Abraham, at first resistant, finally consents to consider the possibility. He declares however that he will first go to Rome, the seat of the Church, and study the ways of God's vicar and his fellow cardinals. Jehannot is dismayed at the thought; he is sure that observation of the conduct of the clergy in Rome will only confirm Abraham in his Judaism. But when the latter returns from his visit, Jehannot has a pleasant surprise. Abraham reports that having noted the scandalous behavior of prelates and priests, all of whom, without exception, he found to be lustful, gluttonous, and greedy, he could only conclude that a church, served by such ministers, that could yet endure must be truly supported by the Holy Spirit. He willingly consents to be baptized. The story is neither antifaith nor anti-God but solely anticlerical and on the surface a defense of the Church. Yet for all that it is hardly calculated to reassure good Christians; not all men, remarking the life-style of the clergy, will come to the same conclusion as the perceptive Abraham.

Filomena's contribution (story 3) carries skepticism to a quasi-philosophical level. Her tale tells of Melchizedek, the wealthy and shrewd Alexandrian Jew, asked by the mighty Saladin to declare which of the great faiths, Judaism, Christianity, or Islam, is the true one. Knowing that his fortune is at stake Melchizedek replies indirectly by relating a parable. A wealthy man, he relates, coming to the end of his years, was faced with a serious problem. Family tradition decreed that he should pass on to his son a precious gold ring that had been handed down for generations as a token of lawful inheritance. But the man had three sons, all of whom he loved with like affection. His solution was to have two copies of the ring made. On his deathbed he gave a ring to each of his sons. So perfect were the imitation rings that they could not be distinguished from the original. Consequently each son was sure he was his father's chosen heir but which one had the rightful claim could never be ascertained. And so, of the three faiths, assuredly one of them is God's true law, but which it is still remains to be determined. This story, which Boccaccio found in the *Novellino*, was effectively retold by Lessing's Nathan der Weise in the eighteenth century, a climate where the message of tolerance might be expected to win sympathetic hearing. But it certainly points up a change of attitude from that of the High Middle Ages, confidently believing that "Christians are right and pagans are wrong." In truth, if its lesson is tolerance it is also agnosticism.[30] Filomena's listeners, perhaps a little uneasy, make no comment on her story.

So it may be said that the first three items establish the tone of the *Decameron*; skeptical, affable, and all but dangerously open-minded. They have also in common a technical mastery that assures the reader's attention; they are all good stories, quite apart from their implications. Generally speaking the remaining tales of the first day are less interesting; they drift off into the anecdotal and the witty riposte. Perhaps an exception should be made for Dioneo's account of the fat abbot (story 4) caught *in flagrante delicto* by one of his monks, himself a lecher. This not only gives us a notion of what we may expect of the free-wheeling narrator but also epitomizes the characteristic Decameronian mixture of sex, resourcefulness, and farce.

Pampinea brings the first day's sequence to an end with a little anecdote meant to illustrate the vanity of womankind and the truth that old men may be good lovers; she then names Filomena her successor. The latter, accepting the charge gracefully, proposes that henceforth the tales should follow a special topic to be prescribed by the ruler of the day; assuming it is agreeable she would suggest for her reign that the stories deal with people who, after suffering under adverse fortune, come out with better results than they had hoped for. The idea meets with unanimous approval. Dioneo, however, asks to be exempted from the general ordinance and to be allowed to tell whatever kind of story suits him; in recompense he is willing to speak last. Filomena, who knows him to be a merry rogue, gladly accepts his amendment. The day closes with a song sung by Emilia (accompanied by Dioneo's lute) in which she expresses complacent delight in her own beauty, a motif echoing Dante's Lia in *Purgatorio* 27.104 ff.[31]

The purpose of the lyrics that conclude each day is a little unclear. One may suspect that the alternation of prose and poetry in Dante's *Vita nuova* had its effect on his admirer, but in sharp contrast to the verses of the Master's book, the lyrics of the *Decameron* are quite irrelevant to the prose content. If the songs are meant to add a little more substance to the characterization of the storytellers they are not particularly successful. Admittedly, the interludes between the days demonstrate that the young people have a life of their own; they can dance, sing, and indulge in badinage as well as simply tell stories. But the songs themselves, all dealing with various aspects of the tender passion, are generalized and too enigmatic to clarify, for example, any of the relationships hinted at in the introduction. The verses are technically deft but their substance is conventional and for the most part derivative. Possibly the courtly tone of the lyrics is intended to draw a line between the narrators, all well bred and patrician, and the world depicted in their tales, democratic and often vulgar. This would reinforce the pointed distinction, made at the end of the book, between the emancipated nature of some of the tales and the strict propriety that governs the conduct of the youthful band. But it may be that the poetry is meant simply to add a certain gilding to the frame, to supply —to change the figure—a stylized punctuation mark between one day and the next.

The nature of the topic dictates some change in the kind of story told in contrast to the freedom of the first day. Of necessity if the workings of the unpredictable goddess Fortune, a theme dear to the heart of the Middle Ages, are to be properly illustrated there must be scope for action. And the second day in fact gives us narratives rich in incident. Many of them could be called adventure stories; characterization is hardly important and the purely anecdotal, with which the first day had tapered off, would be too fragile to support the thesis. One may say in the second day that the plots thicken; the stories *qua* stories are richer in incidents and on the average longer than the stories of the first day, or for that matter, any other of the ten. In the main our *raconteurs* (save of course for Dioneo) scrupulously obey the dictate of their queen; which is to say that their narratives present rather passive protagonists, at first beaten down by the blows of chance and later restored to prosperity through no effort of their own. In some cases, however, they are alert enough to give Fortune a nudge, as it were, and the motif of ingenious opportunism that characterizes the work as a whole is not lost sight of. The story of Zinevra, wife of the merchant Bernabò (ninth of the day, told by the queen herself) illustrates both how disaster can be brought about by another's malice and the turn of Fortune's wheel be reversed by one's own efforts. If Zinevra's resourcefulness is admirable it must be admitted too that the villain does not lack ingenuity either; his stratagem appealed to Shakespeare who put it to good use in *Cymbeline*. [32]

A number of the tales of this eventful day call for special comment. The fifth story, dealing with the rustic Perugian horse trader, Andreuccio, in world-wise and crafty Naples is one of the few tales wherein local color plays a prominent part. Generally speaking, Boccaccio does not dwell on such details; many critics have remarked that his backgrounds tend to be sketchy. But in this account (appropriately set forth by Fiammetta) the ambience is part of the story. [33] One may add that Andreuccio too learns in the course of his misadventures how to give Fortune a helping hand. Innocent and gullible at first, with wits sharpened by adversity, he returns to Perugia not only a richer but a wiser lad—with some loss of innocence, to be sure.

In the juxtaposition of the trials of Lady Beritola and Princess Alatiel (sixth and seventh stories) one may suspect calculation with a touch of mischief on the part of the author. Both heroines are noble women, subjected to undeserved abuse at the hands of Fortune; both suffer shipwreck and exile and for both everything comes out all right in the end. But the contrasts are pointed; Lady Beritola is a faithful

wife and a devoted mother; she preserves her loyalty—and chastity—
through all her vicissitudes. Her character redeems or justifies the
outrageous melodrama of the plot; for Thomas Greene her story
"constitutes a miniature epic of a family."[34] Alatiel is of different mold.
Sent across the Mediterranean by her father to be the bride of a prince,
she is violated no fewer than nine times in the course of her frustrated
and storm-tossed journey (which, incidentally, Millicent Marcus notes,
"approximates the medieval trade routes of the Mediterranean
world");[35] yet, favored by chance at the end, she is able to pass herself
off as a virgin bride, and the moral of the tale is purely Machiavellian:
seeming is as good is being if no one can tell the difference. If this
verges on hypocrisy (elsewhere Boccaccio's target) yet it is the way
of the world. The account of Lady Beritola's miseries brings the ladies
of the band close to tears; their sighs as they follow the saga of Alatiel,
the author opines, may have been prompted by envy as much as
compassion. If constancy has its appeal, apparently so too does promis-
cuity—so long as the tale be well told.

Finally the story of Dioneo, having little to do with the revolutions
of Fortune's wheel, adds another element to the sauce of this savorous
day. His account of the conduct of the emancipated Bartolomea, wife
of the desiccated and impotent Ricciardo da Chinzica, is in effect a
manifesto of women's rights—in the sexual area. A healthy woman has
a right to a vigorous partner and the husband's incompetence (described in racy satirical language by his starved spouse) is ample justification for abandoning him. Bartolomea's unabashed frankness gives her
a special place in the second day's gallery of resourceful women, all
of whom, however, are strong-minded and in one way or another
tenacious and triumphant.

At the close of the second day Emilia sings a song of contented and
requited love and Neifile (who blushes girlishly as Filomena crowns
her), as if to counterbalance the stress on Fortune, sets the theme of
the third day stories of people who through their own efforts achieve
what they sought or retrieve what they have lost. She also suggests that
the company suspend its diversions for the next two days, Friday and
Saturday, for on Friday it is proper they should remember the death
of the Savior and on Saturday "we women usually wash our hair and

take our baths." She prescribes that the storytelling should resume on Sunday and proposes a new site, removed, as we later learn, some two thousand paces where yet another palace stands surrounded by the conventional verdancy.[36] Against this new background—not differing greatly from the old—the stories of the third day are told.

The topic suggested by Emilia is general enough in its terminology but "what people sought" is, in all cases presented, not fame, nor riches, nor power but sexual satisfaction and "their own efforts" is translated to mean "through the use of their wits." Sex dominates the entire day, colored in a few cases by anticlericalism. The first tale combines these motifs; it is told oddly enough by Filostrato and deals with the ingenuity of a simple laborer Masetto, who by pretending to be dumb manages to seduce not only all the nuns but the abbess herself in a small convent of which he is the gardener. Masetto's triumphs are set forth with lively naturalism and his success illustrates once more the vigor of female sexual appetites. A significant passage occurs when, at the beginning of Masetto's service, two nuns come upon him apparently asleep in the garden. It occurs to one of them that he has the proper equipment to justify their finding out if sexual delight is as joyous as it is said to be. The other remonstrates, reminding her friend that their virginity has been promised to God. The adventurous nun replies that many things are promised to Him every day and He gets none of them; if they break their vows "let Him look for others who may keep them." And they proceed to their great experiment, deriving rich satisfaction from it. The ladies of the band, the author notes, hear the story "with blushes and laughter" and with no disapproval.

The second story, told by the competent Pampinea, is a little masterpiece of professional technique; it tells of how a lowly stable boy managed to sleep with his queen and, by alert thinking, escape the vengeance of the king, no simpleton either. The duel of wits ends in a tie, as if to show that astuteness of mind, even as true virtue, knows no distinction of class. An unusually virulent note is heard in the tirade against friars, delivered by the protagonist of the seventh tale, dwelling at some length and with somewhat surprising passion—given the normally temperate tone of the *Decameron*—on their faults, and accusing them specifically of avarice, indolence, lust, and above all hypocrisy. This day, concluding with the famous account of "putting the devil in Hell," whereby sexual intercourse is described in a kind of sacrilegious allegory, is of all the days, the one that, over the years, has contributed most forcefully to the reputation of the *Decameron* as a collection of dirty stories.[37] (It is noteworthy that Momigliano, in compiling his scholastic anthology of forty-nine tales, omits all the stories of the third day.) Other memorable items in the day's harvest must include Fiammetta's account of a seaside seduction (again notable for its realistic Neapolitan background)[38] and the pair illustrating ingenious psychological manipulations: the third tale wherein a clever woman makes use of an unsuspecting priest to bring her prey to her bed, and the fifth, in which a lover employs his dialectical skill to win over a reluctant lady. The ninth story, depicting yet another purposeful female, is of particular interest to English-speaking readers; it supplied Shakespeare with the plot of *All's Well That Ends Well.* Through all the third day erotic desire and tactical guile function in effective cooperation. The day concludes with Lauretta's sad song of her lost lover, evocative of the *Teseida*'s Emilia and "not understood by all the company."[39]

Between the third and the fourth days the author interrupts his narrative to say a few words in his own defense. His complaint is that in spite of his self-effacing modesty in presenting the stories to his public (they are written in the vernacular and in prose and without the author's signature) he has been subject to the attacks of the envious. Some, on reading these stories, have charged him with being too fond of women, some have remarked that such an interest is inappropriate to his years; others have opined that he would be wiser to spend his time with the Muses on Parnassus rather then wasting it in such trivialities. [From which we may judge that the stories of the first three days had already had some circulation.][40] Boccaccio's defense against these charges begins with his telling a parable, thus adding another tale and another storyteller to the *Decameron.* He relates the story of a boy of the Balducci family brought up in rustic isolation by a stern father determined to protect his son from temptation. One day, however, they are obliged to visit Florence and replenish their supplies: the son, now eighteen, is permitted to accompany his father. The youth, never

having been in a city before, is full of questions about everything he
sees. And when a bevy of attractive girls crosses their path he inquires
what they may be. His father tells him to avert his eyes, for they are
wickedness incarnate, and since he would like the lad to know nothing
of women, he tells him they are geese. To which the lad replies that
above all things he has seen the geese are the most beautiful; he begs
his father to get one for him, "so I may feed its pretty mouth."
"Never," his father replies, "you have no idea what mouth you have
to feed." But in his heart he has to admit that nature is stronger than
wisdom. This ancient parable (it goes back to Oriental sources),[41]
which Boccaccio cleverly adapts to his purpose, may fairly be regarded
as representing the polemical thrust of the *Decameron*, which is certainly a statement of the recognition of the power of nature sweeping
aside the barriers that human reason might put in its way. Come what
may, man will have his mate—it is an urgency that must be recognized.

The parable is followed by the author's brief. He admits at once that
he loves women, has loved them since his youth—and as for those who
do not love women, well, they do not know the power of honest love
and he will not concern himself with them. As to his age he is content
to cite the examples of Guido Cavalcanti, Dante Alighieri, and Cino
da Pistoia in whom love of women long endured. And if it is true that
he would do well to stay with the Muses on Parnassus, yet "since we
can neither dwell with the Muses nor they with us, a man, if he must
leave them cannot be blamed if he takes pleasure in the sight of
something that looks like them. Muses are women and even though
women are not the equivalent of the Muses yet at first sight they
resemble them—to say nothing of the fact that women have been the
cause of my writing a thousand verses while the Muses never occasioned a single one."[42] (He concedes, however, that the Muses have
helped him by showing him how to compose those verses and may
even have helped him in the writing of these stories.) And if his critics
would seek to persuade him that his writings bring him no substance,
well, poets have discovered much more in their visions than rich men
in their treasures. He concludes that he will go on with his enterprise;
criticism has not shaken his resolve.

The tale of the geese and its polemical sequel have received a good deal of critical attention. "[The parable] constitutes," Enrico de' Negri affirms, "the real prologue and, so to speak, the ideal substratum of the entire *Decameron*, as much for the choice of content as for its formal elaboration."[43] For Aldo Scaglione it indicates that the author's naturalism "is a conscious program, intellectually formulated and presented in a polemic, militant, aggressive tone, in explicit reaction to medieval prejudice."[44]

What the reader may find a little obscure is the distinction in the author's mind between women and Muses. If the ladies have inspired a thousand verses and the Muses none, what kind of work would the Muses have inspired? Conversely if the Muses have taught him to write his verses and even collaborated in the writing of the *Decameron,* how is their effect on his pen different from that of his cherished "geese"? Perhaps there is a suggestion here that the "Muses" stand for a kind of technical proficiency; they are teachers of the "how" but the substance of inspiration, the "what," lies in womankind—or, if you will, nature. Else why should not a poet dwell forever on Parnassus? Or do the Muses signify—for the author's purpose here—works of high style, with veiled allegories, perhaps even requiring Latin? Carlo Grabher's comment on this question is illuminating: "In [Boccaccio's] reply, so truly serious under its smiling irony, we have the beautiful image of an art, based on a disciplined preparation wherein the Muses have shown what artistic mastery requires, yet drawing its inspiration only from life itself. Boccaccio venerates Parnassus and the divine majesty of poetry, but for him Poetry itself, in its divine inspiration, springs only from living reality."[45]

Having affirmed his position, Boccaccio retires and allows Filostrato, who has proposed as his topic (in defiance of Pampinea's prescription for cheerfulness) the stories of unhappy loves. And in truth the tone of the day runs counter to the blithe nature of the work as a whole; one may wonder if perhaps, in the midst of his professed effort at "consolation," which certainly implies avoidance of the melancholy, the author may yet have yielded to the temptation to try his hand at the tragic. If so he has not been especially successful; most of the tales are lacking in truly tragic weight. Some evidence that the writer is a little out of his element may be seen in the statistical fact that the fourth day is one of the shorter days and furthermore the "tragic" quotient is sharply reduced if we exclude Dioneo's story and the second story, told by Pampinea, which is purely comic in tone even though the protagonist comes to an unhappy end. The truly sad stories are well below the average tale in length; one almost suspects that the author was hurrying through his tribute to melancholy.

Of all the sequence of tales of woe and despair paraded before us at the bidding of the dour Filostrato readers will undoubtedly find the tale of Ghismonda (told by Fiammetta) the most moving, as critics have long found it the most provocative. And it is intriguing no less for the substance of its plot than for certain tangential implications. It is no tale of roguery or duplicity meant to amuse, it is a serious story, and one senses that the author himself takes it seriously.

Ghismonda, Fiammetta relates, was the daughter of Tancredi, prince of Salerno, a good ruler and a wise man save perhaps for his sensibility where his daughter was concerned. Such was his affection for her that he kept her a spinster long after the normal marriageable age; at last however he allowed her to marry the son of the duke of Capua, with whom she had lived only a short time before she was widowed and so returned to her father. She was still beautiful and young and merry but her doting father showed no disposition to find her a new husband. Finally, after taking thought, Ghismonda chooses a lover, selecting for that intimate relationship a young man of the court named Guiscardo, of lowly birth but of admirable character and engaging personal qualities. Knowing that her father would be displeased Ghismonda keeps her relationship secret. Unhappily, chance reveals the affair to her father, who has the young man apprehended.

Tancredi then goes to his daughter and in tears reproaches her for her conduct; her fall from virtue is reprehensible in itself but her choice of a lover of low degree aggravates her fault. Ghismonda replies with an eloquent defense of her actions: she warns her father that she is determined to share her lover's fate whatever it be. Tancredi, skeptical of his daughter's resolve, has Guiscardo executed and sends the heart, cut from the body and placed in a goblet, to Ghismonda; she in the meanwhile prepares a poisonous brew. When she opens the goblet and finds Guiscardo's heart in it, she loses no time. After a moving farewell to her Guiscardo, addressed to the heart, she pours the poison into the goblet and dies—but not before Tancredi, summoned by her ladies in waiting, appears to hear his daughter's last request, to be buried with her lover. After long mourning the grieving father fulfills her request.

Violent passion against a princely background is a classical prescription for tragedy. But Ghismonda cannot be called truly a tragic heroine; there is no tragic flaw nor any cathartic illumination. She is a woman who has determined on a certain course of action and is betrayed by no inner weakness but pure chance. She has no regrets. Led by Moravia,[46] some recent critics contend that the true protagonist of the story is Tancredi, whose jealous possessiveness of his daughter leads to her destruction and who, in fact, does come to understand at great cost the error of his ways. But it seems unlikely that such a reading is in line with Boccaccio's intention—his focus is on Ghismonda throughout and, as Momigliano remarks,[47] Tancredi is neither analyzed nor developed.

At least as significant as the melodramatic action is Ghismonda's apologia, which covers, in a rational dialectic, with a *sangfroid* rather surprising under the circumstances, two arguments of significance. First, it is a defense of love. Ghismonda avows she is a woman of flesh and blood with needs that her father should have understood. Particularly, since having been married and known the joys of love, she could not reasonably have been expected to be deprived of them; her father erred in not finding her another husband. Compelled to shift for herself, she asserts she has made an admirable choice, for Guiscardo, though not nobly born, is in character and behavior truly noble, since nobility is a matter not of birth but of character. The latter thesis is a commonplace in the Middle Ages set forth by the troubadours and given reinforcement in the fourth book of Dante's *Convivio* (indeed Chaucer pursues the same line of argument in his quest for "gentilesse"). As for the defense of her love one may say that Ghismonda, accepting the lesson of young Balducci and his "geese," that love is simply an irresistible natural force, goes on to supplement or refine this basic tenet. If the impulse cannot be controlled it can be channeled by reason, discretion, and good taste. Any one of the "geese" would have satisfied the innocent adolescent but Ghismonda's love can be only for

Guiscardo. So refined, carnal love transcends its origin and becomes a religion of its own. If love were mere appetite Ghismonda could have found a replacement for Guiscardo; as it is, she commits suicide—and in the certainty that she will be reunited with him in Paradise, where surely carnality has no place. Nor does she seem in the least afraid of the condemnation of the Church; love, now purified, justifies her act.

If Ghismonda's saga is not truly tragic it comes the closest of all the stories of the fourth day to meriting that appellation. The story that follows (number 2), a lively tale in its own right, burlesques the concept of tragedy. Pampinea, more eager to amuse her fellows than to please the king, tells the story of the seduction of a silly Venetian woman by Alberto, a cunning friar who persuades his victim that his body houses the Archangel Gabriel. Since the protagonist comes to a bad end, the tale meets Filocolo's prescription but the tone is light-hearted and even irreverent; the seduction seems a kind of parody of the Annunciation and the use of sacred language and images parallels in some sort the initiation of Alibec. The story is told with brio and sharp delineation of Venetian background; the guileful if ultimately luckless Alberto has been carefully studied by Erich Auerbach.[48]

The touching and grisly account of Isabetta and the pot of basil (retold by Keats) is pathetic rather than tragic. Alberto Moravia finds it "the most exemplary love story Boccaccio has written," and cites it in support of his not entirely persuasive view that Boccaccio is not an erotic writer.[49] The ninth story (told by Filostrato himself and presumably the kind of tale he had in mind in setting the day's topic) is another version of the lover's heart eaten by a surviving mistress. It is related by this theme to the story of Ghismonda; perhaps it is fitting that Filostrato and Fiammetta should share a taste for this kind of erotic cannibalism, dear also to Dante.[50] The tale is of literary interest too, being a version of the old Provençal *vida* of the troubadour Guilhem de Cabestanh; the source is cited by the narrator.

The other items of the day are tales of romantic misadventure; it is noteworthy that they present a kind of democracy of misery. In the third, fourth, and fifth stories the protagonists are people of high degree; embarking on the seventh, Emilia avers that Love does not scorn to assert his dominion over the huts of the poor; her heroine is

Simona, a humble weaver's assistant. Neifile, who follows, gives us another girl of the lower classes—although, to her misfortune, her wooer is wellborn and wealthy. Dioneo, not bound by the rules, offers a racy tale of the resourcefulness of an adulterous wife of a surgeon.

As one might expect Filostrato passes the crown to Fiammetta, the only one of the ladies who is given a detailed if conventional physical description (she is a dark-eyed blonde; a type Ariosto and Tasso will admire) and, as might also be expected, she calls for stories of lovers whose vicissitudes have ended in happiness. The day ends with Fiammetta bidding Filostrato to sing a song, knowing it will be sad; she would like to have the melancholy strain limited to one day. Obediently Filostrato sings a song of love betrayed, thus bringing to an appropriate conclusion the one day dedicated to sadness and frustration.

The motif of the fifth day is *au fond* a repetition of that of the second day, differing only in the prescription that the stories must deal with love (as in fact all of the second day also have though, as it were, spontaneously). And, as under Filomena's rule, here too Fortune plays a major role in the narratives, three of which depend on the old recognition theme. For example, in the seventh story the young Armenian prince, sold into slavery, is recognized by a compatriot as he is about to be burned at the stake for seducing his master's daughter. And of course where Fortune plays a part the plots are bound to be full of swift-paced action. Fiammetta's day, about average in length, is highly readable.

A few tales call for special comment not so much for their plots as for their illumination of tangential aspects of Boccaccio's Muse. The first story, for example, is meant to illustrate the refining influence of sexual love—a theme common in troubadour poetry, and treated at length in Boccaccio's *Comedy of the Nymphs.* Young Cymon is oafish in manners and dedicated only to the pursuit of a crude simple life among the rustics. One day in the fair month of May he enters a woodland glade and comes upon the figure of a sleeping girl. Enraptured by the vision, he changes his whole style of life, learning to dress well, mingle gracefully in society, and even dabble in music and the arts as well as participate in all kinds of warfare. Love has civilized him.

It must be said too that love also leads him under its forceful sway to kidnapping, murder, and violence; clearly love's beneficent influence is societal rather than ethical; the story thus exemplifies the fundamental ambiguity of courtly or even romantic love. The discovery of the sleeping beauty with its attendant springtime adornments carries some echoes of *Ameto*, as Muscetta notes[51] (it may be suggestive of classical pastorals to some readers and others may recall Percival's encounter with Blanchefleur in the Arthurian legend), but it seems also to cast a long shadow ahead; the image is surely Botticellian. And on that theme one may even dare to add that the sketch of the perfect gentleman into which Cymon is changed by love suggests a kind of "cortegiano" *avant la lettre*.

The third story, dealing with the vicissitudes of two young Roman lovers, is notable for its evocation of the lawless state of Rome and its *campagna* in the fourteenth century, thick with armed bandits and partisans of the great feuding families. The fourth tale, offered by Filostrato, as if in atonement for the grimness of his own day, is a bit of lighthearted wordplay, telling how Caterina manages to "listen to the nightingale." The appeal of the story lies in the double entendre, though one may admire too the depiction of young love, innocent, insistent, and heedless, and the prudence of Caterina's father, who knows how to make a good bargain out of an embarrassing situation. The eighth item, a "ghost story" warning ladies that a true lover should not be scorned, is interesting for the spectral atmosphere it creates and for its setting in the pine forest of Ravenna already celebrated by Dante.

Most readers would agree that the most moving item of the fifth day is the ninth story, contributed by Fiammetta; it is the tale of Ser Federigo and his falcon, sacrificed in the service of his lady. It is all but unique among the stories of the *Decameron* in that the focus is not on guile or fortune but on true chivalric gentleness; even the note of carnal eroticism is absent. It is small wonder that Tennyson and Longfellow found the tale to their taste; it has an authentic nineteenth-century flavor, compounded of nobility, tenderness, and sad irony. Almansi with reason calls it "one of the most attractive and moving *novelle* in the whole *Decameron*."[52] It seems a little misplaced in the sequence of the fifth day; it properly belongs among the magnanimous examples set before us on the last day, save that the sense of straining for effect is not perceptible. Dioneo's contribution, vivacious and mischievous as ever, is the only tale among the hundred that includes a sodomite in the cast of characters.

Between the end of the fifth day and the resumption of narration on the sixth what passes between the narrators is of special interest. At the conclusion of day 5 the queen calls on Dioneo to sing a song. He offers her a choice of selections, all of which, as one can deduce from their titles, are of a definitely bawdy nature. As Elissa rejects one saucy suggestion after another, her amusement changes to irritation and she finally bids Dioneo to sing something pleasing (and proper) or else he will incur her displeasure. At last obedient, he sings a song on the traditional theme of devoted love. Then at the beginning of the sixth day, as, after their usual diversions (some play chess or backgammon while Dioneo and Fiammetta sing of Troilus and Cressida), they are preparing for the round of stories, a great din is heard in the kitchen. When summoned, Licisca the servant reports in very frank language that she had been scolding Tindaro (another servant) for his absurd notion that one Master John Thursday's bride went to her wedding night a virgin. "Why," she adds, "I haven't a single neighbor who went to her husband a virgin." During her tirade the women laugh uncontrollably and when it is over Dioneo, asked by the queen to give judgment, opines that Licisca is perfectly right and Tindaro is a simpleton.

The action of this provocative interval assuredly underlines the emancipated nature of most of the tales; it may indicate too how close the band of young narrators come to the frontiers of decency. They are, as it were, playing with fire during the whole course of their house party.

The theme of the day, as proclaimed by Elissa, is the witty retort, used in defense or to extricate oneself from some condition of danger or embarrassment. In accordance with the requirement most of the stories are very short, and in fact the sixth is the shortest of all the ten days. Yet its relatively few pages have received a great deal of attention from contemporary critics who see in its substance something more than a mere series of resourceful ripostes. This type of story, Scaglione

observes, noting its earlier appearance in the *Novellino* and its survival
in Sacchetti, "shows the gifts and interest of a society (especially the
Tuscan) that had assimilated the century-long tradition of rhetorical
teachings and developed a genuine cult for a well turned phrase."[53]
Franco Fido makes use of the sixth day to probe the whole problem
of Boccaccio's *ars narrandi* and finds in story 1 ("placed exactly in the
center of the *Decameron*") a *"poetica in nuce"* of the whole book."[54]
Marga Cottino-Jones analyzes the fourth story (admittedly this one can
still make us smile) to explore certain aspects of Boccaccio's stylistic
virtuosity.[55] And for Thomas Greene, the "spontaneous artistry" that
characterizes the Decameronians "in its most modern forms is visible
in the witticisms of the Fifth and Sixth Days."[56] Yet although Dioneo's
day be a magnet for scholars, the reader in search of simple enjoyment
will probably agree with J. H. Whitfield who defines the sixth day as
"arid."[57] Perhaps it is a day that invites study rather than enjoyment
—or commitment.

Two of the anecdotes have a certain accidental interest deriving
from the identity of their protagonists; story 5 recalls a jesting exchange between Giotto and a learned friend, and story 9 records a
cryptic riposte of Guido Cavalcanti. The reader familiar with Boccaccio's gallery of masters may fairly wonder why there is no Dantean
anecdote. This would be just the place for it. Franco Fido's answer to
the question leads to an interesting exploration of the Decameronian
Boccaccio's attitude toward Dante, present but not exalted in the
hundred tales.[58]

If we are inclined to feel that by and large the stories of the sixth
day are too brief to make a lasting impression we are bound to concede
there are two spectacular exceptions. The first is Filostrato's contribution (story 7). It concerns Filippa, a woman of Prato, taken in adultery,
and according to the laws of that town, subject to punishment by death.
When she is called upon to defend herself she replies first of all by
pointing out that although women were most affected by such a
regulation, they were not consulted about it and therefore they are not
bound by it. She then asks her husband to come forward and say if
she has ever denied him his conjugal rights. He concedes she has never
done so and she goes on triumphantly to maintain that if she has served

her mate faithfully, she has a right to dispose of "what is left over; must she give it to the dogs?" This story is certainly the most subversive of all the tales in the *Decameron* and the most eloquent defense of women's liberation. Filippa is the most clear-thinking of all the realistic females of the ten days.[59]

Dioneo's contribution is again noteworthy too; he tells the story of Fra Cipolla, a roguish friar who comes to Cerraldo prepared to dazzle the yokels by showing them a feather of the Archangel Gabriel. A pair of tricksters have substituted a lump of coal for the feather in the good friar's pouch; when he draws it forth he is not in the least embarrassed but welcomes the occasion to display instead one of the coals on which St. Lawrence was roasted. His description of his travels to the Holy Land and the marvels he there beheld is a masterpiece of ingenious double-talk; he is the confidence man par excellence. In his unrepentant use of sacred references he reminds us of Ciappelletto and indeed Millicent Marcus notes the similarity of their names,[60] but of course his irreverent performance, not being under the shadow of death, is more comic and less shocking then the masquerade of his predecessor. One can admire this outsize specimen of an articulate rascal, without any inner uneasiness of conscience. Assuredly Frate Cipolla is one of the half dozen most successfully presented figures of the whole work.

When the young company has had its fill of laughter over the resourcefulness of the engaging friar, Elissa hands her crown over to Dioneo as if gently suggesting the attraction roguery has for innocence. His suggested topic for the following day is "tricks women have played upon their husbands." When some of the ladies object that the theme seems a little improper for them to embroider, Dioneo replies vigorously in defense of his choice. He reminds his critics of the nature of the times they are living in, wherein, within the bounds of decency, all kinds of freedoms are permissible. It is a time, he points out, when divine as well as human laws seem to be suspended and in the name of self-preservation the maximum license is permitted (thus echoing what has been set forth in the introduction concerning the moral-social effects of the plague). Therefore, he concludes, "If you permit yourselves a little freedom in speech—not as a prelude to any unbecoming action but simply to give pleasure to yourselves and others—then I don't see how you can incur any justifiable reproof in the future." He adds, to emphasize his point, that "our company, no matter what has been said, has been irreproachable from the first day to this; with God's help it will continue to be such."[61] Surely, he concludes, the ladies' assurance of their virtue, which is unshakable, should make them unafraid of such a topic—indeed their hesitation might be suspect. In this significant apologia Dioneo is not speaking merely in defense of his choice of argument but also in defense of the author and his book; his somewhat perverse conclusion is no doubt intended to give detractors of the *Decameron* something to think about.

At the suggestion of Elissa all the women of the party follow her to the Vale of the Ladies, a circular glade in the midst of the forest wherein lies a pellucid lake.[62] Tempted by its waters the ladies divest themselves of their garments and bathe. So again the charm of the frame is enhanced by a change of scene; we have yet another *locus amenus*, this time colored with a dash of innocent sensuality. Coming back refreshed, the ladies tease the three men for the march they have stolen on them; and in their turn too the male trio proceeds to the Vale and bathes in its lake. Perhaps in the fact that the sexes bathe separately we may see a reinforcement of Dioneo's assertion of their modest behavior. The day concludes with Elissa's song, telling of frustrated love and somewhat puzzling to her audience.

Dioneo has every reason to be pleased with his choice. The stories of the seventh day, all narrated against the enchanting background of the Vale of the Ladies, present a gallery of resourceful not to say unscrupulous women who easily manipulate or mislead their husbands, be they trusting or justifiably suspicious mates. And for all the initial reluctance of the ladies of the band, their contributions are as spirited as those of the men.

Emilia's heroine (in the first story) makes use of an incantation with a very suggestive double entendre to warn her lover when her husband is in the way. Elissa (story 3), interpolating a diatribe against the manners and morals of friars, uses churchly language to describe the triumph of Brother Rinaldo over his willing victim. Filomena (story 7) adds a mildly sadistic touch to her account of a husband not only gulled but beaten.

All of the tales are well constructed with the emphasis, as the theme requires, on carefully plotted action. A few are notable for special features: Peronella's tirade against her husband (story 2) provides a happy example of the traditional nagging woman, the lively goings-on in the fourth and sixth stories somehow suggest their adaptability to farce or burlesque; the intervention of Simonda's family (story 8), as much deceived as her husband by her resourceful tactics, produces lively and naturalistic dialogue; it serves him right for marrying above himself.

Two of the items call for somewhat more detailed comment. Fiammetta (story 5) contributes an item a cut above the others in subtlety; she tells how a woman very cleverly makes her husband's jealousy an actual aid to her adulterous conduct. It is a good example of the trickster tricked, for it is the husband's original deceit, disguising himself as a priest to hear his wife's confessions, that leads to his downfall. Panfilo's narration of Lydia's seduction of her servant Pyrrhus (ninth story, cast in ancient Greece)[63] concludes with the ancient motif of the magic pear tree with which Chaucer's Merchant has familiarized English readers. Before reaching that point however, Pyrrhus, as shrewd as Lydia, insists on three proofs of her true devotion: she must kill her husband's hawk before his eyes, pluck a lock from his beard, and extract a tooth from his head. Lydia manages to fulfill all these requirements without arousing her husband's suspicions. (He is, one should note, much older than she and therefore fair game.) The setting of such trials whets the curiosity of the reader and assures his interest in the narrative: a reader of today however may be a little disturbed at the vein of sadism that the devices of Lydia seem to reveal. Dioneo concludes the day with a story of a departed soul who comes back from Purgatory to reassure his friend that in the other world "people don't bother their heads about godmothers or godsons" and possibly by implication other transgressions of sexual by-laws, either.

His reign over, Dioneo names Lauretta his successor and, as if to dilute by expansion the tendentious thesis of Dioneo, she proposes for the eighth day "tricks played by men on men or by men on women." Filomena then sings a song inviting her absent lover to return (reminding Branca of Fiammetta of the *Elegy*).[64] Lauretta, reminding the company that the following day is Friday, suggests they follow the example set by Neifile at the end of the second day and resume their storytelling after a two-day rest.

Reassembling on Sunday after having duly attended divine services in a church "not far away," the band takes up the theme suggested by their queen and embarks readily on their eighth day of narration. According to the rules laid down, the majority of the tales (six) deal with tricks played by men on other men and four with tricks played by men on women (in three of these there is a fair exchange of stratagems). Of the whole day's sequence the most memorable story is the seventh, that of the scholar's revenge. It rises above the normal emotional level of the *Decameron*; it is a story of weight and seriousness, standing in marked contrast to the general comic, often disinterested, tone of most of the tales. It is significant that it is the longest story of the collection and perhaps also that it is told by Pampinea, the most mature of the female storytellers.

Briefly the plot turns on the unhappy love affair of the scholar Rinieri, infatuated with Helen, a beautiful but superficial woman. Bored by his attentions, she takes another lover and keeps the scholar shivering in the cold through an entire winter night as he waits for the tryst she has promised him, meanwhile diverting herself pleasantly in bed with her lover, sending her maid at intervals to bid her dupe wait until she can receive him. Rinieri's love changes to hatred and he plans a dreadful revenge. When, predictably, the lady's lover deserts her and she turns to the scholar to help her win him back, he has a ready solution. He suggests that she must take a puppet (which he will have made for her) and at bedtime carry it with her to a stream wherein she must bathe and then, still naked, ascend to the roof of a deserted house and repeat certain incantations. The simple woman obeys his instructions, and Rinieri removes the ladder by which she has climbed and leaves her exposed not only all night but under the burning sun of the following day. When she begs for mercy he lectures her on her behavior, making the point that with his scholarly intelligence he could have taken a worse revenge; he could have made her the object of his embittered pen, which would have brought her to everlasting shame. Only when she is at the point of death does he allow her maid to summon the gardener and his ladder and rescue her mistress. It is the same maid who had treated him so saucily in the course of his humiliation; when she breaks a leg attempting to assist her mistress, Rinieri feels his revenge is complete.

The story has a psychological dimension unique in the whole catalog of tales, pointed up by an unforgettable scene in which the scholar, lurking in the shadow and watching the naked beauty pass by on her way to the pool, feels a strong surge of compassion mingled with lust that all but overcomes his desire for the cruel revenge he has planned. "This is surely one of the most intense and anguished moments of eroticism in the whole *Decameron*," Almansi comments,[65] but in the combination of aesthetic delight, human compassion, and sexual attraction it is something more than mere eroticism. Many critics have seen in this narrative not only an example of the familiar misogynistic motif of a certain current of medieval—and even classical—literature overtly manifest in the scholar's tirade, but also the memory of a bitter personal experience—a theory fortified by the presence of the same ingredients in the *Corbaccio* (in both accounts, as we have noted, the woman is a widow). This is not to say of course that Boccaccio himself ever took any such revenge—or indeed any revenge—but, in the words of Muscetta: "Only if we read [the story] as a dream of vengeance for a disillusionment in love shall we be able to understand the complacent desire to savor in the images and the words an action neither implemented nor implementable in real life but realizable through the power of the pen (as the scholar vaunts)."[66]

Pampinea's contribution is not, however, the only item of special interest in the decalogue of deceit set before us on this sunny Sunday. The first tale underlines a kind of by-law of the code of love: doing it for money is wrong; the revenge taken by an honest German seducer on his venal paramour meets with the approval of both the male and female members of the company. One may note too that it opens the tit-for-tat motif so much more harshly illustrated in the scholar's revenge, and in fact the same theme is present in the second tale, against a rustic background and full of saucy double entendres, and in the tenth, which moves to Sicily and concerns not a scholar but a gullible young Florentine businessman who, like Andreuccio, learns how to exchange innocence for guile. The third story introduces the Bruno-Buffalmacco cycle of pranks. These two rogues are painters in Florence and their favorite pastime is the playing of practical jokes, usually on their simple-minded colleague Calandrino. It is a cycle drawn apparently from popular accounts of such a waggish trio. Elissa, the narrator of the third story, locates the action in "this city of ours which has always been full of strange customs and odd people." Branca[67] identifies the characters with early fourteenth-century Florentine artists. They are, Elissa and the critics would have us believe, exemplifiers of truly Florentine ingenuity and inventive mischief.

In the third story the two pranksters persuade Calandrino that he has found the magic heliotrope that makes him invisible and, pretending they don't see him, stone him mercilessly. In the sixth story Filomena tells how the pair steals Calandrino's pig and puts him through a painful ordeal in the hope of having it returned; in the eighth, Lauretta returns to this irresistible duo to tell of the ingenious trick they play on Master Simon, a doctor freshly returned from Bologna, full of his new importance. Gulling a doctor gives special pleasure to the irreverent wags—and perhaps the notion was not unappealing to Boccaccio either; he seems to have shared Petrarch's low opinion of the medical profession. The eighth day has a strong Florentine coloring; five of the stories have a Florentine background (two others have their scene in the nearby towns of Fiesole and Varlungo), and a Florentine merchant is the hero of the tenth *novella*. If this is meant to suggest that the Florentines are particularly sharp-witted it would probably be in line with the general opinion of the times. On the basis of the Bruno-Buffalmacco cycle, the ingenuity of the inhabitants of the City of the Lily also contains an infusion of cruelty not always as amusing to the reader as it is to the perpetrators of the prank. Panfilo's song of joyous love, recalling Boccaccio's own lyrics of the Fiammetta period, concludes the day.

Emilia's decree that for the ninth day the storytellers may choose any kind of subject that appeals to them might suggest a lack of inventiveness on the part of the young queen, or perhaps may be seen as an indication that we are nearing the end of the house party, for with such liberty of choice, similar to the freedom of the first day, it is clear that we have come full circle. A small detail in the prelude may reinforce our suspicion. As the young people stroll through the pleasant glade on their way to their assembly they meet many animals of the woods that come forth and frolic freely with them, since the absence of hunters (because of the plague) has made them tame. This passing allusion reminds us of what originally brought the band together and again unobtrusively suggests the completion of the circle.

It has been noted, however, that although there are no restrictions on the topic of the tales, in actual fact the ninth day carries on faithfully the motif of "tricks"—ingenuity used either for prankish pleasure or in self-defense. All but two of the ten stories deal with deceit or stratagem in one form or another. And, also in keeping with the familiar pattern, five of the ten deal with illicit sexual relations. For the most part fast-moving and lively, the stories of this penultimate day give no evidence of flagging vigor, yet withal it is safe to say that there is no truly great story told in the course of the afternoon.

The cycle of Bruno and Buffalmacco reappears: the third item, contributed by Filostrato, tells how the playful pair make Calandrino believe he is pregnant and Fiammetta in the fifth story tells how they get their dupe into trouble with his wife, pretending to further his courtship of a girl who has caught his fancy. The sixth story (the substance is that of Chaucer's Reeve's Tale) is fascinating for a kind of geometrical bedazzlement as the various characters move from one bed to another; it is a well-contrived farcical scene, and to a lesser degree the same may be said of story 2 wherein the guilty abbess is betrayed by the odd headdress she is wearing as she chides her errant flock. (It is a repeat of Story 1.4 in plot, with change of sex in the actors.) Two items have a kind of historical literary interest: the fourth story has as its protagonist the well-known if antisocial Cecco Angiolieri (Muscetta notes that Boccaccio presents him sympathetically as he does another—and greater—nonconformist poet, Guido Cavalcanti [6.9]).[68] And in the eighth tale Dante's gluttonous Ciacco, the sodden prophet of *Inferno* 6, reappears in the principal role; Boccaccio treats him with some respect too. The misogynistic note recurs in the short and rather brutal tale of a husband's prophetic dream of his wife slain by a wolf (story 7) and in the parable of Solon, who covertly suggests that wife beating may be a salubrious activity (story 9). Dioneo's brief but racy account of how to change a woman into a mare shows that he has lost none of his brio—nor inventiveness. Perhaps for its explicitness and depiction of the credulous avarice of the peasant this tale stands out above the rest. It may be that another token of time running out is the brevity of the ninth day; next to day 6, made up largely of brief witty retorts, this is the shortest day of the *Decameron*.

At the close of the ninth day when the ladies have had their fill of laughter at the story of Dioneo, which they understood "better than he had wished," Emilia chooses Panfilo to preside over the tenth day. He proposes that the stories deal with "those who have acted liberally or magnanimously in affairs of love or other matters." After which, according to the established pattern, Neifile sings a song of happy youthful love, with echoes of Dante and Guido Cavalcanti.[69]

The nature of Panfilo's choice of subject matter sets the tenth day apart from all the others. No longer are we to hear of clever tricks and calculated stratagems but rather of lofty deeds and achievements. No longer will the dramatis personae be composed of schemers and seducers intent on their own pleasures but instead we shall meet noble characters, unselfish in motivation. Socially too, no less than ethically, we shall find as the narratives unfold that we are on a higher plane than we have been accustomed to; most of the stories deal with individuals of high degree and lords, princes, and prelates come on to the stage replacing the more variegated and predominantly middle-class cast of the preceding days. For this shift in gears it is not hard to think of good reasons. The tenth day is to be the last and it is understandable that Boccaccio would want his parade to end with a bang rather than simply taper off on the same familiar note. It is probable, too, that his intention is palinodic. So far he has set before us a world of characters dedicated in the main to practical, self-advancing interest. With few exceptions they have bent their efforts to the winning of worldly rewards and triumphs, some honestly and legitimately enough but few with any altruistic intent; none, not even the noblest, has been motivated by idealistic, unworldly purpose. This naturalistic picture of society will be corrected and even repudiated by the gallery of high-minded figures presented on the final day—at least

such we may suspect is the author's aim although a reader of today
might in some cases have his reservations about the examples.

So the tenth day is in purpose something like the last book of
Andreas Capellanus, wherein the whole code of seduction set forth in
the earlier books is repudiated. It fits the familiar medieval life design,
too, exemplified by the Provençal poets who after years in the service
of love, retired to monasteries; it is in line with Petrarch's last sonnets,
expressing penitence for the years wasted on the courtship of Laura.
Although the tenth day contains some good stories the reader senses
that the new climate is not quite suited to Boccaccio's Muse; the
storytellers seem less at ease; there is a perceptible feeling of tension
as they vie with each other to see who can portray the noblest subject.

In no fewer than four of the narratives crowned rulers play a major
role in the action. The first story describes the generosity with which
Alfonso of Spain rewards an Italian who has served him well, after
teaching him a lesson on the whims of inscrutable Fortune. Fiammetta
(story 6) appropriately tells the tale of Charles of Anjou, king of
Naples, and his resistance to the lustful temptation that stirs him as he
watches two young girls wading in a pool (the scene is pictorially
effective and seems to cry out for illustration). Pampinea immediately
matches this Guelph episode with the romantic account of King Peter
of Aragon (Charles's Ghibelline adversary) and his tender treatment of
a lovesick girl. The truly chivalrous tale is marred somewhat by the
prosaic ending in which the girl is persuaded to take a husband and
think of Peter only as the prince of her dreams. The ninth story is a
tribute to the great Saladin, who employs magic to restore to his
homeland a Christian prisoner who had befriended him.

Other protagonists, though uncrowned, are of high degree and of
lofty magnanimity. More than royal is the generosity of Gentile dei
Carisendi (fourth story), who restores to life and to her family a
woman he loves—asking nothing in return. A touch of humor enlivens
the *beau geste* of the wellborn bandit Ghino di Tacco, who earns the
gratitude of his captive, the bishop of Cluny, by putting the clerical
gourmet on a severe diet.[70] The fifth story (originally told, as was the
fourth, in the *Filocolo* and appealing to Chaucer's Franklin) represents
a veritable competition of high-minded generosity. Although the ac-

tion hinges on magic the characters, sympathetically portrayed, evoke credibility—and admiration. Of the remaining trio one must say that they transcend the limits of belief; their protagonists have moved from self-conscious altruism to exhibitionism. Nathan, for example, in the third story, carries generosity to absurd extremes: he is ready to give even his life away simply to demonstrate that his liberality knows no bounds. One reads of Gisippus and Titus (eighth story) with less wonder than distaste; the story is meant to depict a perfect friendship but when it results in the callous betrayal of a bride, the virtue of friendship becomes suspect. (The classical background gives Boccaccio an opportunity to display his familiarity with ancient rhetoric; the apologia of Titus is a masterpiece of its tedious kind.) But assuredly in this glittering parade of the exhibitionistic-masochistic, the pathologically submissive Griselda is preeminent.

The enduring and worldwide resonance of the piteous saga of this docile creature has given her name an archetypal status surpassing that of Lucretia or Cornelia.[71] Her story may be briefly told. Walter of Saluzzo, urged by his subjects to take a wife, chooses Griselda, a simple peasant girl, first exacting from her a promise that she will always obey him no matter what he may ask of her. Once married, Walter subjects his spouse to a series of painful and humiliating ordeals; he has her children taken from her, pretending that they are to be killed, and finally he sends her from his home, saying he is planning on taking a new bride—for whom, incidentally, he expects Griselda to serve as an attendant. Griselda accepts it all with superhuman meekness and at last, won over by her abject devotion, Walter reveals that all his persecutions had been simply tests of her wifely obedience. He truly loves her, he declares: the children are brought back and presumably the family lives happily ever after.

Petrarch was so deeply moved by the exemplary conduct of Griselda that he thought her story worthy of translation into Latin and it was his version of the tale that (filtered through a French translation) Chaucer slyly and appropriately gave to his pious (and celibate) Clerk.[72] The favorable view of Petrarch and Chaucer (or at least his cleric) no doubt bespeaks the high esteem in which the Middle Ages held wifely docility, nor does Griselda lack admirers even today.

Critics have seen in this unbelievably submissive creature a Mary figure or a Christ figure or a wistful idealizing evocation of the author's abandoned mother.[73]

There is, on the other hand, another school of thought. Certainly if we were to put Griselda in modern dress, as it were, she would seem to many of us to represent a perfect case of masochistic perversion and we should advise her (accompanied by her sadistic spouse) to consult a psychiatrist. Momigliano, finding the whole story false and inconsistent, called her passivity in the face of what she believes to be the fate of her children simply idiotic and noted that she is apparently quite willing to be an accomplice in a pair of murders.[74] Hauvette, who didn't give the heroine credit for a grain of sense, believed that Boccaccio didn't take his own story seriously,[75] a verdict that seems to be echoed six decades later by Almansi, who suspects the tale may be "a deliberate, we might even say, malicious product of Boccaccio's authorial strategy."[76]

In rebuttal it may be argued that we should not judge Griselda by realistic or even rational standards. The entire tenth day takes us out of the naturalistic world in which most of the Decameronians go about their business and back into the medieval realm of exalted visions. Incidentally, the palinodic tone of the final day is reinforced by the fact that this saint's life comes to us from the lips of Dioneo, the narrator of so many risqué episodes. Like Nathan, Titus, and Gisippus, Griselda is not of this world and should not be judged by its norms. Just the same, an example of virtue pushed beyond the bounds of belief is sure to arouse as much suspicion as admiration. Boccaccio's own view of his creation is a little hard to define. Ostensibly she is to be admired, yet Dioneo remarks that it might have been a better thing for Walter if he had chosen a different kind of bride, and the band of young people seem uncertain what to make of the account, "some taking one side and some the other." The same ambivalence obtained in the case of Ciappelletto, the first person on the Decameronian stage. So it can be claimed that from the arrogant and unprincipled sinner we have moved up the Jacob's ladder of the hundred tales to the humble and saintly peasant girl, from the depiction of an utterly unprincipled man to a uniquely perfect woman. It is an appealing figure, although the intermediate rungs of the ladder are not immediately perceptible—and both sinner and saint are open to contradictory interpretations. If the pair truly represents ethical poles in the intention of the author it is regrettable (but hardly debatable) that most readers not looking for a *sovrasenso* will find Ciappelletto not only more engaging but much more credible than the pathological wife of Walter.

Concluding his reign, Dioneo makes a short speech to the company. He reminds them of their purpose in coming together to flee the plague and enjoy a little relaxation. He congratulates them all on the success of their enterprise and makes the point (speaking surely for his author) that although their stories may have been a little improper and their style merry and carefree yet they have done nothing they need to be ashamed of; their conduct has been exemplary.

He adds that since everyone has now had his turn as king or queen it might be the time to call an end to their holiday. He adduces three reasons for this: to continue might lead to boredom, people might raise their eyebrows if a group of young people overly prolonged their sojourn together, and finally an elitist argument: "Our company has become known to others round about and it may soon be so much enlarged that we can take no joy in it."[77] Of course, he concludes, he is willing to name a successor if the others wish to continue their sport. After a lengthy discussion the company approves the king's suggestion. And so the last day comes to an end following the pattern of the others, with supper, dancing, and song. Fiammetta has the honor of concluding the series of lyric postludes; she sings a song voicing her delight in her lover and her jealous fear lest some other woman take him away from her, she is prepared to do battle with such rivals. Mario Marti observes that Fiammetta's aggressive frankness is in sharp contrast to the meekness of Griselda.[78]

Having concluded his work the author comes forward to say a few words for himself. He addresses himself—as he had in the prologue—to his public of ladies. First of all he defends the character and language of his stories: he has simply reproduced them as he had to and as art demanded. He claims the same license as a painter who paints things as he chooses, having St. George thrust at the dragon in whatever part

of its anatomy he will, and painting Adam male and Eve female.
Further, he reminds his public that these stories are not told in church
nor in schools of philosophy but rather in places of recreation and by
young people (yet sufficiently mature not to be led astray by mere
stories). And they were told at a time (i.e., during the plague) when
"the most respectable people went around wearing their breeches over
their heads for protection—nor was it held against them."[79] He concedes that the stories can be turned to good or evil according to the
mind of the listener; wine is good for the healthy and bad for the sick;
fire is essential to mankind but also dangerous. His stories must be read
at the proper time and by those for whom they were intended.

Some may say, he continues, that certain stories should have been
omitted. "Granted," says Boccaccio, "but I could not and should not
have written any stories but those that were told. The ladies should
have told pretty stories and I would have written pretty stories. And
even if it were assumed that I had been both writer and inventor of
these stories—which I am not—I should not feel ashamed if they were
not all beautiful for there is no master save God who can create perfect
things."[80] And finally, he concludes, the reader may choose the tales
that suit him and skip the others; they all have titles indicating their
content.

To the possible charge that some stories are too long the author
replies that, as he stated at the beginning, they were written for ladies
with time on their hands—and perhaps in need of more lengthy
exposition than an audience of scholars. So too if many of the stories
seem trivial and full of jests, they were written to drive away melancholy. And if some women will protest that he has an evil-speaking
tongue because he has told the truth about friars, it may be that they
have reasons for their objection and he will forgive them. He rests on
the assurance of a lady of his acquaintance who had read most of the
stories that his tongue was the sweetest in the world. And thanking
God who has enabled him to bring his work to an end, he wishes his
ladies well and hopes they will remember him if they have profited
by reading his book.

Boccaccio's statement that he is not the inventor of any of the one
hundred tales is a little ambiguous. Does this disclaimer mean that

within the scaffolding of his work he is simply passing on the responsibility to his frame characters? Or is it simply an acknowledgment that he made up no plots of his own but took what he found in the works of earlier writers or in oral tradition? In any case his remark opens up the whole question of the sources of the *Decameron*'s narratives, which scholars have been zealously exploring for centuries. In his meticulous edition of the work Vittore Branca finds that very few of the tales have what he calls an "authentic" or "precise antecedent." Yet he also conscientiously cites derivations and analogues accumulated by earlier scholars and concludes that situations and motifs are often drawn from medieval literature of the centuries immediately preceding Boccaccio's time, and that they frequently contain material from anecdotes current in contemporary oral circulation, and, somewhat rarely, from classical sources.[81]

It is fair to say that even where we find a recognizable source the treatment given the story by the hand of the master invariably results in an artifact that may well claim to be called original. The saucy story of Masetto, who so joyously plays the role of the mute (3.1), for example, is well known to students of Old Provençal, familiar with William of Poitou's use of the same stratagem, and there are analogues in the *Novellino* and elsewhere. Branca concedes too that the theme was already popular and even cites a proverb in which he detects the nucleus of the ardent nun's easy dismissal of her vow of chastity.[82] Yet the creation of the ambience, the realistic reproduction of the scene, and the ensuing conversation when the nuns discover the sleeping Masetto—these are Boccaccio's own contributions and they make his story truly original. So too in the tragic story of Ghismonda; the detail of the poisoned cup may be an echo of Paulus Diaconus, the reasoning of the heroine derives in part from the code of courtly love; the association of love and death had been sanctified by the example of Tristram and Iseult; yet the background, narrative detail, and the vigorous delineation of the heroine suffice to establish the originality of the tale. Finally, although from the point of view of "motifs" and patterns the docile wife is a familiar figure in medieval literature (we could cite examples from the sundry saints' lives and Old French romances) there is, for better or for worse, no heroine quite like

Griselda, humble, obedient, yet withal on occasion surprisingly eloquent. Unquestionably Boccaccio turned often enough to such predecessors as the *Novellino*, the *Disciplina clericalis*, the *Book of the Seven
Sages*, and perhaps even more often to current gossip—simply as a
primer, one might say; but the resultant artifact may yet rightly be
called his own.

It would not be too much to say that even if we could find readily
recognizable antecedents for all the tales the manner of their telling
would nevertheless justify a claim to originality. For in the pages of
his masterpiece Boccaccio reveals himself as a consummate stylist,
suiting with masterful assurance the tempo and color of his prose to
the various uses of exordium, reflection, conversation, or action. One
may say, oversimplifying a little, that in the *Decameron* two different
kinds of prose are successfully blended: much of the work; the *proemio*,
the introduction, the passages dealing with the frame characters, and
many expositional or descriptive passages in the stories themselves are
in the high style, the sort of prose we found in the *Filocolo*, though
of course more sophisticated. Such passages employ long, complicated
periods, make regular use of the cursus, and are, as Branca has demonstrated, often embellished with divers kinds of ornaments—some passages can be scanned as iambic measures.[83] Yet when the occasion calls
for it—in passages of swift action or in lively conversation—another
manner is employed, crisp, straightforward, anything but "medieval."
A ready example of Boccaccio's technique may be observed in the very
first story. The exordium of Panfilo is elegant and calculated; the
confession of Ciappelletto and the responses of the simple-minded
confessor are straightforward and naturalistic.[84]

As we have noted, Branca has suggested that the less ornate type of
prose may have come from Boccaccio's perusal of diaries and logbooks
of commercial travelers and businessmen of the time. Whatever be its
origin it is something new in Italian prose. The combination of styles
adds an element of aesthetic enjoyment to the reading of the work,
even if the reader is barely conscious of it; so many-faceted is the
language of the master that a contemporary translator has flatly stated
that Boccaccio is untranslatable.[85] Yet though of necessity much is lost
in the carry-over from the Italian, a good English translation can give

the reader a tolerably fair notion of the *richesse* and adaptability of Boccaccio's manner.

An account of the history of the criticism of the *Decameron* would be too lengthy for inclusion in a book of this nature. But some comment on what Italians call "the fortune" of the *Decameron* may not be out of place. Briefly, one may say that the work was widely read before it was deemed worthy of criticism or even mention, and criticized long before it was truly appreciated. Boccaccio's allusion to his detractors preceding the fourth day indicates that the work had a public even while it was yet coming into being, and the number of manuscripts attest to its wide popularity (many of them from the fourteenth and fifteenth centuries: the *editio princeps* is of 1470 approximately).[86]

Yet the early biographers of Boccaccio, who were also critics, writing at the end of the fourteenth century or the beginning of the fifteenth, unanimously ignore or disparage the *Decameron.* The kindest comment comes from Petrarch who patronizingly assumes that it was a youthful work written to please the multitude; he finds Griselda irresistible but does not claim to have read all the stories, "having more serious matters on his mind." Filippo Villani, coming at the end of the fourteenth century, discusses only the Latin works with special praise for the *Genealogies of the Pagan Gods.* He alludes only vaguely to the vernacular works "wherein his mind quite plainly delights in the lustful joys of youth."[87] Leonardo Bruni (1369–1444) is of the same opinion and Giannozzo Manetti (1396–1459) likewise reports that all agree that the *Genealogies* is the best of Boccaccio's works; he too ignores the works in Italian. Such verdicts need hardly surprise us when we recall the exaltation of Latin in the first stage of the new humanism; even Petrarch affected to disparage his own *Rhymes.*

Yet the vitality and popularity of the work, if not its prestige among intellectuals, is documented by the early appearance of imitators or emulators such as the Ser Giovanni who wrote (1378–1385) *Il pecorone.* Giovanni Gherardi (1367–1442), author of *Il paradiso degli Alberti,* Giovanni Sercambi (1347–1424), whose *Novelle* borrow the framework of a plague (in this case that of 1376), and Franco Sacchetti (*Trecentonovelle,* 1399) also reproduce the world of the *Decameron.* In the fifteenth century translations into other tongues testify to the spreading popularity of the work. Laurent de Premierfait translated the work into French as early as 1414. A Catalan version appeared in 1429 and by the middle of the quattrocento some fifty tales had found a Castilian translator; a German version was published at Ulm in 1473. The first English translation (1620, probably by John Florio), is a little late in appearing but, as Herbert G. Wright puts it, "in one way or another news of the *Decameron* had arrived long before then."[88]

By the end of the quattrocento the vernacular had recovered its prestige; men of letters could no longer ignore the *Decameron.* Lorenzo de' Medici, in a percipient and surprisingly modern comment, lauds the work for its inventiveness, abundance, and eloquence in the depiction of human emotions; he goes so far as to call it "sola al mondo" —unique.[89] Lorenzo's appraisal is a high water mark in pre–nineteenth century criticism of the *Decameron.* Critics and editors of the work in the sixteenth and seventeenth centuries focus their attention on matters of style and diction; the *Decameron* becomes involved in the pedantic and polemical "quistione della lingua." Probably the great Muratori speaks for the eighteenth century when he admires the style and elegance of the hundred tales, while deploring "the obscene stories and the sentiments offensive to piety and religion."[90] Baretti praises the language of the work but finds its style objectionable.

In the nineteenth century, which was sympathetic to the Middle Ages and medieval artifacts, the *Decameron* comes into its own. Appreciation of its merits is not limited to Italy; in England, for example, men of letters read and commented on the masterpiece, sometimes with reservations and sometimes uncritically, but always with recognition of the art and scope of the work. Hazlitt and Coleridge were among its early explorers. Walter Savage Landor, whose *Pentameron* (1837) is still instructive as well as readable, does not hesitate to compare the gifts of Boccaccio with those of Ariosto, Shakespeare, or even Dante. In Italy Ugo Foscolo and Vincenzo Gioberti contributed perceptive essays on the *Decameron*; the latter, like Landor, found Boccaccio's range and variety comparable to Ariosto's grand design.

The great landmark in the history of Decameronian studies comes, however, in the midcentury when Francesco De Sanctis, in a chapter of his *History of Italian Literature* (1855), writes an acute, coherent, and sympathetic analysis of the work and its historical significance. Here, for the first time, as Petronio notes, "the art of Boccaccio is not only proclaimed but demonstrated, analyzed, and defined."[91] Simplifying the essay of De Sanctis we may say that it makes three cogent affirmations with regard to Boccaccio's masterpiece. First, in measuring its greatness, De Sanctis does not hesitate to put it beside Dante's poem: where the latter is rightly called a *Divine Comedy* the *Decameron* may merit the definition of a "human comedy." Second, De Sanctis associates the work with its times, which are, as he sees them, characterized by the decay of the idealism of the Middle Ages and the efflorescence of a new materialistic and naturalistic world. And finally, he does not hesitate to say that "art is the only thing in life Boccaccio takes seriously."[92] De Sanctis, to be sure, had forerunners in Foscolo and especially Edgar Quinet but his analysis, well argued and forceful, is singularly authoritative. Generally speaking, he has set the framework for all subsequent criticism down to the present, whether revision or elaboration has been the intention of his successors. Certainly his pronouncements greatly stimulated critical and scholarly interest in the *Decameron.*

Scholars returned to scrupulous study of the text fortified by the sophisticated philological weapons that the nineteenth century devised; this work still goes on. Boccaccio's life became a new field for historians; in this area the work of the Italian scholar Crescini is preeminent although his findings have sometimes been questioned.

The twentieth century cannot be accused of ignoring either Boccaccio or his masterpiece. In Italy, out of an *embarras de richesses*, one may cite the works of Attilio Momigliano, Umberto Bosco, and Benedetto Croce as particularly valuable; the first two for serene and impartial interpretation of the work, Croce for his concept of Boccaccio as a poet, with the recommendation (consistent with the writer's aesthetic theories) that the *Decameron* should be read not as an artifact of its times but on its own merits, sub specie aeternitatis, as it were. Henri Hauvette in French and Edward Hutton in English contributed substantial monographs on the man and his works still useful as introductory essays. But studies of the master were given vigorous new impetus in our century by Vittore Branca, textual scholar, historian, and critic. The title of his best-known work, *Boccaccio medievale*, suggests his approach, somewhat revisionary of De Sanctis.

Among numerous Italian critics of recent years Giovanni Getto merits particular attention; he argues that the "lesson" of the *Decameron* is the "art of living well," that is, to present, as we should say today, the right public image—a kind of social if not strictly ethical morality.[93] Turning to works written in English, Aldo Scaglione's somewhat obliquely entitled *Nature and Love in the Late Middle Ages* is perhaps the best point of departure; with just appreciation of both De Sanctis and Branca, and with many shrewd insights of its own, it is a well-balanced study of Boccaccio's roots and the implications of his work. In the abundance of recent studies it is hard to find a consistent trend; to quote a recent observation "no general agreement among scholars as to the meaning [of the *Decameron*] has yet been reached."[94] A few currents may be noted. There has been evident a basic division between those who see the work as entertainment with concomitant and coincidental depiction of the society from which it springs, essentially in the tradition of De Sanctis, though of course modified by personal insights, and those who look for a hidden meaning, whether allegorical or didactical; one might say "allegorists and moralists."

As for the allegorists, it may be conceded that when De Sanctis equates the *Decameron* with the *Divine Comedy* or at least mentions them in the same breath, he seems to invite a consideration of the presence of allegory in the "Human Comedy." Branca's stress on Boccaccio's medievalism might appear to offer a similar invitation, for allegory is a necessary element in many serious medieval works of art. Besides, it must be admitted that there are occasional suggestions of hidden meaning, at least for eyes that are looking for them (and our age is avid in its search for veiled meanings, Christ figures and the like) within the *Decameron* itself. We cannot fail to note that the book contains a hundred stories even as there are a hundred cantos in the *Divine Comedy* (of which of course Boccaccio was not only an admirer, but a keen student). This fact alone encourages Dantean-allegorical interpretation. A distinguished scholar of our day affirms that "in a certain sense the *Decameron* matches the structure of the *Commedia*. Boccaccio suggests three modes of earthly existence that can be said to correspond to the *Inferno*, *Paradiso* and *Purgatorio*. They do not occur sequentially but are imagined to coexist simultaneously with each other."[95] In this concept plague-stricken Florence would be Hell, the "heaven of the villa" would be Paradise, and the hundred tales, "offered as fictional," would compose Boccaccio's Purgatory. This is an appealing parallel if we keep our eyes firmly fixed on the stage props and the flats. The actors are something else again. The dwellers in the suffering city though wretched are not damned, the young band of escapists is hardly saintly, and the characters in the tales are not penitents cheerfully undergoing purgation. For in the *Decameron* in fact the dimension of eternity, basic to the *Commedia*, is totally lacking. The plague will end, the house party breaks up in a fortnight, and none of the energetic and resourceful figures brought to life by the narrators has any interest whatsoever in eternal bliss.

Inevitably too, certain aspects of "the frame" have attracted the seeker for hidden senses. It is easy to see in the flight from the horrors of the plague a metaphor for the detachment from contingency necessary to the creative artist, or even an affirmation that the writing and reading of stories signifies escape. Indeed if we agree with Charles Singleton that "Boccaccio's art is an art of escape,"[96] this interpretation is hardly allegory at all. Giuseppe Mazzotta, arguing his own original thesis on the nature of Boccaccio's vision, finds that "the retreat into the garden is obviously an effort to cope with loss and a conversion to life."[97] No doubt—but this is hardly more than a translation into abstract terms of the simple naturalistic reaction of a group of frightened young people in a realistic historical situation. All the details of the formation of the group: the time of year, the place of meeting, the remarks of the characters, are quite satisfying on the literal level. They need no gloss. When we take up the *Divine Comedy* we know before we have read ten lines that if we are going to understand the poem we must look beyond the literal: the opening pages of the *Decameron* beget no such urgency.

Again, it is true that a sequence of tales beginning with the depiction of an utter rogue and ending with the portrayal of a "saintly" woman suggests a moral progression vaguely similar to that of the wayfarer Dante from the abyss to the summit. It is hardly surprising that some such trajectory has been postulated.[98] Yet such a view ill accords with the shrewd observation of Thomas K. Seung that "many stories could be shuffled or reassigned within the topical framework of the tales"[99] or with Thomas Greene's observation (with which most readers will concur) that "there is a kind of downward drift running through the stories of the seventh, eighth and ninth days,"[100] a number of which contain elements of sadism and cruelty. As for the polarity of Ciappelletto and Griselda, most readers having no thesis to defend would find the ironic aura surrounding Ciappelletto hard to shake off: he is too lighthearted a rogue to gravitate naturally to the Inferno, while the saintliness of Griselda is somewhat suspect to an unprejudiced eye, unless masochism be a prerequisite for canonization.

The number and the names of the storytellers have quite legitimately led scholars to ponder their possible symbolism.[101] Yet such readings have not been entirely convincing. We might fairly contend, in fact, that if symbolism had been a part of the author's intention he could have made it a little clearer, as he did in the *Comedy of the Florentine Nymphs.* It seems likely that Bosco is right when he affirms that it is as difficult to find allegorical symbolism in the storytellers as it is to find consistency in the depiction of their personalities.[102]

Summing up, it seems not unreasonable to conclude that, while there is recurrent symbolic allusion of one sort or another in the hundred tales, suggestive of meanings under the veil, the case for true allegory (which in Northrop Frye's definition requires that "the events of a narrative obviously and continuously refer to another simultaneous structure of events or ideas")[103] has yet to be made. Basically, the obstacle to a satisfactory allegorical interpretation of the *Decameron* lies in the dissidence between its pattern and its substance. The design of the frame encourages the search for a hidden meaning; the stories themselves and the world they portray invalidate any such reading and bespeak the "realistic disposition" of the author, which Natalino Sapegno finds "the one constant element" in the work.[104] The *Decameron*, like the *Divine Comedy*, is a great cathedral, but the men and women who stroll about in it ignore its suggestive construction and are insensitive to its transcendent implications.

It is not easy either to argue for moral purpose in a work wherein

Scaglione notes "the complete absence of the sense of sin"[105] and in which Rocco Montano finds "no philosophy of any kind in the author's intention."[106] One can make a moralist out of the *Decameron*'s author only by insisting that he consistently and purposefully "ironizes," a thesis as difficult to defend as it is to refute. But as we look at the world of the *Decameron* we shall see that illicit sex is sometimes punished and more often simply enjoyed; rascals thrive or perish according as Fortune or wit serves or fails them. Surveying this world without prejudice, we are bound to conclude with Bosco that "Boccaccio doesn't want to teach anyone anything."[107] Allegorists and moralists alike face the unhappy task of contradicting the straightforward statement of *ipse Johannes*, who tells us that his stories were intended for the solacing perusal of idle hours and, in his conclusion, seems to disclaim any connection between his art and life itself. It is hard to disagree with Singleton's blunt statement: "The *Decameron* has no *sovrasenso*."[108] Contemplating the mass of interpretative criticism that the hundred tales have occasioned in our time, the reader must choose between the axiom that "great writers mean what they say" and the more subversive postulate latent in the title Guido Almansi gives his essay: *The Writer as a Liar.* Opting for the latter alternative, one would be compelled to admit that Giovanni Boccaccio is the greatest liar of them all.

Of course in one sense the *Decameron* is a serious book, as De Sanctis noted: its art is serious. Our contemporary critics from Auerbach on have been on firm and fertile ground when they turned their attention to Boccaccio's tactics and techniques and to his notions, as revealed by his practice, of the fascinating and delicate art of storytelling. It is true too that a work written with no serious intention may yet contain elements suggestive of something more than mere amusement. There is no doubt that some of the characters in the tales are serious enough: Ghismonda certainly, and the scholar Rinieri, and no doubt in their way most of the seducers. And though a writer may be perfectly neutral, his choice of material tells us inevitably something about his vision of the world. When Boccaccio pleads innocently that he did not "invent" the stories he obscures the fact that he chose them; he could easily have assigned a few saints' lives to the women and tales of

NOTES

Books and articles in the notes are cited by authors and short titles. For details of publication see the bibliography.

CHAPTER 1

1. Charles T. Wood, *The Age of Chivalry*, p. 139.
2. *A History of Europe from the Invasions to the XVI Century*, p. 380.
3. *A Distant Mirror*.
4. Translation (of uncertain authorship) from *Petrarch: Selected Sonnets, Odes and Letters*, ed. T. G. Bergin, p. 64.
5. Robert S. Lopez, *Naissance de l'Europe*, p. 267. Such estimates are necessarily conjectural; on the population of Italian cities see further Josiah Cox Russell, *Medieval Regions and Their Cities*, pp. 39–76.
6. Quoted by John A. Symonds, *The Renaissance in Italy*, p. 70.
7. Ibid., p. 220.
8. *Le istorie fiorentine, Tutte le opere* 2.42., p. 120. Translation mine.
9. Ibid., p. 221. Writing in our time, Gene A. Brucker, reckoning the population of Florence as "perhaps 90,000 in 1340," calculates that the city lost "one third and possibly more of her inhabitants in 1348." "Florence and the Black Death," in *Boccaccio: secoli di vita*, p. 22.
10. Fausto Nicolini, "Napoli," in *Enciclopedia italiana*, vol. 24, p. 235.
11. *The Shorter Cambridge Medieval History*, vol. 2, p. 863.
12. *Rhymes* 53. Translation of G. F. Cunningham in *Petrarch: Selected Sonnets, Odes and Letters*, ed. T. G. Bergin, p. 38.

13. Pirenne, *History of Europe*, p. 381.
14. *Feudal Society*, p. 74.

CHAPTER 2

1. Throughout this chapter I have followed the guidance of Vittore Branca's *Profilo biografico*, which summarizes and assesses the findings assembled by earlier scholars, supplementing them with the fruits of his own research.
2. Branca, *Profilo*, p. 6, who cites in support Pier Giorgio Ricci, "Studi sulle opera latine e volgari del Boccaccio," p. 3 ff. Not all scholars concur: Ernest Hatch Wilkins ("Discussion of the Date of the Birth of Boccaccio," p. 314) had concluded that our author "was born in 1313 or 1314, probably in the first half of 1314."
3. Branca, *Profilo*, pp. 3–4.
4. Book 5, chapter 9. See our chapter 4.
5. Chapter 23; see our chapter 7.
6. Villani's brief account is printed in *The Decameron*, eds. Mark Musa and Peter E. Bondanella, pp. 188–191.
7. Branca, *Profilo*, p. 6.
8. Natalino Sapegno, "Boccaccio," in *Dizionario biografico degli italiani*, vol. 10, p. 838.
9. *Genealogies of the Pagan Gods*, 15.10.
10. See Villani's account in *The Decameron*, eds. Musa and Bondanella, pp. 188–191.
11. In the summer or the autumn of that year (Branca, *Profilo*, p. 15). Other authorities have suggested different dates: see Branca, p. 15, n. 35.
12. Branca, *Profilo*, pp. 17–18.
13. *Ep.* 12.
14. *De casibus*, 9.26.
15. Filippo Villani, *Vite d'uomini illustri fiorentini*, p. 419.
16. E. G. Léonard states flatly that Acciaiuoli was the princess's lover, *Dizionario biografico degli italiani*, vol. 1, p. 87. Léonard's entry, pp. 87–90, gives a concise account of the career of this able and ambitious statesman.
17. *Boccace*, p. 101.

18. Branca, *Profilo*, p. 22.
19. *Filocolo*, ed. Antonio Enzo Quaglio, book 1, chapter 1, pp. 63–65. Translation mine.
20. Ibid., p. 718, n. 66.
21. *Boccaccio medievale,* p. 243.
22. Chapter 49, line 80.
23. *Ep.* 5; "probably 28 August, 1341," according to Branca, *Profilo*, p. 55; see also his note.
24. Branca, *Profilo*, pp. 59, 67, 69; the dates are also accepted by Muscetta.
25. *Profilo*, p. 67. Especially noteworthy is Boccaccio's version of a report on the Canary Islands, written by an agent of the Bardi. Boccaccio's version is found in the *Zibaldone magliabecchiano*. *Zibaldone* (pot-pourri) is the name given to a miscellaneous collection of works copied by Boccaccio for his own interest, with a few original items. There are two *zibaldoni* (or two versions of the *zibaldone*) called after the manuscripts containing them: the *magliabecchiano* and the *ricciardiano*. See Texts and Translations of Boccaccio's works.
26. *Ep.* 6, dated by Massèra (*Opere latine minori*, p. 325) as of late 1347 or early 1348.
27. *Boccace et Naples*, p. 43.
28. Branca, *Profilo*, p. 78. Earlier scholars doubted that Boccaccio had actually been in Florence at the time of the plague in spite of his statement in the introduction of the *Decameron*.
29. *Fam.* 21.15; translation of Morris Bishop in *Letters from Petrarch*, p. 182.
30. *Ep.* 8; see Léonard, *Boccace et Naples*, pp. 59 ff.
31. *Ep.* 9.
32. Branca, *Profilo*, p. 97.
33. *Fam.* 19.3; see Bishop, *Letters*, pp. 156–160.
34. *Profilo*, p. 102.
35. *Fam.* 18.15.
36. See Branca, *Profilo*, p. 80 and note.
37. *Ep.* 14. Translation mine.
38. *Sen.* 10.4. Translation from Bishop, *Letters*, p. 274.
39. Branca, *Profilo*, p. 118.
40. Ibid., pp. 109–110.
41. The tale of Leontius is told in detail in R. Pertusi, *Leonzio Pilato fra Petrarca e Boccaccio*. See Branca, *Profilo*, pp. 114–115.

42. From the letter of consolation to Pino de' Rossi, *Ep.* 6 in *Opere in versi*, pp. 1112–1141; quote from pp. 1140–1141.

43. All passages of this letter are from Bishop's *Letters*, pp. 225–227.

44. *Ep.* 12 (*Opere latine minori*); for details of the visit see Léonard, *Boccace et Naples*, pp. 84–117, in which Acciaiuoli appears in a somewhat better light.

45. Branca, *Profilo,* p. 140, quoting a letter of Boccaccio as yet unpublished.

46. *Sen.* 5.1.

47. *Sen.* 6.1,2.

48. See E. H. Wilkins, *Petrarch's Later Years*, pp. 154 ff.

49. Branca, *Profilo*, pp. 163–164, citing Petrarch *Sen.* 10.4 and 5.

50. *Sen.* 17.3. Translations by T. G. Bergin, following Fracassetti's Italian version.

51. *Ep.* 20.

52. *Ep.* 24.

53. For details see Branca, *Profilo*, p. 188.

54. Translations mine, following Latin text in Giannozzo Manetti's *Vita Joannes Boccacii,* published in *Le vite di Dante, Petrarca e Boccaccio*, ed. Angelo Solerti.

55. See Hauvette, *Boccace*, p. 464, n. 1.

56. *Poetical Works by Lord Byron* (Oxford, 1921), p. 228.

57. Summarized from the translation of Hugh Skubikowski in Musa and Bondanella, *The Decameron*, p. 191.

CHAPTER 3

1. Branca, *Profilo*, p. 41.

2. *Caccia di Diana*, ed. Vittore Branca, p. 3.

3. Carlo Muscetta, *Giovanni Boccaccio*, p. 18, somewhat vaguely suggests the date of composition may be 1338–1339 or perhaps a few years earlier.

4. Canto 13, lines 29–30.

5. Muscetta, *Giovanni Boccaccio*, p. 21.

6. *Caccia*, pp. 6–7.

7. Robert Hollander, *Boccaccio's Two Venuses*, pp. 19 ff., suggests other "ironic possibilities" of interpretation.

8. *Caccia*, p. 4 and note on p. 869.
9. See "Bibliografia essenziale," pp. 680–681, of Branca's edition for details.
10. "Mondo aristocratico e mondo comunale nell'ideologia e nell'arte di Giovanni Boccaccio," p. 82.

CHAPTER 4

1. *Filocolo*, ed. Antonio Enzo Quaglio, introduzione, p. 47.
2. *Profilo*, p. 44.
3. *Giovanni Boccaccio*, p. 23.
4. Ettore De Ferri in his introduction to the *Filocolo*, p. x, surveys the conjectures of older scholars: Carducci, Koerting, and others. His conclusion is still valid: "We know that the *Filocolo* was begun in the year of the author's enamorment; we do not know with precision the date of its composition."
5. *The Life of Giovanni Boccaccio*, p. 69.
6. *Profilo*, p. 45.
7. The relationship of the *cantare* to Boccaccio's work is uncertain; see Quaglio, *Filocolo*, p. 55.
8. Ibid.
9. Salinari and Sapegno (*Decameron*, p. 787, n. 2) remark that medieval chroniclers, attributing the founding of the city to Brennus, king of the Gauls, called it "Civitas Marmorea" or "Marmora" because of the abundance of marble used in its construction. Muscetta (*Giovanni Boccaccio*, p. 56) speculates that the version of the story in Venetian vernacular had moved the Spanish capital to Verona to Italianize the tale. It is not clear why Boccaccio prefers "Marmorina." See Quaglio's note 3 to book 1, chapter 10, p. 729; also, De Ferri, *Il Filocolo*, pp. xxi, xxii.
10. The town of Montorio (for Boccaccio Montoro) in the vicinity of Verona still stands.
11. Florio's Greek is hardly convincing. Scholars have argued that the title of the work should be *Filopono* or *Filocopo*. See Quaglio's note 5 to chapter 75 of book 3, p. 842.
12. Ilario's reaction is "a rhetorical invention" according to Quaglio, note 1 to chapter 96 of book 5, p. 968. Perhaps the reference to a Greek

authority is a kind of recognition of the Byzantine origin of the story.

13. See Herbert G. Wright, *Boccaccio in England*, p. 102. The translation of the Questions was reprinted in 1927 (with an introduction by Edward Hutton) under the title *Thirteen Most Pleasant and Delectable Questions of Love* and again in 1950 (with revisions by Thomas Bell) and 1974.

14. Mario Marti, *Giovanni Boccaccio; Opere minori in volgare*, vol. 1, p. 25.

15. These points are made by Paolo Cherchi, "Sulle 'quistioni d'amore' nel *Filocolo*," pp. 210–217 of *Andrea Cappellano, etc.*

16. "The World of Boccaccio's *Filocolo*," p. 339.

17. Salvatore Battaglia, *Giovanni Boccaccio e la riforma della narrativa*, p. 165.

18. *Giovanni Boccaccio*, p. 56.

19. *Boccaccio's Two Venuses*; see pp. 31–40 for his remarks on the *Filocolo*.

20. Edward Hutton, *Giovanni Boccaccio*, p. 63.

21. *Il Trecento*, p. 288.

22. *History of Italian Literature*, p. 103.

23. Quoted by De Ferri, *Il Filocolo*, vol. 2, p. 265, n. 3.

CHAPTER 5

1. See Wright, *Boccaccio in England*, p. 59.

2. My summary is based on the text of Vittore Branca's edition. I have preserved Boccaccio's version of the names of the principal characters.

3. *Profilo*, p. 41. See also introduction to his edition of the *Filostrato*. P. G. Ricci in his edition of the work (in *Opere in versi*) follows Branca, adding that the lady whom Boccaccio had in mind was one Giovanna, to whom he assigned the fictitious name of Filomena. However, in his foreword (p. viii) Ricci concedes that his dating of the work is tentative.

4. *Giovanni Boccaccio*, p. 98.

5. On Chaucer's version of the tale see Wright, *Boccaccio in England*, pp. 59–100. For further critical comment see Monica E. McAlpine, *The Genre of Troilus and Criseyde.*

6. The version of Benoît may be found in R. K. Gordon, *The Story of Troilus*, pp. 3–22. See also the introduction to Nathaniel Edward Griffin and Arthur Beckwith Myrick, *The Filostrato of Giovanni Boc-*

caccio, pp. 1–107. Muscetta (*Giovanni Boccaccio*, p. 4) mentions other versions of the tale with which Boccaccio may have been familiar, notably Guido delle Colonne's *Historia Trojana*, which also draws on Benoît.

7. *The Tranquil Heart*, p. 125.

CHAPTER 6

1. *Teseida delle nozze d'Emilia*, ed. Alberto Limentani, p. 231.
2. Book 2, chapter 2.
3. Translation of Bernadette Marie McCoy, *The Book of Theseus*, p. 336.
4. *Giovanni Boccaccio*, p. 76. See also H. and R. Kahane, "Akritas and Arcita: A Byzantine Source of Boccaccio's Teseida."
5. For a summary of the sources, see Limentani's introduction to his edition, pp. 231–234.
6. Ibid, p. 238.
7. Translation of Bernadette Marie McCoy, *Book of Theseus*, pp. 196–197. I have somewhat altered her wording.
8. Quoted approvingly by Limentani, *Teseida*, p. 234.
9. Ibid., p. 76.
10. *Boccaccio's Two Venuses*, pp. 56 ff.
11. McCoy, *Book of Theseus*, pp. 16–17.
12. Muscetta, for example (*Giovanni Boccaccio*, p. 78), calls it "the incunabulum of the modern 'heroic genre,' without which the [*Orlando*] *Innamorato* [of Boiardo] and the *Furioso* [of Ariosto] would be inconceivable."
13. *History of Italian Literature*, p. 104.
14. *History of Italian Literature*, vol. 1, p. 309.
15. Francesco Torraca, *Per la biografia di Giovanni Boccaccio*, pp. 112 ff.; Giuseppe Billanovich, *Restauri boccacceschi*, pp. 105 ff.
16. *Boccaccio medievale*, p. 65.
17. Billanovich, *Restauri boccacceschi*, p. 65, note. Muscetta himself is tempted by "emiolia," a musical-arithmetical measure.
18. See Wright, *Boccaccio in England*, pp. 44–48.

·   ·   ·

CHAPTER 7

1. *Comedia della ninfe fiorentine*, ed. Antonio Enzo Quaglio, pp. 667–668; Branca, *Profilo*, p. 59.
2. Admetus was the legendary shepherd-king of Thessaly.
3. Lia: "The Christian faith, born of a river, symbol of baptism." Quaglio, *Comedia*, p. 910, n. 24.
4. Literally "of bright color, woven by Indian hands." Quaglio, *Comedia*, p. 916, n. 33, glosses: "probably red, prized purple."
5. Signifying "virtuous fervor"; see Quaglio, *Comedia*, p. 920, n. 5 to chapter 13. The shepherds probably symbolize the worldly life (Acaten) and the ascetic life (Alcesto); see *Decameron, etc.*, p. 936, n. 7.
6. Fiammetta had used the same pretext to introduce the Questions of Love in the *Filocolo*.
7. Quaglio, *Comedia*, p. 925, n. 10.
8. *Decameron, etc.*, pp. 957–958, n. 8. See also our note 3 to chapter 16.
9. These details suffice to unmask Ibrida.
10. *Decameron, etc.*, p. 986, n. 9.
11. Quaglio, *Comedia*, p. 944, n. 57, suspects that the relationship may be both real and symbolic, in the latter sense indicative of a connection between prudence and apathy.
12. Quaglio, *Comedia*, p. 959, n. 90.
13. Such is the deduction of the scholars from Boccaccio's cryptic phraseology. More precise identification of Ameto's mother is impossible. See Quaglio, *Comedia*, p. 959, n. 93.
14. Quaglio, *Comedia*, p. 960, n. 20. There are many echoes of the *Divine Comedy* in these verses.
15. Quaglio (*Comedia*, p. 962, n. 2) remarks: "Ameto's purgation, which is effected gradually by the intervention of the nymphs, follows Dante's precedents, vaguely recalled and skillfully varied; from the purification at the beginning of the *Purgatorio* through the agency of Virgil to the immersion in Lethe at the hands of Matelda and the intervention of Beatrice." However, in the pattern of the action, one may see as well some affinity with the conclusion of *Diana's Hunt*.
16. All we know of Boccaccio's friend is that with Pino de' Rossi he took part in the anti-Guelph conspiracy of 1360 and was subsequently killed. See Quaglio, *Comedia*, p. 964, n. 2, citing Villani, *Cronica* 10.28.

17. Quaglio (*Comedia*, p. 953, n. 85) remarks on the close similarity of Caleone's vision in chapter 35 to certain passages of the *Vita nuova*.

18. Other predecessors of the metamorphosed Ameto have been unearthed by contemporary critics. Branca (*Profilo*, p. 62) notes that Ameto is often "traced" on the pattern of the Ovidian Polyphemus, wooer of Galatea (*Metamorphoses*, 13. 769–869); indeed such echoes are audible in chapter 8. Muscetta (*Giovanni Boccaccio*, pp. 108–109) dwells on Boccaccio's indebtedness to the *Metamorphoses* of Apuleius. However, the presence of Dante is undeniably ubiquitous and, I think, dominant.

19. Specifically, in the first story of the fifth day.

20. *Boccace*, pp. 114–115.

21. *Lo spirito e le lettere*, vol. I, p. 261.

CHAPTER 8

1. *Amorosa visione*, ed. Vittore Branca, p. 6.

2. As in *Inferno* 4.106.

3. *Amorosa visione*, pp. 16, 560.

4. *Giovanni Boccaccio*, p. 111.

5. *Amorosa visione*, p. 560.

6. The *Inferno* has an inscribed gate, too, although the inscription carries a different message. Here, the narrowness of the gate is of biblical origin; the gate to Dante's Purgatory was likewise narrow.

7. Clearly these young men are opposed in significance to the protective lady. What their colors symbolize is uncertain; Branca (*Amorosa visione*, p. 567), takes the colors as referring to the faces of the youths and sees an allusion "to the two aspects of those who allow themselves to be dominated by their passions." Hollander suggests (*Boccaccio's Two Venuses*, p. 215) that "perhaps Boccaccio wanted to figure in them the duplicity of earthly things."

8. Muscetta (*Giovanni Boccaccio*, p. 112) finds "vivacity and movement" only in the female characters mentioned, particularly Cleopatra. Perhaps the parade of strong-minded ladies here observed may be the genesis of *De mulieribus claris*.

9. Muscetta (ibid., p. 113) sees in this passage "an act of homage to French literature," with which Boccaccio was well acquainted.

10. Muscetta (ibid., p. 119) thinks it was the Neapolitan frescoes of Giotto (now lost) that gave Boccaccio the original inspiration.

11. Billanovich goes so far as to theorize that Petrarch's unnamed guide in the *Trionfo d'amore* may have been Boccaccio. ("Dalla *Commedia* e dall' *Amorosa visione ai Trionfi*, pp. 25–26). Hollander (*Boccaccio's Two Venuses*, pp. 207–208) provides a convenient summary of the scholarship on the Boccaccian inspiration of the *Trionfi*.

12. With like reflective pace, Dante had entered the Earthly Paradise, *Purgatorio* 27, as Branca notes (*Amorosa visione*, p. 709).

13. Branca's discussion of the fountain and its streams covers pp. 708–713 of his notes to his edition of the poem, reviewing earlier interpretations and stating his own conclusions. He observes, *inter alia,* that the fountain may derive from the one described by Andreas Capellanus in his treatise on love and certainly points forward to the magic fountains of Boiardo and Ariosto. Its "realistic" inspiration, like that of the garden, may have been the royal park of Castelnuovo. Nor is Dantean influence lacking, see note 12 above.

14. Branca, *Amorosa visione*, p. 711, where he also comments on Crescini's interpretation.

15. In this injunction Scaglione sees "a transparent reminiscence of the struggle of Love and Nature against Reason in the *Roman de la Rose*" (*Nature and Love*, p. 121).

16. Presumably before their union is consummated, "making the conclusion of the *Amorosa visione* the greatest anti-climax in the mediaeval literature of love." (Hollander, *Boccaccio's Two Venuses*, pp. 89–90).

17. *Il Trecento*, p. 332.

18. *Amorosa visione*, p. 737.

19. Ibid., pp. 735–736.

20. Ibid., p. 741.

21. *Boccaccio's Two Venuses*, p. 90.

22. *Nature and Love*, p. 121.

23. *Amorosa visione*, p. 20.

24. *Giovanni Boccaccio*, pp. 119–120.

CHAPTER 9

1. Branca, *Profilo*, p. 67 and note 18 to that page. However, Branca qualifies his dating with a "perhaps"; Muscetta (*Giovanni Boccaccio*,

p. 138) thinks it may be later, "at least in the version that has come down to us."

2. So too Francis MacManus (*Boccaccio*, p. 126): "The first psychological novel in a modern European language."

3. Guido Almansi (*The Writer as a Liar*, p. 155) quotes Antonio Enzo Quaglio (*Le chiose all' Elegia di Madonna Fiammetta*, vol. 2, p. 48): "Seneca is Boccaccio's only real discovery in those years and his Fiammetta is striking confirmation of this fact."

4. *Profilo*, pp. 66–68. Boccaccio copied his Latin version of the report in his *Zibaldone (magliabecchiano)*.

5. Muscetta, *Giovanni Boccaccio*, p. 139, citing Segre; Muscetta notes also the influence of Livy and Cicero.

6. My summary follows the text edited by Carlo Salinari and Natalino Sapegno.

7. In the concept of a wicked Fortune and in the style of Fiammetta's tirade, Mario Marti (*Opere minori in volgare*, p. 42) hears an echo of the medieval *De diversitate fortune* of Arrigo da Settemello.

8. Robert Griffin ("Boccaccio's *Fiammetta*: Pictures at an Exhibition," p. 93, n. 4) remarks "that Boccaccio's cullings from, say, *Phaedra*, draw on contiguously successive passages and advance through that play as the elegy progresses suggests that he may have written *Fiammetta* with 'Seneca Tragicus' freshly in mind or close at hand."

9. Luigi Russo, *Studi sul due e trecento*, p. 208.

10. Giuseppe De Robertis (*Studi*, pp. 52–53) finds in certain passages "a clean simplicity" and notes that the introspective element opens the way to "another prose, of popular taste, in no way latinizing . . . or elaborated."

11. Russo, *Studi sul due e trecento*, p. 208.

CHAPTER 10

1. Muscetta, *Giovanni Boccaccio*, p. 140.

2. Ibid., p. 156.

3. Accordingly, in his edition of the work (*Opere in versi*, pp. 19–148), he puts the *Nymph Song* before *Diana's Hunt*; only some of the poems would precede it, in Ricci's view.

4. In the introduction to his edition of the work, pp. 269–289, the whole question of the dating of the poem, including Ricci's arguments, is discussed.

5. *History of Italian Literature*, p. 106. Wilkins is not alone in finding the passage shocking; Muscetta (*Giovanni Boccaccio*, p. 147) speaks of the "aggressive and sadistic details" unmatched even in the *Decameron*.

6. Thus does the author casually reveal what critics consider the classical nucleus of the story, the seduction of Callisto by Jove (*Metamorphoses* 2.422 ff.). Balduino (*Ninfale fiesolano*, pp. 826–827) notes that this legend recurs frequently in Boccaccian works—at some length in one of the glosses to the *Teseida* and in the *Vision of Love.*

7. Daniel J. Donno, *The Nymph Song of Fiesole*, p. ix.

8. *Storia della letteratura italiana*, p. 88.

9. See Balduino's introduction, *Ninfale fiesolano*, p. 288; also his "Tradizione canterina e tonalità popolareggianti nel *Ninfale fiesolano.* "

10. T. C. Chubb (*The Life of Giovanni Boccaccio*, p. 122) remarks that "both the writings of Lorenzo de' Medici and the painting of Botticelli are foreshadowed in this slender idyll."

11. This scene, Muscetta remarks (*Giovanni Boccaccio*, p. 151, note), "is by general critical conclusions the most poetic one of all the little poem—a page of classical serenity."

12. See Branca, *Profilo*, p. 71.

13. *Boccace*, p. 176. Branca considers this possibility, too (see n. 12).

14. *Il Trecento*, pp. 346–347.

15. Version of Joseph Tusiani, *The Nymphs of Fiesole*, p. 126.

16. *Mimesis*, p. 190.

17. *Boccace*, p. 164.

18. *Boccaccio's Two Venuses*, pp. 70–71 and p. 195, n. 21.

19. Tusiani, *Nymphs of Fiesole*, p. 15.

CHAPTER 11

1. "Sulla datazione del *Corbaccio*," and "Ancora sulla datazione e sul titolo del *Corbaccio.*"

2. *Opere in versi*, p. 1271. Tauno Nurmela and Anthony K. Cassell concur with Ricci. (See Cassell, *The Corbaccio*, p. xxvi.) Muscetta (*Giovanni Boccaccio*, p. 343), however, although tentatively, seems to agree with Padoan.

3. *The Corbaccio*, trans. and ed. Anthony K. Cassell, p. xxvi.
4. Ibid., pp. xxvi–xxvii.
5. "The *Corbaccio*: Notes, etc.," p. 508, n. 12.
6. *European Literature and the Latin Middle Ages*, p. 362.
7. *Giovanni Boccaccio as Man and Author*, p. 67.
8. See "Satire of Satires: Boccaccio's *Corbaccio*."
9. Such sources are exhaustively surveyed in Cassell's notes to his translation. Muscetta (*Giovanni Boccaccio*, p. 344) sees a considerable legacy from the third book of Andreas Capellanus.
10. *Opere in versi*, p. ix.
11. Cassell (*The Corbaccio*, p. 105) conscientiously cites the literary antecedents of this tirade; nevertheless, the passage suggests personal experience.
12. See ibid., p. xxi and note.
13. "The *Corbaccio*: Notes, etc.," p. 506.

CHAPTER 12

1. *Le rime di Giovanni Boccaccio*. Testo critico a cura di Francesco Massèra. Bologna, Romagnoli-Dall'Acqua, 1914. I have followed the later version published by Unione Tipografico-Editrice Torinese, Torino, 1921.
2. *Giovanni Boccaccio. Le rime, L'amorosa visione, La caccia di Diana* a cura di Vittore Branca. Bari, Laterza, 1939.
3. Branca, *Rime*, p. 316.
4. Vincenzo Crescini, quoted by Massèra, *Rime*, p. 51.
5. For specific examples see Gordon Rutledge Silber, *The Influence of Dante and Petrarch on Certain of Boccaccio's Lyrics*.
6. *Rime*, p. 64.
7. Ibid., p. 107.
8. Translation by T. G. Bergin, reprinted with permission from *Lyric Poetry of the Italian Renaissance*, comp. and ed. L. R. Lind, pp. 209–210.
9. See Rosario Ferreri, "Ovidio e le rime del Boccaccio," *Forum Italicum* 7–8 (1973–1974), pp. 46–55.
10. For the history of the criticism of the *Rhymes* see Rosario Ferreri, "Studi sulle rime del Boccaccio," pp. 229–237.

11. *History of Italian Literature*, p. 101.
12. *Il Trecento*, p. 297.
13. *History of Italian Literature*, vol. 1, pp. 316–317.
14. Rosario Ferreri, "Studi sulle rime," p. 222.

CHAPTER 13

1. *Stile e critica*, p. 198.
2. *Trattatello in laude di Dante*, p. 425.
3. Ibid., p. 427.
4. Ibid., introduction, pp. 425–435.
5. A term Ricci dislikes; to him the revised version is "a new writing with its own characteristics." Ibid., p. 428.
6. Following Dante's own account in *Paradiso* 15.
7. Ricci (ibid., p. 863, n. 98) observes that Boccaccio follows a long tradition of premonitory maternal dreams, citing the story of St. Dominic in *Paradiso* 12; in *Paradiso* 9 Dante alludes to a similar but more sinister vision vouchsafed to the mother of Ezzelino da Romano who dreamed that she would bring forth a firebrand.
8. That is, at about the age of forty-six, following Dante's definition of the stages of life (*Convivio* 4. 24, 2–4). The journey to Paris is attested only by Boccaccio.
9. Following Philip H. Wicksteed, *Early Lives of Dante*, with some revision and abridgment.
10. *Opere in versi*, p. 881, n. 495.
11. Skeletal measurements indicate a height of 1.65 meters (about 5′ 4½″); See ibid., n. 484.
12. Ricci (ibid., p. 882, n. 498) rejects the beard.
13. No doubt the source is the Casella episode of *Purgatorio* 2.
14. As Petrarch stresses; see *Africa* 9.73.
15. The reference is to Epistola 9, edited and translated by Paget Toynbee, *The Letters of Dante*, pp. 148–159. Toynbee notes (p. 148) that the letter has been preserved only in one manuscript which contains the *Zibaldone laurenziano* in the handwriting of Boccaccio.
16. The turning from Beatrice to Lady Philosophy in the *Convivio* may have suggested this statement, although Dante is at pains to say

nothing is intended "in derogation" of the *Vita nuova* (*Convivio* 1.1.16).

17. Boccaccio has confined the date assigned to the vision with the date of composition; the *Comedy* was probably begun about 1307 when Dante was forty-one or forty-two.

18. The same anecdote is told again in the *Esposizioni* (in canto 8, literal commentary 13, where the rescuer is identified as one Dino Perini. (*Trattatello*, ed. cit., p. 891, n. 738).

19. Boccaccio's authority is Piero di Giardino, a notary of Ravenna, "for a long time a disciple of Dante." Ibid., p. 875, n. 376 and p. 892, n. 764.

20. Boccaccio quotes from a letter of "Brother Ilario" to Uguccione della Faggiuola. The letter is preserved only in Boccaccio's own transcription in the *Zibaldone laurenziano*. It is likely that the letter was composed by Boccaccio himself. Giuseppe Billanovich ("La leggenda dantesca del Boccaccio") discusses the matter at length, concluding that Brother Ilario is an invention of Boccaccio and recalling that another clerical Ilario had been called upon to sponsor, as it were, the *Filocolo*. The letter has been translated by Wicksteed, who also doubts its authenticity, in *Early Lives of Dante*, pp. 147–151.

21. Again, the source is Brother Ilario's letter.

22. Beatrice had mentioned a distracting "pargoletta" (*Purgatorio* 31.59) and the "rime petrose" testify to the existence (in fact or fancy) of a "mountain woman." The *Compendio* is more specific; there, after speaking of the death of Beatrice, Boccaccio adds: "Nor was our poet impassioned by this love alone; nay, rather was he much disposed to this affection. We find him often to have sighed for other objects in his riper age; and especially after his exile, when he was in Lucca, for a lady whom he calls Pargoletta, and besides this, almost at the end of his life in the Alps of the Casentino, for an Alpine Lady, who, if I have not been misinformed, however beautiful in face, had a goitre." (*Trattatello*, redaz. A, 35; ed. cit., pp. 503–504. Translation from Wicksteed, *Early Lives of Dante*, pp. vii–viii).

23. Ibid.

24. *Opere in versi*, p. 426.

25. Domenico Guerri, for example, in his edition of the work (Bari, 1918) cited by Francesca Flora, *Storia della letteratura italiana*, vol. 1, p. 292.

26. For a full discussion of the sources and genesis of the lectures see Padoan, *Esposizioni*, introduzione, pp. xv–xxxi.
27. *Il Trecento*, p. 365.
28. Padoan, *Esposizioni*, p. xxiii. He notes that traces of such predecessors as Guido da Pisa, Pietro di Dante, L'ottimo and others are easily detectable although unacknowledged.
29. Branca, *Profilo*, p. 192, n. 4.
30. Benvenuto da Imola, quoted by Padoan, *Esposizioni*, p. xv.

CHAPTER 14

1. *Boccaccio on Poetry*, p. v.
2. Branca (*Profilo*, p. 40) notes that an impassioned enthusiasm for erudition characterizes the *Filocolo* as well as the *Genealogie*. And there are assuredly passages in the *Teseida* that adumbrate the encyclopedist.
3. See chapter 19, p. 330.
4. Osgood, *Boccaccio on Poetry*, p. 137.
5. Ibid., p. xii; Branca, *Profilo*, p. 83.
6. *Genealogie deorum gentilium libri*, ed. Vincenzo Romano, p. 151.
7. Osgood, *Boccaccio on Poetry*, p. 190, n. 9.
8. Ibid., p. 142.
9. Ibid., pp. 111–115.
10. Ibid., p. 114.
11. Sapegno, *Il Trecento*, pp. 385–386.
12. Hauvette, *Boccace*, pp. 426–427.
13. Book 11, chapter 4 (vol. 2, pp. 543–544 of Romano's edition). Translation by J. L. Ryan and T. G. Bergin.
14. In book 2, chapters 22–23, Boccaccio discusses the two Venuses at much greater length.
15. Étienne Gilson cites earlier defenses of poetry but sees in the last two books of the *Genealogies* the first effort ever made to isolate the problems. "Poésie et vérité dans la *Genealogia* de Boccace," p. 254.
16. Book 14 covers pp. 14–101 of Osgood's book.
17. The phrase suggests that the author was already preparing his geographical dictionary.
18. Osgood, *Boccaccio on Poetry*, p. 164, n. 8.

19. *Opere in versi*, pp. 974–975.
20. Dante's friendship with Frederick of Aragon seems unlikely; all mentions of this prince in Dante's works (*Convivio* 4.6.20, *De vulgari eloquentia* 1.12.5, *Purgatorio* 7.119–120, *Paradiso* 20.63) are censorious. It is true that in his *Life of Dante* (see chapter 13, p. 224) Boccaccio mentions a rumor that Dante intended to dedicate the *Paradiso* to Frederick; Ricci, however, (*Opere in versi*, p. 972, n. 2) points out that the source of this information is the letter of "Brother Ilario."
21. "Obviously he has not read Plato," Gilson remarks ("Poésie et vérité," p. 258), citing the passage in the *Republic* wherein Plato specifically excludes Homer from his city.
22. My quotations are from Osgood, *Boccaccio on Poetry*, pp. 102–142.
23. Ernest Hatch Wilkins, "The Genealogy of the Genealogical Trees of the *Genealogie Deorum*," in his *The Invention of the Sonnet*, p. 163.
24. See Vittore Branca, "Boccaccio illustratore del suo *Decameron* e la tradizione figurale del suo capolavoro."
25. *Profilo*, p. 106.
26. Daniele Mattalia, "Monti, selve, fonti, etc.," in *Dizionario Bompiani*, vol. 4, p. 807.
27. See Sapegno, *Il Trecento*, p. 391.
28. I have used the facsimile of the fourth edition of the *Genealogie* (Venice, 1494), which contains also the *De montibus*, published by Garland Publishing, New York and London, 1976.

CHAPTER 15

1. *Boccaccio*, p. 246.
2. *De mulieribus claris*, ed. Vittorio Zaccaria, p. 22.
3. Ibid., p. 25. Translation by Guido A. Guarino, *Concerning Famous Women*, p. xxxvii. Guarino's English version, predating Zaccaria's edition, "is based on the edition of Mathias Apiarius, printed in Berne in 1539" (p. xxxi).
4. Zaccaria, *De claris mulieribus*, pp. 3–4.
5. Ibid., p. 27.
6. Sources for the individual items are supplied by Guarino, *Concerning Famous Women*, pp. 253–257 and more exhaustively by Zaccaria, *De mulieribus claris*, pp. 483–557.

7. Zaccaria, *De mulieribus claris*, pp. 5–6.
8. Guarino, *Concerning Famous Women*, p. xvi.
9. Ibid., pp. xvii–xx.
10. *Triumph of Chastity*, lines 154–159. Zaccaria (*De mulieribus claris*, p. 515, n. 15) notes that Boccaccio follows Justin and not Virgil. So too Guarino, *Concerning Famous Women*, p. 255.
11. All brief quotes that follow are from Guarino's translation.
12. Guarino, *Concerning Famous Women*, p. xxvii.
13. Translation of this chapter, free and abridged, is mine.
14. Daniele Mattalia, "(Delle) Donne illustri," in *Dizionario Bompiani*, vol. 2, p. 837.
15. Wright, *Boccaccio in England*, p. 33.
16. *Forty-six Lives*, translated from Boccaccio's *De mulieribus claris* by Henry Parker, Lord Morley, and edited by Herbert G. Wright, London, 1943.
17. Ibid., pp. 43–47.

CHAPTER 16

1. The date of the letter has not been determined. Branca (*Profilo*, p. 180) discusses the matter at length; for him 1372 or 1373 seem likely dates. The text of the letter is published in *Opere latine minori*, pp. 216–221.
2. *Opere in versi*, p. 652.
3. Ibid., p. 654.
4. *Opere latine minori*, p. 217.
5. Ibid., p. 218.
6. W. Leonard Grant, *Neo-Latin Literature and the Pastoral*, p. 98.
7. *Profilo*, p. 101.
8. Grant, *Neo-Latin Literature*, p. 97.
9. *Le lettere edite e inedite di Messer Giovanni Boccaccio*, ed. Francesco Corazzini, p. 264.
10. Grant, *Neo-Latin Literature*, p. 101.
11. My translation is a versified version of a prose draft prepared by Dr. John L. Ryan of lines 76–139 (*Opere latine minori*, pp. 46–47).
12. *Opere latine minori*, p. 218.
13. Grant, *Neo-Latin Literature*, p. 103.
14. *Opere latine minori*, p. 219.

15. Ibid., p. 220.
16. Grant, *Neo-Latin Literature*, p. 106.
17. *Opere latine minori*, p. 220. The daughter, perhaps not the first of Boccaccio's illegitimate children, was born probably "between 1349 and 1350" and died in September 1355 (Branca, *Profilo*, p. 80, n. 47).
18. Grant, *Neo-Latin Literature*, p. 105.
19. *Opere latine minori*, p. 220.
20. Ibid.
21. See note 1 above. Muscetta (*Giovanni Boccaccio*, p. 337) states that the *Carmen* was "sistemata" (put together) in 1367.
22. Daniele Mattalia, "Carme Bucolico, Il," in *Dizionario Bompiani*, vol. 2, p. 128.
23. *Opere latine minori*, p. 286.
24. I. Gollancz, *Boccaccio's Olympia with English Rendering*, pp. 35–39 (covering lines 170–224 of the Latin).
25. Arcesilas: God.
26. P. G. Ricci (*Opere in versi*, pp. 686–687) notes the details of this description, which Boccaccio borrowed from Dante's *Purgatorio* 29. The colors of the various components of Boccaccio's celestial court do not, however, signify what they do in the Purgatorial procession. Perhaps here the aged band of satyrs represents the Hebrew prophets; the purple order could stand for the disciples or the early martyrs in general. The snow-white host could symbolize the souls of children saved, since Olympia and her siblings are a part of it; the saffron order (in the original *crocei coloris*) possibly the other blessed souls.
27. Asylas: Boccaccino, Boccaccio's father.

CHAPTER 17

1. Branca, *Profilo*, p. 107. Muscetta, *Giovanni Boccaccio*, p. 317, dates the first draft between 1356 and 1360 and assigns the final version, dedicated to Cavalcanti, to 1373.
2. *Fates of Illustrious Men*, p. xiii.
3. Ibid., p. x.
4. See, for example, Massimo Miglio, "Boccaccio biografo," in *Boccaccio in Europe*, ed. Gilbert Tournoy, pp. 149–163.
5. *Fates of Illustrious Men*, p. xi.

6. Ibid., pp. x–xi; see also *Opere in versi,* p. 1279.

7. *Fates of Illustrious Men,* loc. cit.

8. A facsimile of the Paris edition of 1520 with an introduction by Louis Brewer Hall has been published by Scholars Facsimiles and Reprints, Gainesville, Florida, 1962. A number of selections from the work may be found in *Opere in versi,* ed. P. G. Ricci, pp. 776–891, with facing page translation in Italian.

9. According to Monica McAlpine (*The Genre of Troilus and Criseyde,* pp. 615–616) it is "the general opinion that Chaucer was familiar with the *De casibus* and that he drew the general plan of the Monk's Tale and half a dozen of its stories from Boccaccio's work."

10. See Wright, *Boccaccio in England,* pp. 5–21 for a discussion of Lydgate's poem.

11. Ibid., p. 4.

12. Catherine P. Bourland, "Boccaccio and the *Decameron* in Castilian and Catalan Literature," p. 13. Quoted by Wright on page 17.

13. *Opere in versi,* p. x.

14. The story of Filippa is found in book 9. My translation is from Ricci's text, *Opere in versi,* pp. 876–886.

15. Wright, *Boccaccio in England,* p. 3.

CHAPTER 18

1. Francesco Corazzini, *Le lettere edite e inedite di Messer Giovanni Boccaccio,* Firenze, Sansoni, 1887.

2. Aldo Francesco Massèra, *Giovanni Boccaccio: Opere latine minori,* Bari, Laterza, 1928. The *epistolae* cover pp. 109–227.

3. Pp. 155–182 of his *Giovanni Boccaccio: L'Ameto, Lettere, Il Corbaccio,* Bari, Laterza, 1940.

4. Specifically: a very brief note to a Certaldese friend in Avignon published by Roberto Abbondanza ("Una lettera autografa del Boccaccio nell'Archivio di Stato di Perugia," *Studi sul Boccaccio* 1 [1963], 5–13); "Epistola in nome della Signoria al Petrarca," published by Ginetta Auzzas, *Studi sul Boccaccio* 4 (1967), pp. 203–240; and a letter as yet unpublished to Donato da Casentino, mentioned by Branca, *Profilo,* p. 140, n. 32.

5. My translation follows the text of P. G. Ricci in *Opere in versi,*

pp. 1240–1256. Ricci's selection contains thirteen letters with facing page translation of the Latin letters in Italian and copious notes. Ricci believes numbers 1, 3, and 4 of Massèra's collection are probably fictitious and assigns Massèra's number 22 to Petrarch (p. 1284).

6. Ricci, ibid., note 5 to pp. 1248–1249, sees an allusion to Petrarch's refusal to take up residence (and a professorship) in Florence. The language here is somewhat reminiscent of Petrarch's *Rhymes* 4, in which he compares the humble birth sites of Christ and Laura.

7. Boccaccio here refers to Petrarch's *Seniles* 17.2, which he was destined never to receive. See *Opere in versi*, p. 1255, n. 7.

8. That is, the story of Griselda, Latinized by Petrarch.

9. Another epitaph, unknown to Massèra, is that written for Pino and Ciampi della Tosa, published by D. De Robertis in *Studi sul Boccaccio* 9 (1975–1976), pp. 43–101. Its pattern is similar to the one Boccaccio wrote for himself.

10. *Opere latine minori*, p. 295.

11. Ibid., p. 303.

12. This is the text of the youthful work mentioned in our chapter 3, p. 67. Massèra thinks it "perhaps the oldest literary exercise of our author." (*Opere latine minori*, p. 361.)

13. Ibid., p. 367. Other scholars would put the date as early as 1341–1342; see Branca, *Boccaccio medievale*, p. 287, n. 1 and Muscetta, *Giovanni Boccaccio*, p. 336.

CHAPTER 19

1. Branca, *Profilo*, p. 80; Muscetta (*Giovanni Boccaccio*, p. 156) is a little less definite, "soon after the plague, within a two year span."

2. Edgar Quinet, *Rivoluzioni d'Italia*, quoted by Giuseppe Petronio in Walter Binni, *I classici italiani*, vol. 1, p. 204.

3. *Decameron*, ed. Vittore Branca.

4. Alberto Moravia, "Boccaccio," in *Critical Perspectives on the Decameron*, ed. Robert S. Dombroski, p. 100. Abridged from Moravia, *Man as an End: A Defense of Humanism*.

5. *A History of Italian Literature*, pp. 108–109.

6. T. G. Bergin, "An Introduction to Boccaccio," in *The Decameron*, eds. Musa and Bondanella, p. 163.

7. This is the title Branca gives to the fifth chapter (p. 134 ff.) of his *Boccaccio medievale*. English versions may be found in Vittore Branca, *Boccaccio: The Man and His Works* ("The Mercantile Epic," pp. 277–307, complete with notes) and in *Critical Perspectives* ("The Epic of the Italian Merchant," pp. 38–47.)

8. Wilkins, *A History of Italian Literature*, p. 109.

9. Guido Cavalcanti (day 6, story 9).

10. Branca, *Profilo*, p. 78; Muscetta, *Giovanni Boccaccio*, p. 159.

11. Branca, *Boccaccio medievale*, pp. 12, 304–305. Hauvette detected also an echo of Thucydides as filtered through Lucretius; see also Muscetta, *Giovanni Boccaccio*, p. 160.

12. Translation mine, as are following quotations from the *Decameron*, all based on the text of Branca's edition here from pp. 15–16.

13. Branca, *Decameron*, pp. 13–14.

14. Umberto Bosco, *Il Decameron: saggio*, p. 17.

15. On such predecessors see Robert J. Clements, "Anatomy of the Novella," in *The Decameron*, eds. Musa and Bondanella, pp. 159–161.

16. I.e., the seventh story of the sixth day; this style of reference will be followed throughout.

17. Branca, *Decameron*, p. 20.

18. The contrast is noted by Hutton, *Giovanni Boccaccio*, p. 297 and Hauvette, *Boccace*, p. 224.

19. *Boccace*, p. 223.

20. The definitions are from Bosco, *Il Decameron*, p. 44.

21. *The Writer as Liar*, p. 17. Hauvette too had noted (*Boccace*, p. 220) that "seul le rôle de Dioneo est à peu près cohérent", remarking that Boccaccio had called himself "spurcissimus Dionaeus" in *Ep.* 2 (*Opere latine minori*, p. 113; "spurcissimum dyoneum").

22. *Decameron*, p. 997, n. 13.

23. *Boccaccio*, p. 164.

24. *Decameron*, introduction, p. xxv. Specifically "Filomena and Filostrato for the predominantly lyric narrative: Elissa and Emilia for the renewal of the epic; Neifile and Lauretta for that of the lyric; Pampinea and Dioneo for the foundation of the pastoral narrative, Fiammetta and Panfilo for the invention of the novel and the purely psychological novel." For his further comments on the frame characters see pp. 992–993, n. 3, and p. 997, n. 1.

25. "Struttura e linguaggio nella novella di Ser Ciappelletto," chapter 2 of *Vita di forme e forme di vita*, p. 34.
26. Branca, *Boccaccio medievale*, p. 158.
27. *Cultural Thematics*, p. 197.
28. *Il Decameron*, p. 52.
29. *Poesia popolare e poesia d'arte*, p. 89.
30. Writing in the seventeenth century, when matters of faith were taken seriously, Robert Burton found in this story evidence of Boccaccio's atheism: *Anatomy of Melancholy*, ed. A. R. Shilleto, vol. 3, p. 445.
31. As Branca observes, *Decameron*, p. 1044.
32. See Wright, *Boccaccio in England*, pp. 220–226.
33. Cesare Segre, for example (*Il Decameron*, p. 10), stresses the point that man is the protagonist of the hundred tales, wherein we shall find no lingering on nature, places, or objects, save where they are functional in the action or characterization. Undeniably Naples leaves its mark on Andreuccio. See Benedetto Croce, *La novella di Andreuccio da Perugia*.
34. "Forms of Accommodation in the *Decameron*," in *Critical Perspectives*, p. 114.
35. *An Allegory of Form*, p. 39 and n. 21.
36. The new site has been variously and inconclusively identified; see Branca, *Decameron*, pp. 1140–1141, n. 7. Giuseppe Mazzotta ("The *Decameron*: The Literal and the Allegorical," p. 56) believes that Boccaccio's introduction to the third day is "a subtle mockery of the religious quest for Eden." On Boccaccio's various *loci amoeni* see Edith G. Kern, "The Gardens in the *Decameron*," and Lucia Marino, *The Decameron "Cornice,"* pp. 79–122.
37. Alibec's story is analyzed in some depth by Almansi, *The Writer as a Liar*, pp. 83–88.
38. Or perhaps simply beach house background. Today it would be moved up to Fregene and told by Moravia—with more abundant clinical detail.
39. See Branca, *Decameron*, p. 1195, n. 7 to p. 342.
40. On the early circulation of the tales see Maria Picchio Simonelli, "Prima diffusione e tradizione manoscritta del *Decameron*," in *Boccaccio: secoli di vita*, pp. 125–142.
41. Branca, *Decameron*, p. 1199, n. 13.

42. Ibid., pp. 350–351.

43. "The Legendary Style of the *Decameron*," in *Critical Perspectives*, pp. 89–90.

44. *Nature and Love*, p. 104.

45. *Boccaccio*, p. 179, translation mine.

46. Quoted by Almansi, *The Writer as Liar*, p. 136.

47. *Il Decameron*, p. 142, n. 4.

48. *Mimesis*, p. 177–196.

49. *Critical Perspectives*, p. 103.

50. See *La vita nuova* 3. The topos of the eaten heart has a long history, perhaps ultimately folkloristic; see Branca's lengthy comment, *Decameron*, pp. 1250–1251, n. 1. A number of tales told on this day (5, 8, 9) suggest popular origin; on the subject see Alessandro Falassi, "Il Boccaccio e il folklore di Certaldo," in *Boccaccio: secoli di vita*, pp. 265–292.

51. Muscetta, *Giovanni Boccaccio*, p. 237. The scene inspired some of Dryden's most effective lines in his adaptation of the tale, "Cymon and Iphigenia."

52. *The Writer as Liar*, p. 15. His is the verdict of centuries; long before Tennyson the story (original with Boccaccio; see Branca, *Decameron*, p. 1305, n. 2) had wide resonance and prestigious adapters: La Fontaine, Hans Sachs, Lope de Vega, and Matthew Prior among them (Wright, *Boccaccio in England*, p. 294, n. 1.) The tale has recently been sympathetically analyzed by Beverly Joseph Layman, "Eloquence of Pattern in Boccaccio's Tale of the Falcon."

53. "Italy in the Middle Ages," in *The Culture of Italy*, p. 91.

54. "Boccaccio's *ars narrandi* in the Sixth Day of the *Decameron*," in *Italian Literature: Roots and Branches*, pp. 225–242.

55. *An Anatomy of Boccaccio's Style*, pp. 83–96.

56. Greene, "Forms of Accommodation," in *Critical Perspectives*, p. 117.

57. *A Short History of Italian Literature*, p. 67.

58. "Dante, personaggio mancato del *Decameron*," in *Boccaccio: secoli di vita*, pp. 177–189.

59. Kenneth Pennington ("A Note to *Decameron* 6:7") remarks that the story derives its humor from Boccaccio's parody of a legal axiom and of a biblical quotation (Matthew 7:6); "otherwise the tale might appear to be a shallow piece of wit." But if her wit is shallow, Filippa herself is not.

60. *An Allegory of Form*, p. 66; see also her note 2 same page for Giuseppe Mazzotta's view. Momigliano, *Il Decameron*, p. 229, had already linked the two deceivers.

61. Branca, *Decameron*, p. 576.

62. On the possible site of the valley see Branca, *Decameron*, p. 1355, n. 8; Lucia Marino sees the Vale as symbolizing "the hidden 'sanctuary of Venus' and as a metonym for art itself" (*The Decameron "Cornice,"* p. 87).

63. One of the few novelle of which the source is "clear and certain," viz., the *Comoedia Lydiae*, transcribed by Boccaccio himself; see Branca, *Decameron*, pp. 1390–1391.

64. Ibid., p. 1401, n. 8.

65. *The Writer as a Liar*, p. 29. Almansi's discussion of the story is perceptive.

66. *Boccaccio*, p. 265.

67. *Decameron*, pp. 1410–1411.

68. *Boccaccio*, p. 278.

69. Muscetta is reminded of Dante's "pargoletta" and Matelda (ibid., p. 284). Hence her association with the "sweet new style." See note 24 above.

70. Both Carisendi and Ghino have Dantean associations: the Carisendi built the Garisenda, the great tower mentioned in *Inferno* 31.136–138, and *Purgatorio* 6.14 contains an allusion to Ghino's ferocity.

71. On Griselda's widespread renown see Vittore Branca, "Origini e fortuna europea della Griselda," in his *Boccaccio medievale*, pp. 308–313.

72. Wright, *Boccaccio in England*, p. 116. For a discussion of Petrarch's treatment of the tale and an English version of his Latin see Emilie Kadish, "Petrarch's *Griselda*: An English Translation."

73. Branca, *Boccaccio medievale*, pp. 18, 97, and elsewhere equates Griselda with the Virgin. The argument for the Christ figure is made by Marga Cottino-Jones in "Fabula versus Figura: Another Interpretation of the Griselda Story," in *The Decameron*, eds. Musa and Bondanella, pp. 295–305. She would derive Griselda's name from Χριστός and εἶδος, signifying Christ image ("Griseida" would be phonemically closer). Muscetta (*Giovanni Boccaccio*, p. 298) believes that for Boccaccio Griselda is the "reintegration" of the figure of his mother. Giuseppe Mazzotta ("The *Decameron*: The Literal and

the Allegorical," p. 65) finds the paradigm of Job present in the story.

74. *Il Decameron*, pp. 403–404, n. 11, and p. 401, n. 1.

75. *Boccace*, p. 301.

76. Almansi, *The Writer as a Liar*, p. 134.

77. Branca, *Decameron*, p. 956.

78. *Decameron*, vol. 2, p. 734, n. 22.

79. Branca, *Decameron*, p. 960.

80. Ibid., p. 962.

81. Ibid., introduction, p. xvi.

82. Ibid., p. 1145, n. 7.

83. See Vittore Branca, "Struttura della prosa: scuola di retorica e ritmo della fantasia," in his *Boccaccio medievale*, pp. 45–85. The chapter appears also in English translation in his *Boccaccio: The Man and His Works*, pp. 223–275. Good studies of Boccaccio's style may be found in Marga Cottino-Jones, *An Anatomy of Boccaccio's Style*.

84. The effect is achieved, however, by the use of sophisticated devices; for a list of such as used in this tale see Cottino-Jones, *An Anatomy of Boccaccio's Style*, p. 23.

85. G. H. McWilliam, "On Translating the *Decameron*," in *Essays in Honor of John Humphreys Whitfield*, p. 71. His own translation (Penguin Classics, 1972) does little to support his statement.

86. See Branca, *Decameron*, pp. 967–972, and also the article by Maria Picchio Simonelli, "Prima diffusione e tradizione manoscritta del *Decameron*" (see note 40). It is generally believed that the so-called Hamiltonian manuscript (edited by Charles Singleton, Johns Hopkins University Press, 1974, and by Vittore Branca, La Crusca, 1976) is by Boccaccio's own hand.

87. *The Decameron*, eds. Musa and Bondanella, p. 191. The volume contains the Lives of Boccaccio by Villani, Giannozzo Manetti, and Ludovico Dolce. My summary of Boccaccio's "fortuna" is based on Giuseppe Petronio's chapter (pp. 171–232) in Walter Binni, *I classici italiani*, vol. 1.

88. *Boccaccio in England*, p. 114.

89. Quoted by Giorgio Petrocchi, *Stile e critica*, p. 240.

90. In Walter Binni, *I classici italiani*, vol. 1, p. 197.

91. Ibid., p. 210.

92. De Sanctis, *History of Italian Literature*, vol. 1, p. 359.

93. This is the thesis of Getto's book *Vita di forme e forme di vita.*

94. Mark Musa and Peter Bondanella, "The Meaning of the *Decameron,*" in their *The Decameron*, p. 323. In their preface the editors describe the essays included in their book as representative of various critical approaches to the *Decameron*, among others, "the philological (Auerbach), the philosophical (Scaglione), the formalist (Clements), the structuralist (Todorov) and the archetypal (Cottino-Jones)." See also Aldo Scaglione, "Giovanni Boccaccio or the Narrative Vocation," in *Boccaccio; secoli di vita*, pp. 81–104, for valuable illumination in this area.

95. Charles Trinkaus, *The Poet as Philosopher*, pp. 128–129.

96. "On Meaning in the *Decameron,*" p. 118.

97. Giuseppe Mazzotta, "The 'Decameron': The Marginality of Literature," in *Critical Perspectives*, p. 131. So too in his "The *Decameron*: The Literal and the Allegorical," Mazzotta finds theological allusions in the tales of Masetto (3.1) and Griselda (10.10).

98. See Ferdinando Neri, "Il disegno ideale del *Decameron,*" in his *Poesia e storia*. However, on scrutiny the "progress" seems rather topical or conceptual than truly ethical.

99. *Cultural Thematics*, p. 221.

100. Thomas Greene, "Forms of Accommodation," in *Critical Perspectives*, p. 123.

101. For example, Angelo Lipari ("The Structure and Real Significance of the *Decameron*"), Joan Ferrante ("The Frame Characters of the *Decameron*: A Progression of Virtues"), and Lucia Marino (*The Decameron "Cornice"*), who finds both literary and moral allegory in the frame.

102. *Il Decameron: saggio*, p. 200.

103. Northrop Frye, "Allegon," in *Princeton Encyclopedia of Poetry and Poetics*, p. 12.

104. In the introduction to his edition of the *Decameron*, p. xvi.

105. *Nature and Love*, pp. 81–82.

106. *Lo spirito e le lettere*, vol. I, p. 270.

107. Bosco, *Saggi sul rinascimento italiano*, p. 80. So too J. H. Whitfield (*Short History of Italian Literature*, p. 72): "[Boccaccio] did not write the *Decameron* with any firm programme of ideas in mind."

108. Singleton, "On Meaning in the *Decameron,*" p. 124.

109. John Larner, *Culture and Society in Italy*, p. 140.

LIST OF WORKS CITED

A. TEXTS AND TRANSLATIONS OF BOCCACCIO'S WORKS

Note: To avoid cumbersome repetition of bibliographical information we list here three books that contain substantial numbers of texts of Boccaccio's works.

1. *Giovanni Boccacio: Opere latine minori* a cura di Francesco Massèra. Bari, Laterza, 1928.
   This book contains: *Buccolicum carmen, Carminum quae supersunt* (eight Latin poems), *Epistolarum quae supersunt* (twenty-four Latin letters), and *Scripta breviora* (the Mythological Allegory and the sketches of Petrarch, St. Peter Damian, and Livy).
2. *Giovanni Boccaccio: Decameron, Filocolo, Ameto, Fiammetta.* Milano and Napoli, Riccardo Ricciardi, 1952.
   This is volume 8 of the series *La letteratura italiana: storia e testi.* It contains the *Decameron,* edited by Enrico Bianchi; *Il Filocolo* (abridged), *L'Ameto o commedia delle ninfe fiorentine* and *L'elegia di Madonna Fiammetta,* all edited by Carlo Salinari and Natalino Sapegno with an introduction and critical note on all the texts by Natalino Sapegno.
3. *Giovanni Boccaccio: Opere in versi, Corbaccio, Trattatello in laude di Dante (Life of Dante), Prose Latine, Epistole* a cura di Pier Giorgio Ricci. Milano and Napoli, Riccardo Ricciardi, 1965.
   This is volume 9 of the series *La letteratura italiana: storia e testi.* It contains twenty items from the *Rime (Lyric Poems); Il ninfale fiesolano (Nymph Song of Fiesole);* cantos 1, 2, 16, 17, and 18 of *Diana's Hunt;* parts 1, 3, 5, 6, and 8 of the *Filostrato;* books 3, 5, 8, 10, and 12 of the

Teseida; cantos 1, 2, 4, 30, 31, 34, 37, 38, 49, and 50 of the *Amorous Vision;* the *Corbaccio;* the *Trattatello in laude di Dante (Life of Dante);* eclogues 1, 3, 14, and 16 of the *Buccolicum carmen;* the introduction, conclusion, and nineteen items from *Concerning Famous Women;* the introductory matter, conclusion, and twenty items from *De casibus virorum illustrium (The Fates of Illustrious Men);* book 14 of the *Genealogies of the Pagan Gods;* and thirteen *Letters.* A facing page translation in Italian is provided for all the Latin texts.

In the list that follows references to these books will be by short title: *Opere latine minori, Decameron etc.,* and *Opere in versi.* I have listed individually the titles published in the series *Tutte le opere* under the direction of Vittore Branca and published by Mondadori (Milano).

Ameto. See *Comedy of the Florentine Nymphs.*

Amorous Vision (Amorosa visione).
   Amorosa visione, a cura di Vittore Branca. Milano, Mondadori, 1974. (In vol. 5 of *Tutte le opere.*)
   See *Opere in versi.* (Selections.)

Buccolicum carmen.
   See *Opere latine minori.*
   See *Opere in versi.* (Selections.)
   Boccaccio's Olympia with English Rendering by I. Gollancz. London, Florence Press, 1913. (Translation of eclogue 14.)

Comedy of the Florentine Nymphs (Commedia delle ninfe fiorentine).
   Comedia delle ninfe fiorentine a cura di Antonio Enzo Quaglio. Milano, Mondadori, 1964. (In vol. 2 of *Tutte le opere.*)
   See *Decameron etc.*

Concerning Famous Women.
   De claris mulieribus a cura di Vittorio Zaccaria. Milano, Mondadori, 1967. (Vol. 10 of *Tutte le opere.*)
   Opere in versi. (Selections.)
   Forty-six Lives. Translated from Boccaccio's *De claris mulieribus* by Henry Parker, Lord Morley and edited by Herbert G. Wright. London, published for the Early English Text Society by Humphrey Milford, Oxford University Press, 1943.

Concerning Famous Women by Giovanni Boccaccio. Translated with introduction and notes by Guido A. Guarino. New Brunswick, Rutgers University Press, 1963.

Corbaccio.
See *Opere in versi.*
Il Corbaccio. Edited by Tauno Nurmela. Suomalaisen Tiedakatemian Toimituksia: Annales Academiae Fennicae, ser. B, 146, Helsinki, 1968.
The Corbaccio: Giovanni Boccaccio. Translated and edited by Anthony K. Cassell. Urbana, Chicago, and London, University of Illinois Press, 1975.

Decameron.
See *Decameron etc.*
Il Decameron a cura di Cesare Segre. Milano, Mursia, 1966.
Il Decameron. Selections annotated by Attilio Momigliano a cura di Edoardo Sanguineti. Torino, G. B. Petrini, 1972.
Il Decameron a cura di Mario Marti. 2 vols. Milano, Rizzoli, 1974.
Decameron. Edizione diplomatico-interpretativa dell' autografo Hamilton 90 a cura di Charles S. Singleton. Baltimore, Johns Hopkins University Press, 1974.
Decameron a cura di Vittore Branca. Milano, Mondadori, 1976. (Vol. 4 of *Tutte le opere.*)
Decameron: edizione critica secondo l'autografo hamiltoniano a cura di Vittore Branca. Firenze, Presso l'Accademia della Crusca, 1976.
Boccaccio, The Decameron. Translated with an introduction by G. H. McWilliam. London, Penguin Books, 1972.
The Decameron. Selected, translated, and edited by Mark Musa and Peter E. Bondanella. New York, W. W. Norton, 1977. (Contains twenty-one novelle.)

Diana's Hunt (La caccia di Diana). Caccia di Diana a cura di Vittore Branca. Milano, Mondadori, 1967. (In vol. 1 of *Tutte le opere.*)

Elegy of Madonna Fiammetta.
See *Decameron etc.*
L'elegia di Madonna Fiammetta a cura di Mario Marti. *Giovanni Boccaccio: opere minori in volgare,* vol. 3. Milano, Rizzoli, 1971.
Amorous Fiammetta by Giovanni Boccaccio. Revised from the only English translation with an introduction by Edward Hutton. New York, privately printed for Rarity Press, 1931.

The Fates of Illustrious Men (De casibus virorum illustrium).
> See *Opere in versi.* (Selections.)
> *De casibus virorum illustrium.* A facsimile reproduction of the Paris edition of 1520. With an introduction by Louis Brewer Hall. Gainesville, Florida, Scholars Facsimiles and Reprints, 1962.
> *Giovanni Boccaccio: The Fates of Illustrious Men.* Translated and abridged by Louis Brewer Hall. New York, Frederick Ungar, 1965.

Filocolo.
> See *Decameron etc.* (Abridged.)
> *Il filocolo* a cura di Ettore De Ferri. In *Collezione dei classici italiani.* 2 vols. Torino, Unione Tipografico-Editrice Torinese, 1927.
> *Filocolo* a cura di Mario Marti. *Giovanni Boccaccio: Opere minori in volgare,* vol. 1. Milano, Rizzoli, 1969.
> *Filocolo* a cura di Antonio Enzo Quaglio. Milano, Mondadori, 1967. (In vol. 1 of *Tutte le opere.*)
> *Thirteen Most Pleasaunt and Delectable Questions of Love.* Entitled a Disport of Diverse Noble Personages written in Italian by M. Iohn Bocace Florentine and Poet Laureat in his booke named PHILOCOPO. Englished anno 1566 by H. G. To which is prefaced an introduction by Edward Hutton. London, Peter Davis, 1927.

Filostrato.
> See *Opere in versi.* (Selections.)
> *Giovanni Boccaccio: Filostrato* a cura di Vittore Branca. Milano, Mondadori, 1964. (In vol. 2 of *Tutte le opere.*)
> *The Filostrato of Giovanni Boccaccio.* A translation with parallel text by Nathaniel Edward Griffin and Arthur Beckwith Myrick with an introduction by Nathaniel Edward Griffin. Philadelphia, University of Pennsylvania Press; London, Humphrey Milford, Oxford University Press, 1929.
> *Giovanni Boccaccio: Il Filostrato.* Translated by R. K. Gordon. In *The Story of Troilus.* Toronto, Buffalo, and London, University of Toronto Press in association with the Mediaeval Academy of America, 1978. (First published by J. M. Dent and Sons, London, 1934.)

Genealogies of the Pagan Gods.
> See *Opere in versi.*
> *Genealogie deorum gentilium libri* a cura di Vincenzo Romano. 2 vols. Bari, Laterza, 1951.

Genealogiae Ioannis Bocatii: cum demonstrationibus in formis arborum designatis. Eiusdem de montibus & silvis, de fontibus, lacubus & fluminibus. Ac etiam de stagnis & paludibus: necnon et de maribus: seu diversis maris nominibus. Venetiis ductu & expensis Nobilis viri .D. Octaviani Scoti civis Modoetiensis. M. CCCC. XCIIII. Septimo kalendas Martias finis impositus fuit huic operi per Bonetum Locatellum. Facsimile reproduction. New York and London, Garland Publishing, 1976.

Boccaccio on Poetry. Being the preface and the 14th and 15th books of Boccaccio's *Genealogia deorum gentilium.* In an English version with introductory essay and commentary by Charles G. Osgood. Princeton, Princeton University Press, 1930. Reprinted by Liberal Arts Press, Indianapolis and New York, Bobbs-Merrill, 1955.

Latin Verse.
See *Opere latine minori.*
"Un nuovo carme del Boccaccio: l'epitaffio per Pino e Ciampi della Tosa," D. De Robertis. *Studi sul Boccaccio* 9 (1975–1976), 43–101.

Lectures on the Divine Comedy.
Boccaccio, Giovanni. *Il comento a la Divina Commedia e gli altri scritti intorno a Dante* a cura di Domenico Guerri. Bari, Laterza, 1918.
Giovanni Boccaccio: Esposizioni sopra la Comedia di Dante a cura di Giorgio Padoan. Milano, Mondadori, 1965. (Vol. 6 of *Tutte le opere.*)

Letters.
See *Opere latine minori.*
See *Opere in versi.* (Contains thirteen letters.)
Le lettere edite e inedite di Messer Giovanni Boccaccio. Edited by Francesco Corazzini. Firenze, Sansoni, 1877.
Giovanni Boccaccio: L'Ameto, Lettere, Il Corbaccio a cura di Nicola Bruscoli. Bari, Laterza, 1940. (Contains three letters.)
"Una lettera autografa del Boccaccio nell'Archivio di Stato di Perugia." Roberto Abbondanza. *Studi sul Boccaccio* 1 (1963), 5–13. "Epistola in nome della Signoria al Petrarca." Ginetta Auzzas. *Studi sul Boccaccio* 4 (1967), 203–240.

Life of Dante (Trattatello in laude di Dante).
See *Opere in versi.*
Trattatello in laude di Dante a cura di Pier Giorgio Ricci. Milano, Mondadori, 1974. (In vol. 3 of *Tutte le opere.*)

English translation in *The Early Lives of Dante*. Translated by Philip H. Wicksteed. London, Alexander Moring, 1904.

Life of Petrarch.
See *Opere latine minori.*

Life of St. Peter Damian.
See *Opere latine minori.*

Lyric Verse (Rime).
See *Opere in versi.* (Contains twenty items.)
Le rime di Giovanni Boccaccio. Testo critico a cura di Francesco Massèra. Torino, Unione Tipografico-Editrice Torinese, 1921.
Giovanni Boccaccio: Le rime, L'amorosa visione, La caccia di Diana a cura di Vittore Branca. Bari, Laterza, 1939. (Slightly revised ed. in *Rime, Caccia di Diana.* Padova, Liviana editre, 1958.)
Translation of number 126 by T. G. Bergin in *Lyric Poetry of the Italian Renaissance* (compiled and edited by L. R. Lind). New Haven and London, Yale University Press, 1954.

Mythological Allegory (Allegoria mitologica).
See *Opere latine minori.*

Nymph Song of Fiesole (Ninfale fiesolano).
See *Opere in versi.* (Following text of Vincenzo Pernicone, *Il filostrato e il ninfale fiesolano.* Bari, Laterza, 1937.)
Giovanni Boccaccio: Ninfale fiesolano a cura di Armando Balduino. Milano, Mondadori, 1974. (In vol. 3 of *Tutte le opere.*)
The Nymph of Fiesole by Giovanni Boccaccio. Translated by Daniel J. Donno. New York, Columbia University Press, 1960.
Giovanni Boccaccio's Nymphs of Fiesole. Translated into verse with an introduction by Joseph Tusiani. Rutherford, Madison, and Teaneck. Fairleigh Dickinson University Press, 1971.

Teseida delle nozze di Emilia.
See *Teseida* in *Opere in versi.* (Selections.)
Teseida delle nozze di Emilia a cura di Alberto Limentani. Milano, Mondadori, 1964. (In vol. 2 of *Tutte le opere.*)
The Book of Theseus, translated by Bernadette Marie McCoy. New York, Medieval Text Association, 1974.

The Vision of Love (Amorosa visione).
  See *Opere in versi.* (Selections.)
  Amorosa visione a cura di Vittore Branca. Milano, Mondadori, 1974. (In vol. 5 of *Tutte le opere.*)

Zibaldone laurenziano.
  Zibaldone laurenziano. Facsimile reproduction by G. Biagi. Firenze, Olschki, 1913.

B. BOOKS AND ARTICLES ABOUT BOCCACCIO
(Names of editors and translators of works cited in A are also listed.)

Almansi, Guido. *The Writer as Liar.* London and Boston, Routledge and Kegan Paul, 1975.
Andreas Capellanus. *The Art of Courtly Love.* Translated with notes and introduction by John J. Parry. New York, Columbia University Press, 1941. (Reprint by Frederick Ungar, New York, 1959.)
Atchity, Kenneth J, ed. See *Italian Literature: Roots and Branches.*
Auerbach, Erich. *Mimesis.* Princeton, Princeton University Press, 1953.

Balduino, Armando, ed. See A under *Nymph Song.*
————. "Tradizione canterina e tonalità popolareggianti nel 'Ninfale fiesolano.' " *Studi sul Boccaccio* 2 (1964), 25–80.
Barricelli, Jean-Pierre. "Satire of Satires: Boccaccio's *Corbaccio.*" *Italian Quarterly* 18, no. 72 (Spring, 1975), 95–111.
Battaglia, Salvatore. *Giovanni Boccaccio e la riforma della narrativa.* Napoli, Liguori, 1969.
Bergin, Thomas G. "An Introduction to Boccaccio." In *The Decameron,* edited by Musa and Bondanella, pp. 151–171. See A under *Decameron.*
————, ed. *Petrarch: Selected Sonnets, Odes and Letters.* Arlington Heights, Illinois, AHM Publishing, 1966.
————, trans. See A under *Lyric Verse.*
————, trans. and A. S. Wilson, trans. *Petrarch's Africa.* New Haven and London, Yale University Press, 1977.
Billanovich, Giuseppe. "Dalla *Commedia* e dall'*Amorosa Visione* ai *Trionfi.*" *Giornale storico della letteratura italiana* 123, fasc. 367–368 (1946), 1–52.
————. "La leggenda dantesca dantesca del Boccaccio." *Studi danteschi,* 28 (1949), 45–144.

————. *Restauri boccacceschi.* Roma, Edizione di Storia e Letteratura, 1945.

Binni, Walter. *I classici italiani nella storia della critica.* Firenze, La Nuova Italia, 1965.

Bishop, Morris, trans. *Letters from Petrarch.* Bloomington and London, University of Indiana Press, 1966.

Bloch, Marc. *Feudal Society.* Translated from the French by L. A. Manyon; foreword by M. M. Postan. Chicago, University of Chicago Press, 1961.

Boccaccio, for works see A above.

Boccaccio in Europe. Proceedings of the Boccaccio Conference, Louvain, December, 1975. Edited by Gilbert Tournoy. Louvain, Leuven University Press, 1977.

Boccaccio: secoli di vita. Atti del congresso internazionale: Boccaccio, 1975, Università di California Los Angeles 17–19 ottobre 1975. Edited by Marga Cottino-Jones and Edward F. Tuttle. Ravenna, Longo, 1977.

Bosco, Umberto. *Il Decameron: saggio.* Catanzaro, Brazia, 1929.

————. *Saggi sul rinascimento italiano.* Firenze, Le Monnier, 1970.

Bondanella, Peter E. see A under *Decameron.*

Bourland, Catherine B. "Boccaccio and the *Decameron* in Castilian and Catalan Literature." *Revue Hispanique,* Tome xii (1905), numéro 41, pp. 1–232.

Branca, Vittore. "Boccaccio illustratore del suo *Decameron* e la tradizione figurale del suo capolavoro." *Italian Quarterly* 21, no. 79 (Winter, 1980), 5–7.

————. *Boccaccio medievale.* Nuova edizione accresciuta. Firenze, Sansoni, 1970.

————. *Boccaccio: The Man and His Works.* Translated by Richard Monges, cotranslator and editor Dennis J. McAuliffe. Foreword by Robert C. Clements. New York, New York University Press, 1976.

————. *Giovanni Boccaccio: Profilo biografico.* Firenze, Sansoni, 1977.

————, ed. See A under *Amorous Vision, Decameron, Diana's Hunt, Filostrato, Lyric Poems.*

Brucker, Gene A. "Florence and the Black Death." In *Boccaccio: secoli di vita,* pp. 21–30.

Bruscoli, Nicola, ed. See A under *Letters.*

Buck, August. "Boccaccios Verteidigung der Dichtung in den *Genealogie deorum.*" In *Boccaccio in Europe,* pp. 53–65.

Burton, Robert. *The Anatomy of Melancholy.* Edited by A. R. Shilleto. 3 vols. London and New York, George Bell and Sons, 1893.

Carswell, Catherine. *The Tranquil Heart: Portrait of Giovanni Boccaccio.* New York, Harcourt, Brace, 1937.

Cassell, Anthony K., trans. See A under *Corbaccio.*

Chandler, S. Bernard and Julius Molinaro, eds. *The Culture of Italy: Mediaeval to Modern.* Toronto, Griffin House, 1979.

Cherchi, Paolo. *Andrea Cappellano, trovatori e altri temi romanzi.* Roma, Bulzoni, 1979.

Chubb, Thomas C. *The Life of Giovanni Boccaccio.* New York, Albert and Charles Boni, 1930.

Clements, Robert J. "Anatomy of the Novella in the *Decameron.*" In *The Decameron,* edited by Musa and Bondanella, pp. 258–269. See A under *Decameron.*

Cottino-Jones, Marga. *An Anatomy of Boccaccio's Style.* Napoli, Cymba, 1968.

———. "The *Corbaccio:* Notes for a Mythical Perspective of Moral Alternatives." *Forum italicum* 4, no. 4 (1970), 490–509.

———. "Fabula versus Figura: Another Interpretation of the Griselda Story." In *The Decameron,* edited by Musa and Bondanella, pp. 295–305.

———, ed. See *Boccaccio: secoli di vita.*

Critical Perspectives on the Decameron. Edited by Robert S. Dombroski. New York, Barnes and Noble, 1977.

Croce, Benedetto. *La novella di Andreuccio da Perugia.* Bari, Laterza, 1911.

———. *Poesia popolare e poesia d'arte.* 5th ed. Bari, Laterza, 1967.

Cunningham, Gilbert F. trans. In T. G. Bergin, *Petrarch: Selected Sonnets, Odes and Letters,* p. 38.

Curtius, Ernst Robert. *European Literature and the Latin Middle Ages.* Translated from the German by Willard R. Trask. New York, Pantheon Books, Bollingen Foundation, 1953.

Dante, *Convivio.* See Wicksteed, Philip.

———. *De vulgari eloquentia.* See Ferrers Howell, A. G.

———. *Letters.* See Toynbee, Paget.

Decameron, The. Edited by Mark Musa and Peter E. Bondanella. See A under *Decameron.*

De Ferri, Ettore, ed. See A under *Filocolo.*

De Robertis, D. See A under Latin Verse.

De Robertis, Giuseppe. *Studi.* Florence, Le Monnier, 1953.

De Sanctis, Francesco. *History of Italian Literature.* Translated by Joan Redfern. 2 vols. New York, Harcourt Brace, 1931.

Dombroski, Robert S., ed. See *Critical Perspectives on the Decameron.*
Donno, Daniel J., trans. See A under *Nymph Song of Fiesole.*

Falassi, Alessandro. "Il Boccaccio e il folklore di Cerraldo." In *Boccaccio: secoli di vita,* pp. 265–292

Ferrante, Joan. "The Frame Characters of the *Decameron:* A Progression of Virtues." *Romance Philology* 19, no. 2 (1965), 212–226.

Ferreri, Rosario. "Ovidio e le 'Rime' di G. Boccaccio," *Forum Italicum* 7–8 (1973–1974), 46–55.

———. "Studi sulle rime del Boccaccio." *Studi sul Boccaccio* 7 (1973), 213–237.

Ferrers Howell, A. G., trans. *De Vulgari Eloquentia.* In *The Latin Works of Dante Alighieri.* London, J. M. Dent and Sons, 1904.

Fido, Franco. "Boccaccio's *ars narrandi* in the Sixth Day of the *Decameron.*" In *Italian Literature: Roots and Branches,* pp. 225–242.

———. "Dante, personaggio mancato del *Decameron.*" In *Boccaccio: secoli di vita,* pp. 177–189.

Flora, Francesco. *Storia della letteratura italiana.* Vol 1: *Dal medioevo alla fine del quattrocento.* Milano, Mondadori, 1948.

Frye, Northrop. "Allegory." In *Princeton Encyclopedia of Poetry and Poetics,* pp. 12–15.

Getto, Giovanni. *Vita di forme e forme di vita nel Decameron.* Torino, G. Petrini, 1958.

Gilson, Étienne. "Poésie et vérité dans la *Genealogia* de Boccace." *Studi sul Boccaccio* 2 (1964), 253–282.

Gollancz, Israel, trans. See A under *Buccolicum carmen.*

Gordon, R. K. *The Story of Troilus.* Toronto, Buffalo, and London, University of Toronto Press, 1978.

Grabher, Carlo. *Boccaccio.* Torino, Unione Tipografico-Editrice Torinese, 1945.

Grant, W. Leonard. *Neo-Latin Literature and the Pastoral.* Chapel Hill, University of North Carolina Press, 1965.

Greene, Thomas M. "Forms of Accommodation in the *Decameron.*" In *Critical Perspectives on the Decameron,* pp. 113–128.

Griffin, Robert. "Boccaccio's *Fiammetta:* Pictures at an Exposition." *Italian Quarterly* 18, no. 72 (Spring, 1975), 75–94.

Guarino, Guido A., trans. See A under *Concerning Famous Women.*

Guerri, Domenico, ed. See A under *Lectures on the Divine Comedy.*

Hauvette, Henri. *Boccace: Étude biographique et littéraire.* Paris, Librairie Armand Colin, 1914.

Hollander, Robert. *Boccaccio's Two Venuses.* New York, Columbia University Press, 1977.

Hutton, Edward. *Giovanni Boccaccio: A Biographical Study.* London and New York, J. Lane, 1910.

————, ed. See A under *Elegy of Madonna Fiammetta, Filocolo.*

Italian Literature: Roots and Branches. Edited by Giose Rimanelli and Kenneth J. Atchity. New Haven and London, Yale University Press, 1976.

Kadish, Emilie. "Petrarch's *Griselda:* An English Translation." *Medievalia* 3 (1977), 1–23.

Kahane, H. and R. "Akritas and Arcita: A Byzantine Source of Boccaccio's *Teseida.*" *Speculum* 20 (1945), 415–425.

Kern, Edith G. "The Gardens in the *Decameron.*" *PMLA* 66 (1951), 505–523.

Larner, John. *Culture and Society in Italy, 1290–1420.* New York, Scribners, 1971.

Layman, Beverly Joseph. "Eloquence of Pattern in Boccaccio's Tale of the Falcon." *Italica* 46.1 (1969), 3–16.

Léonard, E. G. "Acciaiuoli, Niccolò." In *Dizionario biografico degli italiani.* Roma, Istituto dell'enciclopedia italiana, vol. 1, 1960, pp. 87–90.

————. *Boccace et Naples.* Paris, Librarie Droz, 1944.

Limentani, Alberto, ed. See A under *Teseida.*

Lipari, Angelo. "The Structure and Real Significance of the *Decameron.*" In *Essays in Honor of Albert Feuillerat,* edited by Henri Peyre. New Haven, Yale University Press, 1943, pp. 43–83.

Lopez, Robert S. *Naissance de l'Europe.* Paris, Librairie Armand Colin, 1962.

McAlpine, Monica E. *The Genre of Troilus and Criseyde.* Ithaca and London, Cornell University Press. 1978.

McCoy, Bernadette Marie, trans. See A under *Teseida.*

Machiavelli, Niccolò. *Tutte le opere* a cura di Francesco Flora e di Carlo Cordié. 2 vols. Milano, Mondadori, 1949.

MacManus, Francis. *Boccaccio.* New York, Sheed and Ward, 1947.

McWilliam, G. H. "On Translating the *Decameron.*" In *Essays in Honor of John Humphreys Whitfield,* edited by H. C. Davis, et al. London, St. George's Press, 1975, pp. 71–83.

————. trans. See A under *Decameron.*

Marcus, Millicent. *An Allegory of Form.* Saratoga, California, Anma Libri, 1979.

Marino, Lucia. *The Decameron "Cornice": Allusion, Allegory and Iconology.* Ravenna, Longo, 1979.

Marti, Mario, ed. See A under *Decameron, Filocolo.*

Massèra, Aldo Francesco, ed. See preliminary note to A and *Lyric Verse.*

Mattalia, Daniele. "Carme bucolico, Il." In *Dizionario Bompiani delle opere.* Milano, Bompiani, 1947, vol. 2, p. 128.

———. "(Delle) Donne illustri." In *Dizionario Bompiani delle opere.* Milano, Bompiani, 1947, vol. 2, pp. 836–837.

———. "Monti, selve, fonti, etc." In *Dizionario Bompiani delle opere.* Milano, Bompiani, 1947, vol 4, p. 807.

Mazzotta, Giuseppe. "The *Decameron*: The Literal and the Allegorical." *Italian Quarterly* 18, no. 72 (Spring, 1975), 53–73.

———. "The 'Decameron': The Marginality of Literature." *University of Toronto Quarterly* 62 (1972–1973), 64–81. Reprinted in *Critical Perspectives*, pp. 129–143.

Miglio, Massimo. "Boccaccio biografo." In *Boccaccio in Europe*, pp. 149–163.

Momigliano, Attilio. *Storia della letteratura italiana.* Messina and Milano, G. Principato, 1936.

———, ed. See A under *Decameron.*

Montano, Rocco. *Lo spirito e le lettere: disegno storico della letteratura italiana*, vol. I. Milano, Marzorati, 1970.

Moravia, Alberto. *Man as an End: A Defense of Humanism.* London, Secker and Warburg, 1965.

Morley, Lord, trans. See A under *Concerning Famous Women.*

Musa, Mark, ed. and trans. See A under *Decameron.*

Musa, Mark and Peter F. Bondanella. "The Meaning of the *Decameron*." In *The Decameron,* edited by Musa and Bondanella, pp. 322–331.

Muscetta, Carlo. *Giovanni Boccaccio.* 2d ed. Bari, Laterza, 1974.

Myrick, Arthur Beckwith, trans. See A under *Filostrato.*

Negri, Enrico de'. "The Legendary Style of the *Decameron*." In *Critical Perspectives on the Decameron*, pp. 82–98.

Neri, Ferdinando. *Poesia e storia.* Torino, Gambino, 1976.

Nicolini, Fausto. "Napoli." In *Enciclopedia italiana.* Roma, Istituto dell' enciclopedia italiana, 1934, vol. 24, pp. 229–242.

Nurmela, Tauno. See A under *Corbaccio.*

Osgood, Charles G., ed. and trans. See A under *Genealogies of the Pagan Gods.*

Padoan, Giorgio. "Ancora sulla datazione e sul titolo del *Corbaccio. Lettere italiane* 15 (1963), 199–201.

———. "Mondo aristocratico e mondo comunale nell'ideologia e nell'arte di Giovanni Boccaccio." *Studi sul Boccaccio* 6 (1968), 81–219.

———. "Sulla datazione del *Corbaccio*." *Lettere italiane* 15 (1963), 1–27.

———, ed. See A under *Lectures on the Divine Comedy*.

Parker, Henry. See Morley, Lord.

Parry, John J., trans. See Andreas Capellanus.

Pennington, Kenneth. "A Note to *Decameron* 6:7: The Wit of Madonna Filippa." *Speculum* 52, no. 4 (1977), 902–905.

Perella, Nicolas James. "The World of Boccaccio's *Filocolo*." *PMLA* 76, no. 4 (1961), 330–339.

Petrarch, *Africa*. See Thomas Bergin and A. S. Wilson.

———. *Letters*. See Bishop, Morris.

———. *Selected Sonnets, Odes and Letters*. See Bergin, T. G.

Petrocchi, Giorgio. *Stile e critica*. Bari, Adriatica, 1968.

Pirenne, Henri. *A History of Europe from the Invasions to the XVIth Century*. Translated by Bernard Miall. New York, University Books, 1956.

Princeton Encyclopedia of Poetry and Poetics. Edited by Alex Preminger, et al. Princeton, Princeton University Press, 1974.

Quaglio, Antonio Enzo, ed. See A under *Comedy of the Florentine Nymphs* and *Filocolo*.

Quinet, Edgar. "Rivoluzioni d' Italia." In Binni, *I classici italiani*.

Ricci, Pier Giorgio. "Studi sulle opere latine e volgari del Boccaccio." *Rinascimento* 13 (1962), 3–29.

———, ed. See preliminary note to A and *Life of Dante*.

Rimanelli, Giose, ed. See *Italian Literature: Roots and Branches*.

Romano, Vincenzo, ed. See A under *Genealogies of the Pagan Gods*.

Rossi, Vittorio. *Storia della letteratura italiana per uso dei licei*. 3 vols. Milano, Vallardi, 1921.

Russell, Josiah Cox. *Medieval Regions and Their Cities*. Bloomington, Indiana University Press, 1972.

Russo, Luigi. *Studi sul due e trecento*. Roma, Edizioni italiane, 1945.

Salinari, Carlo. See preliminary note to A.

Sanguineti, Edoardo, ed. See A under *Decameron*.

Sapegno, Natalino. "Boccaccio." In *Dizionario biografico degli italiani*. Roma, Istituto dell'enciclopedia italiana, 1963, vol. 10, pp. 838–857.

————. *Il Trecento*. 2d ed. Milano, Vallardi, 1955.

————, ed. See preliminary note to A.

Scaglione, Aldo. "Giovanni Boccaccio or the Narrative Vocation." In *Boccaccio: secoli di vita*, pp. 81–104.

————. "Italy in the Middle Ages." In *The Culture of Italy: Mediaeval and Modern*, edited by S. Bernard Chandler and Julius Molinaro, pp. 44–66.

————. *Nature and Love in the Late Middle Ages*. Berkeley and Los Angeles, University of California Press, 1963.

Segre, Cesare, ed. See A under *Decameron*.

Seung, Thomas K. *Cultural Thematics*. New Haven and London, Yale University Press, 1976.

The Shorter Cambridge Medieval History. Ed. C. W. Previté-Orton. Cambridge at the University Press, 1960.

Silber, Gordon Rutledge. *The Influence of Dante and Petrarch on Certain of Boccaccio's Lyrics*. Menasha, Wisconsin, George Banta Publishing, 1940.

Simonelli, Maria Picchio. "Prima diffusione e tradizione manoscritta del *Decameron*." In *Boccaccio: secoli di vita*, pp. 125–142.

Singleton, Charles S. "On Meaning in the *Decameron*." *Italica* 21, no. 3 (1944), 117–124.

Solerti, Angelo, ed. *Le vite di Dante, Petrarca e Boccaccio scritte fino al secolo decimosesto*. Milano, Vallardi, 1904.

Symonds, John A. *Giovanni Boccaccio as Man and Author*. London, J. C. Nimmo, 1895.

————. *The Renaissance in Italy*. New York, Modern Library, 1935.

Torraca, Francesco. *Per la biografia di Giovanni Boccaccio*. Milano, Società editrice Dante Alighieri di Albrighi, Segati e c., 1912.

Tournoy, Gilbert, ed. See *Boccaccio in Europe*.

Toynbee, Paget, ed. and trans. *Dantis Alagherii Epistolae; The Letters of Dante*. 2nd ed. Oxford at the Clarendon Press, 1966.

Trinkaus, Charles. *The Poet as Philosopher: Petrarch and the Formation of the Renaissance Consciousness*. New Haven and London, Yale University Press, 1979.

Tuchman, Barbara. *A Distant Mirror*. New York, A. A. Knopf, 1978.

Tusiani, Joseph, trans. See A under *Nymph Song of Fiesole*.

Tuttle, Edward F., ed. See *Boccaccio: secoli di vita*.

Villani, Filippo. *Vite d'uomini illustri fiorentini*. Milano, Nicolo Bettoni, 1834. (Biblioteca enciclopedica italiana, vol. 30.)

Whitfield, J. H. *A Short History of Italian Literature.* London, Cassell, 1962.

Wicksteed, Philip H., ed. and trans. *The Convivio of Dante Alighieri.* London, J. Dent, 1909.

——————, trans. See A under *Life of Dante.*

Wilkins, Ernest Hatch. "Discussion of the Date of the Birth of Boccaccio." In *Studies on Petrarch and Boccaccio.* Padova, Antenora, 1978, pp. 306–314. (Originally published in *The Romanic Review* 4 (1913), 343–351.

——————. "The Genealogy of the Genealogical Trees of the *Genealogia Deorum.*" In *The Invention of the Sonnet and Other Studies in Italian Literature.* Roma, Edizioni di Storia e Letteratura, 1959, pp. 163–167. (First published as chapter 6 of *The Trees of the "Genealogia Deorum" of Boccaccio,* Chicago, printed for the members of the Caxton Club, later reprinted with some changes in *Modern Philology* 23 [1925], 61–65.)

——————. *A History of Italian Literature.* Revised ed. Cambridge, Massachusetts and London, Harvard University Press, 1974.

——————. *Petrarch's Later Years.* Cambridge, Massachusetts, The Mediaeval Academy of America, 1959.

Wilson, A. S., trans. See T. G. Bergin, trans.

Wood, Charles T. *The Age of Chivalry.* New York, Universe Books, 1970.

Wright, Herbert G. *Boccaccio in England from Chaucer to Tennyson.* London, University of London, The Athlone Press, 1957.

——————, ed. See A under *Concerning Famous Women.*

Zaccaria, Vittorio, ed. See A under *Concerning Famous Women.*

INDEX